AFROTOPIA

THE ROOTS OF AFRICAN AMERICAN POPULAR HISTORY

Wilson Jeremiah Moses

CAMBRIDGE
UNIVERSITY PRESS

PUBLISHED BY THE PRESS SYNDICATE OF THE UNIVERSITY OF CAMBRIDGE
The Pitt Building, Trumpington Street, Cambridge CB2 1RP, United Kingdom

CAMBRIDGE UNIVERSITY PRESS
The Edinburgh Building, Cambridge CB2 2RU, UK   http://www.cup.cam.ac.uk
40 West 20th Street, New York, NY 10011-4211, USA   http://www.cup.org
10 Stamford Road, Oakleigh, Melbourne 3166, Australia

First published 1998

Printed in the United States of America
Typeset in Baskerville 10/12 pt, in Penta [RF]

A catalog record for this book is available from the British Library.

Library of Congress Cataloging-in-Publication Data

Moses, Wilson Jeremiah, 1942–
Afrotopia : the roots of African American popular history / Wilson
Jeremiah Moses.
p.   cm. – (Cambridge studies in American literature and
culture)
Includes bibliographical references and index.
ISBN 0-521-47408-6. – ISBN 0-521-47941-X (pbk.)
1. Afrocentrism – United States.   2. Afro-Americans –
Historiography.   3. Afro-Americans – Intellectual life.   I. Title.
II. Series.
E185.625.M66   1998
909'.0496 – dc21   97-43389
                                                        CIP

ISBN 0-521-47408-6
ISBN 0-521-47941-X

CONTENTS

vii

ACKNOWLEDGMENTS

═══════

In the course of writing a work of this sort, many debts are incurred. Eric Sundquist encouraged me to submit the manuscript to Cambridge University Press, where it was acquired by Susan Chang. The manuscript was given a most insightful and helpful reading by Anne Sanow, who was my principal guide along the road to publication. Thanks are also due to my patient and skillful production editor, Janis Bolster, and my exceedingly diligent copy editor, Nancy Landau. My wife, Maureen Moses, gave thorough readings to the manuscript and the page proofs and also assisted with the index.

For Kurtz Myers

Mentor, Matchmaker, and Friend
With Respect and Appreciation

INTRODUCTION

This book is concerned with historiographies of progress and decline that have surfaced in African American consciousness – both learned and popular – from the end of the eighteenth to the middle of the twentieth century.[1] The various perspectives on black history under discussion include one that laments the eclipse of a noble past, and one that celebrates a progressive evolution toward a new and brighter day. I have not confined myself to a definition of history as it is practiced by contemporary professional historians, but have reflected broadly on the historical understanding of literate persons outside the academy. These essays are not confined to the investigation of Afrocentrism, although I have referred throughout to the nineteenth-century origins of some of the historical views that are commonly, and misleadingly, designated "Afrocentric." I have also alluded to African American folk histories that extend beyond simple Afrocentrism to encompass a broader Afro-Asiatic consciousness, for example, the traditions of the Moorish Science Temple and the Nation of Islam.

I must confess that I do not share the obsession with ancient Egypt, "Egyptocentrism," that has dominated much discussion of African American folk-historiography in recent years. That is because my concern encompasses something broader and more complex than the simple attempt to explain or defend the idea that Egypt is geographically and culturally part of Africa. I doubt if I could be called an Afrocentrist, except in the sense that I sympathize with the contemporary sufferings of African peoples, and believe that the image of Africa has always affected both external perceptions and self-images of African Americans.

I have not discovered who was the first person to employ the expression "Afrocentrism," but it was not Professor Molefi Asante, although the term has been closely associated with him for almost two decades. Derrick Alridge, a Ph.D. candidate at the Pennsylvania State University, has reminded me that, not only the concept but the actual term "Afrocentrism" was employed by W. E. B. Du Bois, possibly as early as 1961, and definitely by 1962. Mr. Alridge brought to my attention Du Bois's typescript draft of "Proposed plans for an *Encyclopaedia Africana*," which was to be "unashamedly Afro-Centric, but not indifferent to the impact of the outside world upon Africa or to the impact of Africa upon the outside world." As soon as I saw the proposal, I was reminded of a series of documents shared with me some years ago by the distinguished Africanist Adelaide Cromwell: *Information Reports* issued by the Secretariat for an Encyclopedia Africana in Accra, Ghana, under the directorship of Du Bois. I discovered that the phrase "Unashamedly Afrocentric" appeared in *Information Report* No. 2 and elsewhere in the series. It was obviously known to participants in the project along with the entire panoply of issues later associated with Afrocentrism by Dr. Asante.[2]

Dr. Asante's efforts to appropriate the term Afrocentrism began in 1980 with the publication of his *Afrocentricity: The Theory of Social Change*. The work was a brief essay concerned with a historical analysis of African American political theory, and offering some speculations on how African American students and scholars might avoid incorporating Eurocentric biases into their own work. Since 1980 Asante has amended his definition several times, so that recent formulations are vastly more imaginative than his original statement. His second book, *The Afrocentric Idea* (1987), was a creative and in some respects brilliant but rambling theoretical work, much influenced by the revolution in "critical theory" that occurred in American intellectual life during the late 1970s and early 1980s.

The deconstructionist critic Henry Louis Gates found Asante's *Afrocentric Idea* convincing enough, if we are to believe the jacket blurb in which he gushed, "Asante's wide range of references, his delightful examples taken from black traditions, and his sheer pleasure at discussing black culture, all combine to make his argument both cogent and important. This will be a major book." Houston Baker, later the first black president of the Modern Language Association, also provided a blurb – subtly equivocal but cautiously positive: "Asante's dramaturgy presents an alternative model of inquiry. It persuasively suggests a model of rhetorical and scholarly production." Asante did homage in his footnotes to the works of several authors who have been most influential in contemporary critical theory, including Raymond Geuss, Thomas Kuhn, Marvin Harris, Claude Lévi-Strauss, Edmund Husserl, and Michel Foucault. It was not until his third book, *Kemet, Afrocentricity, and Knowledge* (1990), that Asante's writings demonstrated any great concern with establishing a relationship between the culture of ancient Egypt and the so-called African personality of modern times.[3]

It is important to distinguish between Afrocentrism and Egyptocentrism, as Derrick Gilbert, an undergraduate student at Berkeley, once noted. In neither of Asante's first two books on the subject was he particularly fixated with Egypt. In later works, Egypt became increasingly important, but Asante was hardly the first to insist on linking the study of Egypt to the study of the rest of Africa. Egyptians themselves called for the inclusion of Egypt in the Encyclopedia Africana. The director of the United Arab Republic Cultural Centre in Accra wrote to praise Du Bois for having "maintained faith in the African character of Egypt's achievement," and urging that the Encyclopedia Africana keep Egypt within its Afrocentric focus.[4]

As Asante's ideas are impossible to ignore, so too is it, regrettably, impossible to ignore a recent book purporting to treat on the subject of Afrocentrism – Mary Lefkowitz's *Not Out of Africa*. In a withering broadside against this work delivered from the deck of the flagship *Journal of American History* (December 1996), the redoubtable August Meier correctly observed that "Nineteenth century black intellectuals . . . as early as the 1830s and 1840s presented virtually full-blown arguments about Egypt that are today known as Afrocentric." I agree with him that "to argue with the claims of Afrocentrists is one thing, but that to ignore the work of the band of Afro-American intellectuals and popularizers who enunciated a line of thought that was deeply rooted among rank-and-file Negroes would, I believe, reveal an essentially Eurocentric orientation."[5] In *Black Folk Here and There*, St. Clair Drake, the late dean of African American social scientists, provided an informed discussion of the tradition to which Meier refers.[6] The work was published posthumously in 1987–90, and has been studiously ignored since then by the sentimental Egyptocentrists, who are mocked with icy civility in Drake's erudite volumes.

Aside from the dangers of Eurocentrism that Meier observes, a more glaring problem is Lefkowitz's failure to make use of well-established methods of cultural and intellectual history. She is oddly more concerned with attempting to prove that Cleopatra was a pure "Aryan" than with understanding the circumstances that have produced the colorful phenomenon of black Egyptocentrism. The cultural and historical contexts that have given rise to the peculiarities of African American mythologies are of no interest to her. Furthermore, she demonstrates absolutely no interest in the methods that have been developed over the past sixty years for studying similar problems in cultural history, by scholars such as Henry Nash Smith, David Brion Davis, and Carl Bode.[7]

Many African Americans outside the academy, like their white counterparts, tend to be dismissive of academic history as taught in "respectable" educational institutions. They are convinced that history is written by members of a hostile elitist "establishment." Lefkowitz seems intent on confirming them in their belief. Thus, she attacks the Afrocentric pronouncements of the populist leader Marcus Garvey, and makes the astonishing statement, "I do not know if Garvey was the originator of the idea that Europeans had deliberately concealed the truth from blacks."[8] Surely, she does not intend to challenge the view that the education available to African Americans in Garvey's time was historically inferior, and that it largely functioned to inculcate in them a sense of inferiority. In most cases it actively discouraged or disparaged the idea – championed later by Frank Snowden and others – that African individuals, since ancient times, had made contributions to history, and that racism as experienced in America was a relatively recent phenomenon.[9] Garvey certainly was not the originator of the idea that whites in America systematically withheld knowledge from African Americans.

John E. Bruce, a prominent Garveyite and autodidact, who was born a slave in 1856, did not need to be reminded that whites deliberately withheld knowledge from blacks. At the time of Garvey's rise there were hundreds of thousands of former slaves still living in the United States – some of them, like Bruce, became members of or supporters of his movement. These people had living memories of a time when it was illegal to teach black people to read and write. Slave testimony, recorded in the slave narratives collected by the Works Progress Authority, reminds every historian of the systematic denial of knowledge to black Americans under slavery and segregation. Illiterate people have an amazing ability to create a mythology of the past, meaningful to themselves. One need only recall the often illiterate mummers of medieval Europe, who incorporated biblical history into their miracle plays, or the "rude mechanicals" satirized in Shakespeare's *Midsummer Night's Dream*, who incorporated classical mythology into their folk history and folk arts. Slave testimony reveals that a mythology fed by European as much as by African sources sprang up among the enslaved masses of the African American population. By the early twentieth century they had created a folklore in which many famous persons from history or the Bible were claimed for the black race.[10]

Black Egyptocentrists believe that ancient Egyptian culture was as profoundly influenced by black Africa as American popular culture has been influenced by America's black population. Their project, therefore, is simply to prove that the basic elements of Egyptian culture are historically intermeshed with the cultures of other regions of Africa. The glorification and romanticism of ancient Egypt is clearly only a part of what we call Afrocentrism today. It is to be admitted that since the early nineteenth century some black authors have desired to identify with the land of the pharaohs. It is important to note, however, that many black nationalists – especially those with a strong sense of class consciousness – are disinclined to romanticize pharaonic dominion. John H. Bracey, for example, sees little to celebrate in the joys of dragging a block of sandstone up the side of a pyramid.

This study is not concerned with attempts to establish the "racial identities" of Neolithic Egyptians or Ethiopians. Such questions are best left to persons with interests and abilities in the methods of archeology, physical anthropology, and radiocarbon dating. Burkhard Bilger, senior editor of *The Sciences*, a publication of the New York Academy of Sciences, has said as much in the pages of that journal. Bilger observes, as all reasonable persons must, that it is fruitless and unscholarly to impose nineteenth-century American racial categories on Neolithic populations.[11] Scholars as ideologically diverse as Frank Snowden, St. Clair Drake, and Ivan Hannaford have taken this position, and I agree with them. I tend, however, to share the ironic and amused detachment of St. Clair Drake respecting the folksy racial boosterism of the Afrocentrists, rather than the steaming indignation of Snowden.

I have described Afrocentrism as a traditional "historiography of decline" in several versions of Chapter 2, delivered on numerous occasions over the past ten years. Indeed, in some of its manifestations, Afrocentrism may be viewed as a historiography of decline. Gerald Early has credited me with this observation, and I must in turn credit my source. I borrowed the concept from Professor Bryce Lyon of Brown University, who offered a seminar on the topic, which I unfortunately never visited. I was fascinated enough to scan his book on the subject and to explore the theme independently, and along somewhat different lines. Afrocentrism, however, is not always a historiography of decline, and the various permutations of the ideology must always be related to the changing historical circumstances in which it has arisen over the past century and a half. I would associate W. E. B. Du Bois with the historiography of decline, but not inextricably, as Arthur Herman does in *The Idea of Decline in Western History*. Du Bois, whether viewed as a Hegelian idealist or as a Marxist materialist (and he could speak the language of each), was fundamentally a "progressive," albeit capable of the sentimentalism and romantic nostalgia that I have highlighted in my discussion of him.[12]

More than once, I shall remind the reader that Egyptocentrism and Afrocentrism are not the same thing. Egyptocentrism is the sometimes sentimental, at other times cynical, attempt to claim ancient Egyptian ancestry for black Americans. It involves the attempt to reconstruct the peoples of ancient Egypt in terms of traditional American racial perceptions. Afrocentrism, on the other hand, is simply the belief that the African ancestry of black peoples, regardless of where they live, is an inescapable element of their various identities – imposed both from within and from without their own communities. I have attempted to discuss some of the aspects of so-called Afrocentrism that have been sensibly argued by historians and cultural anthropologists. Most aspects of African consciousness among black Americans are, after all, unrelated to the fanciful exaggeration that African Americans are, in some exceptional or exclusive way, heirs to the civilization of the ancient Nile. The heritage of Egypt belongs to all of humanity.

Lefkowitz's agenda is not driven solely by her distaste for black Egyptocentrism or its sometimes irrational exuberance. She and her supporters are motivated by the guild jealousy of Greek and Latin professors, who are upset by the intrusion of Martin Bernal, an Asian specialist, on their turf with the publication of his *Black Athena*. Largely in response to this, Lefkowitz published *Not Out of Africa*, and a subsequent edited volume, *Black Athena Revisited*.[13] Bernal's efforts are of less than marginal interest to the present study, but I am intrigued by the way classicists have reacted to his work. Professors of Greek (who are usually untrained in hieroglyphics, archeology, or physical anthropology) can hardly be considered more qualified to work in Egyptology than Bernal, albeit his guild affiliation in East Asian languages and culture. Bernal, with his appreciable skills as a linguist, at least claims some knowledge of Egyptian language and writing.

As I shall illustrate, concern with ancient Egypt as a feature of African American cultural ideology did not begin with Martin Bernal's *Black Athena*, which is only the latest in a series of works by white authors cited by African Americans in their attempts to authenticate a tie to the monumental history of dynastic Egypt. In the nineteenth century it was Count Constantin Volney who was most frequently cited by Afrocentric enthusiasts.[14] Bernal acknowledges a tradition of black authors who have represented this concern with ancient Egypt, although his treatment of these authors is sketchy and uncritical. St. Clair Drake offers a more sophisticated treatment of this tradition in his sadly neglected *Black Folk Here and There,* presented with irony and gentle wit. To his credit, Bernal has demonstrated his awareness that those aspects of Afrocentrism with which he is concerned are much older than the current heated debate. His purpose, however, was never to offer a complete discussion of African American folk historiography but, rather, to announce his emotional attachment to some of its more Egyptocentric proponents.[15]

Lefkowitz and Bernal have associated the romanticization of Egypt with the rise of black Freemasonry, but when we examine the major writings of African American Masons during its early years, we find that the Egyptians are curiously neglected.[16] The most important works on black Masonic history, such as Charles Wesley's *Prince Hall,* have been more concerned with demonstrating the validity of their charter putatively acquired from British Freemasons in the eighteenth century.[17] It would have been contrary to their purposes to have asserted a separatist or exceptionalist tradition. Furthermore, the founders of African American Freemasonry were clergymen, who identified with biblical Hebrews and did not wish to be associated with pagan Egypt. William Grimshaw's *Official History of Freemasonry Among the Colored People* traced the tradition not to the Great Pyramid but to the Temple of Solomon.[18]

Since Lefkowitz and Bernal have attributed the rise of Black Egyptocentrism to Freemasonry, it is surprising that they have failed to reference the works of either Charles Wesley or William H. Grimshaw, which are present in the collections of most university libraries. More understandable is that they have overlooked a rare book, Martin Delany's 1853 publication entitled *Origins and Objects of Ancient Freemasonry.*[19] Delany, who buttressed with fundamentalist biblical arguments his position that all wisdom could be traced to black Africa, would have provided wonderful grist for Lefkowitz and Bernal's mill. The writings of black Masons would certainly have more relevancy to their arguments than their digressions on the Egyptian themes of Mozart's *Magic Flute.* They have not troubled to explain how a German opera could have had much influence on African Americans at a time when they were banned from opera houses. The work's many instances of gratuitous racism have always been painful to black people, even those like myself who are fond of Mozart.[20]

For a disproportionate part of her argument Lefkowitz has relied on one idiosyncratic example of Egyptocentric black Freemasonry, simply because it suits her position. She is obsessed with George James's popular underground classic, *Stolen Legacy* (1954), a mystical work that has recently been rediscovered, particularly by working-class black males. James appeals to readers who feel alienated from university-based African American studies programs, which they view as controlled by a flashy crew of postmodernists and deconstructionists who have co-opted every aspect of black culture, from feminism to gangsta rap. Young black males have an understandable mistrust for those amazingly ambidextrous black studies spokesmen who write blurbs for Molefi Asante with one hand and denunciations with the other. They feel excluded from the mainstream black studies movement and are attracted to the mysticism of Egyptocentric books, believing that the black studies movement has "sold out." I have frequently encountered the opinion that it has been taken over by showy media specialists, who cynically exploit the rhetoric of blackness while craftily paying lip service to the vernacular Afrocentrism of the grass roots.[21]

Ironically, the appearance of Lefkowitz's book has been heralded with jubilation by paranoid black nationalists and Egyptocentrists. What better proof for their conspiracy theories could they have desired than such a volume? Especially since it is written by a white woman, its very existence is all the proof they require that there really is a conspiracy to steal the legacy of ancient Egypt from African Americans and other African peoples.[22] Demagogues like Maulana Karenga leap at the chance to debate her, thereby enhancing their notoriety and appealing to their constituencies as defenders of the "stolen legacy" of African peoples. In the process, they assist Mary Lefkowitz, once an obscure drudge in the academic backwaters of a classics department, in her quest for status as a "public intellectual." She has received only negligible monetary rewards on the conservative lecture circuit for her efforts, but the damage she has done by contributing to a spirit of paranoia and mistrust will be impossible to counteract.

Glenn Loury, a well-known black moderate who is not an Egyptocentrist, has astutely called attention to an additional problem. He notes that Lefkowitz expresses on more than one occasion her concern that propagating the myth of the stolen legacy "robs the ancient Greeks and their modern descendants of a heritage that rightly belongs to them" (126). With gentle irony Loury muses, "And here I had been thinking it was *my* heritage too!" He continues with the assertion that "the search for a black Shakespeare or a black Tolstoy [is] unnecessary," presumably because their heritage belongs to whoever is capable of appreciating them. Concludes Loury, "I genuinely doubt that Mary Lefkowitz would disagree with these sentiments. Yet I deeply regret that she sometimes writes in *Not Out of Africa* as though she would."[23]

Along with other opponents of Egyptocentric fanaticism, I am apprehensive that Lefkowitz's diatribe will probably result in far more harm than good. It does nothing to dissuade radical Afrocentrists from their sentimental racism, and it is so mean-spirited that it has increased the difficulties of objective scholars in their attempts to minimize the presence of racial romanticism and sentimentalism in university classrooms. Lefkowitz's book has served only to obscure definitions further; it is ahistorical, presentist, synchronic, and absolutely devoid of any of the methods of serious cultural or intellectual history. Like most polemicists, its author finds methodology inconvenient and precise definitions intolerable. Thus she is hardly different from the various demagogues and polemicists who have gathered on the other side of the Afrocentrism debate. Much silliness and ill will has been spewed forth by the likes of Mary Lefkowitz and the black nationalist polemicist Maulana Karenga, who represent two sides of the same hateful coin. As a result, it has become almost impossible for most persons to engage in analytical, dispassionate discussion of the various expressions of those movements – both intellectual and emotional – that constitute what we today refer to as "Afrocentrism."

Racial polemicists of the Lefkowitz–Karenga ilk have assiduously avoided a systematic definition of Afrocentrism, confusing it not only with Egyptocentrism but with affirmative action, multiculturalism, black nationalism, and whatever other issue they may wish to address at a given time. Under the guise of promoting historical objectivity, they spew out whatever tendentious trash they wish on a wide variety of subjects, reflecting nothing more than their own racial and political biases. Afrocentrism provides for such authors a subject heading that is timely and titillating, to which any number of opinions and prejudices may easily be glued. Thus a limitless range of opinion has been attached to the term Afrocentrism by authors across the political spectrum, most of whom are less interested in scholarly investigations of African American cultures and historical traditions than in forwarding myriad self-serving political agendas.

In fairness to Professor Lefkowitz and her cohort, they have correctly (even usefully) pointed out numerous childish errors in the writings of enthusiastic nonacademic authors. They have exposed, for example, the ridiculous contention that European conspirators looted the Alexandrine Library years before it was built. On the other hand, Lefkowitz frequently makes statements that would be challenged by any shrewd undergraduate. For example, speaking of George James, she asserts that "many otherwise well-educated people believe that what he claims is true." Who are these "otherwise well-educated people" to whom she refers? She does not identify them nor does she provide any data as to their numbers. What Lefkowitz achieves is to "darkeneth counsel by words without knowledge."

She has thoughtlessly muddled ideas derived from nineteenth-century ethnography, popular mythology of the 1920s, and cult literature of the 1980s. She makes the generalization that all of these ideas constitute Afrocentrism, and then implies that this "Afrocentrism" is widely being taught in college classrooms. Has it occurred to her that proponents of African American studies are divided into numerous categories, influenced by disciplinary affiliations, ideological backgrounds, and political affiliations? Conservative, feminist, deconstructionist, and Marxist scholars in black studies programs and departments have long and vocally opposed romantic and sentimental Afrochauvinism – indeed, far longer than she has.

If Professor Lefkowitz and the contributors to *Black Athena Revisited* are truly concerned about the use of taxpayers' dollars to teach myth as history, they ought to be courageously focusing on the real challenge. Conservative politicians in both major political parties have decided that the best way to improve American education at the primary and secondary levels is to give "the people" greater control of local school curricula. Their goal is to be accomplished by increasing the power of local public school boards, which will decide, without benefit of "pointy-headed intellectuals," what "truths" their children need to learn. Those who are truly opposed to antiintellectualism should be fighting against such proposals, and against the use of tax dollars to fund vouchers tenderable at private schools run by biblical fundamentalists, flat earth theorists, black chauvinists, white supremacists, and anti-Semites.

Because Jewish intellectuals have been among Afrocentrism's best, although shamefully unacknowledged, friends, one is appalled that Lefkowitz has ignored their role in the development of Afrocentrism. It is amazing that she has taken the work of Martin Bernal, which is a necessary and valid attack on nineteenth-century anti-Semitism, and mindlessly identified it with the very thing that Bernal is fighting. Furthermore, the fact that a lunatic fringe of slimy little anti-Semites have styled themselves "Afrocentrists" provides no logical basis for implying that Afrocentric writing is even peripherally anti-Semitic or for asserting that it is hate literature.[24] Because of the consistent attempts of the Lefkowitz school to associate Afrocentrism with anti-Semitism, the influence of Jewish scholars on the evolution of Afrocentrism is of interest. The work of Franz Boas and Melville Herskovits is particularly relevant to this discussion, and allusions to their work are frequent in these pages.

Professor Vernon Williams, in a recent discussion of the complexity of African American academic interest in Africa, has related this interest to the emergence of modern anthropology under the leadership of Franz Boas.[25] Williams identifies scholarly positions which we would call Afrocentric today, but which were developed by the Jewish American anthropologist Boas, as representing the most advanced anthropological thinking of his time. Williams also discusses the influences of the Protestant American Egyptologist James Breasted, who converted Booker T. Washington to Afrocentrism. Williams recounts the well-known story that Du Bois told to Harold Isaacs: "I did not myself become actively interested in Africa until 1908 or 1910. Franz Boas really influenced me to begin studying this subject and I began really to get into it only after 1915." In his 1946 publication *The World and Africa*, Du Bois quoted at length from Boas, who sounds like a good Afrocentrist.

> It seems likely that at times when the European was still satisfied with rude stone tools, the African had invented or adopted the art or smelting iron. Consider for a moment what this invention has meant for the advance of the human race.... It seems not unlikely that the people who made the marvelous discovery of reducing iron ores by smelting were the African Negroes. Neither ancient Europe, nor ancient western Asia, nor ancient China knew iron, and everything points to its introduction from Africa.[26]

It is startling that anyone would write what purports to be a study of Afrocentrism without discussing the work of Boas, or Herskovits, or Bronislaw Malinowski. It is not necessary to focus here on such points as Boas's contention that iron smelting was first practiced by Africans. Such claims are of less importance to this discussion than the color of Cleopatra's favorite cat. My purpose is to show that Afrocentrism is not a self-contained tradition, recently developed by black zealots. The phenomenon represents an attempt by black and white authors to manipulate history and myth, poetry and art, folklore and religious tradition, regardless of authorship, in ways sympathetic to African peoples. Despite the fulminations of ethno-chauvinists and other prejudiced persons, it remains a fact that the contributions of white scholars, like Boas, Malinowski, and Herskovits, were fundamental to that complex of ideas that we designate today as Afrocentrism.

Students of African and African American history have long appreciated the irony that much of what we now call Afrocentrism was developed during the 1930s by the Jewish American scholar Melville

Herskovits. It is impossible to deny Herskovits's influence on such universally regarded scholars as August Meier, Roger Abrahams, Sterling Stuckey, and Robert Farris Thompson. In 1970 Pat M. Ryan noted the *centrality* of Africa to any discussion of African American culture since publication of Herskovits's *Myth of the Negro Past.*[27] Any college sophomore may find fault with Herskovits, but would be missing the forest for the trees. It is difficult to dismiss Herskovits's central thesis, which Ryan summarizes as a challenge to the myth "that the black population of this continent had no past, that their past had been obliterated, and that this past was negligible or (if at all present) only marginal and insignificant." Ryan noted the strongly controlling influence of Herskovits's theories on black nationalist theoreticians of no less significance than Amiri Baraka, the principal black cultural nationalist of the late 1960s and early 1970s. In his widely read work on African American music, *Blues People* (published under his old name, LeRoi Jones), Baraka footnoted and promulgated the Herskovits claim that the African past was of fundamental importance to the present and future status of African Americans.[28]

Herskovits was not the only scholar associated with this view of the centrality of Africa, which contains the immediate sources of what is now called Afrocentrism. Bronislaw Malinowski, a Pole who became a British subject, made a most significant contribution to the Afrocentric model in an article published in the unassailable *American Journal of Sociology* in 1943, in which he argued that the roots of African culture are detectable wherever African peoples have been dispersed, and that politics of race relations would remain insoluble until policies of education and integration were adjusted to reflect the roots of cultural diversity that separated Europeans and Africans.[29] Nonetheless, Malinowski, like Herskovits and most other mainstream anthropologists, maintained that the influence of Africanisms on New World cultures was not limited to black communities. In 1967 Roger Bastide produced *Les Amériques noires*, published in English as *African Civilizations in the New World* (1971). The work expanded on the Herskovits thesis that both Latin American cultures and North American cultures were profoundly influenced by the presence of their respective "African" populations.[30]

By now, it will be obvious that I use "Afrocentrism" in this study as a term of convenience. I use it to incorporate a wide range of phenomena that predate that term. Although "Afrocentrism" was not invented until the 1960s, the idea of discussing African American culture as a survival of African culture was well established in sociological and anthropological literature before the Second World

War. The idea that African Americans were essentially African, and that the solutions to their problems must be discovered within a Pan-African context is nothing new. Furthermore, Afrocentrism, although not always under that name, has been a factor in recent African American scholarship and culture theory, even among scholars who have eschewed or disparaged the term.

Henry Louis Gates and Sterling Stuckey are two African American scholars who, roughly simultaneous to the appearance of Molefi Asante's *Afrocentric Idea*, busily revived the theses of Herskovits and Malinowski during the 1980s. They both became acceptable advocates of Afrocentric theory, although neither made use of the term Afrocentric to describe his own work. Gates's Afrocentrism, like that of Asante, reflected the influence of numerous white authors, including most prominently, in Gates's case, Robert Farris Thompson and Roger D. Abrahams.[31] In *The Signifying Monkey* (1988), Gates identified himself with positions that were unequivocally Afrocentric and that strikingly reflected the influences of Herskovits and art historian Robert Farris Thompson.

Viewed from the perspective of his most influential work, *The Signifying Monkey*, Henry Louis Gates appears to be a traditional Afrocentrist in the anthropological mode. He resuscitates the Herskovits legacy of the 1930s, contributing to the idea that black American culture is essentially West African. In addition, he has become the unchallenged interpreter and the principal raconteur of black metropolitan life, reveling with obviously sincere delight in the colorful cabaret of African American arts and entertainment – arguing consistently for their Africanity.

> Inadvertently African slavery in the New World satisfied the preconditions for the emergence of a new African culture, a truly Pan-African culture fashioned as a colorful weave of linguistic, institutional, metaphysical, and formal threads. What survived this fascinating process was the most useful and the most compelling of the fragments at hand. Afro-American culture is an African culture with a difference as signified by the catalysts of English, Dutch, French, Portuguese, or Spanish languages and cultures, which informed the precise structures that each discrete New World Pan-African culture assumed.[32]

Sterling Stuckey, like Henry Louis Gates, represents a continuation of the Herskovits tradition in Afrocentric studies. The fundamental assumption of Stuckey's widely influential work, *Slave Culture* (1987), is essentially the same as that of Gates in *Signifying Monkey*. Both view African American culture as an African culture, which came into being as a process of fusing numerous African cultures during the slavery period. Like Gates, Stuckey insists on "the centrality of the African past to the African in America," and asserts that a new African culture emerged out of the fusion of various African cultural forms that were imported into the Americas. Like Gates, Herskovits, and Malinowski, Stuckey is convinced that this new culture was Pan-African and, like Gates, he is willing to entertain very seriously the proposition that "black Americans today are basically African in culture."[33]

When we apply the political and anthropological definitions of Afrocentrism that dominate the work of Herskovits and Malinowski, it can be seen that the concept is hardly limited to Egyptocentrism. Their political-anthropological perspective had long been entertained by African American missionaries like Alexander Crummell and Samuel Williams, nineteenth-century advocates of African emigration. These men's absence from discussions of Afrocentrism is remarkable, as is that of Henry Highland Garnet, who anticipated political Afrocentrism with his 1859 call for the establishment of "a grand center of Negro Nationality" in West Africa.[34] Certainly the African emigrationist tradition that some scholars have referred to as "Black Zionism" is worthy of mention in Lefkowitz's book, since it purports to be a scholarly treatment of Afrocentrism.[35]

Certain nineteenth-century Afrocentrists displayed a marked hostility to Egypt, because the nineteenth-century roots of Afrocentrism were located in biblical fundamentalism rather than in Egyptology. Alexander Crummell had no love for the land of the "frowning pyramids," and sought to remove African Americans from all association with a people he viewed as decadent and accursed. Certain early-twentieth-century black nationalist sects, such as the Moorish Science Temple and the Nation of Islam, have followed a nineteenth-century tradition of biblical interpretation that placed the origins of the black race in Asia. Noble Drew Ali asserted that African Americans were descended from the original Asiatic race of Moabites, which had migrated to Morocco. Elijah Muhammad identified African Americans with "the great Asiatic Nation of the Tribe of Shabazz."[36]

It was an exotic and heady brew of contradictory ideas that invigorated the Afrocentrism of the late nineteenth and early twentieth centuries. But the problems and contradictions essential to this variety of racial chauvinism were not original with black Americans. They inherited it from Western traditions of pseudohistory and national mythology that were certainly as old as Virgil's *Aeneid* – certainly a lot older. When the black historical writer is as well-read and thoughtful as Alexander Crummell, or as much a trickster as William Wells Brown, one expects and one discovers authorial awareness that Afrochauvinism is a very traditional sort of game and often one will encounter even a spirit of playfulness, a dark sense of humor, and a capacity for self-satire among those nineteenth-century Afrocentrists who were truly – to use an outmoded eighteenth-century expression – "men of parts."

The practice of creating a monumental past for one's race or nationality was hardly the invention of African vindicationists. Traditionally, fanciful Englishmen of letters who preferred not to think of their ancestors as crude barbarians could fancy themselves descendants of Trojan heroes.[37] This tradition was embedded in English letters. Geoffrey of Monmouth (1100–54) – acclaimed by some medievalists as "a master of grave, imperturbable lying" – is credited as the source of a charming mythology that gained widespread currency in late medieval and Renaissance England. He was the apparent progenitor of the pseudohistory that located the roots of British culture in the wanderings of the mythical Brutus, a putative descendant of Aeneas who was supposed to have been driven out of Italy and, after some epic peregrinations, to have established a colony on Albion's soil.[38]

Egyptomorphic Afrocentrism represents a universal and eternal human inclination to create pseudoclassical folk mythologies. And yet black Americans have always been ambivalent toward the antidemocratic implications of claiming a pharaonic past. Like most Americans, African Americans are steeped in the egalitarian mythology of the "self-made man," and have a well-developed aversion to the practice of attempting to base one's sense of personal worth on the possession of a noble lineage. The self-reliant tradition represented by a Benjamin Franklin or a Frederick Douglass is fundamentally more appealing to the instincts of black Americans than is the claim of attachment to some collapsing "house of Usher." Black nationalists who cherish proletarian traditions are uncomfortable with the idea of tracing one's descent to an effete pharaoh with ceremonial flail, mascaraed eyes, and "sneer of cold command," compelling faceless hordes to drag blocks of sandstone up the side of a pyramid. For many black Americans it has always been preferable to trace one's ancestry to noble savages or virile barbarians, living out their lives in the pristine cleanliness of an equatorial Eden.

The present study investigates the fascinating and imaginative, if sometimes contradictory, meanings embedded in the so-called Afrocentric tradition. It is important to disentangle this tradition from the mythology of Egyptocentrism, and to describe its truly complex

origins in enlightenment Christianity, eighteenth-century progressivism, and black resistance to white supremacy. Intellectual Pan-
Africanism owes far more to biblical traditions than to Egyptology or
Freemasonry. Much Afrocentrism has focused on West Africa, where
black princesses danced "naked and free, where black skin was not
God's curse," and where human flesh was never sacrificed to the
harsh stone of "frowning pyramids."

The African American vindicationist tradition has often been a
historiography of decline based on the idea that the African race
had fallen from its past greatness. The endeavor to establish the
credentials of the black race by showing that it had contributed to
civilization in the dawn of history has frequently led amateur historians, journalists, and pamphleteers to believe they had to prove that
the pharaohs were black.[39] Nineteenth-century Egyptocentrists developed the school of thought that the sociologist Orlando Patterson
has called "contributionism" and that St. Clair Drake has called
"vindicationism." Its purpose was to prove that black people were
something more than semihumans, cultural parasites who could do
nothing more than crudely imitate the achievements of the white
race.

But black consciousness of the sweep of history was not always
centered in a metaphysic of decline. Black Americans viewed the
cycles of history as providing a means of projecting the future. From
the nineteenth century onward, they vigorously argued the parallels
between their own experiences and those of the peoples of Northern
Europe. The Roman Empire's experiences with barbarians was seen
as presaging the history of the world's darker peoples under European and American imperial influences. African American authors
lost few opportunities to remind their readers of the one-time barbarism of prehistoric Europe, hoping thus to redeem a message of
hope from Africa's image of relative backwardness.

The tendency has always been resisted by some European historians. C. S. Lewis advanced an ahistorical plea against applying the
term "barbarian" to the ancient Germanic and Celtic peoples,
placing the word in inverted commas. "It might otherwise mislead,"
he explained. "It might suggest a far greater difference in race
arts and natural capacity than really existed even in ancient times
between Roman citizens and those who pressed upon the frontiers
of the empire."[40] Other European writers have found the comparison between European and African barbarians useful, as did Joseph Conrad in the opening pages of *Heart of Darkness*, where he
observed that England too had once been "one of the dark places
of earth."

Here and there a military camp lost in the wilderness, like a needle in a bundle of hay – cold, fog, tempests, disease, exile, and death – death skulking in the air, in the water, in the bush . . . think of a decent young citizen in a toga. . . . Land in a swamp, march through the woods, and in some island post feel the savagery, the utter savagery had closed round him – all that mysterious life of the wilderness that stirs in the forest, in the jungles, in the hearts of wild men.[41]

Black American historical consciousness is based not only on an African-centered construction of the past, but on a variety of attempts to fashion visions of a better future. The present work is therefore intended to address *both* the historiography of decline *and* the historiography of progress in African American thought. It assumes, fundamentally, that popular culture is important, and that popular conceptions of history among a people are worth understanding.[42] African American folk history is interesting, not merely because it is quaint or picturesque but because it represents an attempt by an embattled people to promote a sense of collective worth despite a history of persistent oppression. For this reason, I have attempted to write interpretations of African American cultures and historical mythologies that are sympathetic and respectful.

I am certain, I realize, to offend both the advocates and the opponents of sentimental Afrocentrism and romantic Egyptocentrism by stating my belief that they are usually harmless and inoffensive, if sometimes extravagant, folk traditions. They are whimsical, entertaining, and often charming fantasies developed by nineteenth-century journalists, preachers, novelists, and vernacular storytellers. Some professional historians will no doubt wonder why I have chosen to devote time and energy to the historical perceptions of those outside the guild. Others will see my work as part of a tradition that insists that historical consciousness is neither the independent creation nor the exclusive possession of professional scholars.

VARIETIES OF BLACK HISTORICISM

ISSUES OF ANTIMODERNISM AND "PRESENTISM"

Sentimental Afrocentrism

"Afrocentric" was defined in 1962 by the secretariat of the Encyclo-pedia Africana for the purpose of distinguishing a geographical fo-cus from a racial focus. W. E. B. Du Bois, director of the project, had earlier written that his idea was "to prepare and publish an encyclo-pedia not on the vague subject of race, but on the peoples inhabiting the continent of Africa." Du Bois seems to have settled on the term as he attempted to clarify the relationship of the project at hand to other projects that he had proposed or attempted to initiate over the preceding fifty-three years.

In 1909 Du Bois wrote to the venerable West African nationalist Edward Wilmot Blyden, the nineteenth-century prophet of the idea of "African Personality," who many think of today as the father of the Afrocentric idea, proposing an Encyclopedia Africana, but little came of that proposal. Du Bois began a project for an "Encyclopedia of Colored People" in 1934, but that too failed for lack of funds. Both of these early plans manifested a Pan-African or black diaspora orientation, and Du Bois proposed to treat the history and status of all people of African descent, throughout the world. Du Bois obvi-ously wrestled for many years with the concept of an African-centered project, how it should relate to racial propaganda, and whether it should center on the entire black race or on the geo-graphical entity of Africa. The Encyclopedia Africana, as eventually defined in 1961, was to be limited to the continent of Africa. It was to be "a scientific production and not a matter of propaganda; and [was] to have included among its writers the best students of Africa in the world." Sympathetic white scholars were to be consulted, but the encyclopedia was to be written "from the African point of view from people who know and understand the history and culture of Africans."[1]

Molefi Asante's concept of "Afrocentric perspective" would seem to be similar to Du Bois's concept of an "African point of view," but it rejects Du Bois's precise geographical restriction. Asante's enterprise is "based on the African orientation to the cosmos." An African is defined as "one who has the physical and cultural characteristics similar to those presently found in some region of the continent."[2] Its purpose is to affirm the "African personality," and to illustrate the contributions to human progress and civilization by all persons who might have been classified as Negroes under America's traditional system of racial distinctions.[3] One may legitimately ask what, exactly, is meant by such designations as "Afrocentric perspective" or "African personality." Given the remarkable diversity of languages, customs, and physical characteristics among "black" Africans, can we truly speak of African "physical and cultural characteristics" or an "African point of view"? Many Afrocentrists think so, and speak of a "composite African" to whom they ascribe a set of sentimental notions of Africanness that are reminiscent of nineteenth-century romantic racialism.[4]

Among the romantic and sentimental notions commonly attributed to the African personality are a predisposition to communalism, a harmony with nature, and a propensity for artistic expression and emotional experience. This mythology has been a force in Western literature since the Renaissance, and was a component of the negritude movement among Francophone Africans in the 1930s. Contemporary Afrocentrists impatiently dismiss evidence of diversity among African peoples. They insist that underlying similarities unite all African cultures, despite superficial or apparent differences of language and customs. Afrocentrists have been prone to ignore, or to rationalize away, the interethnic warfare and genocide in Uganda, Rwanda, and elsewhere in Africa, with the simplistic and unconscionable assertion that African internal conflicts are no more than the result of European colonial and postcolonial influences.[5]

Proponents of the African perspective frequently display hostility toward anyone who asks them to define what they mean by African personality or African world view. Invariably, their attempts to define what is meant by African people will shift from a geographical to a racial focus. In attempting to define the term "African people" the Afrocentrist seldom means to include Berbers or white South Africans or the southern Asians who have lived on the continent for centuries. He or she refuses to concede that the concept "African" is based on a racial typology rather than a geographical designation. Asante himself concedes that "African" cannot simply refer to any person descended from African ancestors, since all human beings are presumably descended from one primal African stock.[6] There is some evidence that "Negroid" (Afrocentrists prefer the term "Africoid") stocks were present in prehistoric Europe and Asia, as well. Furthermore, it seems likely that Africoid, Caucasoid, and Asian stocks have intermixed in some parts of Africa since the birth of human culture. The definition of who is African always seems to turn less on the question of African ancestry than on the question of biogenetic qualities associated with "blackness."[7]

The Afrocentrist, therefore, must not only answer the question What is an African? but must also solve the riddle put by Marcus Garvey in 1923: "Who and what is a Negro?"[8] Garvey understood that the term "Negro" – or even "African" – cannot be defined simply as the designation for any person endowed with those features that European anthropologists have traditionally called "Negroid" or "Africoid." This has been true, at least in the United States, from the beginning. In colonial Boston, the designation "African" included all "colored" persons, even those who did not physically resemble Africans. The designation "Negro" in nineteenth-century Washington, D.C., applied not only to persons who were dark or black but to anyone who was known to have Negro ancestry. In the United States, many persons customarily designated as African have conformed to the somatic norm image of a European. They have possessed the essential phenotypic traits of a white person.

Afrocentrists feel compelled to include in the category of Africans all individuals who under segregationist law in the United States would have been designated Negroes. They follow the American tradition that makes one drop of Negro blood sufficient to classify a person as "colored," no matter how Caucasoid in appearance. Thus, the designation African, as used by Afrocentrists, accepts the *idea* of "blackness" as it has been institutionalized in the history, customs, and legal traditions of the United States. The Afrocentrist answers the question of who is an African by reference to nineteenth-century American definitions. One is black, simply, if one or both of one's parents are black. Ancestral legacy is more important than physical appearance in determining who is black or African.[9]

Asante follows the traditional, and apparently inescapable, practice of conflating the concepts of black and African. Social and linguistic realities leave him no choice. Asante asserts that "blackness is more than a biological fact; indeed, it is more than a color; it functions as a commitment to a historical project that places the African person back on center and as such it becomes an escape to sanity." Thus he defines blackness in terms of Afrocentrism and Afrocentrism in terms of blackness. The circular definition shifts inevitably from a geographical locus to a biogenetic type, from an innate state of being to a therapeutic ideological commitment. Black, or African, people are defined by Asante as those who possess a set of values to supplement their African provenance and biogenetic heritage. Whether Asante uses the term blackness or Afrocentricity, he refers nonetheless *both* to the hereditary racial traits commonly associated with African ancestry, *and* to a commitment to placing Africans and their point of view "on center." Asante's definition has the advantage of simplicity, but it is far too inclusive. To give it precise meaning, it is necessary to explore what the "project" associated with that definition has meant historically.[10]

Vindicationist and Contributionist Traditions

The term "vindicationist" refers to a unique tradition among people of African ancestry, the project of defending black people from the charge that they have made little or no contribution to the history of human progress. Sometimes vindicationism may imply the even more basic struggle to secure recognition of the fact that black people are human at all. The East African scholar Ali Mazrui addressed the problem of psychic damage in a 1979 BBC lecture series, "The African Condition," where he maintained that blacks, "although not necessarily the worse casualities of brutality" when compared to such groups as German Jews or American Indians, "remain the worst victims of contempt." African people, says Mazrui, have been "psychologically demeaned" by the experiences of slavery, colonialism, and racism to such an extent that "Africans and people of African ancestry might be regarded as the most humiliated in modern history."[11]

Afrocentrists frequently view racial vindication as necessary because the African person is taught, from earliest childhood, to doubt the capacity of black people for "civilization," meaning self-government, mechanical invention, economic independence, and abstract reasoning. The theory that people of African ancestry suffer in some peculiar ways from self-doubt and self-hatred has been expressed by W. E. B. Du Bois, E. Franklin Frazier, Malcolm X, and the psychologist, Kenneth Clarke.[12] This theory of "the damaged black psyche," has been analyzed by Daryl Michael Scott, who observes that even Afrocentrists "while rejecting the self-hatred paradigm as Eurocentric . . . have created what amounts to an Afrocentric version" of this model. Scott asserts, in other words, not that Afrocentrists are inclined to self-hatred, but that they frequently assume that black people, by and large, have damaged psyches. For such theorists, an essential part of their cure for self-hatred involves the adoption of an Afrocentric perspective on history.[13]

In this connection, it may be observed, not without irony, that some apologists for the African personality have accepted an essentially racialist characterization of the Negro, but have attempted to stand it on its head. The Martinican poet Aimé Césaire, celebrated by Asante as "the greatest of all poets," collaborated in the creation of a philosophy called *négritude*, or negritude, which claimed that the very incapacity for rationalism and abstract thought endowed the African with a naturalness and emotional purity that constituted superiority of a sort. Thus Césaire celebrated Africans as

> those who have invented neither gunpowder nor compass
> those who tamed neither steam nor electricity
> those who explored neither the sea nor the sky.[14]

Another negritude poet, Léopold Senghor, once president of the Republic of Senegal, similarly expressed the view that "emotion is Negro and reason is Greek." The views of both poets have been gently but firmly rebuked by the Senegalese anthropologist Cheikh Anta Diop, for although the musings of Césaire and Senghor carry an irony more complex than immediately meets the eye, they nonetheless acquiesce in a tradition of self-disparagement that African scholars should seek to combat.[15]

Because it contests the idea that Africans have invented nothing and have made no contributions to human progress, Afrocentrism is linked to "vindicationism," a tradition that anthropologist St. Clair Drake has identified. Vindicationists, angered by the white supremacist accusation that Africans have never built a civilization, have stressed African contributions to human progress. Black leaders such as Edward Wilmot Blyden and Frederick Douglass have felt they must answer the charge that black people were subhuman creatures, lacking in capacity for "civilization." Unlike the negritude poets, they have seen civilization as one of the essential proofs of the humanity of Africans and their New World descendants. Only occasionally have the vindicationists celebrated the "primitivism" of the preliterate societies of tropical Africa; more typically, they have stressed ties to monumental Egypt and Ethiopia. The term civilization is always related to the architectural imagery of "marble . . . the gilded monuments of Princes." With a few important exceptions, the vindicationists have failed to question the concept of civilization, itself, but have sought to defend Africans by proving the African origin of ancient civilizations and demonstrating the indebtedness of modern humanity to those civilizations.[16]

In *Black Folk Here and There*, St. Clair Drake identifies himself as a vindicationist and acknowledges that his perspective is not impartial. He is, nonetheless, critical of the evangelical spirit that pervades much Afrocentric thinking, and questions a tendency to substitute mythic creativity for systematic analysis. Particularly concerned with the discourse of "Nile Valley Blacks in Antiquity," Drake has focused on subjects of traditional concern to Afrocentrists, such as "The Roles of Egypt and Ethiopia in Black History," "Color Coding in Egypt Before Hellenization," and "The Somatic Norm in Meroitic Society." He takes the eminently reasonable positions that ancient Egypt was a racial and cultural melting pot, and that while ancient Egyptians did not think of themselves as white or black in the sense that those terms are used in the United States today, they displayed a broad range of physical traits closely approximating those of contemporary African Americans rather than the narrower range of physical types found among contemporary Euro-Americans.[17]

What Drake calls vindicationism is similar to what sociologist Orlando Patterson has called "contributionism," a concern among historians with demonstrating that black or African peoples have made a contribution to the progress of mankind. This variety of thinking appeared in a 1789 sermon by John Marrant, which called attention to the African origins of Christian church fathers Cyprian, Origen, Augustine, and Chrysostom. In the twentieth century J. A. Rogers, a West Indian immigrant to the United States, produced a number of works concerned with demonstrating the black ancestry of various world historical figures. Rogers stressed the mulatto parentage of Alexandre Dumas and Aleksandr Pushkin, whose African ancestry was known and acknowledged, along with the supposed Africanity of the pharaoh Akhenaton and the emperor Hannibal, although their racial histories demanded more imaginative reconstruction.[18]

Heroic Monumentalism: The Egyptocentric Mode

Vindicationist history, which focuses on the ancient civilizations of Egypt and Ethiopia, is not a new movement. An 1827 editorial in *Freedom's Journal*, the first black newspaper in the United States, asserted the relationship between black Americans and the ancient Egyptians. "Mankind generally allow that all nations are indebted to the Egyptians for the introduction of the arts and sciences," the editorial stated, "but they are not willing to acknowledge that the Egyptians bore any resemblance to the present race of Africans; though Herodotus 'the father of history,' expressly declares that the Egyptians had black skins and frizzled hair." Since the 1820s, Afrocentrists have displayed remarkable exegetical prowess on those passages in Herodotus that are susceptible to interpretation as implying Egyptian or upper Nilotic origins for early Mediterranean civilization.[19]

Vindicationism has often been concerned with presenting African history in a heroic or monumental mode. It emphasizes the spectacular past and monumental contributions of the ancient civilizations of the Nile, including Ethiopia, Egypt, and Meroe. Black writers of the nineteenth century, including Samuel Ringgold Ward, William Wells Brown, and Frederick Douglass all claimed the ties of African Americans to the builders of Ancient Egypt. J. W. C. Pennington began the practice of identifying the civilizations of the eastern Mediterranean and Tigris–Euphrates with an ancient Negroid race, a tradition maintained in the 1940s by Drusilla Dunjee Houston. The recent fascination of Afrocentrists with the writings of Martin Bernal is only the latest manifestation of their traditional eagerness to celebrate the writings of white authors who are inclined to assert the importance of Egypt (and darker peoples) as contributors to Western history and civilization.[20]

It is frequently remarked that Afrocentric vindicationism in the nineteenth century was characteristically blind to the virtues of sub-Saharan societies.[21] Nineteenth-century vindicationists often chose to define their African heritage exclusively in terms of monumental Egypt. In recent years, however, Afrocentrists have struggled mightily to demonstrate linguistic and cultural connections between ancient Egypt and the societies of tropical Africa. In recent work, Molefi Asante has argued that the cultures of the African diaspora contain numerous and significant survivals of Egyptian civilization.[22]

The literature of vindicationism has burgeoned with irresistible force, especially with the advent of desktop publishing. A common thread in this literature is the affirmation that a central core of Egyptian philosophical and scientific concepts is derived from Central African cultures, and that an essentially African cosmology has been shared by Egypt and the rest of Africa since prehistoric times. The hypothesis is not fundamentally unreasonable, although the attempts at a systematic presentation of this argument have often been more imaginative than convincing. Thus one finds Molefi K. Asante involved in titanic efforts to discover cognates, analogues, and influences in the linguistic and philosophical histories of Nilotic and sub-Saharan Africa.[23] Chief Kwabena Faheem Ashanti asserts in his book *Psychotechnology of Brainwashing* that "African religions are based on African philosophy and ancient black Egyptian theology." Theophile Obenga, in *Ancient Egypt and Black Africa*, presents an extended and systematic assertion that the religion and philosophy of ancient Egypt are linked by "genetic linguistic connections" to the rest of the continent. Asar Jubal, Runoko Rashidi, and Na'im Akbar make similar connections – although mostly by implication rather than systematic demonstration.[24]

"A Grand Center of Negro Nationality"

The idea among African Americans of making Africa into a center of a national or international movement recurs throughout African American history. In 1773, four Boston slaves designating themselves as "Africans" petitioned the General Court of Massachusetts for legislation to set aside one day in a week on which they might work for themselves toward the end of buying their freedom and transporting themselves "to some part of the coast of Africa, where we propose a settlement."[25] In 1787, Prince Hall, grand master of the African Masonic Lodge in Boston, petitioned the General Court to assist his community in a "return to Africa, our native country."[26] In 1815, Paul Cuffe, a Massachusetts sea merchant and shipbuilder, proposed a plan to settle numbers of his fellow African Americans in the British West African colony of Sierra Leone. In 1817, the American Society for Colonizing the Free People of Color was founded by a group of whites, many of whom were opposed to the abolition of slavery and sought simply to rid the United States of the anomaly of a free black population. In response to what they perceived as a plan for forced deportation, three thousand black people reportedly met at the church of Richard Allen in Philadelphia to protest the American Colonization Society's program.[27] During the late 1820s, even the Pan-Africanist David Walker, who possessed a militant racial consciousness, was opposed to colonization.

Events of the 1850s led to renewed interest in an African return, symbolized by an 1854 colonization convention in Cleveland. The United States Congress had severely weakened the rights of Free Africans in the compromise of 1850, then in 1857 the Dred Scott decision seemed to deny them any rights at all. The founding of the African Civilization Society in 1858 signaled a revival of interest in Africa and in repatriationism. In this era of "classical" black nationalism, Henry Highland Garnet called for the establishment of "a grand center for Negro nationality," in either Africa or the New World. Martin Delany left on an exploratory venture to West Africa in 1859, committed to the goal of "Africa for the African race and black men to rule them." During the early years of the Civil War, there was considerable interest in African emigration, promoted by the editors of *The Weekly Anglo-African*. In the late nineteenth century, Bishop Henry McNeal Turner advocated African colonization and worked to strengthen the idea of Pan-African unity between African Americans and continental Africans. The tradition was carried into the twentieth century by Alfred C. Sam and Marcus Garvey. The idea of geopolitical nationhood was seldom accompanied by "cultural nationalism," however. Traditional black nationalists were generally contemptuous of African "tribal" culture and institutions. Their attitude toward Africa has come to be known as "redemptionism."[28]

African Redemptionism: The Hands of Ethiopia

Redemptionism, as St. Clair Drake has observed, was often associated with the language of "Ethiopianism," a teleological approach based on a biblical verse, "Princes shall come out of Egypt; Ethiopia shall soon stretch forth her hands unto God" (Psalms 68:31). The passage was given a prophetic interpretation and became the basis for a progressive theory of history. The eventual triumph of Africa over paganism and primitivism was an inevitable part of the Divine Plan. In the twentieth century, with the decline of traditional Christianity among black intellectuals, a Marxist theory of predestination was substituted for theological historicism, but the faith in the redemption of Africa remained strong among black nationalists and Pan-Africanists.[29]

Rhetoric and programs for the "redemption" of Africa flourished from the late eighteenth through the early twentieth centuries. It made its early appearances in the writings of such Europeanized Africans as Jacobus Capitein and Olaudah Equiano. Among black writers, even those opposed to African resettlement believed that Africa must be redeemed from paganism, and barbarism, before it could be redeemed from European colonialism. David Walker, Maria Stewart, and Robert Young made use of the Ethiopian prophecy in calling for universal African uplift. Alexander Crummell, even after abandoning emigrationism, wrote of the connection between civilization and Christianity as being necessary to the uplift of the continent. African American leaders who were most committed to the redemption of Africa were dedicated to the replacement of "pagan" and "primitive" African cultures with a new bourgeois Christianity that was to be based on scientific and industrial progress.

African redemptionists attempted to reconcile the slogan Africa for the Africans with the modernizing formula of the so-called three C's, Christianity, Commerce, and Civilization. They believed that the military, commercial, and industrial might of the North Atlantic nations had occurred as the result of natural laws of progress, which they associated with the triumph of Protestant culture. They considered Christianity to be the principal cultural ingredient of historical progress. In some cases, notably that of Edward Wilmot Blyden, black nationalists esteemed all the "religions of the book," Judaism, Christianity, and Islam, as superior to indigenous religious customs and beliefs.[30]

Romantic Racialism: Cult of African Moral Superiority

There is a universal appeal to the idea that victims of oppression are superior to those who oppress them. Afrocentrism, like many other modern political movements, has readily incorporated this belief. Afrocentrism has been committed to what Lloyd Monroe, a Ph.D. candidate at Brown University, calls the manipulation of victim status. The roots of such thinking run deep in Western culture. In the Greek classical tradition of *pathe mathos*, suffering was viewed as a source of knowledge. The valuation of suffering also has obvious roots in the Judeo-Christian notion that victimization is the mark of a messiah: "He is despised and rejected of men, a man of sorrows, and acquainted with grief," says the prophet Isaiah. "Blessed are those who have suffered persecution for righteousness' sake, for theirs is the kingdom of heaven," says the Gospel. Afrocentrism frequently attributes a unique moral destiny or humanizing mission to the scattered and driven African peoples. It has often partaken of the sentimental belief that the African race is uniquely peace-loving and gentle, and in this regard has a message for the world. Harriet Beecher Stowe offered the most celebrated rendition of this myth in *Uncle Tom's Cabin*.

The fertile imagination of W. E. B. Du Bois transformed Stowe's long-suffering messiah, Uncle Tom, into "the figure of the Black Mammy, one of the most pitiful of the world's Christs. . . . She was an embodied sorrow, an anomaly crucified on the cross of her own neglected children for the sake of the children of masters who bought and sold her as they bought and sold cattle." The tradition of beatification through suffering leads to Marcus Garvey's celebration of "the black man of sorrows."[31] Martin Luther King also contributed to the cult of African moral superiority when he spoke of "the Negro" as the instrument of a great moral ideal, and cited the historian Arnold Toynbee to the effect that "it may be the Negro who will give the new spiritual dynamic to Western civilization that it so desperately needs to survive."[32]

Afrocentrists have also attributed moral significance to an often cited-passage from Pope's "translation" of Homer, which supposedly indicated some acknowledgment of African moral leadership in the ancient world.

> The Sire of Gods and all the ethereal train
> On the Warm limits of the farthest main
> Now mix with mortals, nor disdain to grace
> The feasts of Ethiopia's blameless race.[33]

Afrocentric moralists have been profoundly influenced by Senegalese scholar Cheikh Anta Diop, who has professed that the material conditions of the Nile Valley produced "in the Negro, a gentle, idealistic, peaceful nature, endowed with a spirit of justice and gaiety." The Egyptians had a "hermaphroditic ontology," reflecting a balance of power between the sexes. The benevolent climate and the androgynous god reflected the "basic traits of the Negro soul and civilization." By the same token, according to Diop, "the ferocity of nature in the Eurasian steppes" produced among all Indo-Europeans, "whether white or yellow," an instinctive love of conquest. The painful conditions of postglacial Europe led Europeans to "conjure up deities maleficent and cruel, jealous and spiteful: Zeus, Yahweh, among others."[34] Michael Bradley has provided an astonishingly creative exposition of the mythology that ascribes to Europeans the qualities of ice and to Africans the qualities of the sun.[35] Chancellor Williams and John Henrik Clarke have spoken of the propensity of Europeans for harshness and cruelty. It is difficult for the present author to entertain such a theory in the face of worldwide murder, rapine, and hatred, which all races, religions, and nationalities practice both intramurally and extramurally, with obvious enthusiasm.[36]

African Diaspora and Culture Diffusion

Basil Davidson is well known for his declaration that the cultures of continental Africa share an underlying unity – a core set of characteristic, if not unique, African values. Anthony Appiah has attacked this position as one of the fundamental fallacies underlying Pan-African and Afrocentric thought. Orlando Patterson has also attacked the cultural uniformity thesis, although he has given some credence to the idea of cultural continuities, as well as discontinuities, in the "western coastal belt of sub-Saharan Africa," the area from which, "it has been well established," most New World blacks derive. Patterson inherited from Melville Herskovits a commitment to charting and interpreting the survival of African cultural traits in the Americas. Herskovits, who dismissed most scholarship that stressed African cultural diversity as "sheer nonsense," asserted that cultural variety, especially among West African peoples, "can be considered unusually great only if we are unaware of the underlying similarities which support local variations."[37] While Herskovits has been the most influential Afrocentric theorist among white anthropologists, one should be aware of the observations of Bronislaw Malinowski, who also took a Pan-African approach to the study of African peoples and implicitly assumed underlying similarities between the various African and New World entities. These autochthonous similarities are not to be confused with the similarities arising from cultural contacts with modern Europe.[38]

Afrocentrism has long been associated with the Herskovits doctrine of cultural Pan-Africanism, which proclaims the existence of a unifying center of consciousness, not only for continental Africans but for Africans throughout the diaspora. Afrocentrism is implicit in Sterling Stuckey's intimation that "black Americans today are basically African in culture." Stuckey engages in a variety of Afrocentrism concerned more with West Africa than with the Nile Valley, and has not argued for a connection to ancient Egypt. In searching for evidence to support his thesis that a unified African culture has survived in the Americas, Stuckey settles on the "ring shout" as his principal metaphor. The ring shout is a religious ritual, widely practiced in Africa, in which the participants form a circle and move in a counterclockwise direction until they are possessed by frenzy, during which they experience what anthropologists call "ceremonial spirit possession."

Stuckey's Afrocentrism is rooted in a fascination with New World survivals of West African culture, regardless of any affinity to Nilotic monumentalism. Stuckey argues that African

> tribalism . . . a lingering memory in the minds of American slaves. . . . enabled them to go back to the sense of community in the traditional African setting and to include all Africans in their common experience of oppression in North America. It is ironic, therefore, that African ethnicity, an obstacle to African nationalism in the twentieth century, was in this way the principal avenue to black unity in ante-bellum America.[39]

The similarity of Stuckey's line of thought to Malinowski's aforementioned theory of Pan-African culture contact is obvious. The same theory underlies the writings of Jahnheinz Jahn and Henry Louis Gates, when they posit that Africans coming into contact with European societies generated a "new African culture, a truly Pan-

African culture, fashioned as a colorful weave of linguistic, institutional, metaphysical, and formal threads." Gates, in asserting that "Afro-American culture is an African culture," is in agreement with Stuckey, although Gates is more inclined to acknowledge the "difference" signified by the influences of the various European cultures with which they interacted.[40] Nonetheless, Gates is able to discover a unifying trope, representing the oneness of West African culture in the myth of Esu Elegbara, the trickster god. Trickster gods are a universal phenomenon; Esu has cognates in Greek, Norse, and Native American mythology. There is a long tradition in African American anthropology and folklore studies that focuses on such trickster tales as the Spider Anansi of the West Indies and the Brer Rabbit of the American South. Gates restates the fundamentals of this approach in attributing a survival of the myth of Esu Elegbara in the legend of the "signifying monkey," which he associates with the West African trickster god.[41]

Gates and Stuckey, with their emphases on the emergence of a new African culture, or cultures, in the New World, follow in the tradition of Carter G. Woodson, Jahnheinz Jahn, and Roger Bastide, who have emphasized the cultural and linguistic continuity at least of sub-Saharan Africa, and who place great emphasis on African survivals in the Americas.[42] More strenuous assertions have been associated with Diop, who argues for the profound importance of cultural continuities between ancient Egypt and contemporary sub-Saharan Africa.[43]

The Antimodernist Paradox: Modernism as Primitivism

Afrocentrism, a movement that places such absolute value on the quality of Africanness, is ironically indebted to the ideology of cultural relativism, which arose at the beginning of the twentieth century. Cultural relativism is the theory, associated with anthropologist Franz Boas and the sociologist William Graham Sumner, that every culture should be viewed as a rationally integrated world view, and that no culture should be condemned by the standards of another. The German scholar Leo Frobenius did much to champion this view with his treatments of African cultures, particularly their erotic beliefs. After the Boas–Herskovits view of culture had become established and the Freudian view of sexual repression had been promulgated, the celebration of African eroticism as represented in the writings of Frobenius became fashionable.[44]

During the early decades of the twentieth century, Western artists and intellectuals began to express a fear that the soil of Europe had become culturally depleted. This attitude was present in the writings of T. S. Eliot, Sigmund Freud, Oswald Spengler, and Ernest Hemingway, obsessed as they were with symbols of wounded manhood and mutilated kings. Artists like Picasso, Modigliani, and Stravinsky made a fetish of the fertility of "primitive" art forms, and borrowed from "barbarian" societies in the hopes of rejuvenating the effete artistic life of Europe. The myth of virile barbarism – which should never be confused with the noble savage mythology of sentimental Christians – had long played a part in African American thought. Alexander Crummell and Edward Wilmot Blyden, inspired by their reading of Tacitus, believed that pristine African villages were in some ways more healthy than European cities.

The spartan virtues that Blyden and Crummell saw among pristine Africans were at some considerable remove from the "bohemian" primitivism of the so-called Harlem Renaissance of the 1920s, which occurred at a time when primitivism of a more libidinous sort had become fashionable in intellectual circles. The fascination with African exoticism and its diffusion, as it was revealed in the poetry and novels of the period, offered a critique of the concept of civilization itself. Many intellectuals of the twenties and thirties, white and black alike, began to question whether civilization was really a good thing. Perhaps, as Oswald Spengler had suggested, civilization really was nothing more than "dead culture." The French *négritude* poets of the thirties began to celebrate their estrangement from civilization and to declare their defiant opposition to Westernization.

Marginalized white artists and intellectuals, notably Carl Van Vechten, Nancy Cunard, Melville Herskovits, and Gertrude Stein, became fascinated with bohemian and proletarian manifestations of black culture during the 1920s. Again, during the 1960s the hippie movement, the desire to discover "Where the Waste Land Ends," to make a counterculture, and to experience the "Greening of America," nourished persistent sentimental myths of an African American primitivism that might have the potential to revitalize American society.

Deeply influenced by Franz Boas and Sigmund Freud, anthropological Pan-Africanism led to the synthesis of modernism and primitivism. The anthropologist Roger Bastide has proclaimed that the African spirit has given "life and vitality" to the entirety of Western civilization. "The European turns increasingly to Africa or Black America for the satisfaction of those vital needs which industrial society can no longer answer."[45] Playwright George Houston Bass referred to the impact of African American culture on the Western world as "the liberation of pelvic motion." Afrocentrism claimed to value the fecundity of African primitivism over the sterility of European civilization and viewed the only prospect for Western cultural health in terms of a symbolic return of the spirit to an Edenic Africa.

Afrocentrism and Mythic Truth

I do not use the term "mythic" in the popular sense to suggest that an idea is false because it is "unscientific." I use myth in the way in which it has long been understood by such classical students of humanity as Plato, Boccaccio, and Shelley, and by such modern anthropologists as Lévi-Strauss and Joseph Campbell. "Myth" and "mythic" are frequently used by cultural historians to indicate a variety of thought that crystallizes truth in the legends and folklore of a culture, endowing its possessors with the power and facility of shorthand communication. The various perspectives currently grouped under the rubric of "Afrocentrism" have long performed these functions among black Americans. Afrocentrism operates as the verbal and moral equivalent of a secret handshake, a sort of Freemasonry whereby one black American can say to another, "Although we have never met before, I believe we think alike. We are brothers and sisters. We know the same folklore, we appreciate the same riddles, laugh at the same jokes. We share the same beliefs, and reverence the same icons."

For some Africans and African Americans these mythologies have had an extended religious function. They have amounted to a variety of utopian or chiliastic belief, with its utopia situated sometimes in a romanticized past, sometimes in a future millennium. The more reasonable American historians recognize in the latest revival of Afrocentrism, patterns described by the late E. L. Tuveson of the University of California/Berkeley, and the late William G. McLoughlin of Brown University, who developed useful methods for looking at the history of American millennial movements, revivals, awakenings, and reforms. The Afrocentric tradition may also be understood within the pattern that Harold Walter Turner describes in his article "Tribal Religious Movements."[46] If we substitute "national" for the patronizing term "tribal," we can see the applicability of Turner's concept not only to African but to European peoples. Perhaps it would be appropriate to apply such terms as primitive or tribal to every group whose national politics are influenced or determined by genealogical and religious mythologies.

The noted sociologist Karl Mannheim attempted to enforce a distinction in his *Ideology and Utopia* (1929), where he associated utopianism with millenarian mass movements based on religious beliefs rather than on bourgeois rationalism and political ideology. There are debates over the meanings of Mannheim's definitions, and not everyone accepts his separation of ideology and utopia into mutually exclusive and discrete categories. T. S. Eliot, for example, in *Notes Towards the Definition of Culture* (Faber and Faber, 1948), was less inclined to separate ideology from religious belief. He viewed religion as the backbone of culture, defining culture as "that which makes life worth living" (p. 27). In the world of real experience, ideological movements are inseparable from the emotional lives, religious enthusiasms, and cultural myths of their followers. Ideologues frequently invent or reinvent mythologies for the purpose of endowing their rational positions with emotional force. Thus, while some of the positions of Afrocentrists are supportable by common sense or scientific evidence, others are associated with millenarian or utopian patterns of thought.

Afrocentrism, like most ideologies, contains both a utopian history and a millenarian future. It fixates on an idealized past before the white man's "Destruction of Black Civilization," and predicts an Ethiopian revival, a messianic era of peace and goodwill, "when the black man comes into his own." Its manifestations represent a millennialist movement and a political ideology, frequently attracting the type of person Eric Hoffer describes in *The True Believer*. Many Afrocentrists have, in fact, undergone the charismatic transformation that the African American psychologist William E. Cross has called "the Negro to Black Conversion Experience."[47] They start out as Saul and end up as Paul, often changing their names as a sign that they have, to use Saint Paul's language, "put off the old man and put on the new man."

Afrocentrists frequently take on the role of proselytizers, eager to share the good news, the truth, the real truth. It is impossible to argue with some of them, convinced as they are that you are the one who is confused. People convert because they find the message appealing, then work backward from what they need to believe through a system of rationalizations, in order to construct "proofs." Converts speak with prophetic conviction, and the more you argue with them, logically, the more passionately they explain to you why you are wrong. Afrocentrism is not a purely intellectual movement; it is a secular religion or, putting it in Karl Mannheim's term, it is a utopia. But it is an ideology as well, and it is embraced primarily by eminently reasonable working-class and middle-class individuals, who are attracted to it, sometimes, in spite of themselves.

Symbols of Dignity and Cultural Literacy

The strongest argument in favor of Afrocentrism is that it guides many of its adherents in the direction of increased cultural literacy. It is the heroic or monumental form of Afrocentrism that is most important in this regard, not the anthropological. The working-class convert to Afrocentrism is usually brought into the movement through contact with some form of vindicationism, as represented by J. A. Rogers or Chancellor Williams. Artists and intellectuals, if they are interested in Afrocentrism at all, tend to be fascinated by the blues antiheroes and sexual exoticism of the anthropological tradition. The working-class convert is more often attracted by the black nationalist content of the Afrocentric message, which thrives on the desire of the African American masses to identify with symbols of power, stability, self-discipline, and high culture.

Cheikh Anta Diop, whom Afrocentrists frequently acknowledge as their spiritual father, embodies the high culture concept. His works, despite their frequently tendentious quality, often encourage an advanced cultural literacy. Diop is notably opposed to the vulgar popular culture stereotypes of black culture that have been dominant since the so-called Harlem Renaissance of the 1920s. Diop is also suspicious of the sentimental black cultural nationalism associated with Léopold Senghor and the French negritude school. More is to be said of the various expressions of the Harlem Renaissance and the negritude ideology in the following chapters.

As does the late African American critic Sterling Brown, Diop condemns the treatment of black folk as jazzy exotic primitives and erotic barbarians. Afrocentrists resent the tendency to define black culture in terms of "primitivism grafted onto decadence." Diop's ardent followers are also opposed to the profane, scatological variety of black ghetto culture that is associated with gangsta rap, "signifying monkeys," and "playing the dozens" (word games based on ritualized insult). The Afrocentrist dreams of appropriating the high culture of classical civilization, and disdains the low culture of gangsta rap. Although some may defend 2 Live Crew on First Amendment grounds, few are sympathetic to the proposition that 2 Live Crew represents black culture. In my personal experiences with black nationalists, including Black Muslims and many Afrocentrists, I have found that they insist, to their credit, that gangsta rap must be understood as social pathology. Unfortunately, many of these same black nationalists have undermined their credibility by their fundamentalist antiintellectualism and their paranoid ravings about the ice man inheritance, Jewish conspiracies, and melanin theory.

One of the great ironies of black American life is that historically, perhaps even today, black nationalism, while urging political separatism, has been a conduit for the transmission of a universal high culture. Classical black nationalists and Afrocentrists since the nineteenth century, including John Russwurm, Frances E. W. Harper, Martin Delany, Alexander Crummell, Edward Wilmot Blyden, Pauline Hopkins, W. E. B. Du Bois, and Marcus Garvey, were committed to a civilizing mission. They made references to Egyptian civilization hoping to focus the minds of black folk on noble and uplifting universal values – what Matthew Arnold called "the best that has been known and said in the world." They were not cultural relativists; they believed that some cultures are better than other cultures, and they were not amused by the spectacle of illiterate schoolboys insulting one another's mothers, just for fun. Many people feel that at least this much can be said in behalf of Afrocentrism: that it focuses young minds on pyramids and temples rather than on priapic displays and foulmouthed monkeys.

Avoiding Presentism: Afrocentrism as a Response to Slavery and Segregation

It is perfectly understandable that the African American culture that grew up in antebellum America, where nine out of every ten African Americans was a slave, gave legitimate expression to feelings of anger and resentment. The editors of *Freedom's Journal* who claimed the glories of Egypt for black Africans were, ironically, mulattos. Society designated them "Free Africans," but in reality they were quasi free, and more than half white, and deprived of both their African and their European heritages. They chose to crusade fiercely to reclaim their African heritage, asserting that knowledge of their past had been deliberately kept from them. They were correct in this assertion, for they and their children were banned by force of law and custom from schools, universities, and libraries.

If there is a reactive anger and resentment in some Afrocentric writing, it is certainly understandable. It grows out of an American educational experience that has sought at times to systematically degrade and mislead black people. As late as 1960, the year when the present author graduated from high school, there were many universities in this country from which he was barred by force of law or other forms of violence. Even in the North, college classrooms were places where black Americans were sometimes driven to the verge of tears by the cruelty of students and teachers. Afrocentrism has always sought to preserve the confidence of African Americans in their own humanity. It sometimes reacts passionately to environments that are hostile, patronizing, or indifferent. Nonetheless, Afrocentric literature is not hate literature; it is a sometimes quaint, sometimes fantastic reminder of the irrational, fantastic attitudes toward race in the Western world. It is a vestige of the segregation era and its racial code, but no more anachronistic than our society's continuing color prejudice.

George James's book *Stolen Legacy* is an admittedly idiosyncratic rhapsody on the mystical legacy of ancient Egypt. It argues that Greek philosophy derives from ancient Egyptian mystery religions that are presumed to have their roots in central Africa. The book has been denounced by Mary Lefkowitz as "hate literature."[48] Such a reaction is presentist and ahistorical. The book is simply the attempt of a frustrated and abused man to demonstrate a black contribution to the common intellectual heritage of mankind. Pseudohistorical though it is, the book is no more malicious than the Freemasonry and Rosicrucianism to which it is indebted. Written in the environment of American segregation and humiliation that black people experienced during the 1940s and 1950s, it is, of course, filled with bitterness, and it would not be remarkable if hatred dripped from every page. As a matter of fact, the book neither advocates nor defends racial hatred. It is, on the contrary, an exotic but poignant attempt to unite African peoples with the rest of humanity, a moving response to segregation and dehumanization, the product of a heart that is filled with tears.

If we were to identify *Stolen Legacy* as hate literature, we would have to identify every work that reflects an ethnocentric mythology as hate literature. We might start with the Bible, since Leviticus enjoins the stoning of homosexuals and denies equality to women. We might join forces with the yahoos who seek to remove Mark Twain's *Huckleberry Finn* from the libraries. We could condemn some of Thomas Jefferson's letters, along with Shakespeare's *Merchant of Venice*, as anti-Semitic, or we might dismiss *Othello* as misogynist hate literature.[49] We might view Milton's *Areopagitica* as a hypocritical, anti-Catholic tract, produced by a regicidal fanatic. Each of the aforementioned classics contains some ideas that most living Americans find embarrassing, offensive, or downright hateful. But we cannot, with any degree of intelligence, sensitivity, or historical consciousness, relegate them to the category of hate literature.

Many classics of the Afrocentric tradition, which argued that the Egyptians were black, were produced at a time when "one drop of Negro blood" was enough to make even the whitest person a Negro. Even today, this inconsistent reasoning remains the basis for classifying appreciable numbers of Americans as "black," while foreigners of similar appearance and derivation are classified as Arabs, Jews, or Egyptians. Justice Thurgood Marshall had a lighter complexion than the Egyptian president Anwar Sadat, but Marshall was classified as "Negro." Congressman Adam Clayton Powell was whiter in appearance than Egyptian president Gamal Abdel Nasser, although Congressman Powell was classified as a Negro.

General Colin Powell, although whiter than most of the self-portrayals of Egyptians in most surviving paintings, can remember a day when he would have been barred from the University of Alabama. And yet many of the same Americans who once denied Ralph Bunche admission to restaurants and tennis courts can become apoplectic at the idea that the pharaohs were Negroes by the American definition. It was in the face of this illogic that the mulatto author J. A. Rogers classified his Pharaohs as black. John G. Jackson was more Caucasian in appearance than most Egyptians, ancient or modern, and many of the pharaohs, if transplanted across time and onto the Chattanooga Choo-Choo in 1945, would have had difficulty obtaining a Pullman berth or being seated in a dining car.[50]

Bad memories are the source of the understandable but indefensible reactions of a few atypical cult authors, who shamelessly exploit the fears and resentments of contemporary readers. Even here it should be remembered, however, that otherwise harmless traditions of Afrocentrism are most likely to be perverted among the unlettered, culturally deprived, and slum-shocked classes of black Americans, or among those who feel strong emotional ties to them. It is extremely unlikely that Afrocentrism will gain much of a following among the black scholars who, although marginalized in the larger society, constitute an establishment within the elite universities. They do not have to live under the vicious, terrifying, humiliating conditions of Southern segregation and lynch law that drove George James over the brink of scholarship and into mysticism during the early 1950s.

But most people do not go over the brink. Most black Americans know Afrocentrism as a warm, folksy cultural tradition that they encounter from early childhood, in their homes and churches, their sewing circles and barbershops. Like most heroic traditions, it is only half believed. It is embraced mainly for its emotional and symbolic significance, and in this sense Afrocentrism possesses the qualities of a cultural mythology. Like the mythic consciousness of Catholics and Jews, it represents an attempt on the part of respectable, honest people to create a group-centered history. Heroic Afrocentrism is really no more than a statement of belief in the humanity of African people. It is no more dangerous than the legends of Moses in the bulrushes, or George Washington and the cherry tree.

The Need for a Cultural Anchor

Religion and mythology are historically inextricable from political thought, no less so than rationalism and empiricism. Since the 1700s, a mystical historiography has been the basis of much that is uplifting and ennobling in African American religion, social life, literature, and the arts. It has tremendous potential for saving us from the romantic racialism and sentimentalism of negritude and jazz culture. I do not mean to disparage the artistic and intellectual merits of jazz as a music form, but it should be obvious that jazz culture, as represented in the lives of Charlie Parker and Billie Holiday, is not a suitable basis for organizing black American communities. It would be just as foolish as asking the masses of white Americans to accept Andy Warhol and Timothy Leary as their cultural models. On the other hand, it is unrealistic to expect that all black life in America can be regimented in accord with the rigorous discipline of the Nation of Islam or the Black Jews. I would not have every African American become a Hasidic black, but no healthy culture can be entirely based on the lifestyles of marginalized intellectuals and jazzy hipsters. It must be based on the stable values of technocratic nerds, middle-class squares, and plain working stiffs.

Afrocentrism offers a cultural anchor to its adherents, similar to that offered by contemporary Protestant fundamentalism to its practitioners. In this connection I must mention the work of Professor Dorothy Nelkin of the Sociology Department of Cornell University, who has devoted much effort to understanding the problem of "creation science" in the schools. I use her model not because I think Afrocentrism is strictly analogous to "creation science," but because both systems represent the search for a cultural anchor. Utopian Afrocentrists, like creation scientists, frequently couch their belief systems in pseudoscientific terms, and they represent the frustration of their adherents as they attempt to cope with the stresses and anxieties of modern urban life. I offer this not as a criticism but simply as a descriptive statement. Afrocentrism often becomes the focus of middle-class attempts to find a cultural anchor in a society where the bizarre is becoming normal. Fundamentalists are often well-educated people, even people with scientific and technical training, who find in religious revivals some insulation from a society they view as corrupt, prurient, and violent.[51]

Thematic Concerns of the Present Work

It is in no spirit of disparagement that I assert a relationship between Afrocentrism and religious movements. All mass cultural movements are at some level related to or analogous to religion, and the religious roots of black American culture have been widely and frequently discussed.[52] In the years immediately following the American revolution, African Americans typically sought solace in the idea that they were people of a new covenant, a newly chosen people whose messianic destiny must in some way be analogous to that of the biblical Hebrews. By the mid-eighteenth century, at least among the literate population, this idea came to be less attractive than the idea that blacks were ethnologically linked to the pharaohs, who had oppressed the biblical Hebrews.

This "ethnological" concern was important to Frederick Douglass, who, despite a fundamental hostility to Afrochauvinists, overlapped their rhetoric when he claimed that ancient Egyptians and African Americans were the same people. In doing so, he sounded chauvinistic, although for the most part his historical theory was egalitarian, whiggish, and "progressive."[53] Douglass seems to have conflated his own spectacular rise, from slavery to celebrity, with the history of African Americans in general. His theory of history was thus a solipsistic metaphysic of progress. Douglass tried to reconcile this left-liberal reform ideology with principles of Afrocentric chauvinism and communal solidarity. He attempted to assume the position of public intellectual, but was never able to escape from the box of racial ambassadorship. Douglass believed that racialism was a reactionary doctrine, but he always remained "a race leader" and was never able to become a true "public intellectual," because the society was not color blind. Douglass's attempt to establish an "ethnological" link between black Americans and the ancient Egyptians was most interesting in that regard and seemed to illustrate the many contradictions in his ideological position.

Sometimes Afrocentrism has taken on a dreamy, mystical quality. Pauline Hopkins, writing at the turn of the century, linked her own Egyptocentric mysticism with intellectual fads that were popular in her contemporary Boston. Her novel *Of One Blood, or The Hidden Self* (1903), a science fiction work, expressed an eminently "progressive" ideology, based on "New Thought," a movement that influenced organized efforts as diverse as Christian Science, Garveyism, and the Peace Mission Movement of Father Divine. Hopkins's ideology, like that of most of her contemporaries, embodied a metaphysical faith in progress, and *Of One Blood* represented an attempt

to reconcile Christian teleology with Pan-African thought. Her efforts were not dissimilar to those of George James, whose eccentric
theories were inspired by Masonic mysticism.

Only a few nineteenth-century black writers were willing to concede any virtue to traditional West African societies. Alexander
Crummell was a notable exception, grafting the myth of the virile
Germanic barbarian onto the virile barbarian of the West African
forest. By the late nineteenth century, developments in the new science of anthropology had led to new ways of perceiving African history and culture. William H. Ferris in *The African Abroad* (1913)
placed Afrocentrism within a social Darwinist framework. Ferris was
typical of twentieth-century black nationalists in his commitment to
the mythologies of progress and change, and in his enthusiasm for
confusing the two ideas. He was also typical of the tragicomic, self-
confounding modern intellectual, a Prufrock full of "high sentence,
but a bit obtuse; / At times, indeed, almost ridiculous – Almost, at
times, the Fool." A disciple of William Graham Sumner, Ferris attempted to transmute Darwinian racialism, along with Hegelian idealism and Carlylean conservatism, into a benevolent ideology of race.
Ferris's contradictions were not only the result of his complicated
agenda, they were emblematic of the ambivalence and indecisiveness
that dominated the lives of many marginalized intellectuals in the
twentieth century.

Charles T. Davis correctly observed in *Black Is the Color of the Cosmos*
(1982) that social science and romantic racialism were linked in
W. E. B. Du Bois's poetry and fiction. Du Bois's religious writings
revealed his ambivalence regarding both the modernism and the
primitivism of the so-called Harlem Renaissance. Du Bois was in unacknowledged harmony with the Afrocentrism of his arch rival, Marcus Garvey, and such working-class cults as the Black Jews of Harlem
and the Black Muslims. These groups still appeal to black puritanical
traditions. Thus the stoicism and Calvinism embedded in Du Bois's
writings offered a corrective to the "modernism" and latitudinarianism of intellectual and artistic elites; but it also led to some of the
more sinister implications of his Pan-Africanism, Afrocentrism, and
black nationalism, as he drifted into Stalinism.

William Edward Burghardt Du Bois launched his career before
the American Negro Academy with a paper called *The Conservation of
Races* (1897), in which Anthony Appiah has accurately enough discerned racialism. Throughout his career, Du Bois published other
Afrocentric volumes, most notably *Black Folk Then and Now* (1939)
and *The World and Africa* (1946). In *The Souls of Black Folk* (1903) he
called on the black peasantry of the South to prevent America from

becoming a "dusty desert of dollars." In many works, he expressed a nostalgia for the lost world of the nineteenth century – a world of manners, refinement, and precapitalistic gentility. Thus, he sounded at times as antimodernist as Henry Adams, Henry James, T. S. Eliot, and Oswald Spengler. Du Bois was not certain that he welcomed "the decline of the West," and he displayed great ambivalence in his views on the history of civilization. Like Eliot, he lamented that the modern world seemed to be degenerating into barbarism and decadence. As did Spengler in *The Hour of Decision* (1934), he argued that primitive "races" had the potential to revitalize a stagnant civilization. Elsewhere, and also in a Spenglerean vein, he referred to the "reeking West, whose day is done."[54]

The Harlem Renaissance literati of the 1920s, in the spirit of the Jazz Age, conflated the modern with the primitive – celebrating both. Encouraged by such critics of sterile bourgeois values as Carl Van Vechten and Gertrude Stein, they paid homage to both the "proletarian" spirit of the working class and the "bohemian" spirit of the jazz artists. Jazz was a musical fauvism that symbolized the merger of the modern and the primitive. It attacked the old-fogeyism of Victorian stuffiness while celebrating, with post-Freudian glee, a primitive sexuality and jungle passion. Inspired by the Dionysian spirit of modernism and the Harlem Renaissance, the French negritude poets sought in artistic primitivism a positive affirmation of a Negro Personality. Since the 1930s, some black artists and intellectuals have followed Léopold Senghor and Aimé Césaire in attempting to transform the white supremacist theories of Count Arthur de Gobineau into a positive myth of black pride and passion. Even before Senghor, they took a perverse pleasure in depicting themselves as exotic savages, or Calibans, cursing an oppressive Western civilization. One observes the tendency in Du Bois's poem "The Riddle of the Sphinx."

> Unthankful we wince in the East
> Unthankful we wail from the westward,
> Unthankfully thankful, we curse,
> In the unworn wastes of the wild.

But, while ever in sympathy with such outpourings of rage, racial vindicationists have been ambivalent toward "Calibanism." The father of contemporary Afrocentrism, Cheikh Anta Diop, has thus suggested that the primitivism of the negritude school may be a concession to, rather than a transformation of, the racialism of Gobineau. There has been continuing tension between the impulse to vindicate African peoples in terms of their primitive sensibilities and the desire to attribute to them a list of solid technical and intellectual achievements.[55]

Black intellectuals of the present day still seek to reconcile the contending forces of primitivism and progressivism. Like black leaders of the past, they must somehow mix the water of a race-specific intellectual agenda with the oil of assimilationist values. This conflict has been dictated, as John Hope Franklin observes, by the history of a segregated American society. African American scholars, even when segregated into black studies departments, seek to contribute to the larger society both as exotic primitives, and as "public intellectuals." As a result, contemporary black intellectuals display what David Nicholson has termed "the schizophrenia inherent in attempting to adhere to conflicting varieties of political correctness." The fundamental contradiction that Afrocentrism shares with twentieth-century civilization as a whole is that it is committed to the simultaneous valorization of primitivism and modernism.[56]

The Afrocentric tradition is related to utopian ideas of progress because it promises a glorious destiny for African people in the future. Ironically, however, it looks backward to a utopia in the past when Africans were the most advanced people on earth. Afrocentrism has conformed in many important respects to Mannheim's definition of a "utopia." It is an irrepressible, class-transcending, charismatic movement, destined to persist for as long as there is an identifiable black population in North America. No ideology is ever entirely free of utopian elements, however, and no system of thought is ever exactly what it seems to be. Afrocentrism and black nationalism are not always exactly what they appear to be in the eyes of their adherents. Afro-Bermudan historian Cyril Griffith once wryly said to me that the unconscious goal of all black nationalist movements in the United States is assimilation. It is my contention that Afrocentrism has always been a vehicle for involving black Americans in the literate culture of the Western world.[57]

I believe it is possible to recapture this venerable ancestral tradition from its modern misuse by an unrepresentative minority of racists, anti-Semites, and pseudointellectuals. Optimally, African American folk history can be a means of focusing the intellects of young African Americans on "the best that has been thought and said" by all the peoples of the world, beginning with an appreciation of the contributions that peoples of African descent have made to the arts and sciences since prehistoric times. Certainly this is consistent with the project of serious scholars like Frank Snowden, who have opposed the extremism of romantic racialism while insisting that people of the black African racial type mixed freely, participated in, and contributed to classical Mediterranean civilization.[58]

Vindicationist Afrocentrism can reinforce a consistent tradition of African American historical skepticism, passed down from John Russwurm through W. E. B. Du Bois to contemporary students of culture. Admittedly, Afrocentrism, in its more aggressive and extremist forms, may sometimes be an uncritical, chauvinistic movement, a born-again, true believer type of enthusiasm similar to creation science, and rationalized with the same sort of evangelical passion. For this very reason it is not likely to be stopped by intellectual arguments or politically correct dogmas from the right or from the left. In my view, it is futile to oppose Afrocentrism. My heart is warmed, not hardened, when I see young men from a culturally impoverished background, dragging around tattered, dog-eared volumes by Cheikh Anta Diop or Drusilla Dunjee Houston. They are learning, often for the first time, the joys of reading, and may eventually extend this newfound enthusiasm to other authors – perhaps to Shakespeare, Pushkin, Voltaire, Ralph Ellison, John Barth, Toni Morrison.

Afrocentrism can be enlisted in the struggle to resist a contemporary tabloid culture, which is obsessed with rape, murder, and tennis shoes. It is culturally more broadening and intellectually more stimulating for young people to spend their time with J. A. Rogers than with ninety percent of what is currently available on television or the internet. Teachers at all levels should attempt to exploit the more elevating and universalistic messages of the vindicationist tradition, and – even more important – its hostility to racism. The best way for a sophisticated college teacher to approach Rogers is not to oppose him but to show students that he was an absolute antiracist, and an accomplished ironist. The bitter joke that underlies all of J. A. Rogers's work is his thorough commitment to the idea that race is a meaningless concept. That is the central thesis of his *Nature Knows No Color Line* and his sprawling three-volume *Sex and Race*. Black people, too, are capable of sarcasm, but people like Mary Lefkowitz have yet to discover this dimension of our humanity.

3

FROM SUPERMAN TO MAN

A HISTORIOGRAPHY OF DECLINE

Historians have long recognized that significant numbers of Christianized "Africans" at the time of the American Revolution viewed themselves as people of a New Covenant, a chosen people whose messianic destiny was overseen by a merciful Providence. Christian teaching revealed that God was always on the side of the oppressed, and that the lowly were destined to be exalted. It is well known that many black people viewed slavery in America as analogous to the bondage of Israel, "away down in Egypt's Land."[1] Ironically, however, African Americans have often been torn by a contradictory desire to identify with the Egyptians as well. Anthropologists and other scholars are fond of reminding us that it is in the nature of mythologies to reconcile contradictions, for mythologies must accommodate the diverse spiritual goals of complex aggregations of people – not to mention the paradoxes within individual psyches.[2]

This need to reconcile contradictions is illustrated in the personal mythology of Olaudah Equiano. Writing under the Christian name of Gustavus Vassa in 1789, he demonstrated his desire to identify with Christian traditions, and a simultaneous need to explain and defend his native West African customs. Although he was the victim of a slave trade instigated and defended by Bible-bearing Christians, he was eager to identify himself and his people with biblical history. His motivations for doing so were complex. First of all, like several other Christianized African writers of the period, he wanted to transfer biblical history and Christian teaching into weapons in his crusade against slavery. Second, he wanted to demonstrate to his European audience that the traditions of his people, "Eboan Africans," were worthy of respect. Finally, he had an apparently sincere belief in the truth of the Bible.

All of these needs he reconciled in his description of indigenous African customs, explaining to his audience that "the natives believe

44

that there is one Creator of all things," and that "we practiced circumcision like the Jews." In the first chapter of his narrative, he devoted a few lines to "the strong analogy" between "the manners and customs of my countrymen and those of the Jews before they reached the land of promise. . . . an analogy which alone would induce me to think that the one people had sprung from another." These similarities, he remarked, had also been noticed by eminent biblical scholars Dr. John Gill and Dr. John Clarke. More recent Afrocentrists, in a similar vein, have cited the work of the Jesuit scholar Joseph J. Williams, *Hebrewisms of West Africa.*[3]

Eighteenth-century black Americans were no less inclined than their Euro-American counterparts to manipulate history in pursuit of an assumed national or racial advantage. African Americans' historical traditions, while to some extent their own invention, were inextricably intertwined with Euro-American historical and religious traditions. No national or ethnic group in the history of the world has ever fashioned a self-identity independent of the perceptions of outsiders. The well-known tendency of African Americans to identify with biblical history was both a product of their cultural assimilation into Western Christianity and a demonstration of their ability to adapt Christianity to their own uses. Thus, black Christians focused dreamily on the song of the black and comely Queen of Sheba, and on the legend of a lost Ethiopian empire on the upper Nile.

Aside from Christian sources, inspiring secular traditions arose that were – despite their pagan sources – attractive even to the most devout Christians. The Episcopal minister Alexander Crummell – whose opinions are more fully described in later chapters of the present work – made lecture notes on his father's Temne tribe, referencing their "great nobility of Character. Indomitable spirit! Unconquerable! British subdued all others around them. Never them! Physique."[4] The images of warrior races in the primeval forest were as gratifying to the bruised egos of a captive people as the images of Ethiopian princes, and black writers laid claim to both. Thus, while many of them focused on Nilotic cultures to illustrate that Africa had a "civilized" past, there was, throughout the nineteenth century, an increasing tendency to focus on West Africa as a region that was also worthy of respect.[5]

In order to fashion a view of themselves and their enslavement within the context of world history, African Americans began to look for patterns in the cycles of progress and decline that seemed to affect all human history. They sought to discover what these patterns might portend about the future history of their cultural progress. The study of history might tell them about the glories of their ancestors in some bygone age, more importantly, it might reveal the possibility of their advancement in the future. African Americans hoped to find within history some explanation of the contemporary African's "barbarian" status and a vindication of their race from the charge of perpetual inferiority.[6]

The problem of black historical identity was not a simple one. Racial and historical mythologies were constructed from the cultural elements in which African Americans were immersed in the late eighteenth and early nineteenth centuries. Christian, Jewish, classical, and Germanic mythologies were combined in the making of an image of Africa suitable to the spiritual needs of Westernized Africans. Thus, it was an exotic and heady brew of contradictory ideas that invigorated the Afrocentrism of those decades. But the problems and contradictions essential to the manufacture of racial chauvinism were not original with black Americans. They inherited them from Western traditions of pseudohistory and national mythology that were as old as Virgil's *Aeneid* and, in fact, much older. African Americans, like their white counterparts, merged Christian beliefs with immeasurably ancient mythologies of classical and Semitic origin.

The process by which African Americans manufactured a religious interpretation of their condition has fascinated generations of historians. In the early 1950s Miles Mark Fisher produced a study of mass historical consciousness that analyzed the content of "Negro Spirituals." Some of his points were conventional and unsurprising, such as the observation that "Go Down Moses" revealed a tendency to view enslavement in America as analogous to the bondage of Israel, "away down in Egypt's Land." But Fisher also advanced a more controversial and Afrocentric thesis. He claimed that songs that spoke of "crossing over Jordan" or "going home" reflected an "all consuming ambition to be sent to Liberia by the American Colonization Society."[7] What Fisher suggested was that enslaved Africans had a black nationalist consciousness, and a sense of national destiny.

Black Americans in the antebellum North revealed attitudes toward history analogous to those of the slaves but derived from American religion of the early colonial period, as well as from slave culture. By the late 1700s many "Free Africans" had adopted Christianity and had begun to fashion their own version of the Judeo-Christian legend of a nation in bondage. Christianity taught that "every valley shall be exalted" and that God was on the side of the lowly. Historians have long known that free African Christians in the North at the time of the American Revolution often described themselves as being inheritors of an ancient covenant, a chosen people, because of their travail. The Afro-Christian reading of Scripture assured them that their destiny must be overseen by a merciful providence, which would deliver them from bondage and bring about the kingdom of God in America.[8]

It is thus common to observe that African American religious rhetoric in the antebellum North was optimistic and future-oriented. African Americans developed a sense of history that they hoped would be useful in influencing their future. Biblical rhetoric was employed to plead the antislavery cause. The people who used this rhetoric were attempting to establish a bond between themselves and fellow Christians, whose assistance they sought in improving their temporal condition. The following statement, issued by the Methodist preacher Richard Allen in 1794, reveals this use of sentimental religious tradition that placed African Americans and their friends within the context of a Judeo-Christian historicism.

> We feel an inexpressible gratitude towards you, who have engaged in the cause of the African race; you have wrought deliverance for many, from more than Egyptian bondage, your labours are unremitted for their complete redemption, from the cruel subjection they are in. . . . You see our race more effectually destroyed, than was in Pharaoh's power to effect, upon Israel's sons; you blow the trumpet against the mighty evil, you make the tyrants tremble. . . . May he, who hath arisen to plead our cause, and engaged you as volunteers in the service, add to your numbers until the princes shall come forth from Egypt, and Ethiopia stretch out her hand unto God.[9]

As this passage illustrates, the sentimental tradition that regarded African Americans as analogous to the Children of Israel existed in somewhat contradictory and uneasy relationship to another cherished mythology. Black Americans wanted to be children of Pharaoh as well as children of Israel. The Egyptians were Africans; biblical authority and many secular authors seemed to agree on this. It was a wonderful thing for an oppressed people to identify themselves with God's chosen people, but it was also attractive to identify with the glories of the ancient Nile. If African Americans cherished the myth that their historical situation bore a contemporary resemblance to that of the Israelites in Egypt, how could they simultaneously nurture the belief that they bore a special historical relationship to Nile Valley civilization and to those same pharaohs who had oppressed the biblical Hebrews?

Black Christians were bothered that the ancient Egyptians had been pagans, worshiping idols and practicing other abominations, such as incest, in the sight of God. Contemporary eighteenth-century Egypt was decadent, and ruled by infidels. Finally, the ancient Egyptians were slaveholders, a matter that was difficult for most African Americans to overlook. An association with Egypt offered a useful sense of history, but it was also troubling to the consciousness of an enlightened eighteenth-century Christian like Phillis Wheatley. Wheatley clearly viewed Egypt as part of Africa, but she was not at all positive about the association. She viewed herself as a child of Israel, delivered from a dark African bondage, which was well symbolized in the following verse.

> 'Twas not long since I left my native shore
> The land of Error and Egyptian gloom:
> Father of mercy! 'twas thy gracious hand
> Brought me in safety from those dark abodes.[10]

These lines, written around 1770, express attitudes concerning Egypt, and Africa in general, that were probably not atypical. There is little evidence that Free Africans expressed much interest in Egypt before the swelling of interest expressed in the larger culture in the early nineteenth century. With the rise of Freemasonry in the United States, African Americans were exposed to a new interpretation of Egyptian culture – external to the doctrines of evangelical Christianity. Since the beginnings of "speculative Freemasonry" in the eighteenth century, Masonic literature had reflected an interest in Egyptian culture. The building trades, and hence the Masonic craft, were intimately related to the construction of ancient Egyptian monuments. Freemasonry in England and in the United States had attempted to reconcile the truths of biblical and Egyptian history, but such attempts were not always well received by orthodox Christians.[11] Many black Masons, like their white counterparts, while acknowledging the importance of the pyramids, preferred to focus on the Temple of Solomon.[12]

Although the discussion of Egyptian mysteries was a subject of some interest within Freemasonry, most American Masons, white and black alike, were ambivalent with respect to pagan cultures and their supposed influences on the craft. The dominant historical model for George Washington and other prominent Masons was, after all, not dynastic Egypt but republican Rome. French Masons were sometimes attracted to the writings of Abbé Terrason, whose works possibly inspired Mozart's fanciful depiction of Egypt in *Die Zauberflöte*. But Masonic lore did not, as a rule, demonstrate an obsession with Nilotic civilization. This may in fact explain why German Masons were so markedly unimpressed, and even offended, by the idiosyncratic and unsanctioned representations of *Die Zauberflöte*.[13]

There is no evidence that speculations concerning Egyptian mysteries were specially attractive on March 6, 1775, to Prince Hall and the fourteen other African Americans who were initiated into a Masonic lodge attached to a British regiment in Boston. On the other hand, it is certainly true that Freemasonry, by its very nature, promised to Hall and his associates a secret knowledge that whites had previously withheld from them. The Egyptian legends associated with Freemasonry took on a special significance for some African Americans during the nineteenth century, but public statements by the founders of African American Freemasonry contained few references to any Egyptian lore, or to any special relationship between Freemasonry and the African peoples.[14]

John Marrant, who was both a Christian preacher and a Mason, addressed the African lodge in Boston in the summer of 1789, lecturing on the ancient origins of Freemasonry. He demonstrated some interest in Egypt, to be sure, but this was not tied to speculative Freemasonry, although European Masons had been showing an interest in Egyptian mysteries for several decades.[15] Marrant was more concerned with the discovery, or the invention, of biblical "proofs" that Freemasonry had existed among black people in ancient times. Responding to the interpretation of Scripture that viewed African people as the accursed descendants of Cain, Marrant assumed a sarcastic tone when he accepted the lineage.

> What was it but [envy] that made Cain murder his brother, whence is it but from these that our modern Cains call us Africans the sons of Cain? (We admit it if you please) and we will find from him and his sons Masonry began, after the fall of his father. . . . no doubt he [Adam] afterwards taught his sons the art of Masonry; for how else could Cain after so much trouble and perplexity have time to study the art of building a city, as he did on the East of Eden. . . . bad as Cain was, yet God took not from him his faculty of studying architecture, arts and sciences – his sons also were endued with the same spirit, and in some convenient place no doubt they met and communed with each other for instruction.[16]

Marrant sought to disarm with levity one of the hackneyed biblical arguments for African inferiority by transforming it into an evidence of the ancient accomplishments of those who putatively carried the mark of Cain. He then went on to demonstrate, in a tone of apparent seriousness, that Nimrod, son of Cush and grandson of Ham (assumed by biblical scholars to be father of the black race), was also a Mason because he had founded the empire of Babylon. Mizraim, the second son of Ham, and therefore also black, must also have been a Mason because he built the city of Thebes. In the Providence of God, the children of Abraham, originally tent dwellers, "practiced very little of the art of architecture till about eighty years before their Exodus, when by the ruling hand of providence they were trained up to the building with stone and brick, in order to make them expert Masons before they possessed the promised land."

It is important to note that Marrant displayed no special interest in the Egyptians as opposed to other "Hamitic" tribes. The interest he did display was based on biblical lore, not the speculative Masonry present in the literature of white Masons. Marrant announced that Moses had been a grand master Mason, but inspired directly by God. He made no mention of Egyptian mysteries. So, too, were Hiram and Solomon grand master Masons, inspired directly by God, himself "the great architect" of Solomon's Temple. Many other patriarchs of the old testament were obviously Masons, for how else could they have built cities and cultivated "all manner of cunning workmanship," unless they had somehow preserved the Masonic wisdom of Adamic civilization before the fall?

Prince Hall and several other leaders of Free African societies in the late eighteenth century were not only Masons but, far more importantly, ministers of Christian churches. It is therefore not surprising that Masons like Prince Hall, Richard Allen, and Absalom Jones, who were also preachers, did not give undue emphasis to profane Egyptian lore in their addresses to the evangelical Christian laity, who might have found such references confusing or bordering on the heretical. Furthermore, the Masons were a secret society that did not disseminate its knowledge to noninitiates, particularly women, who sometimes constituted the bulk of church membership. Thus, one finds in Prince Hall's speeches little that leads to the notion that the founders of black Freemasonry were obsessed with Egypt. The closest thing is a passing reference to "Jethro an Ethiopian [who] gave instruction to his son-in-law Moses," but no rhapsodic outpourings on the wisdom of ancient Egypt. Therefore, contrary to what has been asserted by Mary Lefkowitz and Martin Bernal, it is difficult to prove that the Masonic mysticism of the late eighteenth century laid a foundation for the later insistence that Egyptian civilization had a special link to African Americans.[17]

By the late eighteenth century we begin to see some need to reconcile conflicts in thought and feeling evoked by the image of Egypt, a land of splendor as well as a symbol of heathenism and oppression.

The contradictory attitudes toward Egypt were reconciled in the myth of "Ethiopianism," a teleological view of history with African people at its center. The book of Psalms prophesied that "Princes would come out of Egypt" and that "Ethiopia would soon stretch out her hands unto God." Ethiopia and Egypt, thus associated, were soon merged in the consciousness of many black Christians. Ethiopia was interpreted to mean not only the ancient kingdom by that name, but all of Africa and the entire African race. The Bible verse was seen as a prophecy that the great days of Africa and all her scattered children were in the future. It was seen as a promise that a people of distinction were to come out of Egypt, and that Africans were soon to witness the day of their glory.[18]

In 1798, Napoleon's expedition to Egypt brought with it a team of scholars whose discoveries led to the nineteen volumes of *Description de l'Égypte*, 1809–28. The discovery of the Rosetta Stone in 1799 and Jean François Champolion's 1822 success in deciphering its hieroglyphic text made something of an impact on popular culture in the early nineteenth century. The British museum began to acquire monumental sculptures, and obelisks transported from the Orient were hoisted into prominence in London. It is believed that it was after viewing the damaged statue of Ramses II that Percy B. Shelley framed his famous lines,

My name is Ozymandias, king of kings:
Look on my works, ye Mighty, and despair.

In 1808, ten years before Shelley expressed himself with such melancholy irony, an anonymous member of Boston's African Society expressed his opinions on the pharaohs in less subtle terms. There was neither sentimentality nor nostalgia in his acceptance of the biblical tradition that associated Egypt with oppression, tyranny, and disobedience to God. But William Hamilton, speaking in 1815, avoided reference to the biblical Pharaoh, and painted Egypt in a more positive light. Egypt was part of Africa, "the first fair garden of God's planting," and nurtured by the "fostering care of the sun." In this healthful environment, her population had grown to be an "honest, industrious, peaceable, and well-disposed people." It was "king's shepherds," Hamilton asserted, that "wicked nation," who first brought violence and bloodshed to Africa.[19]

In 1827, *Freedom's Journal*, the first black newspaper in North America, published a front-page feature probably inspired by the first public exhibit of Egyptian mummies in Peale's Museum and Gallery of the Fine Arts in New York in 1826. The article, entitled "Mutability of Human Affairs," reflected on the special relationships between Egypt, Ethiopia, Christianity, and the African race. "Mutability" was a theme with a long history in English letters. From the sixteenth to the early nineteenth century, the term denoted change – not in the happy modern sense that implies progress, but in the sense that implies instability or incoherence. From a historical perspective the word conjured up thoughts of the decay of civilizations. The article's author recognized that the turning wheel of fortune had, many times in the past, reduced great empires to impoverishment and oblivion. For the editors of *Freedom's Journal,* mutability was associated with bittersweet reveries of a golden day when Africa had been the seat of the world's highest high culture.

> During a recent visit to the Egyptian Mummy, my thoughts were insensibly carried back to former times, when Egypt was in her splendor, and the only seat of chivalry, science, arms and civilization. As a descendant of Cush, I could not but mourn over her present degradation, while reflecting upon the mutability of human affairs, and upon the present condition of a people, who, for more than one thousand years, were the most civilized and enlightened.
>
> My heart sickened as I pondered upon the picture which my imagination had drawn – Like Marius surveying the ruins of Carthage, I wept over the fallen state of my people. . . .
>
> All we know of Ethiopia strengthens us in the belief that it was early inhabited by a people, whose manners and customs nearly resembled those of the Egyptians. Many of their divinities were the same; they had the same orders of priesthood and religious ceremonies; they made use of the same characters in writing; their dress was alike; and the regal scepter in both countries was in the form of a plough. . . . The ancient Ethiopians were considered as a blameless race, worshipping the Gods, doing no evil, exercising fortitude, and despising death.[20]

Americans, and particularly African Americans, are reputed to be incurable optimists, and are said to view history as the unstoppable sweep of progress toward the social perfection of a new Jerusalem.[21] The enlightenment belief in the power of science combined with the Protestant belief in the possibility of a perfect Christian state led to a belief that America could become the perfect society. But some historians do not accept the idea that the American perception of history has been so blissfully uncomplicated. They recognize that Americans have always entertained, simultaneously with their progressivism and perfectionism, a less optimistic teleology. Despite the optimism supposedly prevalent in both the American enlightenment and in evangelical Christianity, another, more somber, view of history had a currency in American thought at the end of the eighteenth century.

"The Mutability of Human Affairs," published in *Freedom's Journal*, echoed a theory of history based on the ideas that human fortune is unstable and that history moves in cycles. A society in its growth, development, and decline is similar to a living organism that progresses from infancy through adulthood, then declines into senescence. Historians frequently refer to what is perhaps the only familiar passage from Henry Bolingbroke's *The Patriot King* [1738] to illustrate a dark, fatalistic strain in eighteenth-century historical thinking. "Absolute stability is not to be expected in any thing human. . . . The best instituted governments, like the best constituted animal bodies carry within them the seeds of their destruction."[22]

Examples of the organic model applied to the cycles of history were common in eighteenth-century thought. The unfolding of history was like the development of a plant, and the destiny of civilizations was like the destiny of a flower – it must unfold, blossom, and decay. Johann Gottfried von Herder's *Reflections on the Philosophy of the History of Mankind*, written 1784–91, offers excellent examples of this organic analogy. Herder viewed history as a series of endless cycles, but in each of these cycles there was potential for greater or lesser perfection of certain civilized traits. The cycle that a nation or an individual experienced would play itself out in ways deeply influenced by circumstances of time or place. Within Herder's cycles of repetition, however, there was always hope of a potential for new and enduring improvement of the human condition.

> Every thing that could blossom upon Earth, has blossomed; each in its due season, and its proper sphere: it has withered away, and will blossom again, when its time arrives. The work of Providence pursues its eternal course, according to grand universal laws: and to the consideration of this we proceed with unpresuming steps. . . .
> Reason, however, and the effective joint activity of mankind, keep on their unwearied course; and it may even be deemed a good sign, when the best fruits ripen not prematurely.[23]

The putative optimism that, according to legend, enlightened every corner of the eighteenth-century intellectual environment was real enough. Historians have been correct in recognizing a confidently progressive strain in the ideologies of the emergent United States. It is true that many Americans viewed history in terms of the improvability of the human condition, both morally and scientifi-

cally. For the enlightened Christian, this progressivism was consistent
with a millennial teleology of traditional Christian doctrine. It also
worked nicely with the tendency toward Christian perfectionism that
was a common element of American social thought in the early republic. Societies were improvable and history revealed those forces
that reasonable minds could harness in order to assure their improvement. That a tradition of Christian perfectionism often explained human progress as the inevitable result of the civilizing influence of Christianity is an observation that has often been made.
Optimism prevails in the very documents on which the United States
was founded.[24]

Nonetheless, Thomas Jefferson revealed his exposure to a less optimistic, cyclical notion of history in his *Notes on the State of Virginia*.
He apparently believed that the future of the United States would
never be secure from history's cycle of decay unless the black population could be removed. Jefferson's observations in the *Notes* represented both a theological historicism and a cyclical theory common
in eighteenth-century historiography. He employed the traditional
symbol of the revolving wheel of fortune to illustrate his apprehen-
sion of revolutionary cycles, thus revealing a fear that slavery caused
instability (mutability), which would bring about the decline of the
society. Slavery violated both divine and natural law in two important
respects: it kept human beings in a state of unnatural bondage, and
it threatened the natural order by occasioning the mixing of two
distinct races. Jefferson believed, of course, that slavery could be
abolished only through the drastic measure of exiling the entire
black population to Africa, "beyond the reach of mixture." Both
nature and nature's God were in oppostion to a slaveholding society,
therefore a slaveholding society would contain the seeds of its own
destruction. He invoked religion as well as natural law in calling for
an end to slavery.[25]

> And can the liberties of a nation be thought secure when we
> have removed their only firm basis, a conviction in the minds
> of the people that these liberties are of the gift of God. That
> they are not to be violated but with his wrath, indeed I tremble
> for my country when I reflect that God is just: that his justice
> cannot sleep forever; that considering numbers, nature and
> natural means only, a revolution of the wheel of fortune, an
> exchange of situation is among possible events that it may be-
> come probable by supernatural interference! The Almighty has
> no attribute that can take side with us in such a contest.[26]

This frequently quoted jeremiad from Jefferson's *Notes* exempli-
fied a theological historicism that postulated the direct intervention

of the hand of God in history. It was a product of the same cyclical theory of history that generated the *Freedom's Journal* article on mutability. Among African Americans – even those who could not read – exposure to this tradition was unavoidable. It was common in political oratory, churches, Sunday schools and other places of social interaction. By the early nineteenth century, African Americans had worked out a folk history that was as obsessed with the African past as with the American future. It was a history as concerned with the tragic decline of Ethiopian greatness as with the optimistic hope of racial redemption. From this it may be deduced that African Americans desired a historiography offering a rationale for decline as well as one that offered reassurances of progress.

Among the many places in which Jefferson's generation of Americans encountered the historiography of decline was Constantine François Volney's *Travels in Syria and Egypt* (1783) and his mystical reverie *The Ruins, or Meditation on the Revolutions of Empires and the Law of Nature* (1791). Jefferson was well acquainted with Volney, who on a visit to Monticello in 1796 was appalled by the spectacle of Jefferson threatening his field hands with a whip. Jefferson had been impressed by *The Ruins*, which he volunteered to translate into English. Nothing came of the offer; an English edition of *The Ruins* had already been published in London in 1797 – albeit Volney did not approve the translation. A second English edition, published in Paris in 1802, had an almost immediate influence on African American thought. This was remarkable, because it focused only a moderate amount of attention on the African race. The book took the form of a fantastic vision in which the author was addressed by a supernatural "phantom," or "genius," on the nature of mutability, drawing lessons from the ruins of Egypt.[27]

> And the genius began to enumerate and point out the objects to me: Those piles of ruins, said he, which you see in that narrow valley watered by the Nile, are the remains of opulent cities, the pride of the ancient kingdom of Ethiopia. Behold the wrecks of her metropolis, of Thebes with her hundred palaces, the parent of cities and monument of the caprice of destiny. There a people, now forgotten, discovered, while others were yet barbarians, the elements of the arts and sciences. A race of men now rejected from society for their *sable skin and frizzled hair*, founded on the study of the laws of nature, those civil and religious systems which still govern the universe.[28]

In enormous footnotes to this passage, Volney cited the Greek historians Diodorus Siculus and Lucian to buttress his own contention that "the first learned nation was a nation of Blacks; for it is incontrovertible, that, by the term Ethiopians, the ancients meant to represent a people of black complexion, thick lips, and woolly hair. ... I have suggested," Volney continued, "the same ideas in my *Travels into Syria,* founded upon the black complexion of the Sphinx." Volney has been repeatedly cited by Afrocentric writers since the publication of his work.[29]

Afrocentric authors also responded with enthusiasm to another Frenchmen, Abbé Henri Gregoire, because he promoted the idea that the ancient Egyptians were black in his *De la litterature des Negres: ou Recherches sur leurs facultes Intellectualles* (1808). It is well known that Gregoire sent Jefferson a copy of his book, and that Jefferson, while tolerant of Gregoire's arguments and examples, remained convinced that Africans were physically and intellectually inferior to whites. In Jefferson's view, Africans occupied a position in the "great chain of being" that was but one level removed from the "oranootan." Nonetheless, Jefferson's references to the laws of nature, the wheel of fortune, and the attributes of God all indicated a belief that the cycles of history would work against the American people unless they came to grips with the moral wrong of enslaving even an inferior people.[30]

The African American pamphleteer David Walker responded to Jefferson's *Notes on the State of Virginia* in his *Appeal in Four Articles: Together with a Preamble, to the Colored Citizens of the World, but in Particular and very Expressly to Those of the United States of America.* Adopting and extending Jefferson's rhetoric of theological historicism, Walker predicted a dire fate for the United States of America. Substantial portions of the *Appeal's* eighty pages were addressed to the recently deceased Jefferson. While the *Appeal* was, on one level, an affirmation of Christian progress and the idea that slavery was doomed by the providence of God, on another level it was infused with a cyclical theory of history condensed out of ideas that were in the air. Walker made numerous references to the decline of civilizations brought on by the corrupting influence of slavery. He agreed with Jefferson on one point, however, that the United States could escape from the cycle by ridding itself of slavery.

As history spiraled upward, civilizations would inevitably wither and decay, but mankind in general would experience a continuing advancement in accord with the Christian teleology of progress and perfection toward the messianic era, or in accord with the enlightenment ideal of a republican millennium. David Walker believed that every society might experience its own variety of religious truth, but he was no cultural relativist. He believed there must always be a transcendent reality at the base of every moral system, and that there was only one absolute truth. Egyptians had discovered it, then lost it. The same was true of the Greeks and the Romans. Now the Americans had their chance, and the question was whether they could avoid the pattern of decline that had cursed these previous civilizations, by avoiding the sources of decadence that had precipitated their downfall.[31]

Walker referred to slavery as "that *curse to nations* which has spread terror and devastation through so many nations of antiquity, and which is raging to such a pitch at the present day in Spain and in Portugal" (emphasis in the original). Walker participated in the tradition known as "the black legend," a perspective that viewed the Catholic nations of Spain and Portugal as decadent, the reason for this decadence being the curse of slavery. During the 1820s Spain was experiencing a decline of its already damaged fortunes, brought on by the revolution in her American colonies as well as by the civil disruption known as the Peninsular War. Walker conceived of only one obvious explanation for such disorders. "Though others may lay the cause of the fierceness with which they cut each other's throats to some other circumstances, yet they who believe that God is a God of justice, will believe that SLAVERY *is the principle cause.*"[32]

Walker was as familiar as most of his contemporaries with the Scripture stating that "Ethiopia shall soon stretch out her hands unto God," and alluded to it in the preface to the third edition of his pamphlet. The verse revealed his acceptance of a teleology predicting the ultimate triumph of the African race over its present adversity. In Walker's case, it apparently informed a belief that Africans would assume a position of world leadership, that they were destined for superiority, or that they would become leaders of the world at some future date, which would witness the decline of all haughty and godless Europeans.[33]

Hope of an Ethiopian revival was a constant theme in the writings of Maria Stewart, but in an 1833 speech, at the Masonic Lodge in Boston, she made use of a different historical myth. On this occasion she drew her prophecy from Revelation 18, as she portrayed America as a Babylon and predicted the nation's decline because of its sins against a chosen people.

America has become like the great city of Babylon . . . , She is indeed a seller of slaves and the souls of men; she has made the Africans drunk with the wine of her fornication; she has put them completely beneath her feet, and she means to keep them there; her right hand supports the reins of government, and her left hand the wheel of power, and she is determined not to let go her grasp.

"America has risen to her meridian," she said in the introduction to her literary *Productions* published in 1835. "When you begin to thrive, she will begin to fall." Stewart thus represented a bitter prophetic tradition in African American thought. Her unrequited longing for citizenship rights was transformed into hostility toward the United States, and although she opposed emigration, she felt that African Americans had a separate and distinct national destiny apart from that of other Americans.[34]

Walker and Stewart shared a millennial conception of history that was common to their generation of black people. It is not surprising that Walker and most of his contemporaries were familiar with the prophecy that Ethiopia would soon stretch out her hands, nor is it particularly surprising that he was aware of Thomas Jefferson's gloomy prophecy concerning slavery in *Notes on the State of Virginia*. Literate black people read and discussed a great deal on the subject of slavery – ancient and modern. The reflections on ancient Egypt that appeared in *Freedom's Journal* were certainly familiar to Walker, not only because he was a Boston correspondent for that newspaper, but because they constituted a part of the folk mythology of the masses.

Walker shared *Freedom's Journal*'s view of the ancient Egyptians as "Africans or coloured people, much as we are – some of them yellow and others dark – a mixture of Ethiopians and the natives of Egypt – about the same as you see the coloured people of the United States at the present day." The Egyptians, he argued, were not as evil as the Americans who enslaved the blacks; they had given the Children of Israel some of the best lands in Egypt. Nor were the Egyptians guilty of Jeffersonian hypocrisy on racial mixing. According to biblical authority, Joseph had married the daughter of Potiphera, priest of On. As further proof that "the condition of the Israelites was better under the Egyptians than ours is under the whites," Walker reminded his audience that Pharaoh's daughter had adopted Moses as a son.

Walker's *Appeal* rhapsodized on the past achievements of the African races, "the arts and sciences – wise legislators – the pyramids and other magnificent buildings – the turning of the channel of the river Nile, by the sons of Africa or of Ham." Greece and Rome owed their civilizations to African sages.

I say, when I view retrospectively, the renown of that once mighty people, the children of our great progenitor, I am indeed cheered. Yea further, when I view that mighty son of Africa, HANNIBAL, one of the greatest generals of antiquity, who defeated and cut off so many thousands of the white Romans or murderers, and who carried his victorious arms, to the very gate of Rome, and I give it as my candid opinion, that had Carthage been well united and had given him good support, he would have carried that cruel and barbarous city by storm. But they were dis-united, as the coloured people are now, in the United States of America, the reason our natural enemies are enabled to keep their feet on our throats.[35]

Hosea Easton, in *A Treatise on the Intellectual Character and Civil and Political Condition of the Colored People of the U. States* (1837), accepted the tradition that Noah's grandson, Ham, was "founder of the African race," and had led a colony into Egypt and founded "a mighty Empire." With the passage of time, "the Egyptians communicated their arts to the Greeks; the Greeks taught the Romans." The present inhabitants of Europe were ultimately indebted to Egypt for their "civility and refinement," he argued. The early history of Europe was a maelstrom of barbarism, war and bloodshed, and the respective histories of the African and the European nations bore witness to the inborn traits of the black and the white races. "Had the inhabitants of Egypt, Ethiopia, Carthage, and other kingdoms in Africa, been possessed with the same [sanguinary] disposition [as the Europeans] the probability is that the world now would be in a heathenish darkness." But ancient Africa, he pontificated, had been a utopia of civilization, commerce, and virtue. "The Egyptians alone have done more to cultivate such improvements as comports to the happiness of mankind, than all the descendants of Japhet put together. . . . Nothing but liberal generous principles, can call the energies of an African mind into action."[36]

The question of what had led to the collapse of ancient African glory was a recurrent one in antebellum black writing. White apologists for slavery assumed that Africans had always been backward, and explained this backwardness with reference to the mark of Cain. Africans were children of the first murderer, and thus were doomed to savagery and inferiority. The problem with such an interpretation was that the children of Cain were supposedly destroyed in the Great Deluge, which had been survived only by the children of Noah. Resourceful proslavery preachers thus directed their attention to the biblical story of Noah, according to which Ham, a son of Noah, had mocked his father while Noah was drunken and naked. When Noah awoke from his wine, as the Scripture related, for some reason he cursed not Ham, but Ham's youngest son, Canaan, saying, "a servant of servants shall he be unto his brethren." The curse of Canaan was then generalized to include not only Canaan, the youngest of Ham's children, but selected descendants of Cush, the eldest of Ham's sons.[37]

The Reverend J. W. C. Pennington, a well-known black abolitionist, fretted over the problem of African decline and the curse of Noah in a brief treatise with the inflated title *Text Book of the Origin and History of the Colored People* (1841). Egypt and Ethiopia were indeed black empires, he argued, since "in the Bible, Cush, Ethiopia and black are synonymous names." Herodotus seemed to offer evidence that Ethiopia and Egypt had been "confederated in the same government, and soon became the same people in politics, literature and peculiarities." Pennington also cited biblical authority to the effect that "so far as Nimrod was progenitor of the first generation of Babylonians, (and he was to some extent,) these were evidently related to the Cushites in Africa, since Nimrod was a Cushite." Since those of the Ethiopian race were the progeny of Cush, they could not be descendants of Canaan.[38]

Pennington did not accept the view of David Walker and other Afrocentrists that Carthage had been a black society. Although Carthage was located in Africa, its people were not of the Ethiopian race, argued Pennington, since it had been founded by Phoenicians, who were descendants of Noah's grandson Canaan. Since Pennington, like many other antebellum black nationalists, found it necessary to base his racial theory on the Bible, he was not tempted to make Hannibal black. What Pennington's little book illustrates is that the perspective we today call Afrocentrism had its roots in the Christian Ethiopianism of biblical exegesis, rather than in mystical Freemasonry. It also demonstrates that when the desire for a usable past came into contact with biblical authority, some Afrocentrists sided with the Bible. Pennington apparently had no interest in claiming Hannibal or Carthage, the objects of Noah's curse.

If Noah's curse was not at the source, how did one explain the decline of the once mighty Ethiopian or Cushitic race from its past greatness? Pennington finally decided that one could accept the idea that ancient cultures had declined because of their sinfulness, without subscribing to the idea that the black race was under some special curse, as the apologists for slavery argued. His arguments anticipated those of Alexander Crummell's essay a decade later, "The Negro Race Not Under a Curse." In any event, the cause of the decline of all the pre-Christian empires, white or black, was obviously polytheism, which had led to intellectual and moral degeneracy. The regeneration of Ethiopia would take place as soon as she once again stretched forth her hands unto God.[39]

Samuel Ringgold Ward repeated the common observations that Europe had once lagged behind the darker races, and that it was indebted to the Egyptians for the first gifts of civilization. He asserted not only that Egypt was black, but Assyria, as well, according to biblical testimony, was a black civilization. Because of his Christian biases Ward was "not at all forgetful of the wickedness of the ancient Negroes. In this as in other things they showed their likeness to, their oneness with the human race generally." He did not deny that their sinfulness had led to their downfall, but this did not mean that the black race was burdened with Noah's curse.

> The quietness and peaceableness of the [Assyrian's] country – the reason given for which was, that "they of Ham had dwelt there of old" – is sufficient testimony to the high character of that people; and it agrees exactly with what all know, who know anything of the race; they are aware that Negroes exhibit most prominently those characteristics which accord with quietness and peaceableness. I set a very high value upon this piece of sacred testimony, and am very grateful that it is in the Bible. "Cursed be Canaan" did not hinder this.[40]

The decadence of the Egyptians had nothing to do with Noah's curse, in Ward's view. The cause of their decline was simply the idolatry for which the Egyptians were famous. The Egyptian abominations were not unique, simply a sign of their oneness with all of depraved humanity. "They committed just such sins as did other people, and the impartial Jehovah treated them accordingly. Hence the overthrow of Egypt and the destruction of Assyria" had nothing to do with any perpetual curse on the black race.[41]

Frederick Douglass vigorously contended that the Egyptians were of one people with the rest of Africans. Far from being a cursed people, they were the historical evidence of the potential of the African race. He, too, made the familiar statement that "while the Briton and Gallic races wandered like beasts of prey in the forests, the people of Egypt and Ethiopia rejoiced in well cultivated fields and abundance of corn." Douglass spoke of the glorious civilization that had "sprung forth from the bosom of Africa." He vigorously denounced the attempts of contemporary ethnologists to separate "the Negro race . . . from the various peoples of Africa." He asserted that all African peoples were of the same stock and offered the Lamarckian argument that environmental influences had made equa-

torial Africans appear to be inferior to Egyptians. Plucked from the
unhealthy equatorial environment and nurtured by the healthy
North American climate, New World Negroes were destined to re-
gain the physical and intellectual vigor of their ancient Egyptian
relatives.

Francis Ellen Watkins Harper's *Moses: A Story of the Nile*, viewed the
Egyptians more in terms of their haughty power than their depravity.
She did associate them with the Ethiopian race, and thus, by extension, with African American people. The Israelites seemed to be Caucasian in her mind: she described Moses as "a fair young face, lit
with its lofty faith and high resolves." That Pharaoh's daughter,
Moses' Egyptian foster mother, is African is obvious when she is
moved by deep emotions – for, as everyone knows, Negroes are a
passionate people.

> Her languid eyes glowed with onwonted fire,
> And the bright tropical blood sent its quick
> Flushes o'er the olive of her cheek.[42]

Harper identified the black race with ancient Ethiopia, who "yet
shall stretch her bleeding hands abroad."[43] But, not surprisingly, she
missed the opportunity to paint the Egyptians in heroic tones. It was
the Hebrews with whom she identified, and she did not think in
terms of racializing Egyptian history. Harper's Christian idealism allowed her to view Egypt only as an allegory for the contemporary
United States. In "Our Greatest Want," an essay published in *The
Anglo-African Magazine*, she called for an American Moses, who would
lead the nation towards "the glorious idea of human brotherhood."[44]

On the other hand, a certain class of whites was frequently inclined to nurture the Afrocentric perception of history. Alexander
Everett's oration before the Massachusetts Colonization Society in
1839 may have been no more than the cynical flattery, but Samuel
Ringgold Ward pounced delightedly on it. Everett, like many of the
whites who favored the colonization of black Americans in Africa,
professed a supreme confidence in the capacities of Africans as civilization builders. He referred to the derivation of "this civilization of
which we are so proud," not only from the Greeks and Romans and
Jews but "from Egypt and Ethiopia – in one word, from Africa."[45] It
was not unusual for white colonizationists to recite the bona fides of
the African race. John Payne, a white Virginian, and the Episcopal
bishop at Cape Palmas, Liberia, prepared a series of articles on African glories for a missionary newspaper. Hollis Read, another white
minister, argued that Noah's curse had "no direct application" to

the Negro race. Read reminded his audience that the children of Cush had a noble past in Egypt, Abyssinia, and Carthage; the past greatness of Africa was a "presage of what she shall be."[46]

Volney's *Ruins* and Thomas Babbington Macaulay were the sources of William Wells Brown's opinions on the Egyptians. Brown conjured up the wheel of fortune image in *The Black Man, His Antecedents, His Genius, and His Achievements.* "Britain has risen, while proud Rome, once the mistress of the world, has fallen," he observed. "So has Egypt fallen; and her sable sons and daughters have been scattered into nearly every land where the white man has introduced slavery and disgraced the soil with his footprint." Brown cited such names as Tertullian and Saint Augustine, and spoke of "the image of the Negro . . . engraved upon the monuments of Egypt, not as a bondman, but as the master of art."

> The Sphinx, one of the wonders of the world surviving the wreck of centuries, exhibits these same features at the present day. Minerva the goddess of wisdom was supposed to have been an African princess. Atlas, whose shoulders sustained the globe, and even the great Jupiter Ammon himself, were located by the mythologists in Africa. Though there may not be much in these fables, they teach us, nevertheless who were then considered the nobles of the human race.[47]

On a visit to Paris, Brown had meditated at the classic obelisk of Luxor, which had been removed from Thebes and transplanted to the Place de la Concorde, and "contemplated its hieroglyphic inscription of the noble daring of Sesostris, the African general, who drew kings at his chariot wheels, and left monumental inscriptions from Ethiopia to India." Brown's approach to the comparative histories of Africa and Europe is marked by the ironic opportunism that characterizes so much of his writing. His reading of history allowed him to have his cake and eat it too. Africans were analogous to the robust barbarians of pre-Christian Europe and, at the same time, inheritors of a noble past, predating the rise of Europe. But whether they were descended from virile barbarians or stately Ethiopians, one thing was certain. African Americans were much less than their ancestors had been.

While British warlords were stocking the metropolitan museums with Ozymandian relics, Africans and African Americans viewed such activities with a sense of irony. Brown, although he was certainly no classical scholar, could cite the authority of scholars on the historiography of decline. Brown had somehow discovered Thomas Babbington Macaulay's statement that "when the Britons first became known to the Tyrian mariners they were little superior to the Sandwich Islanders." He had also discovered Caesar's appraisal of the Britons as "the most ignorant people I ever conquered." And he knew that Cicero had advised a friend not to buy slaves from England "because they cannot be taught to read and are the ugliest and most stupid race I ever saw." If once-benighted Europeans could be raised to the level of a glorious civilization, so too could Africans. That was the implicit message of his text on *The Black Man, His Antecedents, His Genius, and His Achievements.* He meditated with obvious relish on the days when British slaves were led through the streets of Rome in chains, and summed up his reflections in a snatch of doggerel.

> You should not the ignorant negro despise;
> Just such your sires appeared in Caesar's eyes.[48]

Brown, torn between two strategies, was uncertain whether he should concentrate on celebrating the African origins of civilization or apologizing for Africa's late entry into progressive history. If he focused on the ancient Egyptians, he must explain their decline; if he focused on contemporary Africans, he must explain their backwardness. Africa's late entry into the march of civilization could be a source of embarrassment, but it also could be viewed in terms of a teleology of progress. Just as Anglo-Saxon achievement had exceeded the accomplishments of the Romans, so might Africans eventually outstrip the English.

"As one man learns from another, so nation learns from nation. Civilization is handed from one people to another,"[49] wrote Brown. World history demonstrated the equality and interdependency of races by virtue of the fact that knowledge and culture were passed on from nation to nation in a cycle of progress. Culture and civilization were seen as transferable from one group to another. To think otherwise was to be guilty of racial prejudice. The African race would necessarily have to travel the identical road that other peoples had traveled from barbarism to civilization. Brown and his contemporaries were not associated with the concept of multiculturalism. They did not use the term "culture" to refer to the distinctive manners and mores of specific peoples. They certainly had not worked out the notion of multiple cultures representing legitimately diverse responses by social groups to specific historical conditions. They tended to view culture or civilization (the terms were used interchangeably) in absolutist terms. As we have seen in the case of David Walker, it was possible to amalgamate the concept of cyclical history with the linear Christian teleology of progress and perfectionism.

There was hope for Africa because, as history had shown, barbarians could be civilized. Culture and civilization, like the Christian message, were viewed as universally transferable from one group to another. Within this view, which assumed the universal oneness of the human family and the fundamental equality of mankind, there was no room for such a concept as multiculturalism. Nor was there room for the concept of "European culture." In fact, it was often argued that certain elements of culture traditionally associated with the North Atlantic would be quickly assimilated by Africans because the African race showed a greater inclination to accept Christianity and civilization than even the white Christian missionaries who were bringing them from Europe and America.

It is not surprising, then, that black Americans would take consolation from reflecting on a time when England's "rude inhabitants lived in caves and huts, when they fed on bark and roots, when their dress was the skins of animals." Although Africans were barbarians, they were not the only people ever to have lagged behind the vanguard of civilization. Europeans, too, had been "wild and bloody savages," and it had "taken ten centuries to change them." Eternal laws of human progress were at work, and they were being effected by the collateral processes of Christianization and civilization. Conceivably, the civilizing process that had required ten centuries in the case of England might be effected much sooner in the case of Ethiopia's stretching forth her hands.[50]

From the beginnings of European colonial expansion in the sixteenth century and throughout the nineteenth century, the attitudes of Europeans and Americans toward uncivilized peoples were fascinatingly inconsistent and contradictory. I refer not only to the obvious contradiction between the ideas of the brutal cannibal and the noble savage, which Shakespeare parodied in *The Tempest.* I refer to more revealing discourses within the thinking of Europeans who were predisposed to think positively about primitives. For when they portrayed primitives as the embodiment of positive values, they revealed much in their own minds about what images of humanity they most valued. They also revealed, as in the cases of Voltaire and Rousseau, a deep cynicism about the value of Civilization and the inevitability of Progress.[51]

The two intertwined but curiously different myths concerning primitives were the Christian pacifism of the noble savage and the warlike ideal of the virile barbarian. There was an element of hostility to civilization in both traditions, which idealized primitives and condemned the softness of more developed societies. The two myths were different in important respects, for although both were based on the idea that primitives possessed fundamental virtues, there was a difference in the virtues that the two mythologies represented. The noble savage represented a nineteenth-century feminine ideal in which Africans, along with other primitives, were often idealized as possessing a feminine softness and a predisposition to that Christian meekness which was destined to inherit the earth.[52]

The virile barbarian is somewhat different from what we have been describing, and is radically opposed to the Christian idealism with which the noble savage is consistent. The concept of barbarism has ancient roots, and etymologists are not certain of the origin of the word "barbarian." The Greeks and then the Romans referred to foreigners as barbarians, which supposedly meant "babblers," speakers of an uncouth, stammering, halting gibberish. According to tradition, the Greeks mocked the speech of foreigners with the nonsense syllables "bar-bar, bar-bar," which were equivalent to the modern English "blah, blah, blah" – anything nonsensical or unintelligible. In time "barbarian" came to mean anything or anyone uncouth and unappreciative of civilization, but it also came to imply a tremendous vigor and strength, unsapped by the sybaritism and softness of city life.

The virile barbarian embodied traits of warlike masculinity, and was thus quite different from the feminized ideal of the noble savage. Presumably traceable to the Roman historian Tacitus, known for his descriptions of the sterling virtues of the Germanic tribes, the concept of primitive virtue was deeply rooted in at least two Greek legends that probably influenced him. First, there was the myth of a "Golden Age" during which primitive mankind existed in innocence and bliss, a result of their uncorrupted simplicity. Ancient Greek mythology also preserved legends of the Hyperboreans, a morally superior people in the north, as well as the Homeric legend of the "blameless Ethiopians," to the south.[53]

Tacitus's construction of the primeval barbarians was presumably influenced by recollections of such myths, which represented archaic moral virtues that were decidedly pagan, and that could be wistfully admired by a warlike, but nostalgic, society. Tacitus was definitely not influenced by the long-suffering ethos of primeval Christianity, nor by the nascent Christian millennialism that would eventually triumph in the Roman world. His writings reflected a stolid, pessimistic discourse, a suspicion that the best days of Roman civilization were in the bygone era of the Republic. His historiography of decline romanticized the barbarians, and endowed them with virtues that he feared were dying out among his fellow citizens. He would not have understood the later sentimental tradition of the noble savage. His virile barbarian was the product of a martial culture. Black vindicationists, who were perhaps becoming impatient with the long-suffering virtues of noble savages, sometimes expressed a fascination with Tacitus's examples of barbarian vigor.

Infected with the tradition that idealized and romanticized the barbarians of pre-Christian Europe, Francis Ellen Watkins Harper was obviously intrigued by the Germanic paganism that was contemporaneously influencing Richard Wagner's creations. There is little evidence, however that Wagner's Ring cycle, which was not completed until 1876, had much effect on the consciousness of nineteenth-century African Americans. The following lines by Harper are nonetheless fascinating.

> In the tempest's lull, I heard a voice;
> I know 'twas Odin's call,
> The Valkyrs are gathering round my bed
> To lead me unto his hall.[54]

Harper's Germanism was apparently little more than a whimsical experiment. There is not much additional evidence of Wagnerism in her thinking or that of her peers, although Du Bois, who studied in Germany, would later be impressed by Wagner and give ample evidence of his influence. Nonetheless, the impact of German romanticism was omnipresent in the English-speaking world of the nineteenth century, and black Americans were subject to its influences. And in any event, whether through exposure to Tacitus's virile barbarians or Longellow's Hiawatha, African American minds were acquainted with the literary convention that attributed a pristine dignity to primitive peoples. Literate black Americans incorporated into their historical consciousness the myth of the tough, virile barbarian, as well as that of the softer noble savage. They adopted a traditional blend of classical and Germanic mythology in which the health of a civilization was somewhat dependent upon a people's ability to retain the pristine vigor of their barbarian ancestors. Only in this way could a civilization escape from the tragic pattern of decline and fall that had overtaken Egypt, and Rome.[55]

Barbarian mythology eventually had to be forced into congruity with the Christian messianic myth. At one level, this was an easy task, since Christianity traditionally sided with those who were simple, childlike, and unworldly. But black Christians had reason to doubt that the meek, however saintly, would ever have a chance to inherit the earth. Witnessing the demise of Hiawatha and his nation before the sweep of white military power did nothing to reinforce their confidence in the triumph of the noble savage. Hence their prefer-ence for the warlike, virile barbarian. The latter were far more attractive than long-suffering saints, even to a bookish Episcopalian like Alexander Crummell. Biographical prefaces to his writings, published during Crummell's lifetime and presumably with his consent, sometimes described him as descended from "the warlike Temne," a heritage presumably well suited to representing the doctrines of "muscular Christianity."

Black Americans and Westernized Africans were wildly inconsistent in their discussion of barbarians. Whether they were speaking of pre-Christian Europe or nineteenth-century Africa, black writers often hedged their bets. They were inclined to blandly manipulate history to their national and racial advantage, just as did European intellectuals. Of course, since Africans were the subjects, rather than the masters, of an empire, they attacked the problem from a different motivation. They hoped to find within history some explanation of their own "barbarian" status and to vindicate their race from the charge of perpetual inferiority. Their ways of discussing African barbarism were influenced by European traditions. On one point they insisted, however, that Africans were becoming literate more rapidly than had the Goths and Vandals; of this they were convinced. And by the late eighteenth century, as Africans and black Americans literate in English began to reflect on the implications of their own rapid advancement under Caucasian auspices, they began to seek some patterns in the cycles of progress and decline that seemed to affect all human history. They sought to discover what this might portend about the future history of their cultural progress, but also what it might tell them about the glories of their ancestors in some bygone age.

Black Americans vigorously argued the parallels between the British and Roman empires' experiences with barbarians. In fact, they never lost an opportunity to conjure up the vanished barbarism of prehistoric Europe, hoping thus to transform impressions of Africa's relative backwardness into a proof of destined greatness. Although Christianity taught that it was the meek, not the warlike, who were destined to inherit the earth, many Christians chose to identify with virile barbarians rather than saintly Uncle Toms. Within this mythology the health of societies and cultures came to be seen as dependent upon a people's ability to retain the pristine vigor of their barbarian ancestors. Barbarian mythology eventually was brought into harmony with the Christian messianic myth, but it was more than a recrudescence of the myth of the noble savage. On the contrary, the African barbarian was to be admired because he was uncontaminated by slave religion that taught servility. This variety of thinking had origins in the black author's secondhand fascination with Tacitus's exaltation of the barbarian tribes of primeval Europe. Thus, black Americans often gloried in the description of their ancestral tribes as warlike, and compared pristine Africans to Tacitus's barbarians.

During the years that Crummell worked as a missionary in West Africa, from 1853 to 1872, he developed a respect for contemporary Africans that was remarkable, given his Christian and Anglophilic biases. Sometimes he seemed convinced of the "backwardness" of traditional, indigenous African peoples, but he insisted that African history was "a history not of ignominy and disgrace but of heathenism and benightedness. And even in that state they exhibited a nobleness of native character."[56] For propaganda purposes, especially when addressing white audiences, Crummell demonstrated an ability to transform "degraded savages" into robust barbarians. Recalling his first footsteps on the continent, Crummell described his initial encounter with native Africans in a way that revealed his shifting perspective, even within the scope of a single paragraph.[57]

> As we crossed the bar and entered a small creek and turning of a sudden a sharp point of land, we saw, just a short distance out of the village, a group of men and women sitting on the ground. They were all wrapped in large striped cotton clothes. Their heads bent toward their knees and talking in deep low guttural tones. As we stept on shore the whole company sprang to their feet, and I saw a group of the tallest human beings I had ever met with. They were Joloffs of the Senegambia region of Africa. Their average height was about 6 ft 3-4, but with their remarkable slenderness, they appeared two or three inches taller. I was much struck with both the depth and the brilliancy of their complexions. Such utter blackness of colour I had never seen in our race. Not either the copper or the ashy blackness which is common to the Negro of America, but black like satin, with a smoothness and thinness of skin that you could easily see the blood mantling in their cheeks.[58]

Crummell's recollection of his first encounter with "native" Africans on their own soil is revealing. His initial reaction was to be contemptuous of this "group of men and women sitting on the ground" in postures suggestive of lowliness, conversing in "guttural tones." But as they rose to their feet, they revealed themselves to him in all their majesty. He discovered within himself an unexpected admiration for the brilliant, satiny blackness of their complexions, and used the heraldic term "mantling" to describe the blood in

their cheeks. Crummell neither accepted the view of native Africans
as brutal primitives, nor did he sentimentalize them as noble savages.
He did, however, describe them as strenuous, virile barbarians, after
the manner of Tacitus, and employed the standard classic-Germanic
mythology in their behalf.

> You have perchance, strengthened your powers with the ro-
> bustness of Tacitus; and you may remember how he refers, in
> plaintive, melancholy tones, to the once virile power of Roman
> manhood and the chaste beauty and excellence of its woman-
> hood, and mourns their sad decline. And, doubtless, you have
> felt the deepest interest in the simple but ingenious testimony
> he bears to the primitive virtues of the Germanic tribes, pagan
> though they were, and which have proven the historic basis of
> their eminence and unfailing grandeur.[59]

He capitalized on the opinions of Tacitus, and Cicero as well,
asserting that the very words in which they "describe the homes and
families of the German tribes [were terms that] can as truly be as-
cribed to the people of the West Coast of Africa." Particularly significant to him were the "maidenly virtue, [and] instinct to chastity" of
the women. He asserted that "in West Africa, every female is a virgin
to the day of her marriage," and that "the harlot class is unknown
in all the tribes."[60] He ventured the assertion "that any one walking
through Pall Mall, London, or Broadway, New York, for a week,
would see more indecency in look and act than he could discover in
an African town in a dozen years." Of course there was polygamy in
Africa, "an unnatural system," but

> heathen though these people are, their system is a most orderly
> one – filled everywhere with industrious activities; the inter-
> course of people regulated by rigid law. The whole continent
> is a beehive. The markets are held regularly at important
> points. Caravans laden with products are constantly crossing
> the entire continent; and large nay at times immense multi-
> tudes are gathered together for sale and barter at their mar-
> kets.[61]

The tribes of Africa possessed "points of interest and superiority,"
and were notable for their "general manly strength, symmetry, bod-
ily beauty." Crummell made an interesting observation on the Vai
tribe, which he had visited in the hinterland, and which he much
admired. They were "not equal to either Dahomeans or Mandin-
goes, in firmness, in manly vigor, personal impress or warlike power,
but still distinguished [for] one peculiarity – beauty of women."[62]

Crummell, whose father "was born in the Kingdom of Timmanee," did not object to descriptions of his ancestors as "warlike." The quality assured that they had the makings of good Christian soldiers, and that he had arisen from a stock comparable to the pristine tribes of pre-Christian Germany. In a brief lecture note on "Africa and Her People" among his papers he left the following description:

> Right opposite Sierra Leone, in Bootrium country, a race of people called Timmanees. I may be excused for speaking of them, notwithstanding my own race. My father etc. *Characteristics*. First met in Sierra Leone. Saw them passing through the street and inquired *who these people*. Great nobility of character. Indomitable spirit! Unconquerable! British subdued all others around them. Never them! Physique!

Germanism was rife in the late-nineteenth-century environment in which early black nationalism thrived, and Crummell readily adapted the romantic notions of barbarism to his own people, painting their character in terms that glorified secular virtues of cultural health and commercial development.

Africans had actually declined under slavery; the slaves had possessed only a mockery of religion. The entire history of black people in the United States was "a history of moral degradation deeper and more damning than their heathen status in Africa. . . . and I unhesitatingly affirm that they would have been more blessed and far superior as pagans in Africa than slaves on the plantations of the South." These were strong words for a Christian, but the African, in Crummell's view, although a "barbarian" and a "pagan," was never so degraded as the slave. If there was any regression in black history, it was the result of slavery; the native character of the West African stood in marked contrast to that of what he called "the debased American Negro."[63]

Pristine Africans were noble, but plantation blacks, by contrast, were with rare and individual exceptions "ignorant, benighted, besotted and filthy, both in the inner and the outer man," people from whom "inner life, is gone: crushed out or beaten out! and only the shreds – the wreck of humanity remains to be seen, and to have one's heart broken when seen." Far too often, the products of American slavery had lost all their African dignity and had become "ignorant, unkempt, dirty, animal-like, repulsive, and half heathen – brutal and degraded." The enslaved Africans were a far cry from the noble Africans of the mother continent, and in Crummell's historiography the American Negro represented a decline not from the

dubious status of an Egyptian pharaoh but from the inherently nobler condition of a virile barbarian.[64]

The analogy of contemporary Africans to European barbarians
appeared in some unlikely places, for example, in the writings of
James Pike, sometime abolitionist, sometime defender of the white
South. Pike was author of *The Prostrate State*, a diatribe against Reconstruction that was denounced by W. E. B. Du Bois as narrow propaganda. Pike did, in fact, combine a hostility to slavery with an antip-
athy to black people, but what is most interesting in the present
context is the analogy he drew between the newly emancipated
freedmen and the barbarians who eventually "overran Rome."

> Shall we, then, be too critical over the spectacle [of Negro
> prodigality in the South]? Perhaps we might more wisely won-
> der that they can do so well in so short a time. The barbarians
> overran Rome. The dark ages followed. But then the day finally
> broke, and civilization followed. The days were long and weary;
> but they came to an end at last. Now we have the printing press,
> the railroad, the telegraph; and these denote an utter revolu-
> tion in the affairs of mankind. Years may now accomplish what
> it formerly took ages to achieve. Under the new lights and in-
> fluences shall not the black man speedily emerge? Who knows?
> We may fear, but we may hope. Nothing in our day is impossi-
> ble.[65]

Advocates of black nationality and culture in the nineteenth century seldom questioned the "progressive" dogma that civilization
was a unilinear teleological progression under "the moral gover-
ment of the universe."[66] Black nationalism of the nineteenth century, was, ironically, tied to cultural monism, and its advocates conceived civilization as a unilinear process. Paradoxically, however, they
believed in the importance of developing a singularly black contribution to the universal civilization. They did not abandon a belief
that Africans in the past had made significant contributions to world
history, but although they frequently referred to the magnificence of
ancient African empires, they reminded themselves that it was not
enough to reflect on archaic glories. It seemed unlikely to them that
the present condition of the African race could be altered solely
through the cultivation of positive self-images. The orientation of
nineteenth-century Afrocentrists was toward the future creation of a
nation state, and it was with the future in mind that they began to
marshal their energies for what they called the "African movement."[67]

Nineteenth-century black leaders who were Africa-centered emulated the military values of Anglo-Saxon masculinity, accepted Christian perfectionist teleology, and manifested their relish for standards of civilization as realized in modern urban societies. These observations must be accompanied with one caveat, however. Crummell and the other major figures of classical black nationalism, while monistic civililizationists, were nonetheless committed to the multicultural ideal of Herder that every nation was capable of fulfilling the highest promise of humanity, according to the environmental circumstances in which it found itself. Only by working out its singular destiny could each of the various races blossom in accord with the will of God, and express its reflection of the divine personality in a distinctive way. Some scholars have seen this as leading to a contradiction in the thinking of Herder, whose particularism was in jarring opposition to his universalism. A similar contradiction is evident in the writings of Alexander Crummell, who encouraged Africans to develop in accord with "universal" standards of European civilization, while at the same calling on them to develop "a new culture and a new civilization."[68]

Crummell's friend Anna Julia Cooper called for restoration of the African race through a union of barbarian vigor with Christian civilization, when she addressed the convocation of the Protestant Episcopal Church in 1886. Such a union would form the basis of whatever excellency modern Europe and America could boast. And like Crummell, she found Tacitus useful, as the following passage makes clear:

> Tacitus dwells on the tender regard for women entertained by these rugged barbarians before they left their northern homes to overrun Europe. Old Norse legends too, and primitive poems, all breathe the same spirit of love of home and veneration for the pure and noble influence there presiding – the wife, the sister, the mother.[69]

This stood in marked contrast to observations made a decade earlier by Frazelia Campbell, principal of the female department of Philadelphia's Institute for Colored Youth, who cautioned young black women against too ready an acceptance of the Germanic myth. Her article, "Tacitus's German Women," was published in the *AME Church Review*.

> At no time has the German woman, either in the age of Tacitus or of Bismarck, been recognized as a responsible being. . . . Among all the tribes, the women are considered irresponsible as to thought and action. . . . Baring-Gould in his very in-

teresting work, *Germany Past and Present,* says of the early Teutonic woman, "She was treated as a household drudge . . .
when her husband died she was expected to burn herself as if
she was of no more use in the world. . . ." Excepting among
the Visigothic tribes, the German women of Tacitus' times had
no inheritance in lands.[70]

Edward Wilmot Blyden, like Campbell, disagreed with those
among his contemporaries who dwelt on romantic conceptions of
the Teutons; he disparaged the "ancient Slavonic superstitions" and
the polygamy under which "women were regarded as slaves, and on
the death of their husbands . . . were expected to ascend the funeral
pile or otherwise put an end to their lives." As for Tacitus's idealization of the barbarians, Blyden was unimpressed. Tacitus demonstrated such endemic vices of prehistoric Europe as slavery and human sacrifice. He conceded the moral shortcomings of native
Africans, but with the proviso that "there is not a single moral defi-
ciency now existing among Africans – not a single practice now in-
dulged in by them – to which we cannot find a parallel in the past
history of Europe." "Out of savages unable to count up to the number of their fingers, and speaking a language containing only nouns
and verbs, arise at length our Newtons and Shakespeares." Such
observations, of course, revealed a blindness to the sophisticated languages and cultures of West Africa, not to mention an insensitivity
to the complexity and depth of Anglo-Saxon and other "primitive"
cultures.

Blyden viewed barbarians, whether they were African or European, as primitives who must be brought under the influence of
progress and civilization. He sought identification with the civilizations of Egypt and Ethiopia, which he linked to the cultures of the
upper Nile, and the rest of Africa; thus, classical Mediterranean civilization was traceable to the African interior. In support of this thesis,
Blyden invoked a Homeric passage that has since become familiar to
black nationalist ideologues and Afrocentric vindicationists:

> The sire of Gods and all the ethereal train
> On the warm limits of the farthest main
> Now mix with mortals, nor disdain to grace
> The feasts of Ethiopia's blameless race
> Twelve days the powers indulge the genial rite,
> Returning with the twelfth revolving night.[71]

In an essay entitled "Africa's Service to the World," Blyden recounted the observations of the ancient Greeks on the heritage of
"Ethiopia's blameless race."[72] Ethiopia, in the discourse that Blyden

inherited, was usually interpreted as referring to all black persons of African descent, and Blyden believed that the heritage of ancient Ethiopia overlapped that of ancient Egypt. It is not surprising that on his visit to Egypt in 1866, Blyden visited the Pyramid of Cheops. Standing in its central hall, he voiced his exultation in the words of the Liberian poet Hilary Teage, and exhorted "every African in the world" to reclaim the glory of the ancient Nile:

From pyramidal hall,
From Karnac's sculptured wall,
From Thebes they loudly call –
Retake your fame.

Evidence of past greatness offered hope of future progress as he stood within the pyramid. "This, thought I, is the work of my African progenitors," Blyden rhapsodized. "Feelings came over me far different from those which I have felt when looking at the mighty works of European genius. I felt that I had a particular heritage in the Great Pyramid." He went on to make what was by the end of the nineteenth century a standard claim of black nationalists, that "illustrious Africans" had created the source of all civilization. Africans were the "stirring characters who sent civilization into Greece," it was they who had invented poetry, history, and mathematics and they who had taught it to Homer, Herodotus, and Euclid. Subsequent generations of Afrocentrists would continue to cite the works of Herodotus, and other Greek authors, as "proof" that the Egyptians and the Ethiopians were of the same black race. Proving that the Egyptians and Ethiopians were of one race was a necessary step in showing that the future of the Negro was foretokened by past greatness.[73]

For Blyden, the fact of Europeans' achievement despite their crude beginnings reinforced a belief in the inevitability of human progress, and a confidence in the future of the African races to achieve future greatness.[74] The greatness of a people and their potential for self-improvement were detectable even in their less advanced stages, and the qualities of their primitive state presaged their ultimate human potential. Although in his earlier work, Blyden tended to discuss native Africans in terms of their improvability, Blyden eventually came to be a staunch defender of African culture in its contemporary state.

The historian Hollis Lynch has noted that Blyden's earlier writings tended to focus on the idea of improving Africa by Europeanizing it.[75] He assumed, in other words, a missionary position with respect to Africa. In later work, such as his *African Life and Customs* (1908), Blyden showed greater sympathy for the merits of indigenous culture. He came to celebrate and defend the traditions and social patterns of African people, which were supposedly uncorrupted by European influences. Thus, he defended the practice of female genital mutilation, which was strongly opposed by more "Westernized" African leaders. Blyden also defended the practice of polygyny, to which he attributed the nonexistence of a prostitute class in Africa. "Under the African marriage system," he asserted, "such a state of things is utterly impossible. There are no 'women of the under world,' no 'slaves of the abyss.' Every woman is above ground protected and sheltered."

Blyden was simply putting a secular, anthropological twist on a Christian tradition of "romantic racialism" that had thrived in the United States throughout the later nineteenth century. This tradition received its best-known expression in Harriet Beecher Stowe's *Uncle Tom's Cabin,* whose protagonist associated the black race with the idea of a natural man, innately predisposed to the assimilation of transcendental Christian truths. Stowe, who was a supporter of African repatriation, believed that the Negro's predisposition to aestheticism, sensuality, and emotional sensitivity would eventually engender a new Christian civilization in Africa.

> Life will awaken there with a gorgeousness and splendor of which our western tribes faintly have conceived. In that far-off land of gold, and gems and spices, and waving palms, and wondrous flowers, and miraculous fertility, will awake new forms of art, new styles of splendor; and the negro race, no longer despised and trodden down, will, perhaps, show forth some of the latest and most magnificent revelations of human life; certainly they will in the gentleness, their lowly docility of heart, their aptitude to repose on a superior mind and rest on a higher power, their childlike simplicity of affection, and facility of forgiveness. In all these, they will exhibit the highest form of the peculiarly Christian life.[76]

Stowe's rhapsodies represented the more benign side of the racism elemental to Count Arthur de Gobineau's thesis in *Essai sur l'Inegalité des Races Humaines,* published 1853–55. Gobineau was at some remove from the conventions of American racial thought that had been present in the writings of Thomas Jefferson and Harriet Beecher Stowe, both of whom had doubted Africans' intelligence but found them not lacking in moral sense. Gobineau questioned not only the intelligence, but also the moral fiber of the black race, and viewed the African personality as dominated by emotionalism and sensuality. A devout Catholic, he accepted the biblical account of creation and rejected evolutionary theory in all its forms. Africans were definitely humans, and not apes, but humans of an inferior sort. Gobineau contributed to the tradition of assigning to Africans the quality of a "feminine" race, while asserting that the European race was "masculine."

But Gobineau endeared himself to black readers like George Wells Parker, who interpreted him as saying that "the Egyptians, the Assyrians, the Grecians and the Etruscans were nothing but half-breeds, mulattoes," and knew that Gobineau had attributed the artistic and scientific achievements of these peoples to an "amalgamation with the black races." Gobineau believed that a small infusion of "Negro blood," with its passionate and aesthetic properties, was essential to creativity in other races. His pontifications on inherent racial traits (if not his opinions on miscegenation) were well received in the United States, following the publication of an American edition of his *Essai* in 1856.[77]

Martin Delany in his first trip to Africa was little interested in describing the traditional societies. In fact, he was more inclined to report on "heathen and slave-trade horrors." He repeated a newspaper report that Badahumg, the king of Dahomey, intended "to make an immense sacrifice of human life to the memory of the late King, his father." Determined to surpass all former monarchs by the magnitude of his sacrifice, Badahumg had ordered a great pit dug, "which was to contain human blood enough to float a canoe." Reportedly, two thousand persons were to be sacrificed. Delany thus supported philanthropic agencies like the African Aid Society of London, which was dedicated to the repatriation of persons of African descent, who would serve as missionaries and lead the indigenous peoples away from their bloodthirsty customs.[78]

Delany focused on ancient history with the publication in 1879 of a ninety-five page booklet, *Principia of Ethnology: The Origin of Races and Color*, which included an examination of the Ethiopian and Egyptian civilizations. Delany's method was idiosyncratic. He attempted to make use of existing anthropological knowledge on the origins of races, but anthropological knowledge in the nineteenth century was speculative, and reflected the limitations of nineteenth-century biological sciences. Thus, although Delany's ethnology contained some fortuitously accurate guesses, it was mostly a repetition of contemporary errors that have since been disproven by modern genetics and microbiology.[79]

Delany's attempt to discover the contributions of Africans to ancient civilization were complicated because he found it difficult to take issue with the biblical account of creation. Thus, he made numerous ironic observations on Scripture, without actually contesting its veracity. Perhaps this derived from his concern for reaching a black audience, people he viewed as "highly susceptible of religion." It may be that his awareness of African American fundamentalism made him especially sensitive to a perceived need to discuss his topic within a religious framework.[80] Since his words on the subject are puzzling, it is best to allow him to speak for himself (emphasis added).

> Man, according to biblical history, commenced his existence in the Creation of Adam. *This narration is acceptable to us.* The descendants of Adam must have been very numerous, as we read of peoples which we cannot comprehend as having had an existence, as "in the land of Nod, on the east of Eden, whither Cain went from the presence of the Lord and dwelt," where we are told his wife bore Enoch, his first born, though until this circumstance, had we known of the existence of but one woman, Eve the first and mother of Cain, who did not even have a daughter, so far as Moses has informed us in Genesis.[81]

While Martin Delany was not incapable of irony, and although he focused his attention on some of the more problematic points in Genesis, we remain puzzled as to whether he intended to reveal any skepticism in his commentary on Cain, his wife, or the population of the land of Nod. In any event, Delany chose to pass quickly over the generations of mankind from Cain to Noah, without any mention of the idea, dismissed by Pennington, that Africans were the special inheritors of Cain's curse. Delany's willingness to treat the biblical account as literally accurate probably had something to do with a convenient assertion he wished to make.

> The Hebrew word Adam (ahdam) signifies red – dark red as some scholars have it. And it is, we believe, a well-settled admission, that the name of the Original Man, was taken from his complexion. On this hypothesis, we accept and believe that the original man was Adam, and his complexion to have been clay color or yellow, more resembling that of the lightest of the pure-blooded North American Indians. And that the peoples from Adam to Noah, including his wife and sons' wives were all of one and the same color, there is to our mind no doubt.[82]

In order to convince his audience of the racial heritage of the ancient civilizations, Delany found it necessary – or convenient – to accept the story of the deluge and of Noah's ark. Again, it is difficult not to detect a tone of veiled skepticism, and it may be that Delany

was consciously humoring his presumably fundamentalist readership. That Ham was black, he accepted without question, because
"history so records." Delany had also "gathered by research" that
Cush settled a colony in Asia, "contiguous to Egypt," and that "he
with his father Ham, is known to have entered through the Isthmus
into Africa." Ham, the original settler of Egypt, was the person on
whom the Egyptians eventually based their god Ammon. It was for
Ham that the Pyramid of Cheops was constructed. The ancient Egyptian empire had extended from the Nile to the Niger.

Delany was at no point deterred from discussing a subject simply
because he knew nothing about it. He misquoted Herodotus as saying that the Egyptians and the Ethiopians were one people, and he
asserted that the Ethiopians were the source of all progress and civilization. As for the other inhabitants of inner Africa, Delany stated
that they were identical with the original Hamitic people.

> And the enquiry naturally presents itself: How do the Afri-
> cans of the present day compare in morals and social polity
> with those of ancient times? We answer, that those south of the
> "Sahara," uncontaminated by influence of the coast, especially
> the Yarubas [Yoruba], are equal in susceptibility and moral in-
> tegrity to the ancient Africans. Those people have all the finer
> elements of the highest civilization.[83]

Delany did not have to explain the debasement of modern Africans, at least not when it came to elements of morality, since he did
not believe that sub-Saharan Africans had lost anything of the moral
excellence of the "blameless Ethiopians." Their women were known
"for their virtue and matrimonial fidelity . . . the basis of female excellence and worth." The men always kept their word. As a whole
they were friendly, sociable, and benevolent. They were universally
polite; obscene, profane or blasphemous language was never heard
among them. Quarreling and fighting were unknown among the
Yoruba, since they were prohibited by law. All the coarser and heav-
ier work was done by men, while the women performed only those
tasks that were "finer and lighter."[84]

Not all discussions of African life were so idealized and romantic
as Delany's. Beginning in the 1850s African missionaries, in many
cases among the most scientific anthropologists of the day, began
making attempts to view African life objectively – neither sentimentally nor pejoratively. T. J. Bowen, a white Baptist missionary, published *Central Africa* in 1857, and Delany claimed to have been influenced by his descriptions of African societies. The Reverend Samuel
Williams, a black missionary to Liberia, was also noteworthy for his

dignified portrayals of African life and customs. Like Blyden, however, he was uncritical of female puberty rituals. Crummell, on the other hand, gave indications of hostility to certain traditional customs and institutions, especially the Gree-Gree cults associated with female circumcision. Much of what Crummell found reprehensible in African life would be condemned just as unequivocally by twentieth-century feminists and progressives, although with a different logic and rhetoric.[85]

Frederick Douglass was even less inclined to romantize black Africa, viewing the contemporary black African as a degenerate suffering under "the vicissitudes of barbarism," which explained "the gaunt, wiry, ape like appearance of some of the genuine Negroes." Douglass believed Africans to be inferior in appearance, intellect, and physique, as a result of the African climate. The African's color resulted from the "vertical sun" and the "damp black soil of the Niger, the Gambia, the Senegal, with their heavy and enervating miasma, rising ever from the rank growing and decaying vegetation."[86] Douglass believed in the improvability of black Africans, and as proof of this invoked the ancient Egyptian, who was superior to the pre-Roman Celts and Germans. But Douglass was not inclined to find evidences of superiority among contemporary tribal Africans. The potential virtues of the African could be demonstrated only by proving that the African was really a degenerate offshoot of the race that had constructed the pyramids.

Douglass, in his dismissal of the "savage" or "barbarian" equatorial Africans, represented an old tradition, unfortunately preserved among many African American leaders to the present day. Like most of his contemporaries, he believed that people were either civilized or uncivilized, and that sub-Saharan Africans, who were by definition uncivilized because they had not built cities comparable to London or New York, were culturally and socially inferior to Europeans. They were also culturally inferior to the ancient Egyptians, who had constructed temples and pyramids. Douglass represented the tendency to think of Egypt as superior to the rest of Africa, and demonstrated a resultant desire to attach black Americans to a romantically conceived ancient Egypt, rather than to an embarrassingly uncivilized contemporary Africa.[87]

Alexander Crummell was more comfortable identifying with barbarians than with Egyptians. Barbarians, whether African or Germanic, were simple and chaste. Identification with the decadent Egyptians brought one uncomfortably close to the idea that the black race might be under a curse. Crummell had bravely confuted the doctrine that black people were the victims of Noah's unrelenting hate, having taken the controversy seriously enough to publish a tract on the subject in 1852. Africa's backwardness was due simply to heathenism, a matter that was in the process of rectification.[88] The African race could be validated without reference to any linkage to the ancient Egyptians; in fact, such an association was degrading. Egypt's collapse was due to its idolatry and abominations; its fall was inevitable, as was the decline of all pre-Christian civilizations. Lacking the inspiration of the personality of Christ, Egypt had not had the internal moral force to progress beyond a certain level, and had inevitably sunk into senility. With the entry of Christ into its history, African progress was destined to become an unbroken linear progression, and the old cyclical patterns of decline and fall could be broken.

It is likely that Crummell rejected the Egyptians for the same reason that Douglass was drawn to them – because they were a mulatto population, and not black enough to meet his definition of a true African.[89] In any event, he was appalled by what little he knew of Egyptian culture. He viewed some of the West Africans as primitive and degraded, but he saw the Egyptians as decadent and depraved. He was willing enough to recite the encomium of Homer referring to "Aethiopia's blameless race," but the Egyptians had "heaped up abominations upon the impurities of their ancestors, until they well nigh reached heaven." The West Africans, on the other hand, he viewed as diamonds in the rough. He cited the German theorist John Frederick Blumenbach to the effect that "there is no savage people, who have distinguished themselves by such examples of perfectability and capacity for scientific cultivation; and consequently that none can approach more nearly to the polished nations of the globe than the Negro."[90]

It was not that Crummell lacked a reserved appreciation for what he called "the cultivation" of Egypt, Babylonia, Greece and Rome, but although he admired the technical accomplishments of these empires, he was revolted by the "vile and infamous" content of their literature and art. Furthermore, he found the condition of women among the ancients "degrading." Crummell did credit the Egyptians with the cultivation and elevation of the ancient Hebrews and witnessed their civilizing influence on Moses as providential. One broad generalization could be made of all pre-Christian societies, however. "They were saturated," wrote Alexander Crummell, "with the spirit of brutality, lust and murder."[91] "The fragments snatched from the almost barren past of Egyptian history, relate chiefly to the murderous exploits of, a Sesostris or a Shiskah [Shishak]; and the remains of its high and unequalled art are the obelisks and the urns, commemorative of bloody conquerors – or the frowning pyramids, upon whose walls are the hieroglyphic representations of War, Conquest, and Slavery." Crummell, unlike Brown, did not view Sesostris as worthy of admiration. The "unequalled art" of the classical empires was only a somber reminder of a confused and bloody past, numerous peccancies, depravities, and abominations.[92]

Having contemplated the relics of the ancient world in the British Museum, Crummell was convinced that the Greeks and Romans had learned their arts and sciences from prior cultures. But far from condemning the Greeks and Romans as cannibals of foreign culture, Crummell viewed them as wise connoisseurs of excellence, because of their ability to judge value and assimilate the eternal verities. He argued that the prosperity of the African race was guaranteed because of its well-known spirit of imitation, and Crummell saw this imitativeness as a good thing.

There was a quality that had been present in all the great nations of the past – the Hebrews, the Greeks, the Romans, and the ancient Britons, and it was clearly latent in the African race; this was the quality of plasticity, or imitativeness.

> This peculiarity of the Negro is often sneered at. It is decried as the simulation of a well-known and grotesque animal. But the traducers of the Negro forget that "the entire Grecian civilization is stratified with the elements of imitation; and that Roman culture is but a copy of a foreign and alien civilization." These great nations laid the whole world under contribution to gain superiority. They seized upon all the spoils of time. They became cosmopolitan thieves. They stole from every quarter. They pounced, with eagle eye, upon excellence wherever discovered, and seized upon it with rapacity. In the Negro character resides, though crudely, precisely the same eclectic quality which characterized those two great, classic nations; and he is thus found in the very best company. The ridicule which visits him goes back directly to them. The advantage, however, is his own. Give him time and opportunity, and in all imitative art he will rival them both.[93]

Following in the tradition of Pennington and Delany rather than that of Crummell, Rufus Perry explained in 1887 the decline of the African race from its ancient greatness in terms of the universal metaphysic of mutability, referring to the "transient nature of the life, and the checkered history of nations." His work was entitled *The Cushite or the Children of Ham (The Negro Race) as seen by the Ancient Historians and Poets*, with an introduction by T. McCants Stewart, another Afrocentrist. Perry's document was founded on the idea that "ancient language is a constructive tale-bearer; that its roots are etymological indices twinkling like the fixed stars to light up the pathway of the scholar engaged in historic research." He seems to have given some credence to the literal veracity of the Bible, and to have regarded classical mythology as providing some glimpses of historical truth. Perry's style of presentation was less imaginative than Delany's, and he offered no observations on the supposed nobility of contemporary Africans. Perry merely cited the usual well-worn sources from Herodotus to Volney, in response to the taunts of white supremacists that subordination was the natural condition of dark people. As a "thoughtful Negro," he hoped to find "something of ancestral greatness with which to repel this goading taunt and kindle in his breast a decent flame of pride of race."[94]

Africanus Horton, a West African contemporary of Blyden, offered the usual evidence from Herodotus concerning the woolly hair and projecting lips of the ancient Egyptians. As did other black writers of the period, he referred to the "Negro cast" to the features of the Sphinx. On the whole, he was, however, more concerned with the virtues of West Africans than with the past glories of Egypt. Horton's theory of history was progressive. He believed that mankind had "emerged from a primitive state of barbarism, and have gradually brought to themselves the benefits of a civilised life." He had little patience with the Greek myth of a golden age when primitive mankind lived in a state of innocence and bliss. Thus, while he wrote at length about the nobility of pristine West Africans, it was always with an eye to their improvement, and his theory of social change was fundamentally progressive.

On the other hand, Horton entertained a theory of decline, based on the standard belief in historical cycles of mutability and decline. Both the glorious past of Egypt and the native intelligence of contemporary Africans offered evidence that the black race could "once more stand on their legs and endeavor to raise their characters in the scale of the civilized world."

> In the examination of the world's history, we are led forcibly to entertain the opinion that human affairs possess a gradual and progressive tendency to deterioration. Nations rise and fall; the once flourishing and civilized degenerates into a semi-barbarous state; and those who have lived in utter barbarism, after a lapse of time become the standing nation.[95]

In the tradition of Blyden and Horton, a Boston journalist, Pauline Hopkins, blended a theory of decline together with a progressive optimism that is evident in the title of her *Primer of Facts Pertaining to the Early Greatness of the African Race and the Possibility of Restoration by its Descendants* (1905), in which she gave up no ground on the Egyptian–Ethiopian issue and consistently maintained the Africanity of Egyptian culture and physiognomy.[96] She asserted that the Venus de Milo and Apollo Belvedere were chiseled from Ethiopian slave models. "Undoubtedly," says a character in one of her speechifying novels, published in 1903, "Afro-Americans are a branch of the wonderful and mysterious Ethiopians who had a prehistoric existence of magnificence, the full record of which is lost in obscurity." She has one of her characters speak her own thoughts when he says, "I know that in connecting Egypt with Ethiopia, one meets with the most bitter denunciation from the most modern scholars. Science has done its best to separate the race from Northern Africa, but the evidence is with the Ethiopians."[97]

Recent critics like Kwame Anthony Appiah have found it easy to place the old Afrocentrists in a double bind, characterizing them as imitative and uncritical when they demonstrated their involvement in monistic, unilinear progressivism, and as naive emulators of European racialism when they sought to appropriate an "Ethiopic" past. But Pauline Hopkins, whose writings Appiah overlooks, summed up the reasons for attempting to link African Americans with Ethiopia, Egypt, and the classical past, when she observed that Africans were "the people whose posterity has been denied a rank among the human race, and has been degraded into a species of talking baboons!"[98]

The contradictions in the thinking of literate nineteenth-century African Americans reflected the complexity of the situation they encountered. People like Hopkins felt obliged to strive toward authenticity as apostles for an African point of view, but they also hoped to see African people benefit from the progressive Victorian culture that surrounded them. Black social thinkers of the nineteenth century were no less tortured and ambivalent than anyone else who reflects with honesty on the human condition. They were faced with the task of reconciling the ironies and contradictions that they perceived in their own lives and in the world surrounding them.

The agenda of nineteenth-century black historicism cannot be separated from the demeaning characterization of African Americans in popular culture. Their rhetoric of Egyptianism and Africanity chronicled the attempts of literate persons to discern patterns of progress, civilization, and decline in human history, as a means of inspiring their own self-confidence at a time when black Americans were emotionally battered by degrading stereotypes. They first sought solace in the idea that they were people of a new covenant, a newly chosen people whose messianic destiny was in some way analogous to that of the biblical Hebrews. But, at least among the literate population, this idea came to be less attractive than the idea that blacks were ethnologically linked to the pharaohs, who had oppressed the biblical Hebrews. Nonetheless, residual notions of the Egyptians as a sinful and decadent people occasioned ambivalence. Black writers adapted their theory of progress by grafting the classical and Germanic mythology of the virile barbarian onto African primitivism.

Amateur historians, journalists, and pamphleteers of the nineteenth and early twentieth centuries found it necessary to argue that the population of early Egypt overlapped the racial category that mid-twentieth-century America would have designated black. The project has seemed important even to such restrained professional black historians as W. L. Hansbury and Frank Snowden.[99] They developed the tradition that sociologist Orlando Patterson has called "contributionism," and that St. Clair Drake has called "vindicationism" – the endeavor to establish the credentials of the black race by showing that it had contributed to civilization since the dawn of history.[100] They sought to provide the necessary refutation of widespread racist beliefs that black people were semihumans, or cultural parasites who could do nothing more than crudely imitate the achievements of the white race.

During and after the First World War new trends in anthropological and historical writing began to make themselves felt in African American thought. There was a reaction to Victorian morality and evangelical Christianity, which had dominated the productions of classical black nationalists after the order of Crummell, Delany, Pennington, and Ward. African American intellectuals were no longer so thoroughly compelled to force their theories into conformity with biblical history, classical mythology, or progressive Christianity. The new generation of more secular vindicationists was led by John E. Bruce, William H. Ferris, and Arthur A. Schomburg, as well as numerous lesser-known pamphleteers and street-corner orators. Several of these figures consolidated their efforts in the black nationalist movement led by Marcus Garvey, during and shortly after the First World War.

In 1916 Marcus Garvey brought his Universal Negro Improvement Association (UNIA) and African Communities League to New York, and began raising funds for a shipping company, the Black Star Line. Garvey hoped to establish business and industrial connections with Africa, and encourage selective emigration from the New

World to that continent. He also intended to develop Africa as a
military and political power. As a young man, Garvey had been introduced to the works of Blyden and had spent some time studying
them in the British Museum, and his theory of history was clearly
influenced by Blyden and other nineteenth-century black thinkers.
Garvey was a brilliant journalist and publicist, and the official UNIA
publication, *Negro World*, afforded many opportunities for senior
journalists, writers, and historians to air their views. Its board of editors included John E. Bruce and William H. Ferris, who had been
protégés of Alexander Crummell and had always associated themselves with Pan-African and black nationalist thought.

Bruce dedicated one of his editorials in *Negro World* to Volney's
Ruins of Empires, where he wrote scathingly of the "tricks" of American translators. Bruce was particularly outraged by the omission of
the "voluminous footnote" to which reference was made earlier in
the present chapter, and he condemned publishers for their practice
of

> expunging from the text all passages which give credit to the
> black or Ethiopian race for any particular virtues. . . . It is there
> stated, in describing the ancient Kingdom of Ethiopia and the
> ruins of Thebes, her opulent metropolis, that "There a people
> now forgotten, discovered while others were yet barbarians, the
> elements of the arts and sciences. A race of men now rejected
> for their sable skin and frizzled hair founded on the study of
> the laws of nature those civil and religious systems which still
> govern the universe." . . . This fact which is so frequently re-
> ferred to in Mr. Volney's writings, may perhaps solve the ques-
> tion as to the origin of all religions, and may even suggest a
> solution to the secret so long concealed beneath the flat nose,
> thick lips, and Negro features of the Egyptian sphinx.[101]

The same Volneyan historiography of decline was expressed in
the title of Joel Augustus Rogers's *From Superman to Man* (1917).
Rogers, who is perhaps the most beloved and influential of the vindicationists, wrote numerous books and newspaper articles which
appeared in the first half of the twentieth century. Like Bruce, he
was an editor of *Negro World* during the 1920s. In 1940 he published
an immensely popular book for young readers, *Your History from the
Beginning of Time to the Present*, presented in a comic book format.
From Superman to Man takes the form of a dialogue between an educated Pullman car porter named Dixon, and a bigoted but tractable
passenger identified only as a senator from Oklahoma. In the course
of the short novel, Dixon is able to persuade the senator of the

nobility of the black past by the force of his logic, and by quoting from Herodotus and reading from Volney and other more recent scholars.[102]

"Civilizations" as [Gustav] Spiller has pointed out "are meteoric, bursting out of obscurity only to plunge back again." Macedonia, for example! In our own day we have seen the decline of Aztec and Inca civilizations. Of the early history of man we know nothing definite. Prior even to paleolithic man there might have been civilizations excelling our own. In the heart of Africa, explorers may yet unearth marks of some extinct Negro civilization in a manner similar to the case of Assyria forgotten for two thousand years, and finally discovered by accident.[103]

Rogers's cyclical theory, as the title of his work suggests, was influenced by Nietzsche as well as Spiller. Rogers was critical of Nietzsche, but admired his statement "Where races are mingled we find the sources of all great civilizations," and the Nietzschean maxim "Have nothing to do with the preposterous race-humbug."[104] Nietzsche, of course, anticipated and almost certainly influenced the following pontification of Oswald Spengler:

Race purity is a grotesque word in view of the fact that for centuries all stocks and species have been mixed and that warlike – that is, healthy – generations with a future before them have from time immemorial always welcomed a stranger into the family if he had "race," to whatever race it was he belonged. Those who talk too much about race no longer have it in them. What is needed is not a pure race, but a strong one, which has a nation within it.[105]

Spengler, like Herder, viewed history as the unfolding of racial destinies through a history that developed in cyclical patterns, and he built on a biological model of the universe in which societies, like living organisms, must experience an eventual decline and decay. He adopted the tradition of Herder and Nietzsche with their disparagement of doctrines of race purity, but Spengler's encouragement of national spirit and warlike temperament was antithetical to their humanitarian and liberal tendencies. On the other hand, Spengler's thinking was congruent with the virile barbarian mythology that occasionally revealed itself in the thought of nineteenth-century black chauvinists, notably Theophilus Gould Steward, a founding member of the American Negro Academy, who preached the doctrine that "war will winnow out his [the Negro's] chaff" (see his "Washington and Crummell," *The Colored American* [November 19, 1898]).

Spengler's *Der Untergang des Abendlandes* translated into a satisfying vision of sunset on a European Atlantis, sinking beneath the waves, but even this did not fully satisfy the emotional needs of ordinary African Americans. They were more gratified by Volney's reflections on monumental *Ruins*, and they were willing to forgive even the most racist authors – Gobineau for example – so long as they acknowledged the blackness of some fleeting pharaonic dynasty. In any event, African and African American thinkers, having already developed their own mythology of decline, felt no particular need of Spengler.

Pixley ka Isaka Seme, a young Zulu studying at Columbia, was thinking in terms of a cyclical organic history when he delivered his prize-winning oration "The Regeneration of Africa" in 1906. His theme was hardly original; it was a creative synthesis of ideas well represented in nineteenth-century racial romanticism.

> Civilization resembles an organic being in its development – it is born, it perishes, and it can propagate itself. More particularly it resembles a plant, it takes root in the teeming earth, and when the seeds fall in other soils new varieties sprout up. The most essential departure of this new civilization is that it shall be thoroughly spiritual and humanistic – indeed a regeneration moral and eternal![106]

Carter G. Woodson, who founded the Association for the Study of Negro Life and History (ASNLH) in 1916, revealed an understanding of the sort of cultural history most African American people desired. The ASNLH was not the first association that attempted to meet the needs of African American people in their search for a usable past. Since the early 1800s African Americans had founded literary and historical societies, and discussion groups. By the late nineteenth century African Americans had established a tradition of taking control of their own history, which found expression in such organizations as the Bethel Literary Society of Washington, D.C., the American Negro Academy, the American Negro Historical Society of Philadelphia, and the Negro Society for Historical Research founded by John E. Bruce and Arthur A. Schomburg in New York. All of these associations laid the groundwork for Woodson's association, and their members provided a readership for its organ, the *Journal of Negro History*.[107]

An early issue of the *Journal* carried an article by George Wells Parker, a Garvey booster and founder of a skeletal institution known as the Hamitic League of the World, which included several Garvey associates among its organizers. The purpose of the society was to "spread the knowledge of the part played by Hamites in the development of human civilization." In the tradition of J. W. C. Pennington and Martin Delany, Parker attributed at least a symbolic validity to the biblical account of the divisions of mankind into three main races, represented by the sons of Noah. Whereas his predecessors had contented themselves with the assertion that the children of Ham were responsible for the cultures of Egypt, Ethiopia, and Babylon, Parker insisted that Hamites had also seeded the culture of ancient Greece.[108]

There was another version of the Hamitic myth, "under cover of which," as W. E. B. Du Bois observed, "millions of Negroes have been characteristically transferred to the 'white' race by some eager scientists." The version of the Hamitic hypothesis to which Du Bois referred began when Gobineau decided to move the children of Ham out of the black and into the white race. The Hamitic hypothesis was developed by the Italian anthropologist G. Sergi, but some black scholars, notably William H. Ferris, found Sergi's formulation ambiguous enough that they were able to adapt it to their vindicationist agenda. It was revived in C. G. Seligman's *Races of Africa* (1930), but Seligman's theory, while fundamentally repugnant, also left enough loopholes that scholars like Du Bois were able to adapt some of Seligman's work to their antiracist needs. In Seligman's formulation, Hamites were presumed to be a Semitic people of the Middle East, who migrated into Africa in ancient times, bringing their civilizing influence. Eventually they were supposed to have intermingled with the indigenous African races until their descendants increasingly bore a resemblance to blacks. Seligman asserted that any culture or civilization to be found in Africa was a result of this Hamitic infusion, and claimed that the Hamites, although they might superficially resemble other Africans, were not "true Negroes."[109]

Parker offered an alternative version of the Hamitic myth in his *Children of the Sun* (1918), where he wrote of an ancient Pelasgiam civilization that had dispersed culture throughout the Mediterranean in a golden age that could be perceived dimly – though unmistakably – through the writings of ancient authors. Parker spoke enthusiastically of the time when "our dusky mother Ethiopia held the stage [and] wooed civilization and gave birth to nations." On his first page Parker provided the obligatory quotation from Volney, and by the fifth paragraph had provided the standard lines from Homer describing Zeus's banquet with "Ethiopia's blameless race." He moved with dispatch through the usual references to European scholars and the Bible, to argue that the cultures of the ancient Middle East derived from a vanished Hamitic civilization. Parker attributed every element of culture or civilization that existed in Europe to a Hamitic infusion, and claimed that Western civilization was the creation of a black people whose blood still invigorated the best European stocks.[110]

Drusilla Dunjee Houston's *Wonderful Ethiopians of the Ancient Cushite Empire* (1926) argued that an antediluvian civilization had flourished from the banks of the Ganges to the Pillars of Hercules, and beyond. Her work, like that of J. A. Rogers, demonstrated amazing diligence in pursuing a wide range of literature produced by white authors both ancient and modern, albeit some of it was highly speculative. Houston argued that the descendants of Ham had preserved the knowledge that had flourished before the deluge, and transmitted it to primitive European societies. Unlike Pennington and the Hamitic hypothesizers of an earlier generation, Houston claimed that the descendants of Noah's grandson Canaan were members of the black race; this included the Phoenicians, "who called themselves Ethiopians, and the Hebrew writers gave them the same name." Houston's work "makes plain" that the gods of Greece and Rome "were also the kings and queens of the ancient Cushite empire of Ethiopians, which was either the successor or the most famous branch of the Atlantic race." They were the founders of Atlantis of old, who spread civilization to the Indians of the Americas. Houston's work was a hymn of praise to the "Wonderful Ethiopians," who were "masters of other lost arts, and who many scientists believe must have understood electricity, who made metal figures that could move and speak and may have invented flying machines, for the flying horse Pegasus and the ram of the golden fleece may not have been mere fairy tales."[111]

As had Pennington, Houston believed that the the antediluvian civilizations had collapsed because of idolatry. In India, particularly, "Siva worship and its abominable rites were a part of the idolatrous religion for which God destroyed the antediluvian world." Siva worship, which involved the burning of widows on their husband's funeral pyres, was not an indigenous religion but had been introduced into India from the Tartar nations to the north. Traces of the original Indian religion were preserved in Buddhism, a religion that predated by millennia the historical Siddhārtha Gautama. Buildings erected by the Cushitic civilization of India would have been considered the eighth wonder of the world had not "Mohammedans destroyed all the ancient monuments of India." Houston represented the anti-Islamic strain of Afrocentrism that is still preserved among many African Americans, most notably in Chancellor Williams's *The Destruction of Black Civilization*, discussed later in this chapter.

The Hamitic or Asiatic strain in the writings of Parker and Houston is by no means unrelated to ideas found in the doctrines of W. D. Fard and Elijah Muhammad, who organized the Nation of Islam in Detroit during the 1920s. Where, exactly, W. D. Fard and Elijah Muhammad derived the idea that the original civilization was created by black Asiatics is unclear, but the idea had been present in African American thought for some time. For example, it had appeared, as we have seen, in J. W. C. Pennington's writings before the Civil War. When Noble Drew Ali founded the Moorish Science Temple in 1913, rejecting such racial designations as "Negroes, black folk, colored people, or Ethiopians," and insisting that he and his followers were "Asiatics," or "Moors," he was not presenting a highly original idea.[112] Two or three years earlier, a Muslim missionary from the Punjab, Mizra Ghulam Ahmad, had attempted to organize the Ahmadiyya movement among African Americans. The so-called Asiatic strain in American black nationalism, like the Egyptocentric strain, represents the desire of many black Americans to justify their self-worth through identification with ancient civilizations rather than with African "tribalism."

During the 1930s and 1940s numerous works on the African origins of civilization appeared, many of which still boast an avid readership. They differed little from the productions of nineteenth-century authors except that they lacked interest in developing a distinctive African American historicism, and devoted little energy to explaining the demise of the ancient black civilizations. Figures such as Charles Seifert, John G. Jackson, and Anna Melissa Graves wrote with lucidity but without the need to reconcile secular history to Scripture. Their purpose, as Sterling Means put it, was "to show, and to prove that these Egyptian Pharaohs were Negro Kings." For a figure like John G. Jackson, the case was not difficult to prove. Although classified and segregated as a Negro, he was so white in appearance that only an irrationally paranoid society could have referred to him as black.[113]

Among the most ambitious, and the more circumspect, of these polemics was Du Bois's *Black Folk Then and Now* (1939). Du Bois cited Homer, Herodotus, and Diodorus as evidence that classical authors were not burdened with the prejudices of contemporary America. He did not depend on classical Greek and Latin authors for evidence on the racial characteristics of the pyramid builders – realizing that Herodotus was born two thousand years after the Great Pyramid was erected, and that Diodorus lived four centuries later. For the benefit of his readers, Du Bois, who was himself literate in Greek, quoted from a reputable translation of Herodotus to indicate that the Egyptians of the fifth century B.C. were "black skinned and wooly haired."[114] Nonetheless, and this must be emphasized, Du Bois did not base his conclusion that the pyramid builders were "Negroid" on the evidence of ancient authors.

Du Bois was skeptical of quasi-historical accounts regardless of whether they were Greek or Hebrew. Thus, he reports in passing but attaches no particular credibility to the legend of the Queen of Sheba's visit to the court of Solomon. It was not from the speculations of ancient Greeks, but from contemporary historical and archeological scholarship that Du Bois derived his opinion as to the ancient raciology of Egypt, "from the early predynastic to the Fifth Dynasty." While he consulted the usual classical authors, Du Bois relied on the evidence of twentieth-century science, rather than on the speculations of classical authors for his arguments. This is evident from the footnotes and bibliographies of *Black Folk Then and Now* and *The World and Africa*, which appeared seven years later in 1946.

Far different in tone and objective than the work of Du Bois was George James's *Stolen Legacy*, published in 1954. Like George Wells Parker in "African Origin of the Grecian Civilization" (1917), James was concerned with arguing that all of Western culture was "stolen" from Nilotic blacks. Both authors agreed with Alexander Crummell's observation of 1877, that the Greeks and Romans were "cosmopolitan thieves," but James lacked Crummell's ironic tone. His work took on a bizarre quality as he attempted to transform the lore of eighteenth-century European Freemasonry into an Afrocentric explanation of the origins of Greek philosophy.[115] Predictably his writings have attracted an enthusiastic readership among African American "true believers," most of whom have lacked the background necessary to contextualize James's writings within the traditions from which they derived or the times that produced them. On the other hand, naive critics of Afrocentrism have overreacted to the writings of James, forgetting the historical context in which they were produced.

Since an interest in mysteries, legends, and speculative Freemasonry is important to the cultural history of black Americans, it is regrettable that George James did not turn his talents to the systematic study of the impact of popular Egyptology on African American Masonic lore. Although "Egyptocentrism" has not been the dominant stream in Afrocentrism, it is nonetheless an interesting one. The Harvard-trained historian Charles Wesley, who was both a Mason and a historian of black fraternal organizations, ignored the presence of Afrocentric ideas in his biography of Prince Hall, and barely acknowledged them in his history of the Alpha Phi Alpha fraternity. Wesley was in a better position than perhaps any other historian to have written a scholarly history of Afrocentrism, but his methodological conservatism and constant striving toward "respectability" did not equip him with an appreciation of or interest in popular culture.[116]

James's *Stolen Legacy* was an understandably "paranoid" response to the paranoid style of American culture, which segregated its population on the basis of racial ancestry. Historically, America has defined a "Negro" as any person having even one remote black ancestor, regardless of how "white" that person may be in appearance. Segregation was justified by the contention that Africans were congenitally inferior to whites, and totally outside the history of progress and civilization. The first point of James's argument was that many of the pharaohs would have fallen into the category "Negro" as defined by the laws of Mississippi, Alabama, and Louisiana. The second point was that the culture of ancient Greece did not arise independently, but was derived from earlier Mediterranean and Middle Eastern civilizations in which Egyptian influences were omnipresent. The first of these positions was correct, although most white people seldom admitted it, and the second was a perfectly conventional idea that could be found in any high school textbook.

The mystical, idiosyncratic, and otherwise "kinky" features of James's work cannot be allowed to overshadow the rational elements in his position. Paranoiacs can be extremely rational – and they are sometimes right. A responsible critique simply cannot remove James's diatribe from the pain and anguish that he, along with millions of other Americans, daily encountered during the segregationist era of the early 1950s. James's work derives from his personal history of humiliation under American law. His purpose was to demonstrate the irrationality of those laws, albeit he chose to do so in ways that may not be understandable to persons who have thankfully never experienced such humiliation.

Stolen Legacy has become the Bible of a small coterie of African Americans, especially young males on the campuses of urban, working-class colleges. I do not use the biblical analogy loosely, because I recognize that to attack James's work in some quarters is equivalent to attacking a sacred text. Because James's work is a product of black authorship, and because it prominently offers a white demonology, it is considerably more popular than that of Martin Bernal, which is nonetheless frequently cited by that same group. Many of the enthusiasts for Bernal's erudite – albeit highly imaginative – work are unaware, however, that his thesis appeared in Parker's *Journal of Negro History* article as well as his perennially popular booklet *Children of the Sun*, both published in 1918.

Students of African American history have shown little interest in the rich folklore of racial vindication that abounded in such nineteenth century publications as the *AME Church Review*. Early issues of *Journal of Negro History* from the time of its founding in 1916 also contained much literature in this tradition, although somewhat more cautious, and usually grounded in the orthodox knowledge of the times. Studies of Afrocentrism have frequently ignored the fact that such nineteenth-century vindicationists as J. W. C. Pennington and Alexander Crummell were critical of Egyptocentrism. More distressing is that many so-called Afrocentrists have ignored the "vindicationist tradition," as represented by Du Bois's *Black Folk Then and Now* or St. Clair Drake's *Black Folk Here and There*. In colleges and universities some apologists for Afrocentrism have become overly dependent on Martin Bernal – whom in many cases they have not read – just as an earlier generation was dependent on Constantin Volney.

Afrocentrism covers a broad terrain, and the sensitive reader meets with many surprises. The popularity of Chancellor Williams's work *The Destruction of Black Civilization* (1974), a prime example of a historiography of decline, demonstrates the complexity of the Afrocentrist tradition and offers some of those surprises. Williams is remarkable for his claim that the first villains in the decline of the African peoples were not Europeans but Asiatic Caucasians, primarily the Arabs. Africans, because of their essentially generous and hospitable nature, were unprepared to resist the brutality of Caucasian imperialism.

> Modern Africans and students of Africa have tended to emphasize the destructive impact of European imperialism in Africa while ignoring the most damaging developments from the Arab impact *before* the general European take-over in the last quarter of the nineteenth century – a relatively recent period. ... There are still countless thousands of blacks who are naive enough to believe that the Arabs' bitter attacks on Western colonialism show their common cause with Black Africa.[117]

It should never be forgotten that cultural black nationalism (in which Afrocentrism is inextricably intertwined) is a tradition that reconciles separatism with assimilationism. This idea I have discussed at considerable length in *Alexander Crummell: A Study of Civilization and Discontent*.[118] Hostile though some Afrocentrists were to the idea of European political and military domination, they were certainly not hostile to the literary and intellectual traditions of the European and American educated classes. Alexander Crummell, Edward Wilmot Blyden, W. E. B. Du Bois, and J. A. Rogers were highly respectful of European high culture. The black nationalism and Pan-Africanism that they advocated was based on the idea of transmitting "the best that has been known and said in the world" to the masses of African Americans. They did not seek to create an Afrocentrism that would separate African peoples from world civilization; they sought to vindicate the rights of black people to participate in the larger community of world civilization, based on evidence of their past contributions to it.

The tradition did not represent a black separatist fantasy, but an attempt to integrate African peoples into the universal history of mankind. Notwithstanding the obvious ethno-chauvinism of such titles as Robert B. Lewis's *Light and Truth: Collected from the Bible and Ancient and Modern History, Containing the Universal History of the Colored and Indian Race* (1844); W. L. Hunter's *Jesus Christ Had Negro Blood in His Veins* (1901); Joseph E. Hayne's *The Ammonian or Hamitic Origin of the Ancient Greeks, Cretans, and All the Celtic Races* (1905); and James Morris Webb's *The Black Man: The Father of Civilization* (1910), racial boosterism was scrupulously balanced by an insistence on the fundamental kinship of all races.

Self-righteous contemporary critics have not found it difficult to place old Afrocentrists of the Alexander Crummell variety in a double bind.[119] They have characterized them as brainwashed pseudo-Europeans when they demonstrated their reverence for Western civilization, and as black chauvinists when they celebrated their "Ethiopic" past or advocated black nationalism. It might, however, be argued that the very contradictions that have been so ruthlessly assailed indicate honesty and complexity of thought. While constantly striving toward authenticity as apostles for an African point of view, nineteenth-century writers were also evangelical pitchmen for European progressivism. My contention is that black people are like all other people. They have been faced with the task of reconciling the ironies and contradictions that we all perceive in our minds and in the worlds that surround us. If black social thinkers have sometimes appeared to be tortured, inconsistent, and ambivalent, that is only evidence that they have reflected with honesty on the human condition.

4

PROGRESS, PROVIDENCE, AND CIVILIZATIONISM

ALEXANDER CRUMMELL, FREDERICK DOUGLASS, AND OTHERS

Lest I give the impression that I believe African American thought in the nineteenth century to have been unremittingly obsessed with the concept of decay, I introduce the historiography of progress in this chapter as a counterbalance to the historiography of decline. The idea of progress seems to hold a perennial fascination for historians, and its significant recent treatments include those of Robert Nisbet, Christopher Lasch, and Bronislaw Bazcko.[1] A classic treatment is that of Herbert Butterfield, who approaches the topic under the rubric of "the whig conception of history." I have used the term "civilizationism" to indicate this whiggish or progressive ideology that dominated African American conceptions of racial uplift during the nineteenth century.[2] "Civilizationism" had both religious and secular forms. The unilinear conception of progress could sometimes assume the rhetoric of Darwinism, as in the case of Frederick Douglass and, later, Marcus Garvey, or it could be viewed in terms of religion, as with Alexander Crummell and Pauline Hopkins, or it could be viewed in terms of an Afrocentric Marxism, which, as we shall see, was the eventual formulation of W. E. B. Du Bois.

The preceding chapter outlined the development of an African American historiography of decline, a feature of which has been explaining why the Egyptians were not recognized as "black," a question that often reflected bitter irony or a sense of "black humor." This focus on Egyptian glories was not the most radical but, actually, the least audacious form of racial fantasy. Racial vindicationists merely asserted that many Egyptians of the third millenium B.C., like the present-day inhabitants of Egypt, were as racially mixed and varied as contemporary American "Negroes." From that point, they proceeded to the rather unremarkable assertion that ancient Egypt had contributed to the history of civilization. This approach to his-

96

tory, even with its insistence on the black racial identity of a few pharaohs, was hardly unconventional.

The misty days of lost civilizations and vaguely recorded histories were grist for the mills of black racial romantics who asserted the existence of a noble "Hamitic" race or a black "Pelasgian" empire that once dominated the ancient world. As seen in Chapter 3, there were two competing but ironically complementary myths concerning the Hamites. One of these myths was pro-black; the other, anti-black. The authors of this tradition envisioned a utopia of the past in which their ancestors, a race of supermen, had erected civilizations from the banks of the Indus to the British Isles. According to various theories, the cultures of the Assyrians, the Babylonians, the Egyptians, the Carthaginians, the Cretans, the Pelasgians, and the Druids had all been black.[3]

Racial enthusiasts asserted that cultural relics of the primal civilization were still to be detected among pristine African warrior tribes. The authors of this tradition explored various theories of decline to explain the descent of the African race from ancient glory into a state of barbarism. They were therefore concerned with interpreting the cycles of history, in order to understand those processes that might lead to a plan for African redemption based on the virile barbarism and ancient dignity of warlike nations of the African interior.

Again as illustrated in the preceding chapter, this version of black history had sources and analogues in religious fundamentalism. Some nineteenth-century racial enthusiasts were concerned with demonstrating that, according to biblical evidence, the great civilizations of the past were Hamitic and therefore creations of the black Afro-Asiatic race. Ancient civilizations were believed to represent the lingering wisdom of Adamic times, transmitted through the sons of Noah. According to some interpretations, all peoples descended from Ham were members of the black race. The great days of Egypt and Babylonia were associated with these peoples, who had for some reason fallen into decline. This decline did not mean, however, that these races were accursed. David Walker was typical in his assertion that in the inevitable cycles of history, they had dragged themselves down in the pride of sinfulness, and lost favor in the sight of God, but they were not necessarily doomed to oblivion.

This biblical fundamentalism, still common in the 1850s, had lost almost all credibility by the late nineteenth century. E. B. Tylor, the celebrated British anthropologist, reflected the unstoppable tide of learned opinion when he disparaged biblical historiographies of decline in 1871 as "degeneration theory." Tylor allowed that "The idea of the original condition of man being one of more or less high culture, must have a certain prominence given to it on account of its considerable hold on public opinion.''[4] By the late nineteenth century, many intellectuals had come to believe that specific nations, and humanity in general, had progressed from savagery to barbarism to civilization in accord with certain immutable laws.[5] The stages of development were eventually codified in 1877 by Lewis H. Morgan, whose formulation of the patterns of progress influenced both Marxists and Darwinists in the later nineteenth century.[6]

Of course, Christian historicism was not wedded to degeneration theory; it could be just as progressive as Marxism or Darwinism. Christian progressivism had its roots in traditional Protestant perfectionism, a world view in which history progressed upward toward the creation of the kingdom of God on earth. If history was cyclical, then the cycles of history spiraled upward, civilizations would rise and fall, but mankind in general would experience a linear advancement, through the power of Christ in history. Thus, the rising fashion of secular progressivism could be reconciled with the Christian teleology of progress and perfectionism. By the end of the nineteenth century, many reform preachers had reconciled the doctrines of Jesus to those of Darwin and Marx.[7]

As Christian intellectuals sought to reconcile scientific knowledge with religious faith, they saw in scientific progress a metaphor for the moral progress of the universe. ''More and more, the world is to be governed by the force of mind,'' wrote the Reverend Amos G. Beman, articulating Christian progressivism's optimism concerning the power of knowledge to solve moral as well as scientific problems.[8] The preachments of Crummell, Pennington, and Beman typify Christian progressivism as a nineteenth-century modernist ideology, which transformed traditional doctrines of divine providence and social millenialism into a gospel of American perfectionism. Their writings illustrate the desire of Christian progressivites to wed the power of faith to the power of mind, through the blending of religious and scientific faith. Progress was synonymous with the triumph of knowledge, both Christian and scientific, and since it was obvious that the progress of Christianity coincided historically with the march of science, it was evident that the future of humanity was destined to be governed by both forces.

By the late nineteenth century, many American intellectuals had either transformed the traditional Christian teleology into – or replaced it with – a scientifically based progressivism. But a series of important social critics, including Henry David Thoreau, Henry Adams, and Jane Addams, developed a tradition of questioning the ascendant ideology of progress. By the early twentieth century, anti-progressivism was evolving into a dogma in its own right. Disillusion-ment with the idea of progress had found significant expression in the writings of Hermann Hesse and Aldous Huxley, *inter alia*. Thus, the Afrocentric anthropologist Donna Richards is not so revolution-ary as she would have us believe, in offering her version of the doc-trine, that progress is a spurious concept, with sinister elements "hid-den beneath a facade of universalistic, scientific, and 'humanistic' rhetoric." She argues, too simplistically, that American and Euro-pean intellectuals reflect the values of their imperialistic, missionary culture and "see themselves as morally obligated to ceaselessly move/change/expand themselves."

> The idea of progress is a "philosophy of change" and, as such, tends to support any innovation, anything "new." Wherever this force leads is by definition "good" – whereas in the context of other world views what could be defined as pro-gressive activity depends on concretized goals. The idea of pro-gress transforms what is merely "change" into "directed move-ment." Participants in Western culture perceive change in this way. Continually influenced by the images of technology, they are provided with directive signposts and the standard which gives order to otherwise directionless motion.[9]

The above observation is reasonably accurate, but it should be tempered with the observation that antiprogressivism and historiog-raphy of decline are strong traditions in Western thought. It should also be remembered that most African and African American intel-lectuals of the nineteenth century were "progressives." They did not define cultures as specific patterns of behavior developed by specific groups of people at specific times and places. They viewed culture and civilization in absolutist fashion and – as the British theoretician E. B. Tylor apparently did – employed the terms interchangeably. Cultural relativism, which judged each culture on its own terms, did not become a dominant theory until after the turn of the century, in the wake of the publication of William Graham Sumner's *Folkways* and the rise of Franz Boas and the Columbia University school of anthropology – matters discussed in Chapter 7. In the earlier nine-teenth century, nations and individuals either possessed culture, or they did not. Cultural progress was synonymous with intellectual and emotional proximity to the arts and sciences of the European me-tropolises – principally London and Paris.[10]

This understanding of progress was not confined to white suprem-acists and European imperialists. In the earlier nineteenth century, many progenitors of what we would today call Afrocentrism were also captivated by the unilinear theory of progress. They were as much interested in the human potential of undeveloped races as in the past glories of ancient nations. Thus, William Wells Brown took comfort in descriptions of Celtic and Germanic peoples in Caesar's time, who despite their erstwhile backwardness, had eventually demonstrated a capacity for improvement. Brown and his contemporaries were not committed to the concept that we would today call "multiculturalism." They were monoculturalists, who believed there was only one road to civilization. They believed that in its pursuit of a higher culture, the African race must necessarily travel the same road that other peoples had traveled from barbarism to civilization, and perhaps back again.

Certain races were, of course, incapable of progress, and these were doomed to disappear, as had happened with many of the Native American peoples, and Pacific Island populations. The issue for vindicators of the African race was not whether Africans had a culture. In the early nineteenth century, even the staunchest defenders of the race were reluctant to make so bold an assertion. Cultural differences were perceived not as matters of legitimate difference, but as stages of relative advancement. The question was whether Africans were capable of advancing in accord with the laws of human progress. Black nationalists were therefore concerned with martialing every sort of argument, sacred and secular, to prove that the African race did not exist outside the laws of progress, and that Africa had, as Alexander Crummell asserted, using the best biblical arguments at his disposal, "a future."

To demonstrate that Africans were not among those races "whose wrecks lie everywhere upon the shores of time," Crummell published his 1852 article "The Negro Race Not Under a Curse." Its purpose was "to show the falsity of the opinion that the sufferings and the slavery of the Negro race are the consequence of the curse of Noah as recorded in Genesis ix. 25." Crummell's argument was that the curse of Noah was pronounced not upon Ham but upon Canaan, the son of Ham. The Negro race were not the descendants of Canaan; "In fact of all the sons of Ham, *Canaan was the only one who never entered Africa.*" As had Pennington, Crummell disassociated Carthage from the African race. This "Phoenician (Canaanitish) colony" arose after the division of the races, "flourished for a space, and then sank into decay." But the contributions of the Phoenicians and other Canaanite peoples to human progress demonstrated that Noah's curse did not imply "mental degradation or intellectual ineptitude." Africa, in any event, was peopled by the descendants of

Ham's other three sons, "Cush, Mizraim, and Phut." Thus did Crummell nullify the foolish notion that Africans were doomed to be "servants of servants" and outside the scope of human progress.[11]

One black author, writing in a sarcastic vein on the familiar themes of the origins of civilization, the fall of the black race, and Noah's curse, wondered why Noah would have singled out only one of his grandsons to curse for what Ham had done, and asserted that Noah "had no right after a drunken carousal, to curse anything, except the wine that had fuddled him."[12] He also scoffed at contemporary ethnology, whether biblical or secular, which asserted that Abyssinians and Ethiopians belonged to the Semitic family of the white race. Since the Negroes are Ethiopians, "*we* belong to a white race." In a passing swipe at Afrocentrics, the author expressed an opinion shared with many of his contemporaries that, since their parents and grandparents "never knew or saw Africa at all, and as we ourselves were not born in Africa, we are not Africans."

> On the other hand the up-holders of an unbroken lineal descent say that this is shocking to their religious, historic and patriotic belief, because they have been accustomed to bask in the sunshine of ancient Egypt, and to gild themselves by the reflected intellect of that renowned people. And shall they give it up to-day? Though degenerated from the full stature of ancestral greatness, shall they not have the poor privilege of tracing back their lineage for 3000 years – suck in the divine afflatus still rising from the mummies – and so keep themselves inflated with Egyptian glory? Yes! certainly! drink it in by all means brethren – but how are you thereby made any the more Egyptian today?[13]

Crummell would certainly have agreed with the foregoing, as he was not given to rhapsodizing on the ancient Egyptians. He believed that Africa's days of glory were yet to come, as he made clear in a 1877 sermon entitled "The Destined Superiority of the Negro." He began with the gloomy observation that in the workings of providence God had allowed the destruction of many nations: "People after people, in rapid succession, have come into constructive being, and as rapidly gone down; lost forever beneath the waves of a relentless destiny."[14] Egypt, Nineveh, Babylon, Pompeii, and Herculaneum, as well as impressive civilizations in the Americas, had passed out of existence, destroyed by God because the sins of these societies had reached "a state of hateful maturity."

> Depravity prepares some races of men for destruction. Every element of good has gone out of them. Even the most primitive

virtues seem to have departed. A putrescent virus has entered
into and vitiated their whole nature. They stand up columnar
ruins! Such a people is doomed. It cannot live. Like the tree
"whose root is rottenness," it stands awaiting the inevitable fall.
That fall is its property. No fierce thunder-bolt is needed, no
complicated apparatus of ethereal artillery. Let the angry
breath of an Archangel but feebly strike it, and, tottering, it
sinks into death and oblivion.[15]

Crummell's sense of history was based in biblical fundamentalism;
he believed that civilization came directly from God, and that nations
declined when they departed from divine law. His respect for the
accomplishments of the pre-Christian era was restrained, and he
viewed the entire Old Testament as a history of decline from an
edenic state and a series of gropings toward an excellence that was
doomed to failure. The Old Testament revealed a mere groping on
the part of the human race after a truth that was entirely unattainable, owing to their fall from the happiness of Eden. The pre-
Christian era could be understood as cycles of inevitable decline,
resulting from the depravity of man. The cycles of history that had
led to the rise and fall of classical civilizations was linked to a fundamentalist Christian view of history, which illustrated mankind's descent from the primal Adamic state.

> There is evidence in the Bible and in profane history, that
> the enlightenment of our first parents was transmitted, for cen-
> turies, to their descendants. . . . It is a wrong idea to suppose
> that the first ages of the world were blind and uncultivated;
> and equally wrong is it to suppose that man *advanced* from
> barbarism to civilization, instead of that he fell from it. Adam
> was doubtless a most complete and proper man; and his de-
> scendants, although they carried with them for many hundred
> years, some of his high enlightenment and rare capability, still
> must have greatly deteriorated from the high capacity of their
> great progenitor.[16]

Crummell rejected the idea that civilization could have arisen
purely as a result of human inventiveness. He apparently rejected
the view of Edward Gibbon that original man had been "naked both
in mind and body," preferring to cite another historian, Georg Barthold Niebuhr, who had written that there "is not in history the record of a single indigenous civilization; there is nowhere, in any reliable document, the report of any people lifting themselves up out of
barbarism. The historic civilizations are all exotic. The torches that

blaze along the line of centuries were kindled each by the one behind."[17] Like many social conservatives of his generation, Crummell
rejected the hypothesis that mankind had arisen from barbarism as
a violation of common sense.

He could find no evidence of a truly autochthonous culture
springing directly from the bosom of the earth, and apparently never
considered the idea that civilization had arisen by gradual stages of
the sort that Tylor envisioned. Nineveh, Babylon, and Egypt were not
"indigenous civilizations," he argued, and it was well known that the
Greeks and Romans were "cosmopolitan thieves," great imitators
who pounced on the wisdom of earlier civilizations.[18] All civilizations
derived ultimately from other civilizations that had preceded them,
and the ultimate source of civilization was in the mind of God. Even
the earliest human societies had been civilized because they had
retained some remnants of the enlightenment that had been Adam's
"crown and glory in Eden," but as these civilizations became idolatrous, "weakness advanced and ruin ensued." Ancient history was
dominated by evil men, violence was glorified, and abominations
were rampant. Thus, all early civilizations had been trapped in cycles
of decline and had been destined to corruption and decay.

The cycles of history had begun to spiral upward only as a result
of "The Greatness of Christ," whose personality generated and sus-
tained a historical progressivism.[19] Crummell's theory of history
placed African Americans in a historiography of decline and redemption. The African race, pagan and debased, still retained some
shadowy perceptions of the eternal verities. From their pagan state,
they had fallen into slavery, where they had been introduced to a
perversion of Christianity called "slave religion." Thus, theirs was a
history of decline from African nobility to American degradation.
"They would have been more blessed and far superior, as pagans, in
Africa than slaves on the plantations of the South."[20] In his later
speeches Crummell lectured youthful audiences against constant
recollection of the past. It was time to look toward the future, and
concentrate on the solution of problems "for the elevation of your
race, for the progress of science and learning; and for the glory of
God."[21]

As a rule, antebellum African American writers shared Crummell's progressive teleology, if not his fundamentalist theology, and
took comfort from a world view in which the cycles of history would
always follow in the direction indicated by the arrow of truth. One
need only be on the right side of God to guarantee a permanently
favored place in the progression of history: "On the wheel of Providence has ever been a dangerous place for tyrants to play their

pranks," wrote J. W. C. Pennington, "while to those who act in concert with God, the higher they ascend on its great circle the safer is their position."[22]

Martin Delany likewise accepted a progressive view of history within which God had intended human problems to be solved by human agency, once their causes had been analyzed and understood. Writing on the condition and destiny of "the colored people," Delany observed that "the world is looking upon us, with feelings of commiseration, sorrow and contempt."[23] He admonished black Americans to observe how white folk have raised "massive buildings," launched swift vessels, "with their white sheets spread to the winds of heaven," built railroads, "travelling with the velocity of a swallow." All of these stood, "rebuking us with scorn." African Americans had been described by Frederick Douglass as "the sick man of America" and by Alexander Crummell as "the withered arm of humanity."[24] With cruel bluntness, Delany observed that throughout the world, "the white race predominates over the colored; or in other words, wherever there is one white person, that one rules and governs two colored persons. This is a living, undeniable truth, to which we call the especial attention of the colored reader in particular."[25]

There was a historical cause for the "ignorant, degraded, and depressed" condition of the African race "as there is no effect without a cause, a comprehensible, remediable cause."[26] Black people were excessively inclined toward a reliance on the supernatural for their deliverance. Blacks had been given to moralizing and to moral appeals, and this had undoubtedly won them commiseration, but it had also made them objects of pity. It was good that we had right on our side, but we must remember that "God sendeth rain upon the just and the unjust." In Comtean fashion Delany called for a social physics, "convinced that the physical laws governing all earthly and temporal affairs, benefit equally the just and the unjust."[27] The "physical laws" by means of which this progressive destiny was to be realized were never systematically outlined in Delany's works, although he frequently attempted to frame his opinions in the rhetoric of science. For example, he encouraged the study of "Political Economy" so that African Americans might become an enterprising people, with a "knowledge of the wealth of nations." He applied a scientific metaphor to the problem of racial elevation, suggesting that history was governed by a social physics.

Martin Delany's theory of history in *Condition of the Colored People* conceded to Europe the authorship of all "useful attainments that the world now makes use of," explaining, "We make no reference to ancient times; we speak of modern things." Oriented toward the future, he called on African Americans to rectify the situation, assuring them that destiny or providence was on their side. While he rejected fatalism and superstition, he nonetheless revealed a mystical belief in the mission and destiny of the African peoples. He cautioned against a passive reliance on divine providence, but he never disassociated himself from a teleological metaphysic. When in 1852 he called for a migration of an enterprising and competitive segment to Africa, he claimed to see "the finger of God" pointing out a temporal destiny to which the African race must aspire in the future, if it was to overcome the degradation of its present condition.[28]

"Human progress, next to human redemption, must, indeed, enter into the economy of every enlightened state and Christian church," wrote J. W. C. Pennington in an 1859 essay on "The Self-Redeeming Power of the Colored Races of the World."

> The race has been preserved mainly by the desperate hope for a better time coming. Their night has been long, and their darkness dense. But their day has been slowly dawning, till, even now, while we speak, the sunbeams appear. Upon this matter it may be remarked, there is a deep conviction resting upon the minds of enlightened colored men throughout the world, that the time has fully come for us to develop our attributes of manhood equally with the other races in the common work of Christian civilization.[29]

Like Crummell, Pennington believed that "adversity to the race, has been a kind of training school." Like Delany, he did not choose to dwell on ancient glories, saying that "the history of a people does not repeat itself, but "it often recalls its people from seeming oblivion," and he heard "the voice of history calling upon us to reproduce the works of our past." God intervened in history to help the righteous and industrious, and presided over a "moral government of Universe," in which "no provision is made for waste of human materials." Thus he condemned on religious grounds the question of whether certain races were incapable of civilization and progress.[30]

Some races, notably certain American Indian nations, had passed into oblivion; other nations, the Chinese, for example, were frozen and stagnant. Blyden, as did Pennington, rejected such ideas as the "law of decay," as an "unfeeling" and superficial theory.[31] Crummell believed that some races had already begun their "funeral marches to the grave."[32] Frederick Douglass reflected an opinion close to that of Crummell, when he celebrated the imitative character of the African American, who, "unlike the Indian, loves civilization. He does not make very great progress in civilization himself, but he likes to be in the midst of it and prefers to share its most galling evils to encountering barbarism."[33] Or as Douglass said on another occasion, "The Indian wraps himself in gloom, and proudly glories in isolation – he retreats before the onward march of civilization. . . . He sees the plowshare of civilization tossing up the bones of his venerated fathers, and dies of a broken heart."[34]

The question of whether Africans were incapable of advancement had been raised, at least by implication, in Thomas Jefferson's "Notes on the State of Virginia," but "the question asked by Mr. Jefferson would never have been propounded had he been acquainted with the philosophy of human progress," wrote James McCune Smith, a black medical doctor, in 1859. The presence of the African population should have been welcomed as "one of the positive elements of natural progress," since "diversity of character and culture" were among the basic factors in human improvement.[35] Amos G. Beman argued another idea central to progressive philosophy, the importance of education, for it was obvious that "more and more, the world is to be governed by the force of mind." And the rate at which humanity could improve was accelerating. Greece and Rome had required centuries to rise from "uncultivated rudeness and barbarism," but "The work formerly requiring ages, may now be done in a day, with all the modern facilities for the improvement of the human race."[36]

What James McCune Smith called "the philosophy of human progress" was expressed nowhere more strongly than in the writings of Frederick Douglass. If Douglass ever revealed the temperament of a "true believer," it was when he expressed his faith in the laws of progress. He was slower than Smith to come to an appreciation for "diversity of character and culture," but grasped with alacrity Beman's conception of "the force of mind." He believed in the inevitability of human advancement through the accumulation of knowledge about the material world, and he possessed a utopian faith in the power of education to make the world better. It should not be surprising that this prophet of intellectual self-reliance and independence was susceptible to the clichés of progressive metaphysics. He was the practical embodiment of progress in his personal odyssey from slavery to freedom. Progressivism, in the creed of Douglass, was sometimes the understandable and forgiveable egocentrism of a self-made man's confusing his own individual triumphs with the progress of a race.[37]

But more than solipsism was at work here. Douglass witnessed, in his lifetime, the stupendous material progress of the United States as it changed from an economy of horse-drawn vehicles and wind-powered sailing vessels to one of railroads and steamships. Via the revolutionary magic of electronic communications, he rejoiced instantaneously at the millennial proclamation that ended slavery in the United States. He witnessed the inexorable tide of history that determined the defeat of an agrarian economy by a rising commercial and industrial commonwealth. He bore witness to the providential triumph of moral revolution as the slave power was overwhelmed by the dawning of American social progressivism. In short, Douglass observed and contributed to the sweeping social changes that made American history synonymous with progress in his life and times.[38]

Douglass was, in fact, a man of his times, representing the self-reliant ideology of many Americans who were born into the era of Jacksonian democracy and nourished on the maxims of Emersonian confidence. He owed much to the romantics' critique of civilization, and embodied something of the notion of noble savagery that flourished in the romantic movement. There was much of the romantic in Douglass's Byronic posturings before his swooning audiences, "with flashing eyes and floating hair." The historian Waldo Martin is correct in speaking of Douglass's ideology as a product of the Enlightenment; so was much ideology of the period, but Douglass was a representative nineteenth-century man.[39]

Although Douglass was closely associated with the transcendentalism and romanticism of the nineteenth-century "American Renaissance," he was intellectually indebted to Enlightenment conceptions of progress.[40] Historians have frequently attributed to the Marquis de Condorcet an eighteenth-century formulation of the idea of progress that was developed in the nineteenth century by August Comte. Both authors assumed that the progress of science must necessarily be accompanied by a progression of morals. The writings of Douglass are hardly rife with references to Condorcet, and any influences of Comtean positivism were probably superficial. Nonetheless, Douglass accepted scientific progress as a determining force in history and, like many progressive intellectuals, linked scientific understanding with moral advancement. On the other hand, he realized "that the moral growth of a nation or an age does not always keep pace with the increase of knowledge" and the "necessity of means to increase human love with human learning."[41]

Douglass's ideology illustrates the origins of American "progressivism," which had its roots in the nineteenth century although it is usually discussed in terms of the first decades of the twentieth. Defined broadly, progressivism encompasses more than the political agenda of the early twentieth century. It is in the nineteenth century that we see the origins of such movements as the social gospel, urban reform, women's rights, labor activism, and the regulation of business. Progressivism, in its broadest sense, is an ideology, a social theory, and a world view that attempts to place humanity at the center of the universe, and that is dominated by a belief that history could be brought under the control of the human will through the agencies of science and scientific planning. Human morality could be improved. Ultimately, it was the moral triumph of the victorious antislavery struggle that validated the theory.

Frederick Douglass's conception of progress was founded in two sets of ideas that converged in nineteenth-century American intellectual life. The first of these was Christian perfectionism, the idea that enlightened religion should construct a righteous empire. This notion was partially derived from the traditional social perfectionism of American religious liberalism. Douglass's religion was indebted to the tradition that had evolved from Puritan rationalism into Franklinian deism, and thence into the transcendental unitarianism of a Ralph Waldo Emerson. It was also tied to the sunburned and sweaty millenarianism of an evangelical tradition, which taught that the kingdom of God could be built in the new Jerusalem of American democracy. Douglass eventually rejected religious interpretations of the meaning of progress, but his intellectual roots were in the tradition of religious liberalism. His intellectual development represented the evolution of religious perfectionism into a secular humanist notion of progress. In his view, the history of Western civilization could be tidily summed up as the triumph of science and reason over tradition and superstition.

This brings us to the other source of Douglass's conception of progress, which was rooted in a scientific metaphysic. Like many Victorian idealists, Douglass professed a faith in the power of reason to replace ancient injustices and atavistic passions with a progressivism both scientific and democratic. For every question in the universe, there was a rational answer, and truth was being constantly revealed by the power of science. The scientific metaphysic was absolutist and led naturally to cultural monism; for just as there could be only one scientific truth in a rational universe, there could be only one cultural truth. Progress and Western civilization were almost synonymous in Douglass's theory. He conformed to the elitist notions of northeastern progressivism that hoped to subsume all of America under one universal morality, which would include feminism, temperance, anti-Catholicism, and a lofty contempt for ethnic politics. Understanding the laws of moral progress, and civilization, led to a replacement of the God who worked through the agency of divine providence, with an impersonal if benevolent Deity who worked through the agency of human reason.

There was something of the Unitarian schoolmarm in Douglass. Influenced greatly by the cold-water feminism of the later nineteenth century, he seems to have rejected utterly any ties to the brawling libertinism of the southern plantation. His romantic impulses, like those of Emerson and Thoreau, were tempered by American "puritanism" and "Victorian" respectability. He held fast to a progressive morality, with its foundations in chastity and temperance – a no-nonsense city on a hill. Douglass and his contemporaries among progressive intellectuals were not engaged in the discourse of American multiculturalism, as we know it today. There was no room in their ideology for "Bohemianism," Irish Catholicism, or bawdy peasant values. Alternative world views were not only different from but inferior to the ideals of enlightened Victorian Protestants. The cultural differences – or deficiencies – associated with the ignorance of southern peasants, Irish immigrants, and other unenlightened, superstitious people, were capable of correction. It was the duty of enlightened progressive missionaries to correct cultural deficiencies and to uplift the ignorant.

Scholars have passionately expressed themselves concerning the significance of Douglass's attitudes on culture, ethnicity, and civilization. Waldo Martin applies the terms "unfortunate" and "utopian" to Douglass's social theory, which in his view lacks sufficient appreciation for proletarian culture and ethnic diversity. Martin is also distressed by Douglass's failure to understand "political powerlessness," his "blindness to Afro-American culture," and his "notion of Euro-American cultural superiority."[42] On the other hand, the sociologist Howard Brotz praises Douglass lavishly for the very elements of philosophy that Martin finds troubling. Brotz endorses Douglass's "objection to multiculturalism," although admitting, "that precise term was not in vogue in his day." Brotz's intention is to utilize the writings of Douglass in a tendentious argument against multicultural education, Lyndon Johnson's long dead Great Society, and programs designed to increase the numbers of black students admitted to higher education.[43]

If one views culture in Matthew Arnold's terms, as "the best which has been thought and said in the world," it would certainly make no sense to talk about a "slave culture." In fact, a common accusation of nineteenth-century black leaders was that slavery deprived its victims of culture. In their view, white Americans withheld "culture" from black Americans, or, even worse, they developed a separate and inferior variety of culture for black consumption. Furthermore, it was commonly believed that culture was an expression of an individual's racial heritage. European culture was perceived by many as an expression of innate racial ability rather than as a result of habits and education. It was within this context that Douglass made the statement that Brotz highlights, in which he expressed categorical hostility to the idea of "different methods of culture."[44]

Douglass's ideas have little if anything to do with the concerns of Brotz or with late-twentieth-century debates over multiculturalism.[45] He was hostile to the biculturalism of the American South because he identified it with the argument that one form of culture was the natural endowment of racially superior masters and another that of racially inferior slaves. Ultimately, black intellectuals, most notably Alain Locke, began to recognize the democratic implications of cultural relativism. We must be careful of simplistic interpretations of Douglass's culture theory. Douglass opposed multiculturalism and cultural pluralism in the 1850s because it was inconsistent with his unilinear theory of moral progressivism. By the late 1860s, as we shall see, he was making statements that would be acceptable to multiculturalists today.

As a doctrinaire believer in progress, Douglass of course rejected cultural relativism, but rejection of cultural relativism had another, more emotional source. It grew out of his belief in the necessity of rejecting the polygenetic theory of evolution.[46] Polygenesis was not one but a number of theories, current in the late-eighteenth and nineteenth centuries, which argued that the various races of mankind had evolved entirely independent of one another. In general, these theories argued that the races actually constituted separate species, differing from one another as distinctly as the horse differed from the donkey. Polygenetic theory even went so far as to argue, in the face of contradictory evidence, that the mulatto children of interracial unions were infertile, as mules are infertile. Polygenesis was sometimes advanced theologically, despite its clear contradiction in Scripture. Sometimes it was argued "scientifically," despite the dearth of supportive evidence. Its basic contentions were always the same, however: that the distinctions between the races were very ancient, that they had existed since the appearance of human beings on the planet, that racial mixing was unnatural, and that racial equality was unattainable.

Polygeneticists argued that cultural behaviors were linked to physical racial traits that were fixed and immutable. They maintained that racial differences indicated unalterable inequalities with respect to cultural attainment or potential. The African race represented an evolutionary dead end, in their theories, and its inferiority was con-

sidered uncorrectable. Black inferiority could never be ameliorated –
neither by evolution nor by racial intermixture. Cultures were unequal because the peoples that produced them were unequal, and
cultural inequalities implied an inequality of inborn moral and intellectual traits. Douglass's rejection of polygenesis led inexorably to his
rejection of the concept of cultural diversity or multiculturalism.

Many nineteenth-century writers maintained a vague belief that
someday a splendid new African culture would arise, different from
and perhaps even superior to what was known in Europe or America.
Few such tendencies to romantic racialism were present with Douglass. The peculiar manners and morals of the African American people could not be separated from slavery. He recognized that most
discussions of plantation folkways had been created by the planter
class as justifications of slavery. Nineteenth-century multiculturalism,
if we may call it that, was thoroughly intermixed with assumptions of
white supremacy. Any talk of cultural relativism was linked in an
illogical fashion to the idea that cultural behavior was an indicator
of racial destiny. To accept cultural difference, as Douglass conceived it, seemed tantamount, in his mind, to accepting racial hierarchy.

In an 1854 address entitled "The Claims of the Negro Ethnologically Considered," Douglass offered a systematic response to polygenesis. He was, and with good reason, fundamentally hostile to the
"science" of "ethnology," because the discipline was so consistently
obsessed with the comparison and ranking of races and cultures. His
natural tendencies toward egalitarianism, individualism, and common sense made him feel that a person's abilities ought to be judged
on the basis of personal achievement rather than racial membership.
Nonetheless, in response to an invitation to speak at the graduation
exercises of Western Reserve College in 1854, he attempted to meet
the ethnologists on their own terms. It should be observed paren-
thetically that polygenesis was only one variety of nineteenth-century
white supremacist thought. There were also monogenetic theories of
black racial and cultural inferiority, but in this essay Douglass framed
his attack on white supremacy in terms of an attack on polygenesis.[47]

Those scientists who were capable of discussing racial differences
without recourse to theories of polygenesis included disciples of
Jean-Baptiste Lamarck, who thought of racial differences as arising
out of environmental conditions. Lamarckians, like everyone else,
were divided between the proponents and opponents of white supremacy, but there was nothing essentially racist in Lamarckian theory, and Douglass utilized Lamarckian arguments to buttress the
fundamentalist religious arguments he used elsewhere. Douglass be-

lieved that environment alone produced differences in the appearances and abilities of the various racial groups.[48] The attractive feature of Lamarckianism was the promise that races could be improved by environmental influences.

This biological progressivism viewed environment as the driving force behind the natural and social history of humankind. Evolution, and therefore evolutionary progress, was a response to environments. The "Afric-American" physician James McCune Smith, accepting the Lamarckian theories current in his time, believed that the "inferiority" of the African could be overcome through the benefits of the North American climate. Smith asserted that "the dark races of the tropics gain in physical development when transported to a temperate climate. . . . This Afric-American race are not only far superior in physical symmetry and development to pure Africans now found on the coast, but actually equal in these respects the white race of Old Dominion, who have never lived in any but a temperate climate."[49] Smith continues:

> The cause of the extreme crispness of the hair of the black may be sought, not merely in the heat of the torrid zone, but in the addition of the low, marshy locations on the coasts of Africa and other tropical localities, in which this close, tight hair is found indigenous. . . . Any one whose observation extends twenty years back, must observe that the hair of the colored population in the Southern and Northern States is growing more and more straight. This is partly the result of extreme culture on their part, and partly the result of the climatic or geological influences under which they live. That these influences – climate and culture – will ultimately produce a uniform character to the hair of the different races upon this proportion of the American continent, is a question even now capable of solution. On the eastern coast of Africa are, living on a marshy sea coast, a race of negroes who speak a language which identifies them with another race who live somewhat farther back, but on land elevated above the sea. These last have hair that is nearly straight, doubtless in consequence of the differences of the climate under which they have, during several centuries, lived.

Smith, in other words, believed that, over the generations, Americans from Africa would eventually lose their "Negroid" characteristics as a result of continued residence in a temperate clime. He remarked on the fact that American newspapers over a period of fifty years more frequently referred to " '*colored people*. . . . ' They are no longer blacks, bordering on bestiality; they are 'colored,' and they are a 'people.' " He entertained the idea that perhaps this terminological shift might reflect "the fact of an already perceptible change in the hue of the skin of this class."[50]

Almost the perfect Lamarckian, Douglass, who admired Smith, offered similar opinions in "Claims of the Negro":

> May not the condition of men explain their various appearances? Need we go behind the vicissitudes of barbarism for an explanation of the gaunt, wiry ape like appearance of some of the genuine Negroes? Need we look higher than a vertical sun, or lower than the damp, black soil of the Niger, the Gambia, the Senegal, with their heavy and enervating miasma, rising ever from the rank growing and decaying vegetation, for an explanation of the Negro's color? If a cause, full and adequate can be found here, *why seek further?*[51]

"Claims of the Negro" revealed Douglass's tendency to link the concept of racial difference to the concept of racial inferiority. Douglass's position with respect to evolutionism was ambivalent and uncertain. He rejected the theory that man was descended from the apes or from an apelike ancestor, but he believed that the human species was mutable and could evolve in response to specific environments. Thus, he dismissed evolution as "scientific moonshine" on one page, while invoking Lamarckian arguments on another.[52] His Lamarckian attitude was revealed in his belief that the migration of a racial stock could bring about rapid changes in its physiognomy. It was differences in environment that brought about variety in the human species.

> One may trace the progress of this difference in the common portraits of the American presidents. Just study those faces, beginning with WASHINGTON; and as you come thro' the JEFFERSONS, the ADAMSES, and the MADISONS, you will find an increasing bony and wiry appearance about those portraits, & a greater remove from that serene amplitude which characterises the countenances of the earlier Presidents. I may be mistaken, but I think this is a correct index of the change going on in the nation at large – converting Englishmen, Germans, Irishmen, and Frenchmen into Americans, and causing them to lose, in a common American character, all traces of their former distinctive national peculiarities.[53]

This argument might have carried some weight if all polygeneticists had believed that racial traits were immutable. They believed no such thing, of course. It is simply that most of them were identified with the belief that the black race constituted an evolutionary dead end, and that Negroes were a stock that could not be improved by environmental influences. In any event, scientific objections were not at the heart of Douglass's concern. He rejected polygenesis because of the political implications of the theory.

> For let it be once granted that the human race are of multitudinous origin, naturally different in their moral, physical, and intellectual capacities, and at once you make plausible a demand for classes, grades and conditions, for different methods of culture, different moral, political, and religious institutions and a chance is left for slavery, as a necessary institution.[54]

Douglass's hostility to cultural pluralism was inextricably bound up with the fact that he could not distinguish between the concepts of polygenesis and cultural pluralism or between cultural pluralism and cultural heirarchy. "Ethnology" had not yet developed into anthropology, with its separation into the subspecialties of cultural and physical anthropology. Nor did nineteenth-century ethnology tend to distinguish between culture and race. Finally, the ethnology with which Douglass was familiar did not link the concepts of democracy and "cultural relativism," as Alain Locke would do in the twentieth century. It insisted that some races were lower than others, and that the lower the race, the lesser its capacity for cultural progress.

Douglass's cultural monism was a rejection of the claims of proslavery propagandists that southern plantation society was the ideal cultural response to the needs and capacities of the Negro race. Ethnologists insisted that cultural differences between Africans and Europeans were evidences of African racial inferiority. Ironically, the only defenders of slave culture in 1850 were white supremacists, who pointed to the banjos and watermelons of "happy contented slaves" as proof that different varieties of culture were suited to different races of mankind. Douglass was also responding to nineteenth-century theories that linked biology to culture. The multiculturalism of the planter class was rooted in the fact that they viewed race and culture as synonymous. Black nationalist cultural separatism was, in the mind of Douglass, a mere concession to the planters' preachments of white supremacy.

"Claims of the Negro" demonstrated Douglass's ability to give himself a crash course on the so-called American school of Ethnology, and to answer its arguments. With the assistance of Henry Wayland, a member of the University of Rochester faculty, he familiarized himself with the writings of Josiah Clark Nott, George Robert

Gliddon, and Jean Louis Agassiz, popular ethnologists of the day, who happened to be polygeneticists.[55] These writers based their theories of racial inferiority on convoluted speculations concerning the origins of mankind, and delighted in "parson skinning" exercises designed to disprove the biblical account of creation. Gliddon was not above using biblical arguments, however, when he thought he could defame the black race by doing so. Douglass, deciding that any stick would do to lambaste the demons of white supremacy, opportunistically latched onto fundamentalist arguments. This was not a bad strategy, but somewhat hypocritical, since it seems to be the only instance in which Douglass showed an inclination to employ the demagogic technique of religious fundamentalism in the midst of a scientific debate.

Douglass knew, of course, that preachers of black inferiority were by no means dependent on the doctrine of polygenesis. White supremacists required neither atheism nor ethnological arguments to bolster a position to which so many Americans were emotionally committed. Theories of white supremacy were manufactured out of religious and secular doctrines with equal facility.[56] Religious thinkers, as Douglass was aware, had long based their racialism on theories that Negroes were descended from Cain, or from the accursed Ham. In other words, one did not have to accept atheism or monogenesis in order to place black folk in a separate and accursed category of creation. Biblical fundamentalists were well represented among white supremacists, and some abolitionists were religious liberals. Such points were useless to Douglass's ad hominem rhetorical strategy, which was to associate proslavery arguments with religious skepticism.

Douglass therefore cast himself as a biblical fundamentalist in order to attack polygenesis, believing that polygenesis was the foundation of theories of scientific racism. There were at least two weaknesses in this line of defense: biblical fundamentalism could easily be reconciled with the doctrine of white supremacy, and, as already noted, not all white supremacist doctrines were based on the theory of polygenesis. In any event, Douglass's argument was disingenuous and opportunistic, because he was not a religious fundamentalist. It was only for pragmatic and rhetorical reasons that Douglass projected himself as a biblical literalist. Furthermore, it should not be assumed that Douglass believed that everyone who attacked the biblical account of creation was in league with slaveholders. He was himself becoming hostile toward the theology and the formal organization of American Protestantism.

Douglass was offended by the fact that American churches frequently defended slavery, and that they were, as a rule, segregated according to race. At the beginning of his public life, Douglass had been licensed to preach in the African Methodist Episcopal Zion (AMEZ) church, but he quickly decided that he was a public intellectual, not a churchman, and far too busy promoting himself to be bothered with promoting Jesus. He soon perceived a truth that Emerson had perceived, that it was possible to practice the trade of public moralist without supporting mainstream evangelical religion. Nonetheless, Douglass was eminently pragmatic about riding on the shoulders of religious moralism, and it is difficult to imagine heterodox public figures like Douglass and Emerson functioning at all unless it was against the backdrop of orthodox nineteenth-century American evangelicalism. One thing is certain: Douglass had no interest in the black preacher's trade, which would have confined him to working in some impoverished parish, ministering to the daily needs of a semiliterate congregation.

This attitude did not endear him to Henry Highland Garnet and that segment of black leadership who were rightly identified not only as churchmen but as "race men." Douglass once gave a glowing tribute to Garnet, saying, "More than fifty years ago when I lived in New Bedford Massachusetts, I went to hear a lecture by Rev. Henry Highland Garnet. He was in every respect a typical negro. Before hearing him I thought I was a man, but after hearing him I knew I was a man and a man among men."[57] Nonetheless, the relationship was troubled by a number of issues as the years passed – both fiscal and ideological. Douglass resented Garnet's fund-raising tour of England, where Douglass had built up a network of contributors to his newspapers. Garnet accused Douglass of deserting the AMEZ ministry, saying, "[He] now derides and ridicules them. Being matchless in mimicry, and unrivaled in buffoonery, he amuses scoffers and infidels by imitating their religious exercise."[58] It is true that Douglass often parodied the speech of those with whom he disagreed, and he made some unkind allusions to the picturesque speaking style of Sojourner Truth in an 1894 address. The story has been frequently retold of how the powerful evangelical orator once challenged Douglass publicly, interrupting one of his declamations in 1852 to ask, "Frederick, is God dead?"[59]

Douglass never admitted to being a Nietzschean or an atheist, but his hostility to the traditionalism and institutional structure of organized religion was part and parcel of the extreme progressive liberalism that he embraced. There was a contradiction in his position, however, for just as he derived his livelihood from his role as a racial leader, he gained his moral validity from the matrix of organized religion that underpinned the moral structure of his public life.[60]

Whether Douglass or Marx or Nietzsche actually believed that God was dead, all of them required a society based on Judeo-Christian mythology, without which their own moral preachments would have struck no emotional chord.

Before the Civil War, Douglass frequently expressed his progressivism in theological terms. He spoke of Providence as an active historical force, working in unexpected and mysterious ways to bring about a more perfect society on earth. There is no way of knowing whether Douglass actually believed such ideas or was simply exploiting the religious beliefs that were so important to the American perfectionist tradition. In "Claims of the Negro" he asserted that moral government of the universe took the form of divine intervention in human affairs.

> There is but one safe road for nations or for individuals. The fate of a wicked man and of a wicked nation is the same. The flaming sword of offended justice falls as certainly upon the nation as upon the man. God has no children whose rights may be safely trampled upon. The sparrow may not fall to the ground without the notice of His eye, and men are more than sparrows.[61]

During the Civil War, however, Douglass seemed less comfortable than did some of his contemporaries with literal apocalypticism. David Blight has argued convincingly that his rhetoric was frequently apocalyptic, but it was more restrained than that of some contemporaries.[62] To firm believers in Providence, the war seemed to be the fulfillment of Jefferson's jeremiad to the slaveholding South that "the Almighty has no attribute that can take sides with us in such a contest." Apocalyptic enthusiasm received its most famous expression in the words of Julia Ward Howe's "Battle Hymn of the Republic," filled with direct references to specific biblical passages, which read as specific prophecies of ongoing events. Lincoln's second inaugural address capitalized on the apocalyptic tradition, when he spoke of the war as a judgment of the Lord. African Methodist Episcopal (AME) Bishop Daniel Alexander Payne also was a true apocalyptist when he wrote,

> Murmur not against the Lord on account of the cruelty and injustice of man. His almighty arm is already stretched out against slavery – against every man, every constitution, and every union that upholds it. His avenging chariot is now moving over the bloody fields of the doomed south, crushing beneath its massive wheels the very foundations of the blasphe-

mous system. Soon slavery shall sink like Pharaoh – even like
that brazen-hearted tyrant, it shall sink to rise no more.[63]

Douglass, by contrast, was unenthusiastic on the question of divine intervention in the war. On January 14, 1862, he spoke vaguely
of the "moral government of the universe," and of the "laws of this
Divine government," which could be transgressed only at the price
of "national sorrow, shame, suffering and death." In an address of
July 4, 1862, he compared the liberation of the slaves to the Hebrew
crossing of the Red Sea, but this seemed to be little more than poetic
flourish.[64] Even his lecture of June 16, 1861, with the promising title
of "The American Apocalypse," was disappointing from an evangelical perspective. It was an abstract, metaphorical reading of Saint
John's Revelation, in an entirely different vein from Julia Ward
Howe's bloodthirsty breathlessness. Douglass converted Saint John's
vision into a mild metaphor for the warfare between good and evil
that takes place within nations and within individual human hearts.
Douglass sought to strip away the "Oriental drapery" of revelation
and "clothe it in the simple and familiar language of common
sense."

After the Civil War, Douglass occasionally made reference to universal moral principles in human affairs, but he now completely rejected the idea of a personal God's intervention in human history.
Eventually he asserted that the works of man were the only agency
through which God's justice could be made manifest. Speaking
along these lines, he drew sharp objections from the African American clergy.[65] In an address of November 1883 entitled "The Philosophy of Reform," he declared that it was man, not God, who was
responsible for human progress. If he was not completely a secular-
ist, he had at least accepted the brand of deism that posited an
impersonal, noninterfering watchmaker God.

> So far as the laws of the universe have been discovered and
> understood, they seem to teach that the mission of man's im-
> provement and perfection has been wholly committed to man
> himself. So is he to be his own savior or his own destroyer. He
> has neither angels to help him nor devils to hinder him.[66]

Douglass's religion became increasingly abstract and metaphorical as he increasingly questioned the linkage between religion
and moral progress. In 1885 he defended the atheist Robert G. Ingersol, out of respect for his liberal racial attitudes, saying it was
better to be "an infidel and a so-called blasphemer than a hypocrite
who steals the livery of the court of heaven to serve the devil in."

Although Douglass continued to employ such concepts as "moral government of the Universe," he was apparently less inclined than formerly to state his metaphysic of progress in theologically dependent terms. His statements once seemed to imply faith in divine intervention, perhaps as a concession to the religious conservativism of mainstream black leadership. Later he apparently rejected the mystical and sought to support his beliefs solely on the basis of reason and evidence. But while he made frequent, opportunistic references to religious myths, he looked increasingly to the sciences for the underpinnings of his progressive ideology.[67]

Before the rise of Darwin, Douglass had linked his theory of progress to Lamarckian evolutionary theory. The advent of Darwinism allowed Douglass to find a new way of arguing African American equality with the rest of the human family. Social Darwinism, like every ideology, could be easily adapted to the rhetoric of black advancement, as we shall later see in our discussion of William H. Ferris and Marcus Garvey. To say that the social Darwinists misinterpreted Darwin's theories is misleading, since Darwin was among the foremost misinterpreters of Darwin. It was Thomas Henry Huxley who created what is today considered the "correct" reading of evolutionary theory with his attacks on "social Darwinism." Darwin was not a social Darwinist. He was, even more ironically, a Lamarckian in some important respects, since he accepted the theory that acquired characteristics could be passed from parents to offspring. Darwin's theory of evolution was not absolutely environmentalistic, since it postulated that a variety of factors contributed to natural selection. Competition, including sexual competition, played a crucial role in his theory of evolution. But Huxley could describe the process of natural selection purely in terms of gradual adaptations to changing environments, and seemed, at times, comfortable doing so without any reference to competition at all.[68]

Douglass, as we have seen, was ambivalent with respect to evolutionary theory, although he accepted the Lamarckian view of evolution because it attributed human diversity to environmental causes. Possibly the advent of Darwinism did lead, as Waldo Martin suggests, to Douglass's developing a greater tolerance for evolutionism.[69] It should be remembered, however, that those ideas that Douglass found congenial in Darwin's theories were already present in Lamarck, who maintained that humanity was monogenetic in its origins, and that human variation was the result of acquired characteristics. It is therefore impossible to say conclusively that Darwinism changed Douglass's views, although Darwin certainly offered support to the monogenetic thesis that was of such importance to him. In any event, by 1883 Douglass no longer dismissed the position of man's descent from an apelike ancestor as "scientific moonshine," saying,

> I do not know that I am an evolutionist, but to this extent I am one. I certainly have more patience with those who trace mankind upward from a low condition, even from lower animals, than with those that start him at a high point of perfection and conduct him to a level with the brutes.[70]

Douglass's progressivism was further developed in an address on Galileo called " 'It Moves,' or the Philosophy of Reform," which was based on "the half suppressed and therefore cowardly and yet confident affirmation of Galileo," who, following his recantation of the view that the earth moves around the sun, is supposed to have said, "And yet it moves."[71] Douglass used Galileo's oppression by the Inquisition as the symbol of the struggle between knowledge and ignorance down through the ages. The oppressiveness represented by the Inquisition or the Salem witch trials was rooted in superstition, the source of all moral backwardness, just as science was the source of all moral progress. The argument was firmly based on the unassailable evidence of technological and scientific progress so apparent to all Victorians.[72] The utopian rationalism that linked education to moral progress was as obvious to Douglass as it had been to Condorcet and John Stuart Mill.

Douglass's commitment to a concept of universal morality dictated the boundaries of his social theory. In fact, he judged the validity of social theory on how well it conformed to the moral dictums that he knew to be true. In his moral universe, legitimate interests were never opposed, and moral precepts were never in conflict. No moral truth could ever be in conflict with another. Nor could moral truths ever be contradicted by science. In practice this seemed to dictate that science must play handmaiden to morality. Ironically, this was the sort of reasoning that had justified the Catholic Inquisition, which he despised.

The pontifical certainty with which Douglass issued his moral proclamations stood in monumental contrast to the vacillation and incongruity of his social and political thought. Douglass's enormous ambivalence with respect to social policy was most evident in his constantly shifting positions on the role of separate institutions in building the African American "nation." Douglass sometimes used the term nation in describing the African American people, but vaguely and imprecisely, for he was not fond of racial or ethnic separatism. It would be a gross oversimplification to view Douglass as an undeviating integrationist, completely untouched by the black nationalist ideology so common among his contemporaries. He was a social integrationist, but he sometimes sponsored separate black institutions. He was an amalgamationist, but he boasted, opportunistically, of his African ancestry. He was an assimilationist, who on the basis of his ethnic heritage made special claims to a place on the public rostrum.

Unlike those among his contemporaries who called themselves "race men," Douglass worked toward a completely amalgamated society. In the view of most black leaders, his idea of the total eradication of race and ethnicity through interbreeding was untimely, and ultimately undesirable. Douglass vacillated wildly in his opinions on ethnic politics, and on cultural institutions in American life in the nineteenth century. His hostility to the traditionalism and institutional structure of organized religion was part and parcel of the extreme progressive liberalism that he embraced.

Douglass's concept of progress in race relations was grounded in a faith that society must inevitably be improved through the triumph of science and reason. He inherited his social theory from an intellectual community that had its roots in a Christian perfectionist tradition, and in utopian conceptions of unilinear cultural progress. It was a blend of positivist social theory, Victorian rationalism, and the Unitarian liberalism of the northeastern intellectual elite. In this positivist tradition, there was no room for cultural or moral relativism. The central contradiction in Douglass's later years is that he derived his livelihood from his role as a racial leader, while increasingly denouncing racial politics. Another contradiction is that his pronouncements derived much moral support from the structure of an evangelical tradition, which always hovered in the background of American culture, while he slipped into an abstract and idiosyncratic deism. Apparently he renounced his one-time faith in an intervening God, whose Providence was active in history. He now believed that "so far as the laws of the universe have been discovered and understood," it did not appear "that divine power is ever exerted to remove evil from the world, how great soever it may be."[73]

Frederick Douglass's moral absolutism was closely related to his cultural absolutism. As an abolitionist, he was hostile to the idea that moral truths might differ according to time or place. Proslavery arguments were sometimes based on a shallow moral relativism that attempted to explain slavery as a "peculiar institution" that could be defended in terms of the special needs of the South. Radical abolitionists spoke of moral absolutes and insisted that slavery was an unmitigated evil. As an abolitionist, Douglass lived in a world of self-

evident moral absolutes, and claimed to believe in a "moral government of the Universe." He believed that moral truths were universal
and accessible through common sense. Thus, he argued that the
triumph of science over unreasoning faith was linked to moral progress and symbolized by the disappearance of witch burning.[74]

As a progressivist, Douglass was also a cultural absolutist, believing
that moral progress, like scientific and technical progress, represented the triumph of reason over superstition. Southern culture was
backward, superstitious, and degraded in his view, and slave culture
was a mere manifestation of slavery's degrading effects. Douglass was
not open to relativistic definitions of culture, which would have allowed him to achieve a higher appreciation of African American
folkways. The intellectual processes that might have been useful in
formulating a defense of African American culture had already been
appropriated in defense of slavery and the southern way of life. Slaveholders characteristically argued in defense of the charms of African
American culture; abolitionists were committed to demonstrating
that the slaves were consigned by their brutal owners to a culture
that was unremittingly dismal.

Harriet Beecher Stowe's thesis in *Uncle Tom's Cabin* was that the
great evil of slavery was its assault on the virtues of Victorian domes-
ticity and the "cult of true womanhood." The bourgeois Victorian
home was the essence of higher civilization, and slavery undermined
the values of the hearthside. Slavery, as a cultural system, constituted
an attack on everything that Stowe or Douglass meant by the term
"culture." It was an assault on "sweetness and light," and "the best
which has been thought and said in the world." For Douglass, as for
Matthew Arnold, "culture" was an elitist concept, and a universal
one. As far as he was concerned, the world required only one universal definition of culture, and that was represented by the arts, sciences, and progressive morality of the Victorian bourgeoisie.

For most black leaders of the nineteenth century the concept of
culture, or civilization, implied evolutionary progression up a hier-
archical ladder. Most black leaders believed that English-speaking
Protestants, despite their many faults, had progressed to the highest
rung on the ladder of culture or civilization. Black nationalists, notably Alexander Crummell and Martin R. Delany, agreed vigorously
with Douglass that racial progress could never be achieved without
an emphasis on personal character and individual responsibility, but
here the similarity ended. Black nationalists accepted the reasoning
of Alexander Crummell, that the African race must collectively develop a distinctive black American culture and civilization. Such efforts could be achieved only by the creation of a social principle and

a true ethnic agenda.[75] In Douglass's mind, such talk of maintaining cultural difference was tantamount to maintaining cultural deficiencies, and as such was viewed as an accommodation to theories of racial inferiority. He thought that acknowledgment of cultural difference implied an acceptance of racial hierarchy; thus, his adamant cultural monism was the natural by-product of his democratic egalitarianism. In his experience, the persons who most often argued for a plurality of cultures were southern planters, who believed in a hierarchy of cultures and meant to relegate Africans to the bottom of the social pyramid.

Douglass would not have defined culture as a variety of adaptations that local groups make to a diversity of environments. He used the terms culture and civilization interchangeably, as did Tylor, to signify one monistic, unilinear civilization that was the common property of all mankind. Civilization was based on a universal system of values in conformity with eternal universal principles of truth. Hostile to any theory that suggested that manners and morals were purely a matter of social convention, Douglass never abandoned the Enlightenment tradition that morality was derived primarily from nature aided by reason. He was vehement in his opposition to the idea that morality was merely a matter of customs, traditions, and training. In other words if there was a cultural relativism, then there must be moral relativism. That proposition simply could not be accommodated within Douglass's transcendental liberalism and progressive moralizing.

Thus, Douglass's cultural absolutism was a direct by-product of his moral absolutism; however, he was not guilty of uncritical acceptance of Anglo-American elite values. Douglass's monistic views were part of his assertion of an egalitarian and unified American nationality. This American nationality must ultimately be based on one single standard of social values, before which all others must give way. In order to assert the primacy of his preferred set of social values, Douglass was forced to rationalize that the preferred values were "progressive" and superior to all others. Neither Douglass nor present-day progressive liberals are willing to admit the possibility that some friction between ethnic groups may be inevitable and legitimate. Douglass apparently never considered the idea that class and ethnic conflicts may arise out of irreconcilable conflicts of interests and values.

I referred at the beginning of this chapter to the Eurocentric cultural universalism that Douglass shared with other nineteenth-century black leaders as "civilizationism." Black nationalists with Afrocentric commitments, like Alexander Crummell, Edward W. Blyden, and Martin R. Delany, believed in a unilinear civilization and in the task of the black elite to "civilize" the "benighted," "ignorant" African race, throughout the world. Later reformers, such as John Mercer Langston and Booker T. Washington, were also cultural monists who thought of world history as one straight line of ascent from barbarism to civilization. They admired educated Anglo-Americans, who were capable of expressing a systematic doctrine of their religion, society, manners, grammar, rhetoric, economics, and logic. The white bourgeois minority were capable of rationalizing their power over the lower classes by means of a cultural argument. Black Americans were only beginning to develop an intellectual class, and most educated blacks, whether separatist or integrationist, resembled Douglass in their emulation of the Anglo-Saxon urban elite.

Since Douglass conceived of every deviation from Anglo-Saxon cultural norms as a reversion to something inferior, he rejected not only multiculturalism but cultural nationalism. Contemporary black nationalists at least paid lip service to the ideal of an Afro-American culture or civilization. Douglass rejected such talk, seeing in it a dangerous doctrine that might all too easily be exploited by white supremacists. Cultural pluralism was too closely associated in his mind with the doctrines of Agassiz, Nott, and Glidden for him to entertain the idea comfortably. In the year of Douglass's address entitled "The Claims of the Negro," Gobineau published his essay *On the Inequality of Human Races.* An American edition of this treatise appeared in 1856. The book attacked Lamarckian environmentalism, and asserted that the cultural ranking of pure races was fixed and immutable. At the same time, he believed that racial mixing, in moderation, could be advantageous because mixed races were potentially more creative. Gobineau questioned Darwinism because he believed in devolution rather than progressive evolution. He also had difficulty rejecting the biblical arguments for monogenesis.[76]

There was, of course, no necessary connection between the doctrines of cultural pluralism and racial inequality, and not all formulations of multiculturalism were as venomous as Gobineau's. Johann Gottlieb Herder's was, at least nominally, more benevolent, asserting that every race had a destiny within human history to make manifest some noble aspect of the divine plan. Herder rejected cultural monism and, in the words of Frederic Barnard, "felt it would be more accurate to speak of specific cultures – in the plural – rather than of culture in general."[77] There was in Herder's scheme no people that was devoid of culture, and he objected to the application of European standards to non-European cultures. Nineteenth-century black nationalists readily seized on such patterns of thought, and frequently expressed them in their writings. Cultural pluralism was broadly influential among Douglass's contemporaries, white and black, albeit most of them had no firsthand acquaintance with Herder.[78]

Douglass, even if he had studied the doctrines of these authors with their talk of divinely ordained missions for every race and nation, would have found such collectivist and deterministic notions unpalatable. He was an antinationalist of Nietzschean proportions, and like Nietzsche, he was fundamentally hostile to ethnic and cultural nationalism. As an individualist and self-made man, he believed that people should be judged on the basis of their abilities and accomplishments rather than trade on their racial or ethnic heritage. He believed that pride in race was a vestige of barbarism that retarded the individual in his or her progress toward universal truth.

Douglass's theories were destined to come under attack from such racial conservationists as Alexander Crummell and W. E. B. Du Bois, who were convinced that American democracy must be based, at least temporarily, on multiculturalism.[79] Crummell, especially, spoke of creating a distinctive black culture, notwithstanding his own unilinear "civilizationism." His conception of a black culture seemed markedly similar to Victorian conceptions. Douglass, for his part, was never entirely free of a collectivist racial consciousness, a strong desire to further the interests of African Americans, and a willingness to engage in identity politics. His attempts as a newspaper editor illustrate the difficulties of attempting to reconcile two mutually hostile varieties of leadership – progressive universalism and ethnic particularism.

In 1847, early in his career, Douglass joined with Martin Delany, the quintessential "race man" of the era and a formidable rival, to found a newspaper, *The North Star*. Denying the charge that black-edited newspapers were guilty of keeping up "an odious and wicked distinction between white and colored persons," Douglass wrote an early editorial under the headline "Colored Newspapers." The editorial did not really answer the objection of critics that self-segregation retarded the progress of full racial equality, however, for Douglass was ambivalent, and half persuaded by those objections himself. The editorial on "Colored Newspapers" thus merely defended its author's individual right to practice the profession of editor; it did not argue for the right or the necessity of an African American journalistic voice, or of creating an independent institutional network in the United States.[80]

Twenty years earlier, the editors of *Freedom's Journal* had launched the nation's first black newspaper, with an unequivocal declaration of ethnic independence: "We wish to plead our own cause. Too long have others spoken for us." *Freedom's Journal* also ran articles on the history of the black race, asserting the ties of modern African Americans to the ancient Egyptians.[81] Douglass, by contrast, did not justify his venture with the rhetoric of black enterprise or self-sufficiency. Despite any feelings of racial-ethnic solidarity, and his desire to demonstrate his uncompromising oneness with the masses of his "oppressed countrymen," he stopped short of endorsing the principle of racial-ethnic institutions, and he deftly avoided associating the defense of his activity with the rhetoric of ethnic boosterism.[82]

In later years, Douglass explicitly counseled against using the press to promote racial and ethnic claims, or the special interests of African Americans. The black press, in his view, ought to define itself as an instrument in the struggle for universal justice, not as a tool for the advancement of ethnic power. Douglass was never comfortable with the idea of serving the specific institutional needs of an African American ethnic group because, unlike the young Du Bois, he did not view history in terms of a contest for power among a heterogenous set of races straining in competition with one another. Thus, his position on institutional separatism was inconsistent and vacillating. He supported black power institutions occasionally, and from perceived necessity, but he was never an enthusiastic supporter of separatism in any form.

When, during the winter of 1851–52, Horace Greeley wrote an editorial urging black folk to "buy out a township in Southern Jersey, or a county in Nebraska," where they might develop a system of independent enterprises, Douglass responded, "Be patient Mr. Greeley, a nation may not be born in a day, without a miracle." It is unlikely that Douglass was praying for the miraculous birth of a black nation. He admitted, in 1853, that the black population were "becoming a nation, in the midst of a nation which disowns them," but he did not greet the development with rejoicing.[83]

He sporadically supported black educational institutions, and was willing, in an editorial of 1854, to join Greeley in calling for an industrial college where black Americans might master a "practical knowledge of three or four of the best paying handicrafts." In that same editorial, he compared the struggle of black Americans to that of other national groups, saying, "If *Hungarians* understand their liberties – if *Irishmen, Italians* and *Frenchmen* may be presumed to understand their moral, physical and intellectual wants for themselves, we, too, may be presumed to understand and to properly appreciate our situation without either egotism or arrogance." Thus, Douglass, as did other integrationists, sometimes implied that the struggles of African Americans were analogous to those of national groups. But while he described black Americans as a "nation," and sometimes compared them to other national groups, he does not seem to have attributed to black Americans any sort of peculiar culture or destiny. They were definitely not a nation in that sense.[84]

When Douglass became involved in separate institutions, he did so halfheartedly, as in the case of the Freedman's Bank. While president of the bank during 1874, Douglass spent his time firing off moral broadsides on racial matters. The absolutist world of moral issues was far more congenial than the surrealistic world of banking and commerce. Douglass found it much more congenial to write and speak on behalf of women's rights and black equality than to master the relativistic morality of the business world. Banking required a person of moral and intellectual flexibility, but the peculiarities of his background imposed severe limitations on Douglass's ability to formulate a practical ethic for the age of Jay Gould and Cornelius Vanderbilt. The leadership of Frederick Douglass was irrelevant to the age of iron and smokestacks. He never truly understood the pragmatic culture of an Andrew Carnegie, whose interpretation of Emerson's "self reliance" led him to his creative amalgamation of atavistic social Darwinism and progressive philanthropy.[85]

Douglass was not sympathetic to the black nationalism of his day. He never accepted the need for a black nation-state any more than he accepted the need for a white nation-state. Although, like most black Americans, Douglass expressed an occasional and opportunistic interest in racial institutions, he did not revel in the concept of black nationalism. It is difficult to deduce exactly what he meant by occasionally applying the word "nation" to African Americans. At times he used "nation" as a synonym for the state, a group of people who occupied the same territory and sought to cooperate for the common good in a spirit of enlightened self-interest. Douglass's conception of the nation-state did not always imply immediate biological mingling of all its peoples. Speaking on "Our Composite Nationality" in 1869, he was apparently not thinking in terms of full-scale amalgamationism, but there was no indication of a polyglot multiculturalism either. The various peoples were supposed to retain their racial and religious differences, while submitting to identical language, manners, and morals.

> We shall spread the network of our science and our civilization over all who seek their shelter, whether from Asia, Africa, or the Isles of the Sea. We shall mould them all, each after his kind into Americans; Indian and Celt, negro and Saxon,

Latin and Teuton, Mongolian and Caucasian, Jew and gentile,
all shall here bow to the same law, speak the same language,
support the same government, enjoy the same liberty, vibrate
with the same national enthusiasm, and seek the same national
ends.[86]

Douglass was clearly attempting to have it both ways. He would
not openly advocate depriving ethnic Americans of their varied ethnic treasures, and yet he clearly envisioned an America in which the
various ethnic groups must abandon the multifarious ethnic peculiarities that gave meaning to their lives. It is difficult to determine
exactly how he believed a nation could reconcile multiculturalism
with cultural monism. Furthermore, his use of terms was unsystematic. Within the space of a single paragraph Douglass used the
term "nation," first to designate "Africans" as a people, then to
designate the United States as a country. In the same paragraph he
classified the Jews first as a nation and then as a race, and seemed by
implication to exclude them from the category "Europeans." He was
not obsessed with consistency of vocabulary.

We are a great nation – not we colored people particularly,
but all of us. We are all together now. We fellow-citizens of a
common country. What a country – fortunate in its institutions,
in its Fifteenth amendment, in its future. We are made up of a
variety of nations – Chinese, Jews, Africans, Europeans, and all
sorts. These different races give the Government a powerful
arm to defend it. They will vie with each other in hardship and
in peril, and will be united in defending it from all its enemies,
whether from within or without.[87]

Aware that the word "nation" was commonly used in the *ethnic
sense*, as a synonym for a group of people rendered distinctive by
culture, kinship, or genealogy, Douglass found it necessary to clarify
that in this sentence he did not intend to endow the term with any
such meaning. He is using the word "nation" in the *political sense*, to
mean a group of "fellow-citizens of a common country." Two sentences later, however, he reverts to the familiar ethnic definition of
nation, as he declares the United States to be "made up of a variety
of nations." Then he calls the United States a "country" (implicitly,
a geographical unit) that was occupied by "nations" (implicitly, ethnic groups), each of them a discrete entity within American society.
That was what he said in 1870, but in 1889 he declared that "a
nation within a nation is an anomaly."[88] Perhaps over a period of
nineteen years he had come to believe that all these Chinese and

Jews and Africans must eventually merge, ceasing to be ethnically distinctive – as he had – in order to become one nation rather than "a variety of nations." Douglass spoke, after all, from the standpoint of an assimilationist Anglo-African mulatto.

As a young man, working in the polyglot environment of Baltimore's shipyards, Douglass had learned that Euro-Americans were not culturally amorphous, but in his later writings it is difficult to feel he paid more than lip service to the idea of "a nation of nations." His conception of Americanism was really a "cultural unitarianism," in which Catholics and Jews as well as evangelical Protestants would, as Thomas Jefferson had once predicted, eventually become deists.[89] Douglass was well advanced in years before the influx of Italian Catholics and Slavic Jews began to change the character of politics and culture in urban centers. Black Americans remained a population of agrarian workers, and their demography had not yet assumed the patterns common to urban immigrants. It would have been impossible for Douglass to apply a "multicultural" analysis to the problems of black Americans. Failing to understand the trends emerging among American immigrant groups, he discouraged ethnic politics, stating that "no part of the American people – Irish, Scotch, Italian or German – could attempt any such political jugglery with less success than ourselves."[90]

Unlike the much younger Booker T. Washington, who instinctively grasped the thought and speech of ethnic politics as he strove to become ward boss of black America, Douglass never conceived of African Americans in terms of an ethnic model. Later scholars, including Franz Boas, Robert E. Park, and W. E. B. Du Bois, came to celebrate the ideal of preserving distinctive ethnic cultures, and there were no necessary assumptions of racial inferiority or superiority in the pronouncements of these authors. They all asserted, perhaps sentimentally, that each race was making its own distinctive and valuable cultural contributions to the American mosaic. Obviously, the plantation culture into which Douglass was born was not the cauldron of ethnicity that dominated urban American life at the end of the nineteenth century. Douglass was born too soon to acknowledge the problem of "unmeltable ethnics," an American dilemma that would later be identified in the writings of American sociologists Daniel Patrick Moynihan and Nathan Glazer.[91] His ideal for America was total subordination to an Anglo-American conception of manners, presumably under the morality of highly literate middle class, Anglo-Saxons, Protestants, and Unitarians.

As Kenneth Warren has shown, one of Douglass's reasons for not entering the world of African American politics in the Reconstruction South was his identification with the thought, speech, and cultural values of the northeastern intellectual elite. He was uncomfortable with the "superstition, bigotry, and priestcraft" that he believed to prevail among the untutored masses. He opposed the corruption of ethnic politics in the same way, and for the same reasons, as other mugwumps and progressives did. It was thus impossible for Douglass to view Tammany Hall or the Chicago ward as offering models for black American political organization. He does not seem to have respected the tough pragmatism of ethnic politicians in derby hats and shirt sleeves, defining their methods in terms of power and pragmatism. Nor could he, as did the younger Jane Addams, discover the richness of class and ethnic diversity in the post–Civil War metropolis. He rejected the idea that some immigrant groups might be unassimilable because of religious beliefs irreconcilable with Anglo-Saxon notions of democracy. Thus, when he spoke on behalf of including the Chinese in the American family, he argued that their religion, Confucianism, was not far removed from American religious liberalism. An interesting idea, and worthy of some development, but betraying an ethnocentric impulse to remake Confucianists into Unitarian universalists.[92]

Although Douglass contributed to the cult of Egyptocentric Afrocentrism, it was his commitment to the total assimilation of the African American population that led him, ironically, to this position. Professor Lefkowitz has approached Douglass's brief observations on Egypt tardily and superficially, and discusses his position on ancient Egypt completely outside the context of his life and times. His position with respect to ancient Egypt can be intelligently discussed only when placed within the context of his racial assimilationism, his mulatto chauvinism, and his Lamarckianism. Douglass was anxious to demonstrate "the resemblance of Egyptians to Negroes," the better to argue the Africans' worthiness for intermarriage and amalgamation with white America.[93]

Douglass recounted Herodotus's opinions on Egypt during his 1854 address at Rochester, in order to demonstrate that he knew the arguments. It seemed reasonable to him that the Egyptians may have been a mulatto population, and as such they proved that mulattoes were not degenerate, but he capped off these reflections with the statement that the issue was not really important. For, in the long run, it really did not matter to Douglass "if the Negro could not prove his relationship to Nubians, Abyssinians and Egyptians."[94] Douglass certainly understood the historical importance of Egyptian civilization and the significance of being able to attribute the pyramids to the enterprise of a black or mulatto people; on the other hand, the idea of a pharaoh was offensive to his egalitarian sensibilities. Douglass was more likely to view Pharaoh as a metaphor for injustice than as a symbol of black pride. His allusions to Pharaoh were usually delivered within the tradition of identifying with Moses and the Children of Israel rather than with their oppressors.[95] During his trip to Europe and the Mediterranean in 1844, Douglass visited Egypt and ascended the Great Pyramid. On the basis of personal observation, he maintained that Egyptians resembled African Americans more closely than Caucasians. He was certainly correct that they looked more like him than they did Chester A. Arthur or Grover Cleveland.[96]

Edward Wilmot Blyden, who also visited the Great Pyramid, was, unlike Douglass, a true Afrocentrist. He was not, however, an Egyptocentrist, although he did believe that the pyramid builders had been black. But among the voluminous writings of Blyden, we find very little about Egypt, other than that which we have already observed in preceding chapters. His Afrocentrism was far more concerned with promoting the Back to Africa movement, the establishment of Liberia and Sierra Leone, and the study of West African peoples and customs. Blyden devoted far more energy to mastering contemporary African languages than to rhapsodizing on pharaonic glories. As a result of his studies in the emerging science of anthropology, he was better prepared than the generation of Douglass and Crummell to grasp the idea that multiculturalism could be separated both from the doctrine of polygenesis and from the idea of racial inferiority.

Blyden, who lived until 1912, eventually grasped the idea of "cultural relativism," which freed him from the standard "progressive" dogma that the humanity of Africans must be justified in terms of their ability to produce a so-called high culture. In a series of articles written for the *Sierra Leone Weekly News*, reprinted as *African Life and Customs*, in 1908, he dismissed as scientifically outdated the polygenetic theories of Nott and Gliddon that Douglass had attempted to refute with biblical rhetoric. Blyden, unlike Douglass, did not view progress as synonymous with the advancement of science, and was even willing – like the negritude poets of the 1920s – to abandon the field of modern science to the European. Blyden believed that progress for Africa and the black race must be developed along African lines. This was the reason for his defense of African "communism," and, to the disapproval of African American feminist intellectuals like Anna Julia Cooper, polygyny and clitorectomy.[97]

Anna Julia Cooper's theory of history was that feudalism and Christianity were the distinctive features of Western civilization that had led to an increasingly wholesome role for women in society. Her praise for the uniquely progressive quality of European civilization illustrates the fact that late-nineteenth-century feminism was not invariably friendly to multiculturalism. As indicated in Chapter 3, Cooper accepted the view that the cultural ingredients of an exalted Victorian womanhood were detectable among the barbarians of Tacitus's time. Medieval Christianity, with its cult of chivalry, was not perfect. It depreciated the value of women by insisting on celibacy for its clergy. On the other hand, it performed the progressive function of "toning down and softening" the barbarian virtues of "a rough and lawless period."

> It seems not too much to say then of the vitalizing and regenerating, and progressive influence of womanhood on the civilization of today, that, while it was foreshadowed among Germanic nations in the far away dawn of their history as a narrow, sickly and stunted growth, it yet owes its catholicity and power, the deepening of its roots and broadening of its branches to Christianity.[98]

Cooper reiterated arguments, familiar to her contemporaries, that educated women were necessary to the refinement of home and family life. She went a step farther, however, insisting that women and their contributions must be enlisted in the advancement of arts and letters in society. She thus condemned Asian societies, where "woman has been uniformly devoted to a life of ignorance, infamy, and complete stagnation." The role of woman in Asia was symbolized by the "Chinese shoe," which dwarfed, cramped, and destroyed a woman's physical powers both physical and mental. Islamic societies were no better, in Cooper's view, owing to inherent traits of the Islamic civilization.[99]

> The Arab was a nomad. Home to him meant his present camping place. That deity [woman] who according to our western ideals, makes and sanctifies the home, was to him a transient bauble to be toyed with so long as it gave him pleasure and then to be thrown aside for a new one. As a personality, an individual soul, capable of eternal growth and unlimited development, and destined to mould and shape the civilization of the future to an incalculable extent, Mahomet did not know woman. There was no hereafter, no paradise for her. The heaven of the Mussulman [sic] is peopled and made gladsome not by the departed wife, or sister, or mother, but by the houri.[100]

A progressive, evolutionary vision of Victorian gender and sexual attitudes was basic to the thinking of most black women in the 1890s.

From our contemporary perspective, the study of comparative gender relations has certainly discovered the weakest point in Afrocentric theory. Polygyny and female genital mutilation cannot be justified with the simple rationalization that they are indigenous to Africa, or an expression of Afrocentric traditions. They are no less reprehensible to present-day secular humanists than they were to Christian feminists of the late nineteenth century.

Francis Ellen Watkins Harper was another author who revealed an evolutionary conception of Victorian Christianity. The terms "multiculturalism" and "Afrocentrism" did not exist in 1892, the year in which she published *Iola Leroy*, and her ideology left no room for such concepts. As did Cooper and most other black women of her generation, Harper advocated an ideology of progress that was unilinear and monistic. She devoted little of her talent to romanticizing the manners and customs of primeval barbarians, whether African or European. Her view of primitives may perhaps be inferred from the words she places in the mouth of a sympathetic character.

> "The negro," said Dr. Gresham, thoughtfully, "is not the only branch of the human race which has been low down in the scale of civilization and freedom, and which has outgrown the measure of his chains. Slavery, polygamy, and human sacrifices have been practiced among Europeans in bygone days; and when Tyndall tells us that out of savages unable to count on the number of their fingers and speaking only a language of nouns and verbs, arise at length our Newtons and Shakespeares, I do not see that the negro could not have learned our language and received our religion without the intervention of ages of slavery."[101]

Like most black Victorians, she thought of progress in terms of the mastery of English language and Protestant religion. Her condemnation, later in the novel, of Mormon polygyny as an "abomination" reveals that multiculturalism never entered her mind. She was committed to mainstream Victorian morality, with its putatively superior conception of woman's sacred sphere within the monogamous heterosexual family.[102] Ironically, her brand of feminism was deeply embedded within the same Anglocentric Christian rhetoric that had been used to advance imperialism and white supremacy. But it was also the rhetoric that Harriet Beecher Stowe had used to fight slavery.

The undeniable strain of Eurocentric civilizationism in the writings of nineteenth-century black authors was both product of and reaction to the brand of multiculturalism present in the European intellectual tradition. This old brand of multiculturalism, opposed by nineteenth-century black writers, was based on the notion that blacks were incapable of mastering European culture. By the first decade of the twentieth century, African and African American intellectuals were beginning to work out a theory of multiculturalism based on the idea that the folkways of "blacks" are different from, rather than inferior to, those of "whites," that variations in environments are the causes of cultural differences, and that these differences are not evidence of genetic inferiority. The nineteenth-century multiculturalism of Nott and Gliddon went hand in hand with antidemocratic ideals, whereas the twentieth-century multiculturalism of Franz Boas and Alain Locke was essentially democratic, and tied to a cultural relativism that was inconceivable to their predecessors.

Edward Wilmot Blyden, born in 1832, was half a generation younger than Douglass and Crummell. Thus in 1908, while writing as an elderly man, he was nonetheless young enough to have profited from the nascent cultural relativism that had begun to affect the intellectual atmosphere. Influenced by the rising tide of social progressivism represented by Jean Finot, whose work he cited, Blyden had, by degrees and over half a century, become a multiculturalist. Nonetheless, Blyden's writings continued to reflect the strain of cultural absolutism that he had always shared with Douglass. He never abandoned his belief in the linkage of sub-Saharan Africa to Egypt, and his vindicationism always betrayed an unconscious Eurocentrism. Blyden in his youth had alluded to Egyptian civilization in his works of racial vindication, precisely because he was not a multiculturalist. Like Frederick Douglass and William Wells Brown, he believed that the most effective way to vindicate the African race was to establish its linkage to Egypt.[103]

But a change was evident in Blyden's later writings. Among the Afrocentrists who had come to prominence in the mid-nineteenth century, he was among the few who had demonstrated an interest in the systematic study of African cultures, and only he seemed to be on the road to discovering relativistic multiculturalism. His view was seemingly contradicted by his belief in progress, but that did not seem to bother him; like most of us, he contained many contradictions. He was a cultural relativist who apologized for tribal polytheism, but he never completely repudiated the Protestantism of his youth. And he remained highly respectful of Islam, which he considered a progressive force. He shared with the quasi-Unitarian Douglass an attraction to that brand of reform social Darwinism that believed in a teleological evolution of society along the arrow-straight lines indicated by Victorian science and American progressivism. Society, in this view, was advancing inexorably, like a railroad, whose steel rails and telegraph wires must meet on the horizon of a progressive utopia with no place for racism.

"We believe that the Negro people, as a race, have a contribution to make to civilization and humanity, which no other race can make," said the young W. E. B. Du Bois. And yet for all this talk of a distinctive African culture and a distinctive African personality, most black intellectuals in fact believed in a unilinear future for Africa, in which the continent's peoples would eventually unite to form a modern, progressive industrial civilization. This world view expressed, in contradictory fashion, tributes to both the multicultural and the unilinear. Primitive peoples might be capable of making contributions to civilization, but they must ultimately join the march of progress. Local cultures might make their contributions to human progress, and great civilizations might rise and fall, but mankind in general must experience a linear advancement. The destiny of African peoples was to make future contributions to the common good of humanity, while advancing its own interests. Booker T. Washington expressed a common belief when he said, "There is no power on earth that can stay our progress." Past contributions of Africans to human history were yet to be fully appreciated, and better understood, but the future was a certainty.[104]

W. E. B. DU BOIS AND ANTIMODERNISM

SECTION 1: ARMINIANISM, ANTINOMIANISM,
AND AFRICANITY IN RELIGION

"A foolish consistency," says Ralph Waldo Emerson, "is the hobgoblin of little minds."[1] Complexity of thought may, conversely, be the mark of a spacious mind, and it is in this spirit that I allude, over the course of this and the next chapter, to the complicated and endlessly inventive thinking of W. E. B. Du Bois. Preeminently a dialectician, he frequently championed apparently opposing positions, sometimes within the scope of a single paragraph.[2] Thus, he could be a spirited advocate of Pan-Africanism, while insisting that African peoples were members of a world community centered in universal values. He could defend African Americans' institutional separatism, while crusading relentlessly for their citizenship rights. He could propose an open and inclusive American society, and still oppose the radical integrationism of Walter White and Thurgood Marshall, who argued that segregation inherently implied inequality. His selective advocacy of separatism led to his eventual rupture with Walter White and the other leadership of the National Association for the Advancement of Colored People (NAACP).

In his 1940 publication *Dusk of Dawn*, Du Bois conceded that Booker T. Washington's emphasis on separate institutional development had always contained elements of validity. Discovery of this fact often surprises those who have not read Du Bois's earlier writings with care. Du Bois had never pledged himself to institutional assimilation, and in his later years he seemed to recognize a similarity between his own ideas and the Stalinist agenda of multinationality within an American union. The Du Bois who preached collectivism in 1896 in "The Conservation of Races" was the same man who in 1888 had offered qualified praise for the single-mindedness of Bismarck and who later, in 1953, was to apologize for the rigidity of Stalin.[3] His antiliberalism is not to be denied, for Du Bois, like Alexander Crummell, frequently advocated the subordination of the individual to cultural and institutional exigencies. It is therefore not surprising that from time to time Du Bois wrote optimistically of the church's past and present role in organizing the political and economic consciousness of black communities.[4]

In his assessment of African American religion, Du Bois represented contradictory tendencies toward modernism and traditionalism. Toward the end of his chapter entitled "The Faith of the Fathers" in *The Souls of Black Folk*, he spoke as the prophet of a new "awakening . . . when the pent-up vigor of ten million souls shall sweep irresistibly toward the Goal."[5] At other locations in that same essay, he wrote almost nostalgically of the waning of a mythical Afro-Christian virtue, which was supposedly giving way to the tawdry values of modern capitalism.[6] He was ambivalent with respect to the role that religion played in African American acculturation, suggesting at times that it symbolized the retention of African traditions, at others viewing it as an evidence of African American acceptance of American values. He posed the question of whether religion had functioned historically as a force for social reform or as a form of escapism.[7]

Much of Du Bois's Afrocentric writing was poetic. It should be understood as an attempt to create a quasi-religious mythology and to found an institutional and authoritative basis for the internal control of black institutions. His commitment to separate institutions, presumably the agencies for the improvement of African and African American society and culture, led to his break with Walter White, Thurgood Marshall, and the leadership of the NAACP. Du Bois is remembered in terms of his embrace of atheistic communism and his crusade against segregation, but as has been said elsewhere, he was much committed to the use of religion as a means of social organization and as a source of a Pan-African spiritual cohesion. Thus, Du Bois, in important respects, bore a greater resemblance to de Maistre than to Marx, for he was committed to manipulation of religious symbols and institutions to give force and cohesion to the political aspirations of black Americans.[8]

The religious rhetoric employed by W. E. B. Du Bois presented an almost perfect example of what the late William Gerald McLoughlin meant by his irreverent oxymoron "Arminianized Calvinism." Arminianism, as McGloughlin employed the term in *The American Evangelicals*, was a variety of American Protestantism that deemphasized strict Calvinist doctrines of predestination and stressed the importance of a Christian's deeds for the attainment of salvation.[9] I am using this term, Arminianized Calvinism, in association with the doctrine of American perfectionism, a concept rooted in the tradition of John Winthrop's City on a Hill. American perfectionism has meant a belief that the Christian must perform responsible civic duties in order to create a "righteous empire" in the United States.[10] By the late nineteenth century the perfectionist impulse to create the kingdom of God in America had evolved into a doctrine called the "Social Gospel."[11]

The more politically and economically sophisticated classes of African Americans were practically predisposed to an "Arminianized" social gospel, which found expression in at least the following forms. African Americans usually felt that their religion should focus not only on spiritual salvation but on the material health, education, and welfare of the community. Their social gospel also supplied a rhetoric to support their moral crusade for civil rights in America. In radical instances the social gospel might even produce a doctrine of Christian socialism, such as was revealed in the writings of Reverdy C. Ransom, Richard R. Wright, Sr., and George Washington Woodby.[12] More commonly, the social gospel supported the black progressives' approach to self-help and internal reform of the black community. It led to the Hampton–Tuskegee doctrine that most of the world's problems could be solved through cleanliness, hard work, and self-restraint.[13]

In contrast to the Arminianized Calvinism of the bourgeois "puritan" leadership was the putatively "antinomian Calvinism" of the masses. The more educated leadership, represented by Daniel Payne, a bishop of the African Methodist Episcopal (AME) church, often voiced their perception of black peasant religion in the South as excessively emotional, otherworldly, escapist, and apolitical. In their view, the religion of the African American masses often fell into patterns of antinomian ritualism.[14] Protestant American antinomianism stems from a doctrine "in which 'the personality of Jesus' became more important than the moral order of God."[15] In its extreme forms it relied on a sentimental belief in justification purely by the emotions experienced during the conversion experience. Among the black masses, this antinomianism was associated with the ritual of the "ring shout," a practice discouraged by Bishop Payne, not only because he saw it as "primitive Africanism" but because he preferred a practical social gospel to the emotionalism associated with ceremonial spirit possession.[16]

In his 1903 study *The Negro Church*, Du Bois asserted that black American rural folk religion was essentially African, "with a simple

Calvinistic creed."[17] In the context of the bulk of his writing, and what we know from other studies of black religion, we may interpret this to mean that black folk-theology was founded on belief in an emotional conversion experience and a personal relationship with Jesus Christ as the source of salvation. In the American evangelical tradition, such an interpretation of the Calvinistic creed was not uncommon, nor was it peculiar to black Americans. Du Bois, of course, believed, as do most present-day scholars, that the folk religion of African Americans, perhaps white Americans as well, was a melding of African and European traditions. African American religion, in his view, was grounded in the "frenzy" of West African rites, but Americanized by an influx of Calvinistic fatalism and otherworldliness.

In one of his unpublished papers, "The New Negro Church," presumably drafted around 1917, Du Bois identified a number of "faults and dangers" that he discerned in most colored churches. "The theology of the average colored church [was] basing itself far too much upon 'Hell and Damnation' – upon an attempt to scare people into being decent and threatening them with the terrors of death and punishment." He dismissed as childish the belief in "the outward and visible punishment of every wrong deed that men do, the repeated declaration that anything can be gotten by anyone at any time by prayer."[18] In his autobiography Du Bois claimed to have abandoned at least organized religion by his thirtieth year. It cannot be denied, however, that he continued to employ Christian symbolism and to address divine authority in his writings until he was into his sixties.[19]

The doctrines of black Christianity and Du Bois's perspective on them were far more complex than the paper of 1917 suggested. True enough, there were many preachers, both middle class and storefront, who thundered hellfire and damnation. But just as frequently, black religion fell into a distinctive antinomianism, in which little was said of punishment for sin, although much was made of seeing Jesus and "feelin' the spirit." Du Bois apparently failed to recognize something that Crummell clearly saw, that "fire sermons" always bear a relationship to the things of this world, and that divine retribution cannot be divorced from the doctrine of works and deeds basic to practical Christianity.[20] Crummell, like Payne, knew that the faith of black Christians was all too frequently limited to the conversion experience, supplemented by recurrent ceremonial spirit possession. The fire sermons could be an antidote to antinomianism and a means of encouraging social responsibility.

In tracing the history of religion among African Americans, Du

Bois made much of the fact that they were first Christianized in large numbers during the waves of conversion that swept America during the eighteenth century.[21] It was the Baptists and the Methodists who were most active among the slave population of the South. Thus, if Du Bois was correct, and if Calvinism was an element in the religion of the masses, it was either a Wesleyanized Calvinism, which had been doctored significantly in the Methodist churches, or it was a Baptist Calvinism, which allowed for considerable creativity on the part of the individual preacher. Baptist and Methodist congregations also made up the largest church bodies in the North, as well, but a small segment of the emerging petit bourgeoisie in that region gravitated to the Presbyterian Church, with its more sedentary forms of worship.

There has been much theorizing to explain why the African American masses usually joined the Baptist and Methodist churches. Melville Herskovits opined that the Methodists and, to a greater extent, the Baptists were most receptive to the syncretization of African forms imported by the enslaved peoples who arrived in the New World. E. Franklin Frazier disagreed vehemently with Herskovits and insisted that the roots of black religion were *entirely* in the American evangelical tradition.[22] Frazier certainly overstated his case, but he correctly understood that black American culture was firmly rooted in Protestantism, and that this Protestant tradition was more than a veneer. The mixture of African and European influences on the religious values of the African American people was fundamental to their institutional life. Furthermore, these influences are complex and of more than one variety. There is certainly a tradition in black American religion that leads to an obsession with vicarious atonement, and ecstatic visionary experiences in which one is "struck dead" and realizes a personal meeting with Jesus.[23] Such religion was often antinomian, but many black Americans, even under slavery, were able to develop and maintain a tradition that emphasized strict personal conduct and the so-called Protestant ethic.

Du Bois, like most Americans, regardless of race – or even religion – was exposed to this Protestant ethic, growing up in the town of Great Barrington, Massachusetts, during the 1870s.[24] The traditions of hard work, cleanliness, and respectability were strong in his mother's family, although occasional falls from grace were inevitable. Du Bois and his mother occasionally attended the local African Methodist Episcopal Zion (AMEZ) church, which was the only black church in town. They belonged to the Congregational church. He explained that "because we lived near the Congregational church and because my mother had many acquaintances there, and because the minister, Scudder, was especially friendly, my mother early joined this church. I think we were the only colored communicants." In the Congregational church he had not found theology oppressive, and had only been required to listen to a weekly sermon "on doing good as a reasonable duty." His funds for his attendance at Fisk University were provided through the offices of a Reverend C. C. Painter, who raised the money by appealing to several Congregational churches in Massachusetts and Connecticut.[25]

He grew up, he tells us, with "an inexcusable ignorance of sex," for which he blamed his New England schooling. At age seventeen he went south to attend "a missionary college [Fisk University] where religious orthodoxy was stressed." All the teachers were white, from New England or from the New Englandized Middle West. He described himself as having been "a bit puritanic" on arriving in "a region with loose sex morals among black and white, while I actually did not know the physical difference between men and women." He later confessed to being "literally raped by the unhappy wife who was my landlady" during one of his summers in rural Tennessee. Nonetheless, he says, "By the time of graduation, I was still a 'believer' in orthodox religion."[26]

Du Bois's years in Germany eroded the orthodoxy of his New England puritanism. He "lived more or less regularly with a shopgirl in Berlin, but was ashamed," and, for the first time, he allowed himself the moderate use of beer and wine.[27] Among his papers one finds a rare instance of frivolity, preserved from his German student days. It is the souvenir advertisement of a Berlin pub in the form of an *ersatz* baggage ticket bearing the following inscription:

Ich kneipe diese Nacht! Solte ich meinen Weg nich mehr finden, so befestigen Sie mir diesen Zettel im Knopfloch und senden mich heim. Name: ———— Wohnung: ———— Das Geld für die Nachtdroschke befindet sich in der rechten Westentasche.[28]

Du Bois attended the lectures of Max Weber while studying in Germany, a decade before Weber published *The Protestant Ethic and the Spirit of Capitalism*, and defined American economic ideals in terms of Benjamin Franklin's Calvinistic background and later preachments. Du Bois reported that he had no contact with the professor while at the University of Berlin, although in 1904, when Weber toured the United States, he visited Du Bois and subsequently solicited an article from him for the journal *Archiv für Sozialwissenschaft u. Politik*. Du Bois's own observations on Benjamin Franklin and the "Protestant ethic" were made in a thirty-nine-page pamphlet he published in 1956. He commented briefly on Franklin's *Almanack*, with apparent admiration for the practical value of the "aphorisms . . . [where] he advised thrift for a poor, hard working people tempted often to waste." These were preachments similar to his own in *The Philadelphia Negro*.[29]

On his return to the United States, Du Bois obtained a professorship of Greek and Latin at an "orthodox Methodist Negro school," Wilberforce University in Ohio, which was operated by the African Methodist Episcopal Church. He says he was "a freethinker," but there is no evidence that he had abandoned religion, either before or during his sojourn at Wilberforce. In *Dusk of Dawn* he speaks of a refusal to lead chapel prayers at one point – a story that has become legendary. Elsewhere, he expresses a hostility, at least to the enthusiastic form of religious revivalism, as he describes being "driven almost to distraction by the wild screams, groans, and shrieks that rise from the chapel below me." Du Bois's recollections of this period in his life provide no clear evidence that he had become irreligious, as he continued to teach Sunday school for several years thereafter. Du Bois recalled encountering much religious hypocrisy and narrow-mindedness at Wilberforce, but it was in the Wilberforce chapel that he made the acquaintance of the venerable Alexander Crummell, who later brought Du Bois into the American Negro Academy. Crummell, an erudite Episcopal clergyman, was likewise disgusted by the excesses of enthusiastic religion.[30]

Du Bois's paternal grandfather, Alexander, had been one of Crummell's supporters in New Haven, Connecticut, during 1842, while Crummell was serving the tiny congregation of St. Luke's and attempting to study as a nonmatriculated student at Yale.[31] There is some evidence that he may have become exposed to the Arminianized Calvinism of the Reverend Nathaniel Taylor's lectures around this time. Taylor stressed, in addition to free will, the doctrine of Christians' participation in their own salvation.[32] Crummell was also possibly influenced by William Whewell's criticisms of the Hobbesian doctrine of natural depravity, while earning the B.A degree at Cambridge University in England. Whewell's doctrines also centered on the seventeenth-century Cambridge Platonists, who believed in the possibility of natural virtue. Crummell's theology represented his own attempt to effect a reconciliation of the Calvinistic idea of natural depravity with the Arminian emphasis on free will. He believed that the Holy Spirit could work, even within the hearts of the unconverted, to promote morality, and he displayed considerable faith in the value of good works. Thus, Crummell's religion, at least by the time he met Du Bois, embodied the watered-down, or Arminianized, Calvinism commonly found in the evangelical wing of the Episcopal Church.[33]

The speech that Crummell delivered at Wilberforce in 1895, later published in the *AME Church Review*, was entitled "The Solution of Problems: The Duty and Destiny of Man." Crummell's address had a decidedly Calvinistic ring with its references to the "agonized strain of the heart of man to pierce the mystery of being," and to "constant anxieties" as the heritage of all God's spiritual creatures. On the other hand, Crummell was what the Episcopalians called a "strict churchman," meaning that he placed considerable emphasis on works in the process of salvation. As Protestants, Episcopalians stressed the need to be constantly aware of one's depravity and dependence on grace as the fundamental source of salvation. Strict church Episcopalians resembled Roman Catholics, however, in their emphasis on the "Law of Moses" as a guide to life. Crummell constantly preached the doctrine of "work out your own salvation," and reminded his congregations that at the Second Coming they would be judged on their deeds. Thus, he preached constantly against the antinomianism that he believed to be a particular plague of the black church, with its constant revivals and incessant enthusiasm.[34]

In 1897, Du Bois joined Crummell in the District of Columbia's Lincoln Memorial Church to inaugurate the American Negro Academy, and delivered his still controversial paper on "The Conservation of Races." The academy membership consisted largely of churchmen, most prominent among them Francis J. Grimké, a Presbyterian clergyman of the time, and Theophilus G. Steward, a Methodist minister and a chaplain in the United States Army. In this environment, Du Bois was exposed to the leadership values of the bourgeois clergy, who emphasized the work ethic and sexual restraint as fundamental building blocks of hoped-for black progress in America.

Although the American Negro Academy was in part a reaction to the power of Booker T. Washington, its founders shared Washington's commitment to the doctrines of enterprising Christianity.[35] Washington eventually published his gospel of work and wealth, under the title *Character Building*, a year before Weber published *The Protestant Ethic*.[36] Unlike Weber, he does not seem to have been directly influenced by Franklin, although his preachments in the Tuskegee Chapel were in the tradition of Franklinism, which equated Protestant morality with the pursuit of material well-being. Washington expressed continual hostility to backwoods revivalism, whose converts often lost their convictions as rapidly as they acquired them. He believed Tuskegee Institute religion must encourage a strict devotion to purposeful labor, and restraint of the passions.

A Calvinistic celebration of work and restraint was in evidence when Du Bois called for "work, continuous and intensive; work, although it be menial and poorly rewarded; work though done in travail of soul and sweat of brow, must be so impressed upon Negro children as the road to salvaton that a child would feel it a greater disgrace to be idle than to do the humblest labor. The homely virtues of honesty, truth and chastity must be instilled in the cradle."[37] Like Washington and unlike Max Weber, Du Bois was more than an observer of the Protestant ethic; he was an enthusiastic advocate of its assumed power to instill the cultural prerequisites for economic progress. The idea surfaced in his biography *John Brown* (1909), where there is a clear recognition of the connections between religion and capitalism. Brown was interpreted as a stern Protestant wool merchant whose puritanical thrift and industry were frustrated by the power of a slave-based cotton hegemony. Historian Herbert Aptheker has opined that "John Brown personified Du Bois's ideal of a religious person," and it is clear that the biography allowed Du Bois to express his own religious views[38] and was a personal expression of religious historicism in the perfectionist tradition.

> To the unraveling of human tangles we would gladly believe that God sends especial men – chosen vessels which come to the world's deliverance. And what could be more fitting than that the human embodiments of freedom, Puritanism and trade – the great new currents sweeping across the black eddies of slavery, should give birth to the man who in years to come pointed the way to liberty and realized that the cost of liberty was less than the price of repression?[39]

This quote's language is hardly Weberian, but it is clearly consistent with the Weber thesis. The linkage of the ideas of freedom, puritanism, and trade were certainly Weberian. Weber had seen the embodiment of Calvinist tradition and Protestant ethic in the personality of Benjamin Franklin, albeit Franklin was a deist. Du Bois believed he could see these same qualities in the personality of John Brown, recognizing a "quaint Calvinistic" patois in the journal of his father, Owen Brown, an earnestly devout and religious man. From his treatment of Brown, it is clear that Du Bois viewed Calvinism and American puritanism in terms of freedom, both political and economic, and saw them as the moral basis of a righteous empire.

Similar respect for the traditions of the puritan Northeast was evident in his first novel, *The Quest of the Silver Fleece*, published in 1911. Much of the plot is centered in a small boarding school for Negro youth, operated in rural Alabama by the missionary New Englander Sarah Smith, "a gaunt, flat, sad-eyed creature, with wisps of gray hair half-covering her baldness, and a face furrowed with care and gathering years." In the course of the novel, Bles and Zora, protégés of Sarah Smith, temporarily leave the South but return to carry on the work of uplift. Zora develops a plan to save Miss Smith's school by establishing a farming cooperative in a nearby swamp. To solicit the support of the black community she must enlist the aid of the local church, but Preacher Jones turns on her and utilizes all the time-honored devices of antinomian, escapist folk religion to undermine her project. Preacher Jones almost succeeds in his attempt, but suddenly his sermon is interrupted by a sharp cry rising from the swamp, and "the sound of great footsteps coming, coming as from the end of the world . . . [and] a rhythmical chanting, wilder and more primitive than song." A wild black prophet emerges from the swamp, an old man "with tufted gray hair and wrinkled leathery skin," to lash the throng with bitter fury.

> "God is done sent me," he declared in passionate tones, "to preach His acceptable time. Faith without works is dead; who is you that dares to set and wait for the Lord to do your work . . ."
> The gaunt speaker turned again to the people. He talked of little children; he pictured their sin and neglect. "God is done sent me to offer you all salvation," he cried, while the people wept and wailed; "not in praying but in works."[40]

This doctrine that "faith without works is dead" is the essence of Du Bois's Arminianized Calvinism. Here the doctrine is colored by the timely appearance of an African prophet, who works to thwart the subversion of a treacherous priest. The doctrine is pushed almost to an extreme in Du Bois's second novel, *Dark Princess* (1928), in which a brilliant young medical student, Matthew Towns, joins a conspiracy of the world's colored peoples and falls in love with one of the conspirators, an Indian princess. At one point in the novel, Matthew goes so far as to declare, "Work is God," but the princess quickly corrects this heresy, saying, "Work is not God – Love is God and Work is his Prophet."[41]

But the work ethic, what Cotton Mather called a Christian's "calling," remained central to Du Bois's religious spirit. In his *Autobiography*, Du Bois mentioned that when asked to participate in religious services at Atlanta University, he wrote his own prayers. Herbert Aptheker has published these documents from manuscripts in the Du Bois papers. The following is most germane to the present discussion:

> God teach us to work. Herein alone do we approach our Creator when we stretch our arms with toil, and strain with eye and ear and brain to catch the thought and do the deed and create the things that make life worth living. Let us quickly learn in our youth, O Father, that in the very doing, the honest humbled determined striving, lies the realness of things, the great glory of life. Of all things there is fear and fading – beauty pales and hope disappoints; but blessed is the worker – his are the kingdoms of earth – Amen.[42]

Such ideals are fairly orthodox within the tradition of African American puritanism. One recalls the sermons of Alexander Crummell, which are dominated by this same gospel of work.

> There are tares to be rooted up from the human heart. Can this be done without labour? The soil of unbelief is to be broken up. Is this a playful pastime? There are passions to be repressed and uprooted, worldliness to be consumed, lust to be annihilated, gross desires to be quenched. Is all this an easy achievement? Can all this giant effort be performed without sweatful toil, without anxious watchfulness . . . ?
>
> Look at the man who, with his hand upon the plough, suffers himself to be constantly led off from his work. How irregular are his furrows! How devious his paths! Every stone throws him out of his course. The smallest tangled root or an old knotted stump could turn it over and thus, looking back, his hand still upon the plough; – everything goes wrong! His work is imperfectly accomplished; tares still remain in the ground; stones are scattered in every direction; and the field of effort which should have given evidence of his skill and faithfulness, indicates, in all directions, carelessness, sloth, inexcusable neglect![43]

Reductionist critics have derided black American adherence to the Protestant ethic as a thoughtless aping of Anglo-American bourgeois values, designed to curry favor with the dominant race. Nothing is so simple. Nationalists and militant separatists have been among the most vocal advocates of the Calvinistic approach to racial uplift. The emphasis that black perfectionists placed on personal character had very little to do with the idea of making one's self acceptable to whites. Black religious leaders were well aware of the hypocrisy of American Protestantism. Some of the strictest Calvinistic rhetoric was delivered by the most militant spokespersons. The Presbyterian minister Francis J. Grimké, for example, denounced Billy Sunday for preaching faith without works, because Sunday refused to denounce racial prejudice.[44] Grimké believed that black folk should adhere to the strictest ideals of temperance, thrift, chastity, and hard work, but not in order to gain acceptance from white folk. The Calvinism of Grimké was designed to develop the backbone of a self-sufficient people, who would have no need to gain the acceptance of whites. Du Bois, too, made it clear that his doctrine of cleanliness, work, and temperance was not intended to impress white folk; it was directed toward "the colored world within."[45]

While Du Bois was rigid in his insistence that the educated classes of black Americans should assume the burdens of a social gospel, he understood the cynicism of the masses regarding the gospel of thrift and industry. Thus, in his novel *The Ordeal of Mansart*, published in 1957, he articulates the position of the alienated black freedman encountered sitting by the roadside eating a stolen chicken. The man boasts of how he will justify himself before God on the judgment day.

> "Gwine to stan' up and talk to God straight as man to man. Gwine to say, 'Massa God, maybe you knows yo' business bettern I. But as ah sees it you ain't doin so well. Looks like to me you done messed up dis world something awful. Starved de good and fed de bad; made scountrels happy and saints sad. Turrible mess. Look at me: born wid nothin, always hungry, beat up and drove to work. Then you frees me and ah thanks you, jumps an prays and hollers! Den you tells me ah ain't free but gotta work. Hell, no! I jest ain't gwine to work! Ef you wants to burn me forevah – well, go ahead. Reckon ah'll last as long as the fire.' "[46]

To understood such antinomian or lawless attitudes was not to condone them. Du Bois was never comfortable with the antinomian amoralism that he attributed, correctly or incorrectly, to a large segment of the black masses. His hostility to the spirit of the so-called Harlem Renaissance, as represented in Claude McKay's *Home to Harlem* and Carl Van Vechten's *Nigger Heaven*, is legendary. Both novels offended his sense of sexual propriety.[47]

In conclusion, then, Du Bois's observations on the Calvinism he detected in the African American subculture reflected the complexity of black American life and religious expression. Calvinistic influences on Du Bois himself appeared in his sociological writings, in his positions on social reform, and in his novels, religious poetry, and prayers. Both as a sociologist and as an activist, he apparently agreed with the position of Booker T. Washington that "the simple Calvinistic creed" to be observed in the religion of the masses was escapist and antinomian. The religion of the masses borrowed from Anglo-American culture that same strain of obsession with the personality of Jesus Christ that Ralph Waldo Emerson once criticized.[48] It was "Calvinistic" in that it was fatalistic, and viewed salvation almost entirely in terms of the conversion experience. It was Wesleyan in that conversion was accompanied by a high level of emotionalism, but black folk-religion was too often removed from the Puritan and Wesleyan traditions of perfectionism that had evolved into the Social Gospel. To the dismay of Washington, Du Bois, Crummell, and Grimké, the black church often failed to express its enthusiasms in terms of social activism. For such bourgeois intellectuals as Du Bois and Grimké the most appealing aspects of Calvinism were its work ethic, capitalist values, and sexual restraint. Predestination and the personal experience of conversion were far less important to them than the Social Gospel, prefigured in the Sermon on the Mount. Their faith was a classic example of William G. McLoughlin's "Arminianized Calvinism."

Du Bois produced a significant body of religious writing. To be sure, his uses of religion were often rhetorical, but it also seems likely that on some levels he remained a believer in the God of his New England childhood. More demonstrably, religion played a part in Du Bois's literary expression throughout his career. In his poetry, pageants, novels, and vignettes he created numerous parables, based on New Testament stories, in order to expose the hypocrisy of American Christianity. More important, however, he continually preached a doctrine of Calvinist Puritanism, insisting that the first steps toward black power would have to result from the strengthening of church and family values. These he conceived in terms of the strict traditional mores that he first learned in Great Barrington, Massachusetts, and later encountered in the transplanted New England environment of Fisk University, "a missionary college where religious orthodoxy was stressed."[49] The burden of his religious writings identified him as in irreconcilable opposition to both the modernism and the primitivism of the so-called Harlem Renaissance. It placed him in opposition to an often antinomian storefront religion. It put him in unacknowledged ideological harmony with such working-class cults as the Black Jews of Harlem and the Black Muslims, groups that still appeal to black puritanical traditions and that stand in opposition to the latitudinarianism of intellectual and artistic elites. Du Bois's internal religious beliefs, like those of most complicated people, remain an unsearchable mystery, and his writings on religion always reflect the complexity of his "spiritual strivings."

SECTION 2: BARBARISM, CIVILIZATION, AND DECADENCE

One sometimes wonders if Du Bois ever regretted writing the passage in *The Souls of Black Folk* that has been quoted with such stupefying frequency, in which he confesses to struggling with "double consciousness," the conflicts of being "an American, a Negro; two souls, two thoughts, two unreconciled strivings; two warring ideals in one dark body."[50] This was almost certainly an instance of rhetorical oversimplification because, like all persons of intellectual depth, "the Doctor" experienced numerous conflicts within his complex identity. Much additional turmoil, equally evident and at least equally as important, stormed constantly within his soul. There was a warfare between his loyalties as social democrat and racial romantic, another battle between his impulses as traditionalist and iconoclast. There was a tension between his austerity and his enthusiasm, another between his elitism and his folkishness, and yet another between his blatant Prussianism and his latent bohemianism.

Du Bois's evolving philosophy eventually encompassed liberalism, Afrocentrism, and communism. Lerone Bennett accurately observed Du Bois's liberal strain by focusing on his noted role as a founder and officer of the NAACP.[51] And Bennett correctly appreciated Du Bois's importance as editor of the NAACP journal, *The Crisis*, where he championed racial integration and ethnic tolerance. Bennett played down Du Bois's communism and Pan-Africanism. Martin Luther King, on the other hand, insisted that "it is time to cease muting the fact that Du Bois was a genius and chose to be a communist. Our irrational obsessive anti-communism has led us into too many quagmires to be retained as if it were a mode of scientific thinking." Charles T. Davis noted the tendencies toward black nationalism and romantic racialism, so evident in Du Bois's poetry and fiction.[52] As a Pan-Africanist, Du Bois had more in common with Marcus Garvey than he cared to admit. Like Garvey, he was a Pan-African chauvinist with a penchant for the theatrical, and, like Garvey, he was faced with the problem of controlling his authoritarian emotions in observance of egalitarian niceties and democratic protocols.

Du Bois was a trained social scientist, with a Ph.D. from Harvard and two years of advanced studies at the University of Berlin, but he also displayed excellent polemical gifts and the skills of a poet. He wrote with convincing sincerity on the "midnight beauty" that he saw in the faces of peasants in rural Tennessee, and he wrote with conviction on the color and the fantasy that he discovered in the African American consciousness. His rhapsodies on black mass culture were always more sympathetic, however, when they focused on small farmers in the South than when directed at the behavior of the urban proletariat. In his youth, he worked as a country schoolteacher in Tennessee, and years later he wrote:

I bent with tears and pitying hands
Above those dusky star-eyed children,
Crinkly haired, with sweet-sad baby voices
Pleading low for light and love and living
And I crooned:
  Little children weeping there,
  God shall find thy faces fair;
  Guerdon for thy deep distress,
  He shall send His tenderness . . . [53]

But Du Bois's tenderness was often hidden behind the dark veil of a stern patriarchal formalism, which manifested itself in his earliest writings. Dogmatic, prickly, fastidious, and impatient, Du Bois sought to impose universal discipline on black Americans in order to lead them into an era of political and economic power. "Bismarck was my hero," he admitted in his *Autobiography*, remembering how he had chosen the German chancellor as the subject of his Fisk University commencement oration in 1888. "He had made a nation out of a mass of bickering peoples. He had dominated the whole development with his strength until he crowned an emperor at Versailles." Du Bois's fascination with the strong man, the political or military leader who could bend nations to his will and force a squabbling *Pöbel* into a national entity, was to be a recurrent theme in his work. Thus, one witnesses his youthful homage to the "unbending righteousness" of Alexander Crummell, and his admiration in later years for the dictator Joseph Stalin, and for Kwame Nkrumah, the Leninist czar.[54]

In 1897, at the age of twenty-nine, Du Bois appeared before the American Negro Academy to deliver a paper entitled "On the Conservation of Races." He insisted that the individual must be subordinated to the race, and that the African race must work as one union of "200,000,000 black hearts beating in one glad song of jubilee." He called on black Americans "to take their just place in the van of Pan-Negroism" and embrace a collectivist racial ideal, rather than "the individualistic philosophy of the Declaration of Independence and the laissez faire philosophy of Adam Smith." The goal of racial leadership was to be realized within an American Negro Academy, a group of "unselfish men and pure and noble women" who would be "firm in leadership."[55]

In another early work, *The Negro Church* (1903), Du Bois had more to say about leadership and authority when he descanted on the power of religion embodied in the African priest or medicine man. Unfortunately, the power of the priest had never fully realized its potential in Africa, and that was a partial explanation for the failure of the Negro race to deliver its full message to the world. Africa had never been able to fashion an enduring political authority. This failure had led to questions about the Africans' capacity for self-government and made them vulnerable to outside domination through colonization and the slave trade. "The central fact of African life [was] its failure to integrate – to unite and systematize itself in some conquering whole which should dominate the wayward parts." The "central problem of civilization" was embodied in this need for conquest and domination, "and some consolidation of power in religion."[56]

The Africans who were transported into the New World were sometimes Muslims, sometimes Christians, but were for the most part tied to the traditional religions of their respective ancestral clans. Some of the transported Africans were priests, Du Bois posited, and along with them "a degraded form of African religion and witchcraft appeared." The Negro church in the United States represented the survival, however faint, of the "vast power of the priest." It therefore seemed legitimate to assert that the Negro chuch in America was essentially an African institution. The Obeah sorcery of the West Indies was a survival of an ancient religion that had found expression not only in West Africa, but in ancient Egypt as well. Du Bois proclaimed that the religious expression of the black peasants of the South represented "the sole surviving social institution of the African fatherland," and it was from this fact that it derived its "extraordinary growth and vitality."[57]

If Du Bois was influenced by Alexander Crummell and the American Negro Academy in stressing the idea of a civilizing mission to be carried out by a strong-minded elite, he was equally attracted by a more Germanic conception of *Kultur*, which implied the idea of a folk spirit rising up out of the souls of the masses. Influenced by the nationalist traditions in German scholarship that had dominated lectures while he was at the University of Berlin, Du Bois began to adapt the concept of *Volksgeist* (folk soul or people's spirit) to the black American and the Pan-African condition. Like Johann Gottfried von

Herder, Du Bois was attached to a conception of the people as a mystical or metaphysical entity, a communal consciousness that would manifest itself in the form of folk art, folk tales, myths, and legends.[58]

Anthony Appiah has asserted that classical black nationalists were influenced by racist theories in Herder, although he has not shared with his readers the direct lines whereby these influences were transmitted. Herder was certainly not a racist by the standards of his time, as Hans Kohn has demonstrated. In fact, Herder, among other fathers of German nationalism, was somewhat more humane and far less anti-black than some of his enlightened American contemporaries. In any event, the relationship between black nationalism and German nationalism, to which I have alluded in numerous writings over the past quarter century, is one of cognates and analogues, not necessarily one of direct influences. W. E. B. Du Bois, like most African American nationalists, expressed ideas congruent with those of Herder, which may or may not have had anything to do with his German education. But, like Herder, he betrayed a mystical belief that every branch of the human family was destined to make a distinctive racial contribution to human progress.[59]

The title of his best-known series of essays, *The Souls of Black Folk,* could be loosely translated as *Der Schwarze Volksgeist.* In this work, Du Bois looked to the roots of black culture as preserved in the rural South as the source of that power which he hoped would eventually transform the world. The African American people were portrayed as the "sole repository of simple faith and virtue in a dusty desert of dollars." But, as always, Du Bois found himself caught up in an internal dialectic – morally uncomfortable with the idea of elite "civilization" while calling for a talented tenth; emotionally uncomfortable with popular "culture," and yet intellectually committed to the idea of *Volksgeist.* He therefore made no systematic attempt to distinguish between the concepts of culture and civilization in his essay "What Is Civilization? Africa's Answer."[60] Some scholars were making such a distinction, notably Robert E. Park and Oswald Spengler. Both had used "culture" to denote the sacred intimacy of vigorous local ethnic groups, and "civilization" to denote the secular impersonal life of disjointed cosmopolitan societies.[61] In this essay, Du Bois used the terms interchangeably, however. His search for a core set of African values was in the tradition of Wilhelm and Jacob Grimm, who attempted to valorize a core ethnic personality and mythology, but wedded this adulation of racial singularities to a curious spirit of cosmopolitanism.[62]

In "What Is Civilization? Africa's Answer," published in 1925, Du

Bois overcame the uncertainty present in "The Conservation of Races" as to whether "The Negro" had made past contributions to the progress of world civilization. In this essay, he insisted that Africans had made such contributions, and his argument, interestingly, was not Egyptocentric. Increasingly, he looked to sub-Saharan Africa for sources of the primal culture that had lifted the world out of barbarism. In fact, as we shall presently see, he identified black people as the only race to make spontaneously the great leap from barbarism to civilization. From the work of Franz Boas and Edward Wilmot Blyden, and later that of the Gold Coast intellectual Casely Hayford, he derived the idea of focusing on West Africa as a source of human progress and potential human advancement in the future. Du Bois is to be contrasted with Alexander Crummell, who had, as we have seen, vehemently argued that no leap from barbarism to civilization had ever occurred. Crummell's religious orthodoxy taught him that early human cultures derived their knowledge from the primal "Adamic civilization."[63]

Du Bois identified three primal cultural leaps originating in Africa and subsequently running through world civilization, to the enduring benefit of all humanity. These three things, "the essential elements of African culture," were: "Beginnings; the village unit; and Art in sculpture [and] in music." Within the tradition of racial vindicationism, it had always been important to demonstrate that black Africans had made a special contribution to the general history of mankind. Du Bois was still cautious in making such claims, however, and the mind grows restless at the task of deciphering the following nicely constructed sequence of ideas:

> Wherever one finds the first faint steps of human culture, the first successful fight against wild beasts, the striving against weather and disease, there one sees black men. To be sure they were not the only beginners, but they seem to have been the successful and persistent ones. Thus Africa appears as the Father of mankind, and the people who eventually settled there, wherever they may have wandered before and since – along the Ganges, the Euphrates, and the Nile, in Cyprus and about the Mediterranean shores – form the largest and often the only group of human beings successfully advancing from animal savagery toward primitive civilization.[64]

In "What Is Civilization?" Du Bois was circumspect in his assertion that Africans had initiated human progress by forging the primal civilization; but then, on the other hand, he did not deny the idea either. He did not say they were the only group to achieve such progress; he said they were "often the only group." He did state that while "probably the properties of iron have been discovered in the world many times," it seemed "likely" that Africans were making use of iron technology while Europe was still in its Stone Age. This was a task that neither Egypt, nor Western Asia, nor ancient China had achieved, and it was "a moment big with promise for the uplift of the human race." Without iron, modern industrial progress would have been impossible, "and this marvelous discovery was made by African Negroes."

With respect to the idea of "progress," Du Bois wanted to have his cake and eat it too. Like many intellectuals of his generation, he was skeptical regarding Victorian notions of progress. He was not beyond the influences of a new cultural relativism that rejected the idea that some societies were better or more advanced than others. Nonetheless, in "What Is Civilization" he clung to the idea of progress, and was determined to show that black folk had contributed to the evolution of civilization. His theory of history was "progressive" and evolutionary. He did not challenge the view that various stages of human advancement can be identified with such terms as "animal savagery," "primitive civilization," and "modern civilization." Therefore, on the one hand, he seemed to question the commonly accepted definitions of progress and civilization, while, on the other, he asserted that Africa was the source of progress and civilization.

However, in defining the second of Africa's gifts to the world, Du Bois revealed that the ideas of modernity and progress were not essential to his theory of African contributionism. Africans, he stated, had given the world the village unit. He presented an idealistic vision of the West African village as "a perfect human thing." The genius of the African village was its ability to reconcile oppositions, that it "socialized the individual completely, and yet because the village was small this socialization did not submerge and kill individuality." This was an implicit critique of modernism, and of urban society: "When the city socializes the modern man he becomes mechanical, and cities tend to be all alike. When the nation attempts to socialize the modern man the result is often a soulless Leviathan." Unlike modern theorists of Afrocentricity, Du Bois did not view individualism as a European invention. He saw individualism as an essential feature of the village culture, and accused Africa of producing a society that was individualistic to a fault. "Africa paid for her individualistic village culture . . . by the slave trade."[65]

The description of modern urbanized civilization as a Leviathan that swallows up the individual was reminiscent of ideas developed by such of Du Bois's contemporaries as Robert E. Park, Oswald Spengler, and Ferdinand Tönnies. In pointing out the differences between the African village and the modern city, Du Bois was making the same sort of distinction that Tönnies had made in differentiating *Gemeinschaft* and *Gesellschaft*. It was this difference that was at the root of Park's culture – civilization distinction. A similar idea was at the root of Spengler's distinction between living culture and dead civilization. In each case the author recognized the importance of a society's bringing the individual into some sort of harmony with society. Park and Tönnies were particularly attracted by the idea of the small town as an institution that performed such functions effectively. Their theories were a critique of modern societies that, because of their cosmopolitanism, produced disorientation and anomie. In a similar vein, Spengler saw the socializing functions of healthy organic cultures as distinct from the mechanical groupings of "civilizations." Eventually Spengler defined civilization as "dead culture," meaning that the elements of society were no longer integral and organically interrelated. Du Bois never specifically endorsed Spengler's pejorative definition of civilization, but he did critique modern civilization as disintegrated, and he idealized the small village as a place where "religion, industry, government, education, and art . . . were bred as integral interrelated things."[66]

The third gift "out of Africa and out of the souls of black folk was music and rhythm." Du Bois wrote with breathless enthusiasm of "the terrible beautiful music" that he had heard forty years earlier in a rustic church in backwoods Tennessee. "It was the demoniac possession of infinite music. . . . I stood and wept, and when in a flash of silence, a woman leapt into the air and shrieked as the dying shriek, I sat down cold with terror and hot with new ecstasy." He personalized his sense of a tie to the music of Africa by referring to a "heathen melody" that had been passed down in his family by his grandfather's grandmother. "The child sang it to his children and they to their children's children, and so 200 years it has traveled down to us and we sing it to our children, knowing as little as our fathers what its words may mean, but knowing well the meaning of its music."[67]

Do ba-no co-ba, ge-ne me, ge-ne me!
Do ba-no co-ba, ge-ne me, ge-ne me!
Ben d'nuli, nuli, ben d'le!

He alluded to "the tom-tom in O'Neill's Emperor Jones," and he praised the audience of a church in New York for listening spellbound to the music of Henry Burleigh sung by a white choir. By now he was able even to celebrate the sound of "a Negro orchestra playing Jazz." Du Bois was trying hard to understand folk and popular culture, and perhaps he was succeeding, but he simply did not seem to have much natural affinity to the spirit of jazz.

> Your head may revolt, your ancient conventions scream in protest, but your heart and body leap to rhythm. It is a new and mighty art which Africa gave America and America is giving the world. It has circled the world, it has set hundreds of millions of feet a-dancing – it is a "new" and "American" art which has already influenced all music and is destined to do more.[68]

He was much more convincing when he spoke of black music in terms of what he called "The Sorrow Songs." But he was not insensitive to the fact that composers who made use of Negro themes were gaining acceptance by white theater- and concertgoers. He was capable of making a passing allusion to W. C. Handy, but Du Bois's best known treatments of black music are his essay on the "Sorrow Songs" in *The Souls of Black Folk,* and his treatment of the British mulatto composer Samuel Coleridge-Taylor, who wrote "classical" music on African themes. Coleridge-Taylor was something of a culture hero to the black bourgeoisie in the earlier years of the twentieth century. Despite the assimilation that he represented in body and in mind, Coleridge-Taylor also represented a variety of cultural Pan-Africanism that they found acceptable.[69]

If Du Bois was fascinated by the musical Pan-Africanism of Coleridge-Taylor, he was influenced by the sociopolitical Pan-Africanism of Joseph Ephraim Casely Hayford. Hayford, a barrister in the British colony of the Gold Coast in West Africa, had organized a Pan-African Conference in 1905, which Du Bois had not attended.[70] In 1911, Hayford had written a book called *Ethiopia Unbound,* in which he mocked some of Du Bois's ideas, put forth in *The Souls of Black Folk,* especially that of "double consciousness." In that same book, Hayford made an obvious allusion to an image, which Du Bois had employed at the end of his second chapter, of "a figure veiled and bowed" who sits in the king's highway. Hayford criticized Du Bois as a prodigal son, who instead of hastening to his father's house "sits sulkily by the wayside over Jordan apples." Hayford had described Du Bois's attitude toward the race question as "pathetic," referring especially to the passage in which Du Bois had described his sense of "twoness" as an American and an African. Hayford dismissed this as the pathetic cry of a man who had foolishly elected to remain in a limbo of unreconcilable strivings.

To be a puzzle to others is not to be a puzzle unto one's self. The sphinx in the Temple of the Sphinx in ancient Egypt is a recumbent figure with the head of a lion, but the features of King Chephron, the Master of Egypt, somewhere about 3960 B.C. Now, fancy Candace, Queen of Ethiopia, or Chephron, the Master of Egypt, being troubled with a double consciousness. Watch that symbolic, reposeful figure yonder, and you can but see one soul, one ideal, one striving, one line of natural, rational progress. Look again, and you must agree that the idea of a double consciousness is absurd with these representative types.[71]

Ironically, the ambimorphous symbolism of the Sphinx seemed to mock the absolutist ideal that Hayford sought to advance. Double consciousness and the timeless problems of mixed identity were not unfamiliar to the ancient Egyptians. In fact, the pharaohs themselves wore a double crown, symbolic of the mixed cultural identity of Egypt, where the ethnic heritages of the black upper and the brown lower Nile were combined.

For his part, Du Bois developed an admiration for Hayford, and cited his works in subsequent publications.[72] He also paid tribute to the work of other black scholars, even William H. Ferris, a black graduate of Yale University and a member of the American Negro Academy, who had challenged some of Du Bois's ideas in "The Conservation of Races."[73] Ferris was the author of a massive collection of essays, which he called *The African Abroad*, published in 1911. This two-volume work constituted an operational definition of Pan-Africanism, with its disquisitions on Africa and Egypt and its impressive discussions of leading black men and ideas of the day.[74]

In "The Conservation of Races," Du Bois had balked at an unequivocal declaration of any ties between Egypt and central Africa, but when he published *The Negro* eighteen years later, he seemed more convinced. He buttressed his work with social scientific references and quotations from the works of Leo Frobenius and Franz Boas. He cited A. F. Chamberlain's "The Contribution of the Negro to Human Civilization" as "one of the special works on which the author has relied for his statements or which amplify his point of view." One of the views expressed by Chamberlain that particularly pleased him was a statement that "the Egyptian race . . . had a considerable amount of Negro blood, and one of the reasons why no civilization of the type of that of the Nile arose in other parts of the continent, if such a thing were possible, was that Egypt acted as a

sort of channel by which the genius of Negroland was drafted off
into the service of Mediterranean and Asiatic culture."[75]

Du Bois was now convinced of the upper Nilotic origins of Egyptian high culture. The Egyptians, he wrote,

> certainly were not white in any sense of the modern use of that
> word – neither in color nor physical measurement, in hair nor
> countenance, in language nor social customs. They stood in
> relationship nearest the Negro race in earliest times, and then
> gradually through the infiltration of Mediterranean and Se-
> mitic elements became what can be described in America as a
> light mulatto stock of Octoroons or Quadroons.[76]

Europeans boasted that they were the sole inventors of human progress, but Africa, true mother of civilization had only been sleeping.
"Who raised the fools to their glory?" asked Du Bois in a poem
entitled "The Riddle of the Sphinx." It was "black men of Egypt
and Ind, / Ethiopia's sons of the evening, Indians and yellow Chinese, / Arabian children of morning, / And mongrels of Rome and
Greece?" / "Ah, well!" In the coming world revolution, "they who
raised the boasters [would] drag them down again."[77]

Du Bois was fifty-six years old when he first set foot on African
soil. He traveled in 1924 as minister plenipotentiary and envoy extraordinary, representing President Calvin Coolidge at the inaugu-
ration of Liberia's president Charles King. Once again, Du Bois
waxed poetic:

> Africa is the spiritual Frontier of human kind – oh the wild and
> beautiful adventures of its taming! But oh! the cost thereof –
> the endless, endless cost! Then will come a day – an old and
> ever, ever young day when there will spring in Africa a civiliza-
> tion without coal, without noise, where machinery will sing and
> never rush and roar, and where men will sleep and think and
> dance and lie prone before the rising sons, and women will be
> happy.
>   The objects of life will be revolutionized. Our duty will not
> consist in getting up at seven, working furiously for six, ten and
> twelve hours, eating in sullen ravenousness or extraordinary
> repletion. No – we shall dream the day away and in cool dawns,
> in little swift hours, do all our work.[78]

During the five years preceding his first trip to Africa, Du Bois
had been involved in organizing a series of Pan-African congresses.
He was not the first to engage in such activities, as there had been
previous attempts to organize a worldwide union of black peoples.

One of these was the London Conference of 1900 organized by the Trinidad barrister Sylvester Williams and the Methodist bishop Alexander Walters. It was at this conference that Du Bois made his famous statement, "The problem of the twentieth century is the problem of the color line."[79] Nineteen years later Du Bois began the series of Pan-African congresses that met in Paris, 1919; London, Brussels, and Paris, 1921; London, Paris, and Lisbon, 1923; and New York, 1927.[80] The proceedings of these conferences were of varied significance. Du Bois believed that the conference of 1919 had at least planted the idea that the former German colonies ought to be administered by an international organization "instead of being handled by various colonial powers. Out of this idea came the Mandates Commission."[81] Du Bois made no grandiose claims for the Pan-African movement, it represented simply "the centralization of race effort and the recognition of a racial fount." The slogan Africa for the Africans did not mean "any lessening of effort in our own problem at home." Pan-Africanism, as he defined it, was "not a separatist movement" and was not intended to encourage the deportation of "any large number of colored Americans."[82] Within a month of this disclaimer, Du Bois was denounced by Marcus Garvey, who was pushing his own variety of Pan-Africanism.[83]

The feud between Du Bois and Garvey was largely, but not entirely, a clash of egos. The two men shared a fascination with nineteenth-century imperialist conceptions of power and authority. Du Bois was less inclined than was Garvey to take his theater into the street, but the pages of *The Crisis*, like those of *Negro World*, were filled with Afrocentric rhetoric and racial romanticism. Both men claimed to represent the true interests of the masses of poor black Americans. Du Bois constantly presented sentimentalized portraits of southern peasants, while Garvey mixed with and rubbed elbows with the urban workers. Both men were no doubt sincere in their commitments to uplifting the race, but neither was completely convincing as an advocate of popular culture. Both were reminiscent of the nineteenth-century prophets of African civilizationism, an ideal that was to be imposed from the top down, rather than growing organically from the bottom up. Both Garvey and Du Bois betrayed more attachment to the symbols of cosmopolitan civilization than to the homely folkways of the American Negro. Neither of them supported the cabaret culture or the new sexual freedom that thrived in the cities of the Jazz Age. They were in competition for control of high culture symbolism and monumental imagery, and they were of one mind in their disparagement of the raunchy folksiness of gutbucket blues.

Du Bois, like Garvey, thus became involved in the culture wars of Harlem in the 1920s. His early involvement in the German rhetoric of *Volksgeist* had prepared Du Bois intellectually for a promotion of cultural nationalism based on the folk culture of the rural South. He was, however, ill-prepared to sympathize with the blues culture that had arisen in the South and was flourishing in the North. His roots in classical "civilizationist" black nationalism did not prepare him to embrace the proletarian-bohemian culture celebrated by Carl Van Vechten and his circle, which included individuals of unconventional sexual orientation. Aside from his professed disbelief in the existence of homosexuals, Du Bois was not entirely unfamiliar with alternative lifestyles. As we have seen, he had first encountered "loose sexual customs" when he went south to college, and had committed adultery while teaching during a summer in rural Tennessee.[84] During his years in Berlin he had practically lived with a young German "shopgirl." Still, his reviews of the novels of Claude McKay and Carl Van Vechten, with their mild, nonexplicit allusions to ribaldry, were immoderately hostile. In 1928, as if fearing the charge of prudishness, Du Bois produced his *Dark Princess*, a representative Harlem Renaissance novel, although he chose to locate much of the action in Chicago. The hero's extramarital affair was central to the development of *Dark Princess*, and the passage in which the hero and heroine make love on an oriental rug, although it leaves much to the imagination, is arguably more erotic than the sketchy sexual encounters in McKay's *Home to Harlem*. Du Bois's objections to McKay's creations was not that McKay's characters deviated from bourgeois ideals of Victorian chastity, but that their sexual encouters were casual and untouched by romantic love. There was no room in Du Bois's cultural nationalism for the tomcat sexual adventurism that he, correctly or incorrectly, associated with blues culture.

Du Bois had completely accepted the blackness of the Egyptians by 1939, when he published *Black Folk Then and Now*. In this book he provided a broad survey of Egyptian history, written from respectable secondary sources. Much of the material was incorporated into Du Bois's third major work on Africa, *The World and Africa*, published seven years later. In both works, he insisted that Egyptian culture had originated among the blacks of inner Africa, then flowed down the Nile to the Mediterranean. He also demonstrated considerable interest in the cultures of western and southern Africa, which he continued to depict as admirable in their own right, aside from any ties that may have developed between them and Egypt or the Islamic world. He continued to speak of the gifts of black folk to America and to the world. Du Bois had anticipated by two decades the assertions of Oswald Spengler and Hermann Hesse that Europeans were becoming culturally impoverished.[85] He came to speak of the modern European ethos as dry, dull, and moneygrubbing, and idealistically presented the Negro as the world-saving remnant of cultural health.

The First World War provided Du Bois, and many other intellectuals, with ample opportunity to reflect on the ruined claims of European cultural supremacy. At the time of America's entry into the Great War, Du Bois still conceded that European civilization had advanced beyond the rest of the world economically, industrially, and militarily. But European supremacy in certain areas did not mean that Europeans were "better, nobler, greater and more gifted than other folk." Europe was great "because of the foundations which the mighty past had furnished her to build upon: The iron trade of black Africa; the religion and empire building of yellow Asia; the art and science of the dago Mediterranean shore, east south and west as well as north." Europe had risen only when she had built securely on her non-European past, but when she had departed from the wisdom of Africa and the Orient, she had "shown the cloven hoof of poor crucified humanity." Similar observations were made by other intellectuals who adopted a cultural relativism, or at least stressed the fundamental humanity underlying all cultures, and came to view the very concept of "civilization" as an ethnocentric mythology that had been undermined by the Great War.[86]

Du Bois revealed occasional sympathy for the idea of cultural relativism, but he did not reject the concept of civilization, nor did he draw too fine a distinction between the two concepts.[87] In fact, his views seemed to resemble those of Sigmund Freud, who said in 1927, "I scorn to distinguish between culture and civilization."[88] History for Du Bois, as for most progressives, was the struggle of humanity to triumph over animal savagery. He viewed civilization as the process whereby human beings developed progressively higher forms of culture, not only in the material but also in the moral realm. The war demonstrated a failure of Europe to realize the highest ideals of civilization; it did not lead Du Bois to question the validity of the concept of civilization.

If Du Bois believed that black folk had much to gain from racial integration as a means of discovering the higher cultural ideals of Europe and America, he never fully accepted the idea of integration as a panacea for America's racial problems. In his 1897 address "The Conservation of Races," he had asserted that voluntary separatism and racial solidarity were often desirable. "If the Negro is going to develop his own power and gifts . . . [and] also to unite for ideals higher than the world has realized in art and industry and social life, then he must unite and work with Negroes and build a new and great Negro ethos." He did not desire to see the black race drowned in a sea of white culture, because he felt that black folk had much to teach the world. Indeed, in his 1924 publication *The Gift of Black Folk*, he provided evidence and argument that black folk had already given much to America. Thus, while he was committed to continuing the fight for integration, he also recognized a need for continuing to build racial institutions.

The idea of separate institutions was fundamentally unacceptable to the board of directors of the NAACP, and Du Bois's advocacy of them led to his being forced out of the editorship of *The Crisis* at the age of sixty-six. Leading the opposition to Du Bois was Walter White, a man of undoubted courage and intelligence but a bitter foe of all institutional separatism, whether voluntary or involuntary. In the process of his battles with the board, and with Walter White, Du Bois attempted to have the association pass a resolution in support of black churches, colleges, businesses, and industrial enterprises. He asserted that the NAACP should support them "not with the idea of perpetuating artificial separations of mankind but rather with the distinct object of proving Negro efficiency, showing Negro ability and discipline and demonstrating how useless and wasteful race segregation is." The board responded by passing a much abbreviated resolution that made no mention of the need for institutional development. The resolution correctly opposed "both the principle and the practice of enforced segregation," but ignored the issue of black institutions as bases for the development of an ethnic power base.[89]

Du Bois used the phrase "a nation within a nation" to describe the African American's status in "An Essay Toward a History of the Black Man in the Great War." The phrase had been used by Alexander Crummell in "The Social Principle Among a People," and similar phraseology may be traced to Martin Delany.[90] Crummell had spoken against "the dogma . . . that the colored people of this country should forget as soon as possible, that they are colored people." Crummell not only had denounced the doctrine as dogmatic folly, but had gone on to describe it as "disintegrating and socially destructive." Black folk were "shut out from the cultivated social life of the superior classes," and were thus forced to depend upon themselves for higher forms of social-intellectual discourse.

Du Bois had practically rewritten these sentences in his essay "Jim Crow," published in *The Crisis* of January 1919. Like Crummell, he recognized that "much of the objection to segregation and Jim

Crowism was in other days the fact that compelling Negroes to associate only with Negroes meant to exclude them from contact with
the best culture of the day." With the passage of time, conditions
had changed and "culture [was] no longer the monopoly of the
white, nor [were] poverty and ignorance the sole heritage of the
black. Crummell had rejected "the demand that colored men
should give up all distinctive effort, as colored men, in schools,
churches, associations and friendly societies." Resurrecting Crummell's ideas again in 1934, Du Bois said, "The real battle is a matter
of study and thought; of the building of loyalties; of the long training
of men; of the growth of institutions; of the inculcation of racial and
national ideals."[91]

In 1934, Du Bois left the NAACP and the city of New York to
return to Atlanta University, where he was able to act on his principles of dedication to black institution building. He traveled frequently in the rural South, carrying his own lunch to avoid having to
eat in segregated restaurants, and bringing along coveralls and me-
chanic's tools so that he could service his own automobile in the
event of breakdown. He returned to Fisk University in 1938 as a
commencement speaker, delivering an oration, "The Revelation of
St. Orgne the Damned." It was, as its title indicated, a mystical and
visionary address in which he called on the graduating class to dedicate itself to "racial unity and loyalty." At the end of the decade, Du
Bois published his autobiography, *Dusk of Dawn*, in which he advocated the development of black cooperatives and community-
controlled institutions, saying:

> In the African communal group, ties of family and blood, of
> mother and child of group relationship, made the group lead-
> ership strong, even if not always toward the highest culture. In
> the case of the more artificial group among American Negroes,
> there are sources of strength in common memories of suffering
> in the past; in present threats of degradation and extinction; in
> common ambitions and ideals; in emulation and the determi-
> nation to prove ability and desert. Here in subtle but real ways
> the communalism of African clan can be transferred to the
> Negro American group.[92]

This statement was clearly both nationalistic and Afrocentric; it
demonstrated a continuing commitment to the "nation within a nation" model of Alexander Crummell, but Du Bois added an element
that Crummell had never envisioned. He presupposed an African
heritage as the basis for building national strength within a regenerated African American community. The black American would even-

tually pass on to the world a blend of its African and its American heritages. Black Americans, by "achieving new social institutions," would "teach industrial and cultural democracy to a world that bitterly needs it" and "move pari passu with the modern world into a new heaven and a new earth."[93]

Du Bois's black nationalism reached one of its peaks when in 1947, acting as an official representative of the NAACP, he delivered an appeal to the United Nations on behalf of the "thirteen million American citizens of Negro descent." The purpose was to "ask that organization in the proper way to take cognizance of a situation which deprives this group of their rights as men and citizens." He described "the so-called American Negro group" as having been welded by its common history "almost into a nation within a nation," and thus possessing a "hereditary cultural unity, born of slavery, of common suffering, . . . and prolonged policies of segregation and discrimination." He reminded the UN that in terms of sheer numbers this "nation" was larger than Canada, Hungary, or the Netherlands, and almost as large as Yugoslavia or Turkey: "In sheer numbers then we are a group which has a right to be heard; and while we rejoice that other smaller nations can stand and make their wants known in the United Nations, we maintain equally that our voice should not be suppressed or ignored."[94]

In later years, Du Bois repudiated what he had once said about the essentially individualistic nature of African culture. Years earlier, he had theorized that the cause of Africa's historic weakness before the onslaught of slavery, colonialism, and racism was that no African Bismarck had arisen, no king or priest sufficiently strong to forcefully merge his interests with the destiny of the tribe. His communalism, socialism, and Afrocentrism were now blended into one holistic doctrine of Pan-African socialism. Whereas in 1919 he had attributed the fall of Africa before the slave trade to an excess of individualism, in 1958 he denied that an African individualism, or even an African freedom, had existed within traditional societies. He insisted that Africa had never harbored more than a trace of "private enterprise or individual initiative. It was the tribe which carried on trade through individuals, and the chief was mouthpiece of the common will."[95]

In 1958, Du Bois was too ill to attend the All Africa Conference that Kwame Nkrumah convened in Accra, Ghana, but from a hospital bed in Moscow he sent a message. His wife, Shirley Graham Du Bois, read his address before the assembly, the only American allowed such an honor. In the address, Du Bois once again turned to the writings of the now deceased Casely Hayford as a source for his Pan-Africanist ideas. From Casely Hayford he borrowed his conception of the African patriarch, who had become a key figure in his theories. In the coming unified Africa, the individual would have to give up his or her individual interests for the good of the whole, and so, too, must each African tribe "give up a part of its heritage for the good of the whole." He called on Africans to achieve a new unity, based on their common heritage of oppression, saying, "Your bond is no mere color of skin but the deeper experience of wage slavery and contempt." He described traditional African life as a world in which "no tribesman was free. All were servants of the tribe of whom the chief was father and voice."[96]

In Kwame Nkrumah, Du Bois hoped to have found his African Bismarck, his Stalinist czar, the "father and voice" of sufficient strength to bring unity to a continent of squabbling tribes. He hoped Nkrumah would create a new variety of socialism based on the hereditary communalism of West African institutions. As Stalin had forged "one nation out of [Russia's] 140 groups without destroying their individuality," so would Nkrumah overcome the divisive tribalism encouraged by British imperialists. If brutal methods were required, Du Bois could accept the necessity, just as he had accepted the repressive methods of Stalin. Scarred and embittered by his own experiences with caste and class humiliation, Du Bois sympathized with men like Stalin and Nkrumah, who had risen from humble beginnings and were often snubbed by persons of more aristocratic background. Nkrumah's credibility was reinforced, in Du Bois's opinion, when he was opposed by Joseph Appiah, an Oxford-educated Ashanti prince, married to the daughter of Sir Richard Stafford Cripps.[97] And Du Bois made no apologies when Nkrumah sent his political enemies to prison.

One ought not readily accept the idea that Du Bois joined the Communist Party and applied for Ghanaian citizenship because he was "disillusioned and disheartened."[98] His commitment to an Afrocentric brand of socialism under strong leadership was the natural culmination of remarkably consistent theorizing over seventy years. Du Bois believed that the tide of history was on the side of communism, and in his final days he accepted the invitation extended to him by Casely Hayford a half-century earlier, and returned to the Fatherland when another Gold Coast leader, Kwame Nkrumah, renewed the invitation. He turned his face

> From reeking West whose day is done
> Who stink and stagger in their dung.[99]

It was within the context of his final years in Ghana that Du Bois and his associates used the term "Afrocentric," but when, exactly, the term was invented is unknown to me. Du Bois's final years in

Ghana were devoted, of course, to his work on the Encyclopedia Africana, which is discussed in Chapter 1 of this study. It was reasonable that the editors of the Encyclopedia Africana, in their attempts to define the project, should discuss whether it should include all peoples of African descent or should be limited to the continent itself. Over the years, Du Bois often referred to his plans for an Encyclopedia of the Negro or an Encyclopedia Africana. When he wrote to Blyden in 1909 to describe what he had in mind, he seemed to be using the terms interchangeably, but he seemed to mean a project that would be Pan-African in scope, covering both the mother continent and the diaspora. This same universal plan was implicit in 1940 when he described the project for an Encyclopedia of the Negro in *Phylon*.[100]

When Du Bois finally decided on Encyclopedia Africana, in 1961, and undertook concrete plans for its realization, he attempted to sort out the confusion by identifying the various projects with which he had been involved up to that point. This he did in a newspaper article, where he clearly defined the scope of the project to be undertaken in Ghana, saying, "My plan is to prepare and publish an encyclopedia not on the vague subject of race, but on the peoples inhabiting the continent of Africa."[101] It was in 1962, after his arrival in Ghana, that he used the term "Afrocentric" to designate "the African continent as such: the geographical entity," although "not indifferent to either the impact of the outside world upon Africa, or to the impact of Africa on the outside world."[102]

An appreciation of irony and contradiction were evident in what Du Bois wrote during the almost fifty years he spent on defining the parameters of this evolving project. Not only was he compelled to treat the two definitions of Pan-Africanism (geographical and racial), he must also reflect on the old question posed by Garvey: "Who and what is a Negro?" In an editorial note published in *Phylon* in 1940, Du Bois toyed with the paradoxes, carefully distinguishing between culture and color. Would it be appropriate to include a person like Pushkin?

> In the narrow sense of the word and according to continental usage, Pushkin was in no sense a Negro; and the mere fact that he was an octoroon had little to do with his cultural development. On the other hand, according to usage in America and according to the biological school of racial theory, the fact that this great literary figure was the result of miscegenation is of vital interest.[103]

He dryly opined that the encyclopedia must include Frederick Douglass, "although his father was white," and that it could not very well exclude Alexander Dumas, "although he was a quadroon." There were also numerous octoroons "who would unquestionably be included in this Encyclopaedia by popular demand. . . . [Although] all of these were octoroons with quite as little Negro blood as Pushkin." If only persons of "unmixed Negro descent" were allowed, it would have been necessary "to omit most of the members of the advisory committee, who have been promoting this encyclopaedia." The problem of defining "Negro" must be solved by an editorial board, whose concept might include "persons with a slight amount of Negro blood who had been culturally identified with the Negro race, and omit mulattoes and even Negroes without apparent mixture, like Ra Nehesi, Pharaoh of Egypt, who although a full-blooded black, had no cultural connection with Negroes."[104]

Conclusion

Early in his career, Du Bois had no difficulty in bringing his cultural theory into harmony with that of Alexander Crummell and the stern conservative ministers who dominated the American Negro Academy. His theory of history from beginning to end was tied up with the problem of power and authority. This was evident in the tendencies he betrayed towards puritanism and authoritarianism, in his *Autobiography*.[105] He developed a political theory in which individuals must always be subordinated to collective goals and racial destiny. His admiration for Egypt was tied to his reverence for power and authority, for Egypt was the African culture that had most successfully represented imperial might. The irony of Egyptian history was that it had channeled the essence of African genius into the Mediterranean, where other civilizations had built their glory on Africa's gifts. The tragedy of Africa was that conquering kingdoms below the Sahara were constantly overthrown before they could integrate their political, social, and religious power.

This is not to say that Du Bois was at all times bereft of liberal values. Notwithstanding his later recollections, his youthful admiration for Bismarck had not been unequivocal or lacking in ambivalence. The young Du Bois possessed the liberal's aversion to Prussian stolidity, and we should be cautious about giving full value to his later recollection of his youthful passion for Bismarck. In *Dusk of Dawn* (1940) he recalled that "Bismarck was my hero," thus undervaluing his own youthful insightfulness. In fact, the precocious twenty-year-old described his subject, with sarcastic understatement, as "one of the strangest personalities the world has ever seen," and made the vitriolic remark that "no lie ever stood between him and success," thus protecting himself from future accusations of hero worship. With uncanny prescience he concluded that Bismarck had "made Germany a nation that knows not the first principle of self-government. . . . [His life] carries with it a warning lest we sacrifice a lasting good to temporary advantage; lest we raise a nation and forget the people." Du Bois might well have remembered those words when, later in life, he became an apologist for Joseph Stalin.[106]

In appraising Du Bois's 1953 eulogy on Joseph Stalin, two points must be made: Du Bois was not alone in overlooking the crimes of Stalin; he penned his eulogy with a clear memory of the compromises that had been made a few years earlier between Stalin and the leaders of the "free world." Winston Churchill, Franklin D. Roosevelt, and later Harry S. Truman had similarly chosen to overlook Stalin's offenses. Du Bois was wrong, as were others, to ignore the evils of Stalinism. Du Bois's humanitarian sentiments were in conflict with a rigid authoritarianism in his later years, and there were other contradictions.

While, on the one hand, Du Bois aligned himself with a latitudinarian ideology, professing a contempt for puritanism and religious conservatism, he continually betrayed a commitment to traditional evangelical reform, even after his conversion to communism. One notes, for example, a very late poem in which he utilized the rhetoric of puritan outrage in his critique of an American capitalist structure that had

> Enslaved the Black and killed the Red
> And armed the Rich to loot the Dead
> Worshipped the whores of Hollywood
> Where once the Virgin Mary stood
> and lynched the Christ.[107]

At the end of his life, Du Bois remained the great synthesizer, linking his Afrocentrism to his cosmopolitan socialism by advancing the idea that local African cultures contained the elements on which an international Marxist utopia could be built. His historiography was essentially progressive, although it included a theory of decline in which decadent civilizations must necessarily fall as new ones rose to challenge their arrogance. His dream of a new world order, while frequently expressed in terms of the "scientific," was never divorced from the racial messianism that had dominated the thought of Blyden, Crummell, and the preceding generation of Pan-Africanists.

AFROCENTRISM, COSMOPOLITANISM, AND CULTURAL LITERACY IN THE AMERICAN NEGRO ACADEMY

On August 23, 1941, William H. Ferris died, penniless and obscure, in his room at 10 West 123 Street, Harlem. His obituary in *The Journal of Negro History* described him as "a man whose career it is difficult to estimate. . . . His body was saved from the Potter's Field through the action of the treasurer of Yale, a member of Ferris's class of 1895." Ferris was one of those figures in African American history who may easily be reduced by the heartless to an Amos-and-Andy caricature of the "miseducated Negro." He has, in fact, usually been handled by historians in just that fashion. Stephen Fox, writing with precocious arrogance, described him as "an interesting, erratic individual [who] spent much of his time freeloading, an embarrassing illustration of the classically educated, unemployed Negro." In 1913 Ferris published his major work, in two volumes, *The African Abroad or His Evolution in Western Civilization, Tracing His Development Under Caucasian Milieu,* which Fox describes as "a chaotically organized mass of material, with some significant details and insights." In all fairness to their author, these remarks only paraphrase opinions handed down by Ferris's black contemporaries. More recently, Rayford Logan in *The Dictionary of American Negro Biography* acknowledged Ferris as an innovative researcher and a serious bibliophile, whose contributions to the history of the African diaspora informed much subsequent research in the field.[1]

"Full of high sentence, but a bit obtuse; At times, indeed, almost ridiculous – Almost, at times, the Fool," Ferris was an unwitting satire of himself. He was pompous, self-pitying, long-winded, and, worst of all, guilty of coining the bizarre term "Negrosaxon." But although Ferris was not entirely devoid of the buffoonish quality Fox ascribes to him, he also embodied a heroic struggle for the life of the mind. Viewed from one perspective, his problems typified the perennial problems of black intellectuals. On the other hand, it may be useful to remove Ferris from the one-dimensionality of an exclusively black interpretation. The image he generated, unwillingly but certainly not unaware, reflects an American attitude that emerges at least as early as Washington Irving's creation of Ichabod Crane – the depiction of the scholar as buffoon. In a more contemporary vein, he was the ineffectual Prufrockean, the tragic symbol of defeated idealism.

Ferris was a vigorous advocate both of general education and of what we today have come to call "cultural literacy," and an Afro-centrist. The two ideas were not so contradictory as the typical pre-sentist diatribe would have us believe. His educational accomplishments included master's degrees from Yale and Harvard, no mean feat for a black man at the turn of the century. He had spent his years at Yale and Harvard well, and he was able to do more than regurgitate the common wisdom of his day. He was influenced by such teachers as the renowned social Darwinist William Graham Sumner, but he was able to adapt Sumnerism to his own uses as a black nationalist. Recognizing that there was nothing inherently racist in Darwinism, he worked out a conception of black American progress, reconciled evolutionism with a muscular Christianity, and demonstrated the truism that black nationalism is often a conduit for European ideas of culture and civilization.[2]

Ferris was thoroughly committed to the advancement of Euro-American cultural literacy, even though African Americans in his day were frequently barred from libraries, museums, and concert halls. He also advocated the study of African and African American life and history, although the pursuit was usually met with sneers and derision from educated whites. He was a journalist and a lecturer, specializing in topics in the literature, history, and sociology of Africans, Afro-Europeans, and African Americans. Eventually he became associated with Pan-Africanism, joined the stridently black nationalist movement led by Marcus Garvey in the 1920s, and became a high-ranking officer of the Universal Negro Improvement Association. His columns in the official Garveyite newspaper, *Negro World*, emphasized topics that we would refer to today as "black studies" or "Afrocentric studies."

Ferris's struggle to transmit core educational values and general cultural literacy was central to discussions of black education at the beginning of this century. There was much opposition to his mission, as became apparent when Booker T. Washington began to seize power as a leader of black America. Washington, the founder of Tuskegee Institute in Alabama, stood for practical education, primarily in such areas as business, agriculture, and applied technology. He argued against undue emphasis on classical education and the liberal arts; he called for industrial training, saying that those who wasted their time on Greek and Latin were likely to find themselves forced into menial occupations, whereas those who pursued industrial sciences would prosper. Steven Fox has suggested that the following statement by Washington was a direct commentary on the unhappy vicissitudes of Ferris.

> I remember one young man in particular who graduated from Yale University and afterward took a post-graduate course at Harvard, and who began his career by delivering a series of lectures on "The Mistakes of Booker T. Washington." It was not long, however, before he found that he could not live continuously on my mistakes. Then he discovered that in all his long schooling he had not fitted himself to perform any kind of useful and productive labour. After he had failed in several other directions he appealed to me, and I tried to find something for him to do. It is pretty hard, however, to help a young man who has started wrong. Once he gets the idea that – because he has crammed his head full with mere book knowledge – the world owes him a living, it is hard for him to change. The last I heard of the young man in question, he was trying to eke out a miserable existence as a book agent while he was looking about for a position somewhere with the Government as a janitor or for some other equally humble occupation.[3]

Washington's depiction of Ferris is a caricature, and caricature usually sacrifices complexity in order to achieve force. Washington himself has often been caricatured, as in Dudley Randall's verse characterization of his educational philosophy, which is frequently anthologized and widely accepted as gospel. Randall invents a dialogue between Washington and Du Bois, in which Washington is made to say, "It shows a mighty lot of cheek/To study Chemistry and Greek," then encourages black youth to stay on the plantation hoeing "Mr. Charlie's" cotton or cooking for "Miss Ann."[4]

Washington, of course, never advised anything of the sort – certainly not for the more talented portion of African American youth. It is true that he was no promoter of strictly liberal arts education, neither in the abstract sciences nor in the literary disciplines. But his educational philosophy was, in some respects, progressive and pragmatic, in both its methods and its goals. He insisted that young people might do well to study chemistry, genetics, and other highly technical fields, but felt that if they wasted their time on Greek and astronomy, rather than on engineering and agriculture, they were almost certain to end up shining shoes, scrubbing floors, or follow-

ing other unskilled occupations. Washington never disparaged any
sort of honest and gainful employment, however, and he provided a
solid "cultural literacy" education in the liberal arts at Tuskegee.
Alexander's Magazine, a Tuskegee subsidized periodical published in
Boston, made occasional references to the successes of Tuskegee
graduates in their subsequent studies at northern universities like
Harvard and Cornell.[5] Washington did, however, encourage the mechanical arts and applied technologies over the abstract arts and
sciences, albeit some critics have insisted that the skills taught at
Tuskegee were "more congenial to the premachine age than to the
twentieth century."[6]

Ferris was a protégé of Alexander Crummell, the bookish, Tacitus-
quoting, one-time missionary to Africa whose views have been discussed from time to time in this volume. Presumably of "unadulterated" African ancestry, Crummell had been born free in New York
in 1819, the son of an African father and a "free black" mother. He
seemed to Ferris the incarnate refutation of the stereotypical African
– both in his moral character and his physical traits:

> He was one of those rugged, adamantine spirits, who stand
> against the world for a principle, but he was gracious, courte-
> ous, tender and sympathetic withal. Tall, slender, symmetrical,
> erect in bearing, with a graceful and elastic walk, with a refined
> and aristocratic face that was lighted up by keen penetrating
> but kindly eyes, and surrounded by the gray hair and beard
> which gave him a venerable appearance, with a rich, ringing,
> resonant baritone voice, with an unmistakable good breeding
> and a conversation that flavored of books and literature and
> art, Dr. Crummell was a man you could never forget, once you
> had met him or heard him preach. . . . Sprung from the fierce
> Timene Tribes, who on the west coast of Africa cut to pieces a
> British regiment near Sierra Leone several years ago, he pos-
> sessed the tireless energy, the untamed spirit and the fearless
> daring that made his warrior ancestors dreaded.[7]

Ferris's attempt was to depict Crummell as representing the pristine African spirit, although, in fact, Crummell embodied the contradictions between Euro-American assimilation and black nationalist
politics. His formal introduction to "high culture" began when his
parents sent him to New York's African Free School during the
1820s, and was completed at Cambridge University in England,
where he took a degree in 1853. He then embarked on the African
phase of his career, serving for almost twenty years as a missionary,

farmer, trade school administrator, and businessman in Liberia, West Africa.

Crummell returned from Africa in 1872, and established St. Luke's congregation of the Protestant Episcopal Church in Washington, D.C., but he was often alienated from the black bourgeoisie of Washington. His intellectual attainments and international reputation did not shield him from the hostility of a class of people who were color-conscious, obsessed with clothing, and given to vying with one another for social position. Crummell did little to conceal his contempt and was accused of coldness, sarcasm, and too frequent absences on speaking tours. When he preached at home, he denounced drinking, adultery, "grossness," and "abominations" from the pulpit. There was considerable rejoicing among some members of his congregation when he stepped down after twenty-two years.[8]

Crummell's African expertise was acknowledged in the fall of 1895 at the Congress on Africa held in connection with the famed Atlanta Exposition, at which Booker T. Washington also spoke. He delivered two addresses that, once again, demonstrated the ironies of turn-of-the-century Pan-Africanism and the contradictions in Crummell's brand of Afrocentrism. Crummell was hardly unique or idiosyncratic when he called for the civilization of Africa under Christian auspices. He insisted on the importance of Christianity as a "civilizing agency," but also insisted on the independence of the African Church and the necessity of "an indigenous missionary agency . . . . for most men know the spirit of their own race better than strangers." Thus he revealed the commitment to political self-determination, and the countervailing commitment to cultural assimilation, that he shared with such figures as Edward Wilmot Blyden and W. E. B. Du Bois.[9]

In 1894, Crummell proposed organizing an "African Society" "for the preservation of traditions, folk-lore, ancestral remembrances, etc." Nothing came of the plan because, as Crummell saw it, "the dinning of the 'colonization' cause into the ears of the colored people, the reiteration of the idle dogma that Africa is THE home of the black race in this land, has served to prejudice the race against the very name of Africa." Crummell continued, however, to advocate a broad view of Negro destiny, and to link the fates of Africans and African Americans together in his philosophy. On December 18, 1896, Crummell and several friends met in his home to organize the American Negro Academy. William H. Ferris and Du Bois were elected as two of the original thirty-one who were to be invited to join.[10]

Similar in spirit to the old African Civilization Society founded in the 1850s, the American Negro Academy dedicated itself to traditional Pan-African principles at its first official organizational meeting in 1897. It was "civilizationist" in that it stood for the cultural uplift of the African-derived peoples, wherever dispersed. It pre-echoed the rhetoric of Marcus Garvey's Universal Negro Improvement Association, which later elevated two of the academy's founding members, Ferris and John E. Bruce, to exalted status. Crummell's inaugural address was entitled "Civilization, the Primal Need of the Race." In it he called for an elite but self-sacrificing cadre of leaders "to guide both the opinions and habits of the crude masses." The kinship between this principle and Du Bois's Jesuitical ideal of a "Talented Tenth," as servants of the servants of God, was not accidental.[11]

Crummell's theory of education was a blend of elitism and pragmatism. In testimony before a House Committee on Education in January 1880, he had insisted that "the great, eminent, universal need of the black race in this country is training in skilled labor, in mechanical knowledge and handcraft." Opportunities for higher education had increased greatly since the end of the Civil War, he observed. The "colleges of the East [were] with rare exceptions open to black youth," although in many cases educated people were "forced at last to gain a livelihood as servants." He called on Congress to establish scholarships for black youth of "genius and talent which fit them for mechanism, agriculture, or to become engineers or workers in metal; – let them appropriate a special fund for their support in some agricultural school or some institution where they can learn scientific agriculture or engineering."[12]

In his 1886 sermon "Common Sense in Common Schooling," he once again voiced his opposition to mindless miseducation along classical lines. Although he rejoiced in the "singular and burning aptitude of the black race for schools and learning," he nonetheless cautioned his listeners against "too much of a good thing." Colored people, like other classes of Americans, were beginning to "run wild about the higher culture." The fault seemed to be widespread throughout society, and many fond parents were ruining their children by craving for them one kind of education and neglecting another, which was at least "quite as important." On the one hand, Crummell recognized the need for a class of "trained and superior men and women" who would constitute a "cultured and refined" level of society, but this was no need for "disproportion or extravagance." Thus, he recognized the need for leaders and thinkers, but identified "industry and practicality" as the "greater, wider need of the race."[13]

Crummell made it clear, however, that he had never intended to disparage the pursuit of classical education with the founding of the American Negro Academy, which was one of a number of societies established by African Americans during the nineteenth century to encourage the life of the mind and defend black Americans from charges of intellectual and moral inferiority. Crummell's academy, however, was organized in such a way as to make clear its opposition to Booker T. Washington's educational theories and the philosophical materialism on which they were based.[14] Members of this academy, like Du Bois, Ferris, and Crummell, advocated an assertive position on civil rights. In his first annual address before the American Negro Academy, Crummell said:

> Labor, just like eating and drinking, is one of the inevitabilities of life; one of its positive necessities. And the Negro has had it for centuries; but it has never given him manhood. . . . The great need of the Negro in our day and time is intelligent impatience at the exploitation of his labor. . . . What he needs is CIVILIZATION. He needs the increase of his higher wants, of his mental and spiritual needs. . . . The Negro mind, imprisoned for nigh three hundred years, needs breadth and freedom, largeness, altitude, and elasticity; not stint nor rigidity, nor contractedness.[15]

It has been observed that the passing of Frederick Douglass in the spring of 1895 marked the end of an era in black American political ideology, and cleared the way for Booker T. Washington's assumption of the race's symbolic leadership.[16] Washington's Atlanta Exposition Address, delivered later that year, marked a departure from the crusading idealism of the abolitionist era in the direction of a materialistic, and occasionally servile, pragmatism. The manifesto was nonetheless initially hailed by the young W. E. B. Du Bois as "a phenomenal success" and "a word fitly spoken." Edward W. Blyden sent Washington his pontifical congratulations on his "wonderful address," calling him the new "Father of his country" and adding, "your work in some respects is greater than his," for while George Washington freed one race from foreign domination, Booker T. Washington was destined "to free two races from false views of life." William J. Cansler, a black teacher in Knoxville, Tennessee, bestowed a more realistic distinction on Washington, declaring, "Upon you has fallen the mantle of the illustrious [Frederick] Douglas[s], to you we accord the title as leader, all intelligent and thinking colored men will follow."

The first stirrings of the American Negro Academy in 1896 beto-

kened an implicit denial of both the symbolic leadership of Douglass
and the belief that his mantle should be passed on to Washington.[17]
The idea of a national academy was first proposed to Alexander
Crummell by William H. Crogman and Richard R. Wright in 1894,
but Crummell is reported to have termed it "completely impractica-
ble."[18] Why he should have expressed such a view is unclear, but
perhaps he was correct, because the academy never did manage to
become the center of black American literary and intellectual activity. It is unlikely that Douglass would have hailed the founding of an
American Negro Academy with enthusiasm. He had often expressed
opposition to institutional separatism, and Alexander Crummell possibly sensed that such a national organization would have lacked
authority without Douglass's support. Within months of Douglass's
death, however, Crummell moved to implement the idea.

In his later years, Douglass had been almost paranoid in his opposition to black institutional separatism. Crummell took issue with
him and had made his position clear in an essay called "The Social
Principle Among a People." He spoke against "the dogma which I
have heard frequently from the lips of leaders, personal and dear,
but mistaken, friends, that the colored people of this country should
forget as soon as possible, that they are colored people." He reminded his audience, in case they needed to be reminded, that black
people were denied travel accommodation, employment opportunities, and the right to vote. One might "Turn madman, and go into
a lunatic asylum, and then, perchance," forget that they were black.

> But not only is this dogma folly, it is disintegrating and so-
> cially destructive. For shut out, for instance, as I am and you
> are from the cultivated social life of the superior classes of this
> country, if I forget that I am a black man, if you ignore the fact
> of race, and we both ostrich-like, stick our heads in the sand,
> or stalk along high-headed oblivious of the actual distinctions
> which do exist in American society, what are you or I to do for
> our social nature? What will become of the measure of social
> life among ourselves which we now possess? Where are we to
> find our friends? Where find our circles for society and cheer-
> ful intercourse? . . . we are a nation set apart in this country.[19]

The academy's ideology was, thus, in some respects, more consistent with Washington's doctrine of accommodation to segregation
than with Douglass's program of social assimilation. Where it differed from Washington's policy was in its absolute insistence on access to the culture-bearing institutions of American bourgeois society. This meant full participation in the life of the mind in America,

to the universities, to concert halls, and to "the rooms where women come and go talking of Michelangelo."[20]

Booker T. Washington was invited to the organizational meeting of the American Negro Academy on March 5, 1897, but it is probable that a number of those who did attend were relieved that he begged off, pleading prior commitments. Francis Grimké, who already feared that Crummell and Washington were irreparably estranged, still hoped to act as a go-between and thus encouraged John W. Cromwell to issue the invitation.[21] It may be that Washington felt he had nothing to gain from joining an organization in which he must meet with other black men as equals. Or perhaps he felt, as he would insist on a similar occasion twenty years later, that his presence "might restrict freedom of discussion, and might, also, tend to make the conference go in directions which it would not like to go." Neither Wright nor Crogman were present at the academy's first meeting, despite their authorship of the idea, perhaps having become more fully aware of the political embarrassments involved. Crummell, who was becoming increasingly open in his hostility to Washington, had nothing to lose. He had privately referred to Washington as a racial traitor while expressing public doubts respecting his educational policies.[22] Washington had responded with a swift display of his increasing power, even gaining access to the Episcopal journals as instruments to undermine Crummell's base within his own denomination.

The speedy and unanimous election of Alexander Crummell to the presidency of the academy must be seen within the context of a partisan struggle. If there was any doubt as to this, Crummell promptly removed it by politicizing his opening address, attacking Washington's ideology of economic determinism and industrial materialism. He decried those leaders who "were constantly dogmatizing theories of sense and matter. . . . Blind men! For they fail to see that neither property, nor money, nor station, nor office" were capable of saving the race.[23] In his second address to the convention, Crummell attacked the intellectual pedestrianism of the "Gradgrinds" who said that "the Negro has no business in the higher walks of scholarship."[24]

That evening the academy heard Du Bois's Afrocentric paper entitled "The Conservation of Races," which had been solicited by the organizational committee. It was a declaration that Du Bois intended to support the racial collectivism and separatism of Crummell, whose opposition to the assimilationism of Douglass was well known. The paper was filled with racial romanticism, and its attack on "the individualistic philosophy of the Declaration of Independence and the laissez-faire philosophy of Adam Smith" was more a disavowal of Douglass than of Washington. In fact, there was little, if anything, in the speech that repudiated Washington, for while Crummell and Du Bois disavowed Washington's antiintellectualism, they endorsed his doctrine of self-help, and even his accommodation to some forms of institutional segregation. It was more a public repudiation of Douglass's assimilationism than of Washington's accommodationism.[25]

Du Bois's Afrocentric rhapsody at the academy's first convocation was a manifesto for ethnic separatism and racial exceptionalism, and a call for enlightened despotism within a Pan-African culture. Du Bois presented the document as a "study-in-honor" of Crummell and as a declaration of solidarity with his racial ideals. The address celebrated ideas with which the senior black nationalist had long been associated: the firm belief in collective identity, the preachment of self-help, the unabashed advocacy of racialism. The ideas Du Bois expressed were closer to the spirit of Joseph de Maistre than of Thomas Jefferson, whose libertarian ideas it explicitly criticized.[26]

William H. Ferris made his first impression on African American history during the lengthy discussion following Du Bois's reading of "The Conservation of Races." His reception that occasion, as on many others, was mixed. Ferris took exception to Du Bois's central idea, the need for the African race to make a distinct contribution to human history. He insisted that it would be "not by developing all that is the Negro, but all that will be useful to civilization." Ferris then rambled on over a number of subjects including the cause of the decline of ancient civilizations, which he attributed to the loss of vitality through sexual immorality. It was this "more than anything else that had caused the Persians and the Orientals to decline in vitality." As he continued to wax in prolixity, the stenographer eventually decided "that some of Mr. Ferris's remarks be left out, as nonpertinent." Du Bois interrupted to ask if there would be any limit to discussion, but Ferris heedlessly rambled on.[27]

Ferris's performances were often embarrassing to his associates, but despite his name-dropping, his rambling style, and his repetition of elitist clichés, he was not an ignorant man. The pressures under which he existed have destroyed many a lesser man, regardless of race. His life and writings provide singular insight into the tribulations of a classically educated African American on the eve of the First World War – this even though his personal reflections were flamboyant, affected, and self-consciously straining toward a sophistication that he never quite achieved. Ferris had assimilated from the learned literature of his time a great deal of knowledge about the relationship of Africa, and African peoples, to the larger world of literary and intellectual life.

The American Negro Academy reflected the "cultural literacy" program of Crummell, who, although politically assertive and possessed of a fighting spirit, was decidedly not a man of the people. His sometimes strident racial romanticism was not complemented by any appreciation for the folkways of the black American masses. His elitist ideology was inseparable from his religious opinions, and, as we have seen, he viewed slave culture as degraded and useless, consisting of nothing more than systematic introduction into licentiousness and irresponsibility.[28] The unadulterated native African possessed a certain barbarian vigor, and a spirit of enterprise, which many black Americans had unfortunately lost. Crummell viewed the religion of the masses as dangerously escapist, based as it was on waves of revivalism that were purely emotional. It represented an obsession with spirit possession, a reliance on visions of Jesus, and a heretical "antinomianism," a belief that heaven could be attained purely by faith in Jesus' vicarious atonement.[29]

The issue of Crummell's idealism versus Washington's materialism was in the minds of everyone in the assembly. Crummell's inaugural address was reminiscent of the Cambridge Platonism that was revived by William Whewell, whose lectures he had attended while at the university. With an anti-Lockean rhetoric reminiscent of Whewell's, he attacked those men who "are constantly dogmatizing theories of sense and matter as the salvable hope of the race."[30] He had insisted that "neither property, nor money, nor station, nor office, nor lineage [were] vitalizing qualities in the changeless hopes of humanity." It was the ability to "grasp the grand conceptions of being" that would inspire a people to change their destinies. It was "the absorption of a people, of a nation, of a race, in large majestic and abiding things that lift[ed] them up to the skies." He read the history of Europe as the triumph of lofty ideals of Aristotle, Plato, and Euclid. "These were the great idealists; and as such, they were the great progenitors of all modern civilization, the majestic agents of God for the civil upbuilding of men and nations. For civilization is in its origins, ideal."[31]

Crummell's philosophical idealism was observed by contemporaries. In the opinion of T. G. Steward, who was present at the meeting of March 5, the conflict between Crummell and Washington originated in basic philosophical differences. Crummell was a Platonic idealist, whereas the practical Washington belonged, in Steward's view, to an Aristotelian tradition. "Washington says a man's life depends upon what he has," continued Stewart; "Crummell says life is but the manifestation of what a man is. Washington is practical and objective; Crummell is idealistic and subjective. Washington looks at the branches and deals with applications; Crummell studies the root and the trunk and deals with principles. Washington is a disciple of Aristotle; Crummell is a follower of Socrates and Plato." This was more than inflated rhetoric. The academy ideology reflected Crummell's long-standing opposition to Jeffersonian egalitarianism and Lockean materialism. During his years at Cambridge, Crummell had been influenced by the lectures of William Whewell, who sought to revitalize the Cambridge Platonism of the nineteenth century. Du Bois was not a Cambridge Platonic idealist; he was, however, a Berlin-educated, Hegel-influenced idealist, and a Hegelian strain is readily identifiable in his theory of history and the quasi-religious vignettes of *Darkwater*.[32]

There can be no doubt as to Crummell's belief that ideas were the forces that drove history, and that it was the responsibility of educated leadership to give ideas substance in everyday life. The educated classes had a duty consisting of "lifting up this people of ours to the grand plane of civilization . . . to a height of noble thought, grand civility, a chaste and elevating culture [and] refinement."[33] The ideas that were responsible for the glory of civilization were present from all eternity in the mind of God, and given historical expression through the progress of civilization. "The Conservation of Races" was a restatement of a mystical Christian idea that Crummell had long preached, the idea that races were "the organisms and ordinance of God." In Crummell's ideology, as in "The Conservation of Races," we find the idea that each race represented an expression of some divine ideal or plan for the advancement of civilization. There could be no doubt, as Du Bois put it, "as to the widespread prevalence of the race idea, the race spirit, the race ideal."

The problem of idealism and the practicality of conserving races within the environmental reality of the United States were taken up in the discussion that ensued. One extemporaneous commentator from the floor opined that while "in an academy the only ideas will be idealistic ideas," Du Bois's position was "too idealistic." He did not see how black people could "live in the United States and still maintain the identity of the race." He did not believe that the ideal of racial integrity was destined to survive in the material environment. The "law of environment" and the fact that "mere race distinctions are of no consequence" seemed to indicate that "here on the American continent, where we have a conglomeration of the races of the world, it is a fact that we are erasing these distinctions."[34] Du Bois and his audience had ample evidence that these distinctions were not being erased; history seemed to be moving in exactly the opposite direction as the Supreme Court handed down its *Plessy* v. *Ferguson* decision of 1896.

The cultural literacy debate among Afro-Americans began as a contest between the venerable, erudite British-educated black nationalist Alexander Crummell and the brilliant young Machiavellian Booker T. Washington. Though each in his own way sought to bring enlightenment to the masses, Crummell was convinced that black leadership's mission was to descend "from the heights of Olympus, lifting up the masses "to the grand plane of civilization," bringing them up to the height of "noble thought, grand civility, a chaste and elevating culture, refinement, and the impulses of irrepressible progress." The academy attacked not only Washington's materialism and economic determinism, but the idea of a "Negro Curriculum," the idea that education should be whittled down to meet only the most basic of practical needs of the moment, rather than preparing African Americans for new adventures in education. The academicians' quarrel with Washington was not that he taught basic skills to country schoolchildren, but that he disparaged the importance of pushing them to their limits in the direction of cultural literacy. Crummell, Ferris, and Du Bois advocated education in the broad contours of Western civilization, approached through history, the literary disciplines, and the social sciences. The problem with the position of the academy was its undue respect for a "gentleman's" education, an excessive regard for the mastery of Latin declensions and Greek syntax.

Washington's educational theories were, arguably, more "progressive" in some respects than those of Crummell's academicians. Washington did, in fact, anticipate one of the cardinal principles of Deweyan progressive education when he encouraged learning by experience. Rather than stifle his pupils with rote memorization of case endings, he tried to impress them with the joys of practical knowledge. Fundamental training in personal hygiene, English grammar, and basic mathematics constituted the needs of the overwhelming majority of black children, and the Bookerites were committed to providing for these. He understood, nonetheless, an obligation to broaden his pupil's cultural horizons, to bring to children of slaves in isolated backwaters some knowledge of the larger world and their places in it.

Washington also understood that teaching cultural literacy in the rural South might call for flexible methods, as the following anecdote illustrates. He admitted that his methods up to a certain point in time had reflected the fashion of the day, and consisted of asking the pupils to learn and then recite what was in their textbook. He had been involved in "a rather stupid geography lesson" that consisted of "asking my pupils a lot of dull and tiresome questions, getting them to define and name lakes, capes, peninsulas, islands and so forth." The students had shown little interest and the day was hot and sultry, so when the recess period came, Washington was "as anxious as the children to get outside of the close and stuffy room and into the open air."

The school was near a piece of wet and marshy land, and as soon as the door was opened, the children scampered off into the marshes to wade in the cool water, and Washington, becoming "infected with the general fever," soon found himself "following the children at a rapid rate and entering into the full enjoyment of the . . . vivid tingling sense of the living out-doors." Soon, he noted that one of the boys who had been among the dullest in the classroom became the leader of a sort of exploring party.

> Under his leadership we began to discover, as we waded along the stream, dozens of islands, capes, and peninsulas, with here and there a little lake or bay, which, as some of the pupils pointed out, would furnish a safe harbour for ships if the stream were only large enough. Soon every one of the children was busy pointing out and naming the natural divisions of land and water. And then, after a few days, we got pieces of wood and bark and let them float down the stream; we imagined them to be great ships carrying their cargoes of merchandise from one part of the world to another. We studied the way the stream wandered about in the level land, and noticed how the little sand bars and the corresponding harbours were formed by the particles of sand and earth which were rolled down by the stream. We located cities on these harbours and tried to find water-power where we might build up manufacturing centers.[35]

This congenial self-portrait of the man who later came to be known as the aloof, Machiavellian manipulator of the Tuskegee machine, is no doubt self-flattering, but in some sense accurate. The principles tested here on elementary pupils were consistent with those that Washington later established at Tuskegee, where students were encouraged to learn by doing, and where abstract learning was supplemented by practical experience. It is not surprising that the final result of this lesson in geography was to evolve in the direction of economics, so that the end of geography was to be an understanding of shipping, commerce, industrialization, urbanization, and manufacturing.

The commitment to cultural literacy demonstrated in Washington's narrative was impressive in two ways. First, it assumed, a priori, that the children of peasants were entitled to receive the broadening knowledge of which elementary geography was symbolic. Second, it demonstrated Washington's sensitive and practical teaching methods, well before John Dewey published *My Pedagogic Creed.* If Washington's pupils became more culturally literate that afternoon, their success demonstrated that Washington's much maligned concept of "working with the hands" was not inimical to book learning. The ability of elementary pupils to apply geological terms to the miniature lakes, capes, and peninsulas in the wetlands adjacent to their school presupposed their familiarity with basic concepts that had been taught them during the preceding morning. Without prior knowledge of geography, the idea of making a game of their lesson would never have occurred to them. The story implies the mutually reinforcing nature of classical and pragmatic teaching methods, and we may be certain that the canny Washington had long deliberated over his story's implications.[36]

Although Washington was caricatured as antiintellectual by some of his opponents, his efforts were radical and dangerous for the time and place in which he had chosen to work. He was well aware that white supremacists opposed his efforts, even at such a modest level. Thomas Dixon, author of *The Klansman,* had clearly penetrated beneath the surface and had achieved an accurate reading of Washington's educational philosophy.

> Mr. Washington is not training Negroes to take their place in the industrial system of the South in which the white man can direct or control him. He is not training his students to be servants and come at the beck and call of any man. He is training them *all* to be masters of men, to be independent, to own and operate their own industries, plant their own fields, buy and sell their own goods, and in every shape and form destroy the last vestige of dependence on the white man for anything.[37]

Washington did, in fact, promote cultural literacy collaterally with economic aspiration; his mask of modesty concealed the radical goal of broadening horizons and expanding minds. His methods were as progressive as those of John Dewey or Maria Montessori.

W. E. B. Du Bois's classic, *The Souls of Black Folk,* may be measured against the spirit of Washington's woodland idyll. Confronted with the stolid resistance of some of the African American peasantry to liberal education, Du Bois sometimes attempted to persuade them with abstract arguments.

> I loved my school, and the fine faith the children had in the wisdom of their teacher was truly marvelous. We read and spelled together, wrote a little, picked flowers, sang, and listened to stories of the world beyond the hill. At times the school would dwindle away, and . . . When the Lawrences stopped, I knew that the doubts of the old folks about booklearning had conquered again, and so, toiling up the hill, and getting as far into the cabin as possible, I put Cicero's *pro Archia Poeta* "into the simplest English possible [which] usually convinced them – for a week or so."[38]

The self-mockery with which Du Bois described his youthful adventures as a Tennessee schoolteacher was perhaps a bit too stringent. Like Washington, he knew that the experiences of African Americans had left many of them tragically alienated from the benefits of a generous and liberal education. Du Bois and his "Talented Tenth," might attempt to uplift the masses to culture's Olympian heights – to paraphrase Crummell's metaphor – but, alas, all too often their well-meaning efforts were greeted with a combination of respectful silence or good-natured indifference.[39]

Nonetheless, the exemplars of the Talented Tenth who were represented in the American Negro Academy were intrepidly committed to their civilizing mission. William S. Scarborough, professor of classics at Wilberforce University, set forth representative ideas in his manifesto on "The Educated Negro and His Mission." The document revealed the cosmopolitan, or Eurocentric, concerns of the academy, and asserted that there could be no racially specific definitions of a scholar.

> The Negro who is an educated man must be a practical man, and zealous in getting to work to show that thinking and doing go together. . . . to show that the educated man has taken for his motto that highest one – "Ich dien" – I serve – a service by leadership and made both necessary and fitting by attainments and worth.
>
> This idea of service to the race is peculiarly the mission of the educated Negro. In no other way can education be justified for the race.[40]

The sources Scarborough cited and the concerns he expressed indicated a blending of the ideals of racial mission and cosmopolitanism. "There are no two definitions of a scholar to be applied to different races," wrote Scarborough in the same essay. "The Negro scholar must be the same as any other – endowed as Milton would have him with a "complete and generous education." Members of the American Negro Academy were obliged to promote the high cultural tradition, but along with a world view sympathetic to the universal uplift of African peoples. The academy was Eurocentric in the sense that it valorized Milton and the ancient classics, but it was Afrocentric in that it sought to promote the interests of African peoples and to validate their world view.

William H. Ferris's *The African Abroad* was the most impressive blending of Afrocentric and cosmopolitan ideals produced by an academy member, but it must be said that Ferris's writings demonstrate the difficulty of defining exactly what is meant by Afrocentrism. Certainly Ferris can be forced into the stereotype of the black chauvinist, but that is to distort his ideological purpose. His life was an illustration of the fact that political black nationalism is seldom at odds with cultural assimilation, and Ferris's volumes were thoroughly immersed in the elitist, Eurocentric traditions. They were cosmopolitan yet black nationalistic, and sought to encourage black interaction with Western civilization. Ferris's Afrocentrism did not imply self-limitation, strident ethnochauvinism, intellectual ghettoization, or a sour-grapes attitude toward Caucasian accomplishments.

The African Abroad revealed an impressive knowledge of contemporary African and Afro-Caribbean writers, who participated in the Afrocentric tradition. One chapter contained a catalogue of "Some Prominent Colored People of Today" and another a list of "Some Distinguished Foreign Negroes." Ferris's purpose was to guide present and future researchers in the discovery of names and sources. Among those Afrocentric scholars he mentioned were P. K. Isaka Seme of South Africa, Mojola Agbebi of Lagos, Duse Mohamed of Sudan, and Arthur A. Schomburg, a West Indian. With some of these figures, Ferris interacted closely; others, he apparently knew by name only. His familiarity with the activities of such a far-flung fraternity made him a useful reporter on the Pan-African movement during the 1920s as he became active in the Garvey movement. His theoretical and biographical essays seem logical places to begin any study of the international black intellectual community – their collateral involvement is both in the Western humanistic tradition and in Afrocentrism.[41]

Throughout *The African Abroad,* Ferris quoted extensively from white authors whom he had read on the subject of African history. Volney made a mandatory appearance, of course, but Ferris was far more interested in the speculations of recent and contemporary authors. Franz Boas was cited on African prehistory, and mention was made of his assertion that black Africans were smelting iron while Europe lingered in a state of savagery. Although he was interested in Egypt, and while he accepted the opinion of Volney that the ancient Egyptians had been black, Ferris was far more interested in Ethiopia. He paid careful attention to the work of G. A. Hoskins, *Travels in Ethiopia above the Second Cataract of the Nile.* Browsing the historical works that Ferris excerpted or paraphrased in his volume, one witnesses the extent to which the same arguments, based on the same sources, have been repeatedly utilized by both the proponents and the opponents of black inferiority since the eighteenth century. Ferris was sometimes undiscriminating in his use of sources and tendentious in his arguments, but he was no worse than those who opposed him. He responded to the arguments of Hoskins that the ancient Ethiopians were not Negroes with arguments that seem perfectly commonsensical.[42]

> Mr. Hoskins said that the Ethiopians represent themselves with red skin, flowing hair, and Egyptian features rather than with the black complexions, receding forehead, woolly hair, thick lips and flat noses of the African Negro as he is depicted in school geographies. But I have met a score of native Africans, students in English and American universities, and none look like the African depicted in geographies and works of ethnology.

Who and what was a Negro? The question was a persistent one. In many geography books, only Africans who demonstrated extreme prognathism – and usually represented by drawings, rather than photographs – were considered "typical." White America continued a very inclusive definition of "Negro" when speaking of African Americans; a very exclusive definition when speaking of East Africa. That, of course, had been a central irony of the vindicationist argument all along. In the nineteenth century, the Hamitic hypothesis had been a poetic biblical argument as easily manipulated by blacks as by whites; in the twentieth, it was regenerated as a pseudoscientific theory, developed in order to transmogrify black peoples into whites. Ferris was thus in that tradition of black vindicationists who creatively found ways of converting the Hamitic hypothesis to their own ends.

To effect his transformation of the Hamitic hypothesis, and to bolster his credibility, Ferris reprinted extensively from works by well-credentialed anthropologists. He devoted the first three chapters of *The African Abroad*, volume two, to discussions of prehistoric contributions of Africanoid people to civilization. He relied heavily on the writings of anthropologists William Z. Ripley and Giuseppe Sergi. Ferris's attacks on the held views of white supremacy employed a dual strategy. He argued, on the one hand, that there were no pure or fixed races, but he averred on the other that the primal races of Europe, according to the known archeological evidence, revealed Africanoid physiognomy.[43]

Far from becoming a participant in racist mythologies or attempting to develop a theory of black supremacy, Ferris accepted a position consistent with the progressivism of his day when he praised William Z. Ripley for showing "that separate and distinct races have no existence except in the heated imaginations of the Bourbons of the South." His reading led him to the belief that the raciology used to separate Africans from all contributions to human progress was not scientifically supportable. He also was aware that the definitions of races were so unfounded that it was impossible to attribute the origins of civilization to any existing group. He insisted, as good Afrocentrists usually do, that the first civilizations, flourishing in the river valleys of Africa and the Middle East, were built by peoples with detectable traces of "Negro blood." At the same time, he subscribed to the idea that race is essentially myth.[44]

Ferris, like many authors, was inclined to hedge his bets. Thus he worked to employ anthropology as an argument for the unity of the human species and, simultaneously, as an argument to demonstrate the contributions of Africans to world history. Although he was not a trained archeologist, Ferris had studied sociology at Yale with the famous social Darwinist William Graham Sumner, and thought highly of his *Folkways*, an early and influential treatment of what later came to be called "cultural relativism." Because Sumner was a social Darwinist, he is frequently associated with theories of racism and imperialism that dominated much American thought during the years of his greatest influence. But Sumner opposed imperialism, and, as we shall see in Chapter 7, his ideas on race and ethnicity were more complex than is usually supposed. Ferris credited him with teaching his students "not to accept all that we read in books on sociology, anthropology, and ethnology.[45]

Ferris's efforts to deconstruct the idea of race anticipated those of J. A. Rogers, who became, as Ferris later did, a literary editor at Marcus Garvey's *Negro World*. As a popularizer of African and Afro-American history, Rogers retains an unrivaled position in black popular culture. His work was occasionally flamboyant, but hardly bizarre, as he made sarcastic claims regarding the possibility of "Negro" ancestry for five American presidents, or the African heritage of Beethoven. It is sometimes difficult to tell just how seriously Rogers intends to be taken, but his work has provided much amusement to generations of African Americans. I suspect that his tone is essentially ironic, and that it epitomizes the underlying bitter joke common to so much racial vindicationism. There really is no such thing as a Negro, or as Marcus Garvey put it, with a sarcasm that humorless white supremacists cannot appreciate,

> the custom of these anthropologists is whenever a black man, whether he be Moroccan, Algerian, Senegalese or what not, accomplishes anything of importance, he is no longer a Negro. The question, therefore, suggests itself, "Who and what is a Negro?" The answer is, "A Negro is a person of dark complexion or race, who has not accomplished anything and to whom others are not obligated for any useful service."[46]

Garveyites like William H. Ferris preserved Blyden and Crummell's nineteenth-century agenda of seeking to "civilize," or "uplift," or "improve" Africa. They did not fully appreciate the implications of Sumner's incipient cultural relativism, nor could they anticipate the thrust of early-twentieth-century thinking in which a new generation would insist that Africa was fortunate for not having been "civilized." They would hold up the ideal of a soft Motherland, which had been blessed in its escape from the historical process of "Civilization," rather than a virile Fatherland, rooted in the ideal of Tacitus's barbarians. But if romancing the primitivist ideal began to touch the thinking of Africans and "Africans Abroad" during these years, the traditional idea of attaining "civilization" lingered on. The early modernist period (regardless of how it is defined) is therefore extraordinarily rich with historical problems owing to the absolute inconsistency with which Africans and Africans of the diaspora either denied or attempted to reconcile ambiguities, ambivalencies, and contradictions.

Ferris's ambitious volumes have their strengths, and their weaknesses as well. Their strengths represent Ferris's ability, despite his clerical training, to escape the religious straitjacket that had often restricted the intellectual movements of his nineteenth-century predecessors. He conceived the Bible as a fairly reliable historical source, but he weighed the evidences of the Bible against the findings of modern anthropology. Another strength of Ferris's work was its encyclopedic quality; it is a unique introduction to the knowledge of its times relating to African people. Although its author was a vindicationist, his appraisals of contemporary scholarship were fair and objective and framed in the language of the social sciences.

The African Abroad is imbued, nonetheless, with certain conceptual weaknesses, which reflect the author's pre–First World War perspective. Ferris did not address popular culture, folk culture, or the cult of primitivism, all of which were emerging in the modernistic world of the arts and were soon to have their impact on the social sciences. This should not be surprising, since primitivism had made its appearance in France long before it began to affect the English-speaking world. Even in France, primitivism thrived in the arts before it influenced the social sciences; it appeared in the paintings of Paul Gauguin before it cropped up in the popular ethnology of Jean Finot.[47]

In the years following the First World War, Africans and Afro-Americans became increasingly aware of the European crisis of self-confidence, and the fragility of Western civilization. The point has been repeatedly made in this volume that European intellectuals, from the time of Wagner's flourishing to that of Stravinski's, have attempted to rediscover the primitive vigor somewhere in their ancestral past. This tendency became more pronounced as intellectuals began seeking for some means to revitalize the culturally impoverished postwar civilization. This resulted in two seemingly contradictory but interdependent movements – one of which celebrated everything that was modern and progressive; another that valorized everything that was natural and primitive.[48]

This contradictory worship of the modern and the primitive generated an interesting and curious tension within Pan-African thought – for as Afrocentrists absorbed the prevailing critical attitudes toward European civilization and modern progress, they were forced to participate in the crisis of Western self-confidence. Ferris, especially during and after the First World War, had to stifle a hostility to the "dead white males" who had created the Western intellectual tradition. Typical of the African vindicationists of his generation, he experienced the Garveyite impulse to repudiate the Western tradition in order to defend the African. On the other hand, he was in the habit of using his Afrocentric arguments to demonstrate the participation of black people in the common heritage of Western civilization. Ferris reflected the Prufrockian contradictions and complexities of modern consciousness.

Although cosmopolitanism and Afrocentrism are often seen today as conflicting agendas in the education of black Americans, they were not necessarily viewed in this way by black nationalists at the beginning of this century. In fact, a figure like Ferris illustrates that the black masses are receptive to the values of the white bourgeoisie. Ferris's work with several black newspapers enabled him to be a useful reinforcer of Anglo-American bourgeois values among the Afro-Americans who conceived themselves as being upwardly mobile. Particularly as literary editor of *Negro World* during the 1920s, Ferris demonstrated the cosmopolitanism of Garveyism, and demonstrated that many of the cultural traits usually seen as the special province of educated elites were attractive to the black masses.[49]

Contemporary ideological biases, on the right and, regrettably, on the left as well, often do an injustice to African American authors by advancing "presentist" interpretations of their writings. The ideological biases of academic conservatives like Professor Lefkowitz are far more pernicious than those of leftists revealing an open contempt for or condescension toward black writers and the ideas they express. Left-liberals, like Professor Appiah, often attack works such as "The Conservation of Races" or *The African Abroad* from a presentist perspective, ignoring the fact that the programs of a hundred years ago focused on a set of social goals that seemed appropriate at the time. Racial boosters, in their quest for heroes and role models, indiscriminately praise everything African Americans have written. Those in this latter category are often guilty of ignoring ideas that are offensive to present-day tastes. In fact, early Afrocentrism is infused with elitism and is consciously directed at the institutionalization of high-cultural racial mythology.

Nowhere did the aspirations of William H. Ferris appear more preposterous than when he invented the term "Negrosaxon." He devoted a chapter of *The African Abroad* to the subject of "Why the term 'Negrosaxon,' or Colored, better Characterizes the Colored People of Mixed Descent in America than the term Negro."

> The term "Negro" suggests physical and spiritual kinship to the ape, the monkey, the baboon, the chimpanzee, the ourangoutan, and gorilla. The term "Negrosaxon" denotes the physical kinship of half of the colored people of America and the spiritual kinship of ninety per cent of the colored people of America to the noble Anglo-Saxon race.[50]

The reader wishes desperately to believe that Ferris was being ironic, but after many careful readings one is forced to the embarrassing acceptance of the fact that Ferris was excruciatingly serious. Recognizing that many African Americans, such as Crummell, would never accept a term that seemed to boast of bastardy, Ferris mercifully abandoned it. We are relieved to find him several years later accepting the position of the Garvey movement, which discouraged the use of terms such as "colored" and "Afro-American" and promoted "black," "African," and "Negro." It should be neither surprising nor embarrassing that a black man, born only five years after the abolition of slavery, should carry a few psychological scars. It is surprising that he bore so few – being a product of a society whose founding philosopher had compared black men to orangutans, and advised shipping the entire population back to Africa.[51]

In the Garvey movement, Ferris did what he could to promote high culture and cosmopolitanism among African Americans. In Marcus Garvey he found a willing collaborator in the enterprise of making the wider world of economics, politics, and literature more accessible to black Americans. It should never be forgotten that Garveyism embodied a splendid contradiction. In constant dialectic with its black particularism, the movement contained a rhetoric of universalism. The presence of cultural assimilationists like Ferris in positions of influence within the movement demonstrates the complexity of its attitudes to race and its ability to merge Afrocentric and Eurocentric world views. In *The African Abroad* and later as editor of *Negro World,* Ferris generously noted the Africans and African Americans who, in his view, had made notable contributions to Western culture, mostly in the world of arts and letters. His purpose was never to promote an isolation of Africans from other peoples, but to demonstrate the willingness and capacity of his contemporaries to assimilate to Euro-American manners and taste, while retaining a commitment to the political empowerment of the Pan-African world.

In Ferris's two volumes of speeches, pep talks, book reviews, philosophical meanderings, and lengthy – but scrupulously acknowledged – excerpts from the scholarship of others, there is more than a mere scholarly exercise. There is insight into the mind of the Talented Tenth far more poignant than anything available in the writings of Du Bois. Some painfully moving lines occur, as in "A Chapter from my Autobiography – My Boyish Dreams and Youthful Resolutions," where the author says:

> All I am or ever hope to be is expressed in this volume. It was not wholly written from other books, for I left my library behind me during my eleven months' lecture tour through the South. My only literary companions were a slender volume containing selections from Ruskin's "Modern Painters" and a little pamphlet upon "The Inspiration of the Bible." This book, then, was written out of my heart, out of my experience with men and women. It expresses my life dreams, hopes and aspirations. Upon this volume, then, I will stake the reality or unreality of my youthful dreams and experiences.[52]

If students of the history of Afrocentrism can attempt to understand the agony of "the African abroad" with compassion, and with an appreciation for irony, if they can appreciate that African Americans are endowed by their experience with a profoundly bitter sense of humor, they will perhaps come to a more sympathetic view of the ungainly pilgrimage of William H. Ferris, who, although he died impoverished and alone, devoted his life to the pursuit of a humane and liberal ideal of culture, an obsession that was tragically comic but quixotically heroic.

7

CALIBAN'S UTOPIA

MODERNISM, RELATIVISM, AND PRIMITIVISM

====

"Generally, his appearance was repulsive, Caliban like," wrote W. A. Domingo on observing a nervous and shaking Marcus Garvey address a New York gathering in April 1916. He gave the impression of the typical immigrant bumpkin, on first arriving in the metropolis, "dressed in a much crumpled and misfitting suit," and at one point falling off the stage. But Garvey learned quickly, and by late autumn of that year the "ambitious, wide-awake and energetic" young man had made a mighty impression on audiences throughout the United States as an accomplished lecturer. He preached the doctrine of "rehabilitating Africa in the interest of the Negro." His attentive sympathizers were made up of various types who were predisposed to hear his message describing "The Tragedy of White Injustice." He appealed, significantly, to intellectuals like William H. Ferris, who first heard him speak in Chicago while working there as associate editor of a magazine called *The Champion*, and to John E. Bruce, also a Crummell protégé. But Garvey's message appealed not only to the marginalized intellectual elite; it also appealed to the working class, the petit bourgeoisie, and the displaced peasants from the rural South, many of whom were born before the Civil War and could recall slavery.[1]

In 1921 Ferris became assistant president general of the Universal Negro Improvement Association (UNIA), which Garvey had founded to promote his plans for the redemption of Africa and the economic salvation of the African race. The organization operated numerous businesses, and sold stock in an ill-fated Black Star Line, which planned to operate as a transatlantic shipping corporation. It was widely believed that the purpose of "Garveyism," as the movement came to be called, was the complete repatriation of the African American population in Africa. The aims were not quite that clear-cut, and repatriation was never the only element of the UNIA program. The purpose was to establish black economic power, centered in an African geopolitical base. The organization also had a paramilitary arm. The Black Star Line purchased several ships, some of which were unseaworthy, and the enterprise eventually collapsed under the weight of administrative incompetency. In two areas, however, Garvey demonstrated real genius. These were journalism and publicity, and he had arrived in America with training and experience in both.

Garvey was drawn to that stream in Afrocentric vindicationism which insisted that the ancient Egyptians had been black, but for Garvey, as for many people of his mind-set, "black" could be a flexible metaphor. Sometimes "black" meant "black" – purely, physically, unadulteratedly, pigmentationally black – in other words, "Negro," and he could use the term in such a way as to exclude and heap contempt on mulattoes. At other times, "black" could be used broadly and metaphorically to include not only mulattoes but Asians, Africans – at times, even Jews.[2] What was important to Garvey was to undermine the myth of Teutonic supremacy, which lay at the roots of white supremacy as he had experienced it in the United States and during several years he had spent in London. This, and only this, was the purpose of identifying Tutankhamen as a black man, or for his claim that "the Negro once ruled the world, when white men were savages and barbarians living in caves." He was understandably disgusted by newspaper reports such as the one he described in the following:

> Professor George A. Kersnor, head of the Harvard-Boston expedition to the Egyptian Soudan, returned to America early in 1923 and, after describing the genius of the Ethiopians and their high culture during the period of 750 B.C. to 350 A.D. in middle Africa, he declared the Ethiopians were not African Negroes. He described them as dark colored races . . . showing a mixture of black blood. Imagine a dark colored race . . . showing a mixture of black blood. Imagine a dark colored man in middle Africa being anything else but a Negro.[3]

When Garvey accused whites of using every means to keep Negroes in ignorance of their past, he struck a vital chord. It cannot be overstressed that slavery was still a living memory in the minds of many Garvey supporters and fellow travelers. A Baltimore slave, born in 1845, would have been twenty at the time of his or her emancipation by constitutional amendment, and at the age of seventy-one could have attended a Garveyite rally. Most of Garvey's followers had never been enslaved themselves, but many were the children of slaves, who had been forbidden to learn reading, writing, or any form of history. Many Garvey sympathizers had grown up in the rural South, a region that effectively discouraged literacy among its black population. African Americans did not need Garvey to convince them that some portion of their legacy had been stolen. To speak to black audiences of a deliberate white conspiracy for the suppression of knowledge was more than mystical Afrocentrism, more than metaphor.

> For two hundred and fifty years they never taught us any lessons except that of the white man's. They hid the very Christian bible and religion from us except that which told us that black men were created to be hewers of wood and drawers of water. For two hundred and fifty years they used us for slavery and serfdom, but there is a day of reckoning and there is a God almighty.[4]

Inspired by his early reading in the works of Blyden, his contact with Sudanese nationalist Duse Mohammed Ali, his grudging admiration for some of the writings of Du Bois, and his later contact with Ferris and Bruce, Garvey was psychologically primed to engage in Egyptocentric rhetoric. During the three years of his confinement in Atlanta penitentiary, after the collapse of his extravagantly mismanaged financial empire, he published a collection of verse, *The Tragedy of White Injustice*. Among the devices of poetic diction, hyperbole was perhaps the one for which Garvey demonstrated the most pronounced talent.

> Millenniums ago, when the white man slept,
> The great torch of light Asia kept.
> Africa at various periods shone
> Above them all as bright as the noonday sun;
> Coming from the darkened cave and hut,
> The white man opened the gate that was shut.

> Gradually light bore down upon him
> The ancient savage who was once dim;
> When he commenced to see and move around,
> He found the book of knowledge on the ground . . .

Garvey's Africa-centered program made him and his movement paradigmatic of Afrocentrism, but it would be incorrect to make him the yardstick against which all other Afrocentric activities must be measured. His cultural program was simply a repetition of ideas that African American publications had featured since the early nineteenth century. Garvey did not commonly pay tribute to the anthropological variety of Afrocentrism; he showed little tendency to discuss, let alone celebrate, the New World retention of African folk traits. Anthropological Afrocentrism, as we shall presently see, was beginning to figure prominently in the writings of Du Bois and other "cultural retentionists." Garvey's Afrocentrism was almost exclusively "high cultural," and therefore committed to the commemoration of Nilotic cultures as the sources of world civilization. Garvey's ideology clearly had need for a monumental past, and he had no inclination to question the idea that city-building empires were superior to other cultures.

Garvey accepted the traditional Afrocentric goal that had developed throughout the nineteenth century, and sought to establish in Africa "a grand center for Negro Nationality."[5] He seemed, at times, to emulate uncritically the values of European nationalism, during a period when those values were beginning to be questioned. We cannot rid ourselves of the image of him in his *fin de siècle* military garb associated with the pageantry of imperial Europe. His conception of African liberation seems melodramatic, romantic, sentimental, and ironically "Eurocentric." The obstacle to his goal of Pan-African unity existed not only because of white opposition, but because of cultural and political differences, many of them legitimate, among various African populations. Nonetheless, there was a commonsense basis to Garvey's Pan-African economic and political theories. Like Booker T. Washington, whom he much admired, Garvey recognized that moral suasion alone could not alleviate the "Negro's problems," and that African peoples must acquire economic and industrial power. The problems created by slavery, colonialism and racism would never be solved purely on the basis of Frederick Douglass's program of constant agitation from a position of powerless morality.[6]

As had Delany before him, Garvey attempted to analyze the sources of Europe's imperial power and industrial might. It seemed clear to him that the ability of France and England to expand their imperial dominions over darker peoples was not due to any innate superiority, but to the mastery of certain laws of nature that they had come to understand. They were, in short, more politically disciplined, more technically sophisticated, and more habituated to literary culture than the colored peoples they dominated. The difficulties of the black world were therefore to be alleviated neither through protest, nor through submission, but through discipline and organization. The cultivation of racial ideals of patriotism and unity would awaken Africans to the necessity of competition with Asians and Europeans. Garvey believed that African peoples must accept the responsibility for throwing off their own shackles, rather than plead for emancipation. They would never accomplish this, however, so long as they persisted in "the looseness, laxity, and immorality that are peculiar to our group."[7]

Garvey was by no means uncritical of Europeans, although he admired their industrial efficiency and military prowess. He certainly was aware of the critique of postwar Western civilization associated with the spirit of Oswald Spengler's *The Decline of the West.* The wasteland of a world war symbolized the weakness of European civilization and its susceptibility to its own destructive impulses. Garvey made the observation that the human race is "discontented with the civilization of today," at least six years before Freud's *Das Unbehagen in der Kultur* was translated as *Civilization and Its Discontents.* He warned, "If the Negro is not careful he will drink in all the poison of modern civilization and die from the effects of it." He revealed the ambivalence of "classical" black nationalism, which had always existed uneasily between the opposites of cultural assimilationism and political separatism.[8]

Many African American intellectuals at this time were attempting to reconcile in their philosophies the contradictory elements of traditionalism and modernism. Alexander Crummell, writing in the 1880s, had dismissed the traditional values of the Negro American past as "chaff and sawdust," inimical to the quest for black power, and had called for new social institutions and cultural traditions resembling those of whites. Du Bois and Ferris, as we have seen, recognized the need for some assimilation of Euro-American traditions in arts and letters, and it was to this end that much of their writing was directed. Nonetheless, all African American leaders by the end of the First World War would have agreed with Garvey's statement that while it was "true that economically and scientifically certain races are more progressive than others . . . that does not imply superiority." The Anglo-Saxon could not claim superiority merely because "he introduced submarines to destroy life, or the Teuton because he compounded liquid gas to outdo in the art of killing."[9]

It should not be assumed that the brutalities of the First World War, horrific though they were, had led African Americans to a total rejection of Western or American civilization. The criticism of European civilization was, in fact, simply another aspect of black participation in white bourgeois culture. Even before the war, Europe and America were riven by their own internal critiques, and black intellectuals, like white intellectuals, had always been inclined to find fault with modern civilization. Crummell, Blyden, and Delany hoped that someday a glorious new African culture would arise, different from and superior to what was known in Europe or America, but they were always somewhat vague as to how this civilization would look.

In sum, the intellectual tradition of nineteenth-century black nationalism – and this includes Garvey – wavered between hostility and admiration for Victorian bourgeois civilization. Alexander Crummell would not have objected to Matthew Arnold's definition of culture as "the best that has been thought and said in the world," although he recognized the common tendency of Arnold's class to exclude black people from that tradition. His Occasional Paper "Civilization, the Primal Need of the Race" nonetheless encouraged the emulation of Victorian bourgeois culture, as did Du Bois's *The Conservation of Races.* The papers of other academicians lauded European efficiency, the precision of the machine process, and the intellectual certainties of modern science, all the while aware of the Europeans' characterization of them as "Hottentots in bowler hats." African American intellectuals were, in a word, "ambivalent." A central feature of "modernism" is cultural ambivalence, however.

Modernism did not suddenly come into existence during or after the First World War; it arose, as David Shi has observed, during the later decades of the nineteenth century "out of a widespread recognition that Western civilization was entering an era of bewildering change."[10] Of course, every era is an era of bewildering change, and every age of Western civilization has been an age of anxiety. "Sophocles long ago" had heard "the turbid ebb and flow, of human misery," as Matthew Arnold realized, listening to the sea at Dover Beach in 1867.

> The Sea of Faith
> Was once, too, at the full, and round earth's shore
> Lay like the folds of a bright girdle furl'd
> But now I only hear
> Its melancholy, long, withdrawing roar,
> Retreating, to the breath
> Of the long night wind, down the vast edges drear
> And naked shingles of the world. . . .
>
> And we are here as on a darkling plain
> Swept with confused alarms of struggle and flight,
> Where ignorant armies clash by night.

Crummell was certainly acute enough to understand these commonplace sentiments of Matthew Arnold, and he was sufficiently attuned to his intellectual universe not to elevate evangelical faith over Victorian rationalism. While he would never have agreed that the tide of faith was receding, he recognized that traditional faith was confronting new challenges. He observed that life "in its present state, in its material condition, in its political aspects, is full of enigmas."[11] Art and literature represented to him the "agonized strain" and "baffled endeavors" of humanity to penetrate the mysteries of existence. Science constantly discovered "bars and hindrances" to understanding and was "astounded at times at prodigious mysteries." "The fashion of our life, it is true, fills us with perplexities, and breeds constant anxieties." Such ideas do not of themselves constitute "modernism," but they reflect the skepticism that was central to the late Victorian critique of scientific, cultural, and religious absolutism. Traditional Afrocentrism had been founded on absolutist conceptions of history, culture, and progress, and was thus challenged by *fin de siècle* intellectualism.

Traditional Afrocentrism, with its emphasis on winning biblical or Egyptological arguments, was in conflict with modernism, which questioned the meaning of such debates. Classical black nationalism had sought to justify African and African American humanity by demonstrating the participation of black people in civilization. Paradoxically, modernism questioned the value of civilization, itself. Civilization had failed the test of its morality as its religious traditions seemed to weaken; it was failing the test of its sapience as science seemed to be unable to retain the certainty and order it had known in the age of Newton. Culture and civilization seemed to be losing their control over human behavior as the civil order among nations descended into chaos, leaving Europe a heap of broken images on a stark wasteland of barbed wire and shell craters.

Skepticism regarding Euro-American assertions of moral superiority certainly was not alien to the consciousness of African Americans, although they had a tremendous emotional investment in the gradually evolving democratic ethos of America. Traditionally, they had placed their hopes in a Christian perfectionist teleology, in which they took consolation from every indication that America might be developing a more inclusive democracy. American ideals had not yet been realized, and it was natural enough that in the second decade of the twentieth century black intellectuals should reveal a continuing ambivalence respecting American progress and civilization. On the other hand, by the 1920s, African American ideology increasingly displayed a modernist world view, and a forward-looking, almost mystical, confidence in a teleology of racial progress. American society seemed to be progressing toward greater tolerance and fairness in many areas of life. There was hope that racial prejudice, along with other outmoded nineteenth-century superstitions might come to be viewed as old-fashioned. Modern rationalism might, perhaps, lead society to question the racial superstitions of the past, just as it questioned Victorian sexuality and gender roles – just as it seemed to be questioning traditional standards of taste in music, literature, and the plastic arts.

Modernism implied a selective nostalgia for certain elements of the past, revealed in its sentimental invention of the primitive. The idealization of the primitive, beginning with the South Sea idylls of Gauguin, linked together the modern and the primitive in the artistic consciousness, as did "fauvism," a later development. In their rebellion against Victorianism, black artists and intellectuals constructed a picture of an African Eden where innocent primitives danced "naked and free" from both the oppression of racism and the trammels of sexual repression. The concept of modernism was thus, ironically, linked to very old traditions of noble savages and virile barbarians.

Primitivism was everywhere linked to modernism. Igor Stravinsky's *Le Sacre du printemps*, a ballet that fabricated an ancient primitive fertility ritual of human sacrifice, provoked a riot when it was performed in Paris in 1913, much to the pleasure of progressive artists and intellectuals. Claude Debussy experimented with what he believed to be African American musical forms in his "Golliwog's Cakewalk," 1908. In 1912, James Reese Europe appeared at Carnegie Hall to represent the increasing fashionability of primitive jazz forms, and the linkage of proletarianism with bohemianism. It should not be surprising that by the First World War, Afrocentrism would begin to demonstrate clear affinities to primitivism, and that both the Harlem Renaissance and the subsequent negritude movement would be not only modernistic but primitivistic.

By the time of the Garvey movement, Africans and African Americans were becoming aware that they were living in a "Jazz Age." They were also increasingly aware of the fact that certain European artists, notably Modigliani and Picasso, were looking to primitive arts for artistic and cultural inspiration. Simultaneously, academic intellectuals led by Franz Boas were focusing on "primitive" peoples as topics of scholarly enterprise. It was within this context that a new idea began to develop among artists and intellectuals of Africa and Afro-America: it was the idea that Africa did not have to be justified purely in terms of its Nilotic civilizations. Aware that the work of Oswald Spengler had fostered a tendency to view the First World War as symbolizing "the decline of the West," many Pan-African intellectuals began to express enthusiasm for the exotic vigor of "pagan African tribalism" that earlier generations had disparaged.

W. E. B. Du Bois and, to an even a greater extent, a younger generation led by Langston Hughes, Countee Cullen, and Alain Locke,
and later Zora Neale Hurston, experimented vigorously with alternatives to monumental Egyptocentrism.

"What is Africa to Me?" asked Countee Cullen rhetorically in his
poem "Heritage." Then he proceeded to give an answer in which
nineteenth-century images of Africa did not fade, but suffered a sea
change into something rich and strange – a hot, passionate vision of
seductive color and animal sensuality. The pagan darkness that cov-
ered the land was viewed as neither gross nor repugnant, but as an
invitation to "go native," to surrender to the hot Negro blood
pounding against one's temples. Speaking in a voice that seemed to
be at once effete and rebellious, the poet recognizes his alienation
from the civilized Christian world in which he lives, but acknowledges his distance from the mother continent. Expressing simultaneously an enchantment with and a fear of the Africanity within
himself, he reflects wistfully that he is not capable of being as African
as he would like to be, but, alas, is "civilized."

The rise of cultural relativism now made it possible to view African
culture as simply different from European culture, perhaps, in some
respects, superior to it; but certainly not inferior. Frederick Douglass
would have considered such an idea preposterous; Alexander Crummell was somewhat more ambivalent; but the much younger Edward
Wilmot Blyden expressed a full-fledged cultural relativism in his *African Life and Customs* (1908). But while the concept of cultural relativism did not flourish until the beginning of the twentieth century,
it was already present in the eighteenth. J. G. Herder, who insisted
that there was no such thing as race and that humanity was one vast
brotherhood, had maintained nonetheless a faith in the reality of
national cultures, each having a value in its own right. He seemed
certain that scientific investigation would eventually demonstrate
that there was but one species of Man, but was equally certain that
every nation had a divine mission to work out as an expression of its
own culture. Herder suggested cultural relativism, of a sort, when he
invoked divine Providence as the agent of human diversity, and
maintained that every form of culture had its place in the divine
plan.[12]

Arthur de Gobineau was no proponent of cultural relativism, but
after Herder he became the principal spokesman for the idea that
various peoples had distinctive innate aptitudes that determined
their cultures. Unlike Herder, Gobineau argued vigorously for the
concept of racial inequality, and placed Africans at that bottom of
the scale of humanity. He viewed Africans as, by nature, high-

spirited, excitable, easily panicked, and possessed of a sensuality that made them – at an instinctive level – artistic. He suspected, however, that a tincture of Negro blood might be useful as a stimulant to passion and creativity when infused into superior breeds of mankind. As we have witnessed intermittently, some Afrocentric scholars were willing to forgive Gobineau his racism because of his willingness to concede that the Egyptians were a mulatto population. We shall presently witness how Gobineau was resurrected by Francophone Africans in the twentieth century as a patron saint of negritude – a form of Afrocentrism that flourished in the 1930s.[13]

Negritude was inconceivable without relativism, and Edward B. Tylor's definition of culture as the entire product of human social behavior may have been "a necessary stage in the growth of modern relativism," according to historian George Stocking. Clearly enough, by defining culture as the entire output of socially learned behavior, Tylor departed from the concept of culture as consisting only of the products of classical education. Tylor was by no means identified with the crusade for racial equality, however, and his texts would not have met Frederick Douglass's standards of fairness and objectivity. William Willis has noted Tylor's belief that the mental inferiority of colored peoples had prevented them from evolving as far as whites. Even Willis grants, however, that Tylor developed a "comparative method" that assumed the cultures of contemporary colored peoples to be equivalent to those of primeval whites. If he was indeed a forerunner of the "scientific antiracism" associated with the cultural relativism of Franz Boas and his students, Tylor was not an antiracist. Nonetheless, Tylor's approach planted the idea in some minds that the customs of primitives might be seen as something other than definitive proof of innate genetic inferiority; they were, after all, comparable to cultural traits of once primitive whites.[14]

Lewis H. Morgan is also credited with contributing to the development of cultural relativism. He is famous for his division of human progress into three progressive stages – savagery, barbarism, and civilization – and for his influences on Karl Marx and Friedrich Engels. The theory was given in detail in Morgan's work of 1877, *Ancient Society,* in which he discussed numerous primitive peoples, but demonstrated little interest in Africa. Morgan revealed a belief that civilization is unilinear, and that its line of progression is everywhere the same, which would seem to imply cultural absolutism, rather than cultural relativism. On the other hand, he implied that primitive cultures, judged on their own terms, contained a "principle of intelligence." He made the following statement, which is based on some undeniably absolutist assumptions, but which appraises primitive cultures in the egalitarian spirit central to cultural relativism:[15]

> The principle of intelligence, although conditioned in its powers within narrow limits of variation, seeks ideal standards invariably the same. Its operations, consequently, have been uniform through all the stages of human progress. No argument for the unity of origin of mankind can be made, which, in its nature, is more satisfactory. A common principle of intelligence meets us in the savage, in the barbarian, and in civilized man.[16]

Although the statement is tinctured with white supremacy, Morgan rejected polygenesis and accepted the idea that accident was a factor in human progress. Nonetheless, the following passage from the same work illustrates why it is impossible to attribute to him the complete egalitarianism that cultural relativism has come to imply.

> The Aryan family represents the central stream of human progress, because it produced the highest type of mankind, and because it has proved its intrinsic superiority by gradually assuming the control of the earth. And yet civilization must be regarded as an accident of circumstances.

William Graham Sumner, who is most often discussed in connection with his social Darwinism and his "root hog or die" philosophy, is usually identified with the American conservative tradition. African American social thinkers have thus been suspicious of his approach to culture. Actually, Sumner made an important contribution to the theory of cultural relativism as he began to develop the concept of "folkways" at the turn of the century. There was a tangentially egalitarian implication to Sumner's views. He placed the concept "primitive society" in quotation marks, as if to imply that the established distinctions between primitives and civilized peoples were chimerical. He sneered at ethnocentrism, the view that "one's group is the center of everything, and all others are scaled and rated with reference to it."[17]

There are few statements of the cultural relativist position more forthright than the foregoing sentence, which asserted that cultural values are largely subjective, and dependent on point of view. Sumner acknowledged that culture was something possessed by all societies, and that all cultures, regardless of how "primitive," represented the reasonable adjustments of populations to their environments. His approach to culture was a departure from the elitist notions of

Matthew Arnold and almost seemed a resurrection of the cultural egalitarianism of Herder, who attacked the idea of universal, unilinear civilization and wrote:

> Men of all quarters of the globe, who have perished over the ages, you have not lived solely to manure the earth with your ashes, so that at the end of time your posterity should be made happy by European culture. The very thought of a superior European culture is a blatant insult to the majesty of nature.[18]

The sociologist Robert E. Park, who was strongly influenced by Sumner, understood much better than Sumner that the acceptance of cultural relativism undermined the theory of white cultural supremacy. Nonetheless, Park was associated with the absolutist idea that many of the problems in African American life arose not from legitimate cultural differences but from social disorganization. In this view, many characteristics of the black community were attributable to the disruption of institutions through which culture is transmitted. In accord with this line of thinking, African American cultural differences resulted from incomplete or imperfect assimilation of European cultural ideas, an idea that received pronounced expression from Park's student, the black sociologist E. Franklin Frazier. Park is thus associated with the two contradictory traditions of cosmopolitanism and multiculturalism. Matters are complicated even more by his being undeniably influenced by conventional attitudes of romantic racialism regarding the singular cultural propensities of African peoples.[19]

"The Negro is the lady of the races," wrote Park, who, although known for his social egalitarianism, expressed an idea reminiscent of Gobineau. The view that Africans were an essentially sensuous, emotional, and artistic people, was not peculiar to Gobineau, or to Frenchmen; the idea was already old by the eighteenth century, as manifested in the Prester John myths of the Middle Ages and the noble savage of Afra Behn's *Oroonoko*. Harriet Beecher Stowe adopted the idea of the aesthetically predisposed and essentially feminine character of the African. Such ideas could be expressed by even the most militant antislavery advocates. Feminized images of the African were common among antebellum white authors and intellectuals, including abolitionists, as historian George Frederickson has shown. Historian Dean Grodzins observes that Theodore Parker, who endorsed John Brown and encouraged violent resistance to slavery, once described the African as "the most pacific of men on the face of the earth; the least revengeful, the most merciful, the slowest to strike, and the readiest to forgive." Parker also made the following public statement:[20]

> The African is the most docile and pliant of all the races of men; none has so little ferocity. . . . No race is so strong in the affectional instinct which attaches man to man by tender ties; none so easy, indolent, confiding, so little warlike. Hence it is that the white men have kidnapped the black and made him their prey.[21]

Edward Wilmot Blyden accepted these nineteenth-century conceptions as he developed his theory of the "African Personality," proclaiming that the contributions of Africans were destined to be not in the area of the sciences, but in the softer disciplines. Mention has been made of Blyden's conception of the "African Personality" in the course of these chapters. Alexander Crummell, W. E. B. Du Bois, Boas, and Park all abided by the nineteenth-century tradition that linked the African personality, in a congenital sense, with aestheticism and femininity. As noted in Chapter 3, Frederick Douglass was correct in seeing the dangers of multiculturalism defined in biological terms and linked specifically to race.[22]

The varieties of multiculturalism and cultural relativism that have nurtured Afrocentrism originated and achieved respectability as a result of the growth of American social science. The rise of anthropology and sociology in the first half of the twentieth century coincided with the arrival of the first generation of Catholics and Jews in the universities. The social scientists of this generation were struggling not only for ideas, but for jobs. Far more than they realized, they were spiritually influenced by urban ethnic politics, most notably in New York and Chicago, where competing ethnic groups squared off in the wards and at city hall, jostling for pieces of "honest graft." Social scientists did not like to accept such a cynical notion of American democracy or their connectedness to it, but ethnic politics unconsciously affected their professional behavior and intellectual activities. Multiculturalism in the emerging disciplines of sociology and anthropology was a powerful argument in behalf of the more ethnically inclusive patterns of American intellectual life that developed after 1900. The process of white ethnic inclusion in the universities created an environment that was sympathetic to certain aspects of the American civil rights struggle, although not necessarily receptive to the employment of African Americans in university professorships.[23]

It is the standard view that Franz Boas was the pivotal figure in creating the concept of cultural relativism. His theories are credited with a supposed tendency among twentieth-century anthropologists toward granting a status of equality to the behavior and values of "primitive" peoples. George Stocking has been a strong proponent of this interpretation of the importance of Boas. William Willis has issued a caveat regarding Boas's multiculturalism, even implying that Boas only tended toward multiculturalism near the end of his career. According to Willis, Boas "advocated pluralism within white societies and pacific internationalism among them" as a reaction to Nazism. Willis and other scholars have seemingly suggested that Boas's cultural relativism had more to do with fears of anti-Semitism than with egalitarian attitudes toward primitives or colored peoples. However, in the view of historian Vernon Williams, and of the present author, it cannot be denied that Boas's early work was an important step in the development of cultural relativism and a direct influence on Afrocentrism, as eventually expressed in the work of Molefi Asante and Henry Louis Gates. Boas's more immediate influences on the development of Afrocentrism in Du Bois has been previously alluded to. Any mention of Boas in connection with Afrocentrism leads naturally to some discussion of his student Melville Herskovits.[24]

Herskovits's early work illustrates my perhaps belabored point that cultural relativism and multiculturalism bear no essential or necessary relationships to Afrocentrism. Herskovits's 1925 essay "The Negro's Americanism" granted that there were some culturally distinct aspects of African American life, but called them "merely a remnant from the peasant days in the South." He considered such cultural differences to be healthy and useful to American civilization as a whole. "Of the African culture," Herskovits pontificated, there was "not a trace." His concern was to stress the degree to which assimilation of African Americans had taken place, and to assert that they had been culturally "absorbed as all great racial and social groups in this country have been." In that same essay, he asserted one specific point of comparison to another ethnic group: "The social ostracism to which they are subjected is only different in extent from that to which the Jew is subjected."[25]

By the 1930s, however, Herskovits was thoroughly identified with the view that African American culture was essentially African. His field research in Central America, beginning in 1928 and 1929, followed up by further research in West Africa and Haiti, had convinced him that West African culture was preserved in the Americas. Although he believed that the farther north one traveled, the fewer Africanisms survived, he was nonetheless convinced that African culture could be detected in the United States as well. The strongest North American survivals were in such isolated parts of the South as rural Georgia and the South Carolina Sea Islands. He now took the position that it was essential for public policy makers, educators, and psychologists to know something of the African background. "The more we can learn of this African background the better the understanding we shall have of those aspects of the ancestral culture that, in the case of the Negro as of all our other minority folk, has not been entirely lost, but continues in some measure to function significantly."[26]

Zora Neale Hurston was another Boas student of considerable importance, but her work, although dazzlingly brilliant as an experiment in merging social science with literary imagination, is maddeningly unconcerned with the articulation of theory – Afrocentric or otherwise. Her fieldwork in the area of folklore would seem almost necessarily to have brought her into contact with questions related to multiculturalism, but she seems to have been uninterested in addressing the issue of African retentions in abstract, theoretical terms. Her witty and ironic treatments of African American life, through the medium of the novel, reveal little fascination with the debate over the cultural relativism of her mentor. Nor do they project the Afrocentric attitudes that characterize the work of Herskovitz. Hurston reveals the folkish tendency of the anthropologist to savor the speech and attitudes of ordinary people at the grass-roots level in constructing her novel *Moses, Man of the Mountain*. But this novel, while it makes much playful and creative use of the African American *Volksgeist*, is almost a statement of anti-Afrocentrism. In *Moses*, Hurston reverts to the nineteenth-century religious mythology found also in F. E. W. Harper's *Moses: A Story of the Nile*, and identifies blacks with Israel suffering under Egyptian bondage.

Perhaps the explanation for Hurston's underdevelopment as a theorist lies in the guild ethnocentrism that seemed to accompany disciplinary antiracism in the academy. No attempt was made by members of the Boas network to carve out a place for the likes of Zora Neale Hurston in their profession. Their conceptions of cultural democracy had not yet evolved to the point where they could conceive of a truly multiethnic university. One should not, therefore, be too sanguine in the discussion of Franz Boas and his students' academic politics. Anthropological antiracism was a core value of their intellectual discipline, but antiracism seldom entered into the professional life of the guild. William Willis has mentioned Herskovits's failure to train black students and has accused him of Machiavellian professional politics – matters of considerable significance.[27] The Boasians seem to have done little better than William Graham Sumner, who allowed William H. Ferris in his classes but gave no indication of considering Ferris worthy of becoming his doctoral student. Nonetheless, Ferris, as we have seen, had positive recollections of the famed social Darwinist because of Sumner's detachment, fairness, and refusal to accept hasty conclusions concerning black inferiority.

The tendency of some researchers to rifle the papers of dead scholars, or to search for anecdotal evidence of their privately expressed racial or religious prejudices, is understandable. Some researchers have made much of the fact that Bronislaw Malinowski made negative comments about "the niggers" in his diary, and it is painful to be made aware of his secretly held attitudes. These skeletons in the closet of antiracist anthropology are, naturally, disturbing and reveal a great deal about the obstacles to black professional advancement within the discipline that have existed in American academic life. Of undeniable importance, however, was Malinowski's public advocacy of human rights, which had an influence on much subsequent thinking in the social sciences and in public policy. Of greatest importance to the present work is Malinowski's association with the rise of social scientific Pan-Africanism.[28]

Malinowski used the term "Pan-Africanism" much as we use "Afrocentrism" today. He believed, as did Herskovits, that the study of African Americans within the wider context of African culture could be useful in the fight against racial oppression. Malinowski indicted the United States as a caste-oriented society and asserted that its "legal discrimination" produced "brutality and abuses," generated "dishonesty and graft," and led to "forced labor with all its inherent evils." He therefore advocated "political action" for raising the status of Africans and breaking down the caste system, while maintaining the need for independent institutions. He seemingly addressed the same paradox identified by Du Bois during the earlier decades of the century, for he posited that black people living in white-dominated societies had two seemingly contradictory but legitimate needs – access to integrated institutions, and institutions of their own. He believed that black-controlled institutions should in some way reflect African traditions, although he "might not agree with some enthusiastic anthropologists who still find a good deal of African background in the culture of the American Negro."[29]

Malinowski wrote, as did Boas and Herskovits, from his own ethnic perspective. Malinowski identified himself in 1943 as "a Pole," whose country was undergoing the experience of "suppressed subject nationality." He introduced "as a parallel and paradigm" to the Pan-African problem, "the aspirations of European nationality, but not of nationalism." Poles did "not desire anything like fusion with our conquerors or masters," but claimed the "right of decision as regards our destiny, our civilization, our careers, and our mode of enjoying life." It is possible to trace much of the antiracist and "Afrocentric" thrust of post–Second World War anthropology to the reactions of antiracist Jewish scholars to Nazism. Once again I restate my point, that the origins of Afrocentrism are historically associated with the struggle against racism and anti-Semitism.[30]

Historically, cultural relativism and multiculturalism are only marginally related to the Egyptocentrism and biblically based forms of Afrocentrism that thrived in the late nineteenth and early twentieth centuries. The version of Afrocentrism that arose among anthropologists was practically unconcerned with Nilotic Africa, but tended to focus on West African cultures and institutions and their relationship to black America. This version of Afrocentrism was closely related to the struggle against anti-Semitism, and Jewish anthropologists, such as Boas and Herskovits, openly made the association. Finally, as we shall see in Chapter 8 of the present volume, Africans and African Americans adopted the anthropological model during the 1920s and 1930s, and became less obsessed with the Nilotic and biblical models of Afrocentrism.

Extreme modernists during this period were also primitivists, who self-consciously nourished an image of themselves as Calibans whose rhetoric was to curse the civilization of Prospero the colonizer.[31] Many came to glory in the depiction of Africa as savage, rather than attempting to argue for the existence of an African civilization. In some quarters, Afrocentrism began to position itself as anticivilizationist, while in other quarters it maintained its traditional civilizationist perspective. At the risk of oversimplification, we may say that a rift developed among Afrocentrists, characterized by a fundamental difference in the perspectives of two Francophone Africans: Cheikh Anta Diop and Léopold Senghor. Diop persisted in the racial vindicationism of the nineteenth century, seeking to demonstrate the essential role of black people in the development of Nilotic civilization. Senghor, and numerous others, celebrated the primitive, gloried in the idea that Africans had never been infected with technological culture, and proclaimed the hope that they would never be infected with the sickness of civilization.

BARBARISM GRAFTED ONTO DECADENCE

It is ironic that around the time Domingo mockingly described Garvey as a Caliban, the metaphorical imputation of savagery was being transformed from a curse into a badge of honor and radical authenticity among African and African American intellectuals. Many were beginning to portray themselves as antimodernists or anticivilizationists. Gwendolyn Bennett in "Heritage," Countee Cullen in his poem of the same name, and Langston Hughes, in "Nude Young Dancer," sentimentalized the primitivism of the West African forest, and all proclaimed their exasperation with bourgeois civilization. Bennett wrote the following:

> I want to hear the chanting
> Around a heathen fire
> Of a strange black race.[1]

The poetry of such authors manipulated and transformed traditional racial stereotypes. In this it resembled the devices of Vachel Lindsay in his poem "The Congo: A Study of the Negro Race" (1914), which depicted the Africans "basic savagery," "their irrepressible high spirits," the "hope of their religion." The work alternated scenes of African American life with flashes of jungle savagery, "tatooed canibals," and "skull-faced witch doctors."

> Boomlay, boomlay, boomlay Boom
> A roaring, epic rag-time tune
> From the mouth of the Congo
> To the Mountains of the Moon.[2]

There were critics who applauded the primitivist theme when produced by black poets, but balked at its presentation by Lindsay, who was white. Lindsay's racial romanticism did, indeed, employ racialist stereotypes, but it also attributed strength and vigor to the African personality, and lamented the process whereby it became "civilized." New Negro artists and intellectuals were as ambivalent about civilization as they were about savagery. Simultaneously, they promoted both, and their Afrocentrism romanticized both myths of the African past.[3]

Mythologies often fuse contradictions, and the two themes of civilizationism and primitivism, notwithstanding their apparent opposition, were myths that coexisted in the minds of individual black intellectuals. Langston Hughes's poem "The Negro Speaks of Rivers" fused the civilizationist with the primitive tradition. It identified the African as a pyramid builder, but also as a drowsy primitive, on the banks of the Congo. The same fusing of primitivism and civilizationism can be observed in Du Bois's poem "The Riddle of the Sphinx." In this poem the African is depicted in one line as the languid, "dark daughter of the lotus leaves," and in another, as a vigorous civilization builder. Civilizationism and primitivism are, as we have seen, contrapuntal themes, frequently interwoven in the work of Du Bois and finding ultimate expression in his version of Pan-African socialism, which allowed its adherents to be simultaneously civilized, primitive, modern, traditional, and progressive.[4]

The intermingling of modernism and primitivism was symbolized in the terms "Harlem Renaissance" and "New Negro movement." Both terms have been used almost interchangeably, in recognition of the importance of Harlem as a center of black artistic and intellectual life during and after the First World War. It should not be forgotten, however, that Washington, D.C., because of the location of Howard University, was also an important center. Some scholars have protested the term "Harlem Renaissance." As for "New Negro," even during the 1920s there was no agreement on what it meant, or when it first was used. Professor Fred McElroy finds an early occurence of the phrase "New Negro" in an 1890 publication by Edward M. Brawley. Booker T. Washington affixed his name to an anthology called *A New Negro for a New Century* in 1900. William Pickens published his book *The New Negro: His Political and Mental Status* in 1916, and Marcus Garvey frequently used the phrase in his speeches and editorials. The two decades preceding the First World War saw the rise of the New Thought movement, believed to have influenced Marcus Garvey. The phrase "New Era" is applied to the period as frequently as that other common designation of the 1920s, the "Jazz Age." The fashionability of the term New Negro as a self-designation among black artists and intellectuals of the twenties may demonstrate their fascination with "modernism"; on the other hand, it may have represented nothing more than America's superstitious obsession with newness for the sake of newness.[5]

No person was better qualified during the 1920s than Alain Locke to define the New Negro movement, or to appreciate its paradoxes. This he did when he oversaw publication of the celebrated March 1925 issue of *Survey Graphic*, "Harlem: Mecca of the New Negro," which after considerable editing and expansion was reissued as a book, *The New Negro*. The magazine included essays by several historians and cultural critics: Locke, Du Bois, Herskovits, J. A. Rogers, and W. A. Domingo; it also included poetry by Countee Cullen, Ann Spencer, Langston Hughes, and others. It included photographs of African art and modernistic-primitivistic drawings by Winold Reiss. There was also a sketch in the heroic-proletarian-bolshevik mode by Mahonri Young. The book version included several drawings and "decorative designs" by Aaron Douglas, which represented the fashionable merger of modernist and the primitivist styles, and a jazzy drawing by Miguel Covarrubias. Locke prefaced the collection with an interpretive essay on the New Negro, which was substantially the same in both editions.[6]

Locke was a philosopher by training, not a social scientist, but his intellectual affinities place him, at times, closer to sociology or anthropology than to the discipline in which he took his Harvard Ph.D. William B. Harvey thus defines Locke's field of study as "philosophical anthropology." In 1923, Locke acknowledged that Matthew Arnold's definition of culture was "famous," "authoritative," and "beautifully defined," but expressed dissatisfaction with it because of its externality and elitism. Indeed, Locke's writings demonstrate a career-long interest in the anthropological perspective on culture, and he was deeply impressed with the idea of cultural relativity, as became evident in his article "The Concept of Race as Applied to Social Culture," published shortly before *The New Negro*.[7]

Most students of Locke's writings believe he had identified himself with cultural relativity by the 1920s, and his statements on the subject became increasingly strong over the years. In 1924 he called for "the study of any given culture . . . in terms of its own culture elements" and for "its organic interpretation in terms of its own intrinsic values." William B. Harvey observes that in "Values and Imperatives" (1935), Locke called for opposition to value absolutism, saying "the effective antidote to value absolutism lies in a systematic and realistic demonstration that values are rooted in attitudes, not in reality, and pertain to ourselves, not to the world." In 1942, he attacked "value dogmatism," and called for "value pluralism," its "corollary of relativity," and its "practical corollaries" of "tolerance and value reciprocity," as instruments of "intellectual Democracy."[8]

In 1944, Locke published "Cultural Relativism and Ideological Peace." In this paper, he argued that

> the increasing proximity of cultures in the modern world makes all the more necessary some corrective adjustment of their "pyschological distance."
>
> No single factor could serve this end more acceptably and effectively than a relativistic concept of culture, which by first disestablishing the use of one's own culture as a contrast norm for other cultures, leads through the appreciation of the functional significance of other values in their respective cultures to the eventual discovery and recognition of certain functional common denominators.[9]

Such ideas resembled those of Sumner in *Folkways,* and of Finot in *Race Prejudice.* They were alien to Douglass and would have been greeted by Crummell with extreme suspicion. Crummell's faith was based in a Christian teleology; Douglass's, in a more transcendental religiosity. Each man was, however, in his own way, a monoculturalist, committed to a unlinear theory of history.

At the dawn of the twenty-first century, Locke's reasoning that cultural relativism is at the basis of all multiculturalism has not found universal acceptance. At least one contemporary pluralist, identified with anthropological Afrocentrism, has been untouched by the argument that a relativistic approach to cultural values will necessarily lead to a discovery of the universal absolutes valued by all human beings. Henry Louis Gates, for example, has stated in the strongest possible terms that relativism "makes the project of cross cultural understanding unintelligible," and that "if relativism is right then multiculturalism is impossible."[10] Cultural relativism has come under attack from the left, by Patricia Rengel, chief legislative counsel of Amnesty International USA, who speaks of the need to "meet the challenge of some Asian governments that continue to argue cultural relativism."[11] Further attacks on cultural relativism have come from African feminists in response to the threat that oppression of women may be falsely defended on the grounds of cultural relativism. Conservative intellectuals oversimplify both cultural relativism and Afrocentrism when they attempt to establish a fundamental link between these two discourses. Although a reasonable connection did, in fact, exist between Locke's Afrocentrism and his cultural relativism, there is no inevitable connection between the two ideas – either in the past or in the present.

While some scholars have seen the thrust of *The New Negro* as basically integrationist, others have associated Locke with a milder form of intellectual black nationalism.[12] Locke, who was no intellectual lightweight, recognized the paradox of his own position. He was the champion of "Aframerican culture," but his position was subsidized by the wealthy white widow Charlotte Osgood Mason, known as "Godmother" of the Harlem Renaissance.[13] She was well situated to put her definitive stamp on the movement, and her stamp was decidedly Afrocentric. Michael Winston notes that "because Mason was convinced that Western civilization was collapsing because of 'artificial values' and technological excess, she was committed to the preservation and propagation of the values of 'primitive peoples.' "[14] In Charlotte Mason, we see the fundamental role played by white benefactors in the promotion of Afrocentrism during the New Era. We also notice, however, that the role Mason played was to move the New Negro movement in the direction of the modernist-primitivist synthesis, and to encourage the anthropological rather than the Nilotic monumental strain of Afrocentrism.

The modernist-primitivist strain of Afrocentrism was encouraged by several other whites in the circle dominated by Locke. Among them was Albert C. Barnes, a millionaire art collector who filled his private galleries at Merion, Pennsylvania, with masterpieces of Impressionist and modern art. More important to Locke, of course, was Barnes's sincere fascination with African sculpture and his contribution of several reproductions of works from his collection to the "Harlem Number" of *Survey Graphic*. Fancying himself something of a culture critic as well, Barnes was dedicated to assaulting a group he identified as "the long-haired phonies and that fading class of egoists, the art patrons." The lines he wrote for the Harlem Number were primitivist clichés, taken from the nineteenth-century vocabulary of sentimental racism:

> The most important element to be considered is the psychological complexion of the Negro as he inherited it from his primitive ancestors and which he maintains to this day. The outstanding characteristics are his tremendous emotional endowment, his luxuriant and free imagination and a truly great power of individual expression. He has in superlative measure that fire and light which coming from within, bathes his whole world, colors his images and impels him to expression.

Embarrassing and dated though these words appear, they clearly indicate that benevolent racialism was an important element in the thinking of at least one white Afrocentrist. Locke, to his credit, was

not so fully caught up in the cult of exotic primitivism that dominated the era that he could not take issue with such opinions. He
challenged the sentimentalism of Barnes in *The New Negro*, where he
wrote: "The characteristic African art expressions are rigid, controlled, disciplined, abstract, heavily conventionalized; those of the
Aframerican, – free, exuberant, emotional, sentimental, and human." In other words, opined Locke, the "emotional temper" of
the African and that of the American Negro were "exactly opposite."[15]

This was not, however, his definitive statement on the subject. For
many years he had confessed to a belief in racial temperament,
which should be seen not as a genetic endowment but as an out-
growth of cultural experience. In the later 1920s, Locke expressed a
belief not only in "racial temperament," but in the survival among
African Americans of African culture. He maintained that although
acculturated with respect to American religion, mores, and language, the African American nonetheless retained an "African temperament, creeping back in the overtones of his half-articulate
speech and action, which gave his life and ways the characteristic
qualities instantly recognized as peculiarly and representatively his."[16]

Locke attributed African Americans' interest in African art to European interest in the same. Indeed, his own collection of African
art would not have been possible if Charlotte Mason had not provided the money. He asserted that African Americans, in general,
had not been interested in African art until white interest had given
it respectability. He acknowledged the importance of white authen-
tication in the Harlem Number, where he cited the influences of
African art on European ethnologists, artists, and critics, and cited a
long list of important names. What was most interesting about Alain
Locke's *New Negro* was its marginalization of the Garvey movement.
The book contained few traces of Nilotic monumentalism; even the
essay contributed by J. A. Rogers on the subject of jazz was concerned with the exotic primitive strain in African American culture –
not with the the the monumental themes of his *From Superman to Man*
published some eight years earlier.

Hughes was one Harlem Renaissance figure who managed successfully to live with both the traditional biblical-classical Afrocentrism and the exotic-modernist mode. He gloried in a conception of
black culture as modernistic jazz culture, as a merger of the cubistic
and the primitive spirit, and as a meeting of proletarianism and bohemianism. In "The Negro Speaks of Rivers," on the other hand,
he redeemed the old biblical and Afrocentric traditionalism, speaking of "bathing in the Euphrates, when dawns were young," and

raising pyramids above the Nile. The painter Aaron Douglas also
merged the modernist-primitivist with the traditional-vindicationist
traditions when he illustrated "The Negro Speaks of Rivers" and
filled his own "More Stately Mansions" with the images of pyramid
and sphinx.

W. E. B. Du Bois also blended monumentalism and exoticism, albeit with a heavy stress on the former, in his poem "The Riddle of
the Sphinx":

> Dark daughter of the lotus leaves that watch the Southern sea!
> Wan spirit of a prisoned soul a-panting to be free!
> The muttered music of thy streams, the whisper of the deep
> Have kissed each other in God's name and kissed a world to
>   sleep.

He portrayed Africa as a Titaness, but placed her under the
dreamy powers of the lotus flowers taken from Homer's *Odyssey*. He
gave her attributes sentimentally associated with the wistful Negro
temperament. The poem recalled classic Afrocentric images of
"black men of Egypt," and "Ethiopia's children of morning." But
while Du Bois felt free to play with exotic primitive stereotypes, he
insisted on endowing them with heroic overtones. He took umbrage
at attempts by whites to reduce black culture to blues culture, or to
confine the African temperament to the level of the speakeasy or the
cabaret. As has been noted elsewhere, he was extremely critical of
Carl Van Vechten, a white patron and sponsor of several Harlem
Renaissance figures, whose novel *Nigger Heaven* Du Bois denounced
as a slander on the black race and a violation of its "hospitality."

Du Bois admitted to admiration for some other white authors; the
German anthropologist Leo Frobenius was a major influence. Du
Bois noted Frobenius's studies in the bibliography of *The Negro*, in
1915, and he quoted him extensively in later works. Du Bois adopted
Frobenius's fanciful practice of referring to Africa's "West Coast
around the great Gulf of Guinea" as "Atlantis." He was captivated
by the poetic, sometimes exotic, at times even erotic elements in
Frobenius's treatment of Africa, for Du Bois – a man of his times –
was not opposed, in principle, to the characterization of Africa or
Africans in connection with that lush primitivism so often present in
the New Negro movement.[17]

"Grafting primitivism on decadence," wrote Sterling Brown in
retrospect, the black authors of the Harlem Renaissance often found
that the easiest path to recognition was to follow in the tradition of
the "exotic primitivism," whose origins Brown attributed to white
authors. He called Van Vechten's *Nigger Heaven* "flamboyant and

erotic.'' Works by other white authors in the genre were characterized as ''sophisticated racist burlesque . . . weird . . . voodistic . . . or-
giastic . . . absurd fantasies of American Negroes reverting at slightest
provocation to ancestral savagery.'' Even Sherwood Anderson was
accused of using African American characters as foils for ''white neu-
roticism,'' inviting a Freudian interpretation of white America's Jazz
Age as a wish fulfillment fantasy. Alain Locke concurred in acknowledging the pandering tendencies of some black writers, and accused
them of ''seeking a forced growth according to the exotic tastes of a
pampered and decadent public.''[18]

Was the Harlem Renaissance successful in promoting an Afrocentric image acceptable to black artists and intellectuals? That depends,
of course, on how one defines the various cultural programs of that
obviously diverse group during the years under consideration. It has
long been noted that although the movement was successful in inspiring a generation of white cultural iconoclasts like Carl Van Vechten and Charlotte Mason, it did not successfully advance black institutional development. Nathan Huggins in his book *Harlem
Renaissance* insisted that the attempt to create a ''New Negro'' failed
''because of naive assumptions about culture unrelated to economic
and social realities.'' He concluded that ''the most important gift
that the renaissance has left to us [is] a lesson from its failures.''[19]
David Lewis claimed in his book *When Harlem Was in Vogue,* that ''the
Depression accelerated a failure that was inevitable.'' It could never
''have succeeded as a positive social force . . . neither culture nor
color could alter the pariah status of those whose ancestors had been
African slaves.''[20]

Harold Cruse argued in *The Crisis of the Negro Intellectual* (1967)
that the Harlem Renaissance was a failure and that among the chief
reasons for its failure was its inability to establish either an economic
foundation or an ideological base.[21] Control of African American
artistic and intellectual life during the 1920s and 1930s was in the
hands of Euro-Americans. It would be naive to assume that the patterns that predominated in the 1920s would not be reproduced in
more recent years. There is a fundamental conflict within the movement between those who would like to see it controlled by forces
outside the university, and those who are content to have its patterns
dictated by those who are within. Pan-African studies of the *Stolen
Legacy* school draw their strength outside the academy, and conform
to the Garveyite separatist pattern of Afrocentrism. The more aca-
demically integrated mode of African American studies is to be
found in the anthropologically and folklorically based Afrocentrism
of Henry Louis Gates and Sterling Stuckey.

Defensiveness, ambivalence, and sometimes disappointment have characterized the reactions of black scholars to the Harlem Renaissance from the very beginning. So pervasive have these feelings been that the literary scholar Houston Baker has posited the existence of a conspiratorial white intellectual establishment, whose "hypothetical injunction" to critics is that they demonstrate the failures of the movement. Be that as it may, there have been few students of the Renaissance who have felt it was entirely without merit. On the other hand, few have been able to offer praise without qualification. Du Bois felt obliged to respond to an attack on the "Renaissance" by H. L. Mencken in 1927, but the intellectual accomplishments he listed were confined neither to Harlem nor to the 1920s. Du Bois praised not only such obvious documents of literary success as the poetry of Claude McKay, but also Booker T. Washington's *Up From Slavery*, published twenty-seven years earlier. Du Bois closed his observations with the remark that "on the whole . . . , we Negroes are quite well pleased with our Renaissance. And we have not yet finished."[22]

He most certainly had not finished. Within a few months Du Bois was condemning the same Claude McKay he had so recently lauded, for pandering to white prurience. McKay's best-selling novel *Home to Harlem* (1928) dealt with the peregrinations of Jake, a good-natured drifter whose encounters with women were opportunistic, but not malign. There was nothing truly salacious in the novel, which contained no profane language and no explicit sexual scenes. It is difficult to fathom what it was that Du Bois found so offensive, since his own *Dark Princess* of 1928 contained its own brand of illicit eroticism, and presented a far more aggressive attack on bourgeois morality. By the early thirties, as Meyer Weinberg has noted, the doctor had drastically revised his position on the entire Renaissance. In 1933, Du Bois pontificated the axiom that the Renaissance had failed, and delivered the following withering denunciation in a speech at Fisk University:[23]

> Why was it that the Renaissance of literature which began among Negroes ten years ago, has never taken real and lasting root? It was because it was a transplanted and exotic thing. It was a literature written for the benefit of white people and at the behest of white readers, and started out privately from the white point of view. It never had a real Negro constituency, and it did not grow out of the inmost heart and frank experience of Negroes.[24]

There was merit to Du Bois's argument, but he was, of course, not immune to the very criticism that he leveled at others. What exactly did he mean when he spoke of writing "out of the inmost heart and frank experience of Negroes"? His own attempts to write such a literature have hardly met with the unqualified praise of African American critics. Furthermore, Du Bois would have had much greater difficulty gaining exposure for his writings without his editorship of *The Crisis*, the institutional support of the NAACP, or the favor of white-controlled publishing houses, who advertised and distributed his books in various genres. Ironically, while accepting the support of white patrons, he accused others of writing "at the behest of white readers."

Marcus Garvey, who ran his own publishing operations, was one who did not miss the irony. He called Du Bois a tool of white people and a hater of black people. Du Bois had rebuffed Garvey's friendly overtures on many occasions, and finally attacked him as "either a lunatic or a traitor." Garvey eventually took off the gloves and responded in kind. One of the most interesting points about the rivalry between the two men, however, is that Garvey and Du Bois shared the same high-cultural aspirations for African American writing, and thus had overlapping opinions on McKay's racy depictions of the emerging Harlem ghetto:

> The white people have these Negroes to write [this] kind of stuff . . . so that the Negro can still be regarded as a monkey or some imbecile creature. Whenever authors of the Negro race write good literature for publication the white publishers refuse to publish it, but wherever the Negro is sufficiently known to attract attention he is advised to write in the way that the white man wants. That is just what happened to Claude McKay.[25]

Garvey considered McKay a sycophant, writing racially treasonous literature at the behest of the "hypothetical injunctions" of white folk. By 1928 Garvey had, of course, been deported, and many black leaders considered him a racial traitor because of his collaboration with reactionary white individuals and organizations. Garvey naturally did not see himself as serving the interests of a white establishment by launching this attack on McKay. He projected such criticism away from himself and onto "these Negroes" who wrote "in the way that the white man wants." Of course, he included Du Bois in this category, but not himself.

The Harlem Renaissance was perceived as a failure by the sociologist E. Franklin Frazier, who anticipated the observations of Harold

Cruse. It was ridiculous to speak of a truly African American art, so long as white people were footing the bill.

> There is much talk at the present time about the New Negro. He is generally thought of as the creative artist who is giving expression to all the stored-up aesthetic emotion of the race. . . . While the New Negro who is expressing himself in art promises in the words of one of his chief exponents not to compete with the white man either politically or economically, the Negro business man seeks the salvation of his race in economic enterprise. . . . Sometimes the New Negro of the artistic type calls the Negro business man a Babbitt, while the latter calls the former a mystic. But the Negro business man is winning out, for he is dealing with economic realities. He can boast of the fact that he is independent of white support, while the Negro artist still seeks it.[26]

It is of considerable interest that Frazier spoke of the "Negro business man" not only as dealing with realities but as assertively entering into competition with whites. The black artist, on the other hand, was seen as mindlessly parroting the shibboleths of white bohemia. One recognizes that Frazier's opinion on both the artistic movement and the black businessman were to change radically by the time he published *Black Bourgeoisie* in 1957. Nonetheless, during the twenties, Frazier, like other critics of the New Negro renaissance, viewed the movement as fundamentally compromised because it had been dependent on white support. When we appraise the past discourse on the Harlem Renaissance, we discover that the entire debate on its validity from the 1920s to the present day has been dominated by this discussion of the "hypothetical injunction" of white sponsors. Not only have the artists themselves been accused of pandering to white establishmentarian, mainstream injunctions; those who have criticized the movement from the perspectives of their various disciplines have been accused of submitting to "disciplinary control and power politics."

There can be no denying that the cultural activity of black artists and intellectuals in the Harlem Renaissance was responsive to the demands of white sponsorship, just as the present-day interpretation of the period is under "disciplinary control, and power politics." White intellectuals, artists, journal editors, and power brokers promoted, for the most part, those images of black life consistent with their conception of a Jazz Age. There was a privileging of the folkish, the proletarian, and the bohemian conceptions of African Americans, the sorts of images usually represented in the writings of Langston Hughes and Claude McKay. The New Negro, as represented in Locke's anthology, was more intellectually accessible and emotionally understandable to the white avant garde than the New Negro who appeared on the pages of *Negro World.*

In most black studies programs today, a seminar on the New Negro is not likely to signal a focus on the "high cultural" Afrocentrism of the Garveyite William H. Ferris. In fact, Ferris's name may not even ring a bell with many so-called experts on the Harlem Renaissance.[27] It is popular culture, the blues tradition, and folklore that have gained the greatest acceptance in the American university because black artists and "public intellectuals" have been networking for many years with the class of whites that Martin Kilson calls "eccentric elites." Kilson observes that Carl Van Vechten's bohemian clique in the 1920s, as well as "homosexual and feminist subcultures," have provided avenues through which whites have been exposed to African American culture. For this reason, among others, monumental Afrocentrism is unlikely to matter a great deal in the majority of African American studies departments and programs.[28]

In the 1920s black artists and intellectuals believed themselves to be championing the African American masses, but celebration of proletarian traditions did not, in itself, constitute an acceptance of mass values. These were manifested in the religious movements of the period, finding expression in the Baptist and Methodist churches, the enthusiastic sects, and the marginal black nationalistic groups including the Moorish Templars and Black Jews. The exotic lives of numbers runners and blues singers were only one side of African American culture. The bourgeois aspirations of a William H. Ferris were ironically more attuned to the ordinary working poeple than were the bohemian pretensions of a Claude McKay. The culture of black intellectuals, while claiming its connection to the culture of the masses, was more closely tied to that of marginalized white bohemians. Thus, during the 1920s and again in the 1960s, although artists and intellectuals attempted to assert their validity by stressing their ties to the black proletariat and its culture, they were really more closely tied to bohemian New York than to the Pentecostal churches.[29]

Harlem Renaissance exoticism was the harbinger of negritude, a movement that originated among French-speaking Africans and defined the African personality in terms of a warm emotionalism, a moist sensuality, and a soft, dreamy poetic quality. Its primary focus was on West Africa rather than the Nile, and it advanced the cult of primitivism rather than Egyptocentric monumentalism. The Francophone Africans were familiar with such ideas and emotions long before the Harlem Renaissance, of course, for French intellectual history was not devoid of racialism – sentimental or otherwise. Nonetheless, French authors of the negritude school were gracious enough to acknowledge the influence of Harlem in the 1920s on their own movement of the following decade.

Negritude was a direct repudiation of "civilizationism," a term I have used elsewhere and that has since been adopted by other scholars to refer to a belief in a single standard of human accomplishment, measured by the symbols of European "progress."[30] Within the civilizationist world view, African history could be justified only by pondering over biblical references to the wanderings of the children of Ham, or brooding with Constantin Volney over the ruins of Nilotic empires. Negritude offered an alternative by completely rejecting the idea that humanity was equivalent to "civilization." In fact, one of the premises of Negritude was that civilization was a kind of malady. The idea was not preposterous; Garvey had suggested it, and after him Countee Cullen, and even Sigmund Freud.

The negritude movement, which began toward the end of the Harlem Renaissance and flourished from the 1930s through the 1950s, was not always associated with this critique of civilization. Its spokesman, Aimé Césaire, followed in the path of Du Bois, who along the lines of Frobenius had presented an idealized African landscape, and, posing to himself the question "What Is Civilzation?" had offered the community of the African village as "a perfect human thing." So, too, Césaire, who rhapsodized on a concept of African communalism. Traditional, "non-European civilizations," asserted Césaire, were "communal societies, never societies of the many for the few." In a direct repudiation of Martin Delany's nineteenth-century standard of progress, he celebrated a people who had "invented neither gunpowder nor compass," and the people who had "tamed neither the sea nor the sky."[31]

Césaire was influenced, as were some African American writers, by Leo Frobenius and Oswald Spengler – Frobenius because he had asserted the relativistic principle that Africa had a great civilization of its own and that its great works could stand comparison with those of any culture; Spengler because he predicted that the West would collapse, just as the once mighty Roman Empire had, and this betokened a great day for the rising star of Ethiopia. A. James Arnold has made similar observations and notes a Spenglerian ring in the following lines, where Césaire senses the decline of Europe, "horribly fatigued by its immense labors . . . in the illusion of victory, trumpeting its own defeats."

Léopold Senghor took his negritude a step farther than the relativism of Césaire – who in fact moved toward absolutism – as he celebrated as virtues of the African personality all the stereotypical traits that survived as the heritage of nineteenth-century racialism. As had the leaders of the Harlem Renaissance, Senghor linked "primitivism" with "modernism," and hailed the twentieth century as "the period of the discovery of African-Negro civilization." He used the term civilization interchangeably with culture, and he used both words incessantly as he sought to define the spirit of African Negro culture as "machineless civilization." He replicated the patterns of Locke and Du Bois by referring to the "admiration of certain European intellectuals for African-Negro literature and art," although with the observation that this admiration "often consists of misconceptions." What exactly these misconceptions were, Senghor did not say; he seemed to reiterate the string of clichés he had inherited from the most conventional of European racial romantics.

Senghor cited the authority of Gobineau, who had defined the African as "the most energetic creature seized with artistic emotion." Senghor, concurring, spoke of the Negro as "a man of nature . . . a sensualist, a being whose senses are exposed." The African was "first of all sounds, odors, rhythms, forms, and colors." He denied believing "that the Negro is traditionally devoid of reason, as one would have me believe." He insisted, however, that African reasoning was not "discursive"; it was "synthetic," not "antagonistic" but "sympathetic." The African had found "another path to knowledge." The European mode of reason was "analytical through use"; African reasoning was "intuitive through participation."

Cheikh Anta Diop, the ideological father of contemporary Afrocentrism, found the concessions of Senghor and Césaire to the conventional racism of Gobineau unacceptable, and accused "Negro-African thinkers in the period between the two world Wars" of accepting the inanities of Gobineau because the

> "Negritude" poets did not, at that time, have the scientific
> means to refute or to question these types of errors. Scientific
> truth had been White for such a long time that, with the help
> and writings of Lucien Levy-Bruhl, all these affirmations made
> under the scientific banner had to be accepted as such by our
> submissive peoples. Therefore the "Negritude" movement ac-
> cepted this so-called inferiority and boldly assumed it in full
> view of the world. Aimé Césaire shouted: "those who explored
> neither the seas nor the sky," and Léopold Senghor: "Emotion
> is Negro and reason is Greek."[32]

In reality, the positions of the negritude poets had nothing to do with lacking the "scientific means" to refute Gobineau, whose opinions had already become disreputable by 1937, when Jacques Barzun felt it necessary to mount a qualified defense of them in his *Race: A Study in Superstition.*[33] It was only in the minds of the negritude poets and the racial theorists of Nazi Germany that Gobineau retained any respectability at all. In fact, Diop could not entirely reject negritude, himself, since he hoped, as we saw in Chapter 1, to reclaim those elements of traditional romantic racism that seemed to paint the African personality in a favorable light. Diop's "authentic anthropology" is, in some respects, a reaction to the follies of Gobineau-derived negritude, in other respects, it is an extension of them. Diop and his disciples reinforce the sentimentalism of the negritude school, on the one hand, while their "authentic anthropology" simultaneously seeks to return Afrocentrism to the "civilizationist" values of classical black nationalism.

With the writings of Diop we enter the era of contemporary Afrocentrism, and it is difficult to find any works that carry the concept beyond the Diop synthesis. John Henrik Clarke and Molefi Asante are complete Diopists. And yet, what is so amazing about the position of Diop and those who follow after him is that they reiterate the position of white American colonizationists in the nineteenth century.

In 1864, the Reverend Hollis Read, a retired white missionary to Africa, published his volume *The Negro Problem Solved,* an argument for resettling the black American population in Africa. Read offered a classic vindication of the African race that both reiterated all the arguments of his predecessors and anticipated all the major premises of Afrocentrism in the twentieth century. To demonstrate an essential element of Afrocentrism's provenance, and to reiterate my repeatedly stated point that the ideology was always able to find encouragement from white sponsors, I close this chapter with a lengthy quotation from Read, who repudiated Gobineau and affirmed Constantine Volney.

> [Learned authorities have shown] "that there was a time when the black race of man were pioneers, or, at least, the equals of any other races, in all the arts, and acquirements of man's primitive civilization" a time when "learning, commerce, arts, and acquirements of man's primitive civilization" – a time when "learning, commerce, arts, manufactures, and all that characterizes a state of civilization, were associated with the black race; a race now associated only with degradation and

barbarous ignorance. As evidence of this, we can triumphantly point to the magnificent kingdoms of Meroe, Nubia, and Ethiopia, and the no less stately monuments of time, scattered along, from the pyramids of Egypt, through all Southern Asia, to Japan; temples, statues, images, cavern palaces, far surpassing any work of modern art. These are the monuments of the skill and workmanship of a crisp-haired and a thick-lipped race.[34]

In these lines by a nineteenth-century "white Afrocentrist" all the elements of classical monumental Afrocentrism are present, coexisting with the tradition of the noble, yet emotional, primitive. Borrowing from a description by Harriet Beecher Stowe, Read linked the African race to superior moral instincts and a lush "gorgeous splendor" of temperament, derived from their native climate of "spices and waving palms." Both the idea of the African as primal civilizer and the African as sensitive, morally superior primitive are present. Whatever else may be said of Diop, or of the current revitalizers of the Afrocentric tradition, they cannot be accused of having "invented" a racist, black supremacist doctrine. They have simply inherited the clichés of nineteenth-century racialism, which still predominate in American popular culture. These ideas, developed by black and white authors alike, have attempted to vindicate the "sons and daughters of Sheba's race" through creative uses of the Bible, the classics, the changing fashions of anthropological theory, and the constant mythologies of the civilization that has produced them.

CONCLUSION

AFROCENTRISM, ANTIMODERNISM, AND UTOPIA

The foregoing pages have offered a somewhat lengthy definition, although a much abbreviated history, of Afrocentrism, a term that became fashionable as a result of the efforts of its repackager, Professor Molefi Asante, during the 1980s. It is important to note that the term was used at least as early as 1962 in connection with the Encyclopedia Africana project under the sponsorship of Kwame Nkrumah and the editorship of W. E. Burghardt Du Bois. The context of its employment was a discussion of whether the encyclopedia would deal with the entire "African diaspora" or be limited to the continent itself. It was decided that the project would be centered on Africa as a geographical entity. It would be "unashamedly Afro-Centric, but not indifferent to the impact of the outside world upon Africa or to the impact of Africa upon the outside world." Thus, within the historical context of 1962, the term "Afrocentric" was used to designate a geographical, rather than a purely racial, focus.[1]

The Encyclopedia Africana was planned as a work "authentically African in its point of view and at the same time a product of scientific scholarship."[2] The planners were concerned with revising popular as well as scholarly images of sub-Saharan Africa, depicted as the "dark continent" by condescending missionaries and biased anthropologists. Sympathetic whites supported the revisionist goal in principle, and the proposed undertaking has been compared to such projects as the *Encyclopedia Judaica* or the *Catholic Encyclopedia*.[3] Dedicated to producing an "accurate interpretation" within a framework of objectivity, the editors intended to present the early history of Egypt in connection with the rest of Africa, although the project was not Egyptocentric.[4]

Afrocentrism is not equivalent to Egyptocentrism – a point I have reiterated endlessly in these pages – although Egypt has figured prominently in the writings of some Afrocentrists. In appraising the history of Egyptocentrism, as it appeared in *Freedom's Journal* in 1829, or in the writings of William Wells Brown, Frederick Douglass, or Edward Wilmot Blyden in the mid-nineteenth century, it is important to remember that the authors were responding to nineteenth-century "ethnographic" and religious debates. Their contributions to these debates were in no way inferior to the "held views" of the times. Within these discourses it was frequently impossible to distinguish between ethnology and theology, and the ways in which the debates were framed reflected this contemporary reality.

At the time of the Encyclopedia Africana's founding, the problem of Africa's image had been compounded by a revolution in communications and entertainment. Movie audiences had experienced some forty-five years of the Tarzan movies, based on novels by social Darwinist Edgar Rice Burroughs. Tarzan, a white man raised from infancy by gorillas, was depicted as mentally, morally, and physically superior to Africans, who were portrayed as cruel brutes or superstitious children. Another "classic" movie, *Trader Horn*, appropriately celebrated for its magnificent shots of thundering herds on the great plains, was typically racist in its portrayal of Africans as ignoble savages, living in a state of "natural submission" to a sexy blonde female, whom they worshiped as their goddess.[5]

Nowadays, when Africa is mentioned, few people think of *Trader Horn*. The new images that abound are more accurate but, alas, far worse. The contemporary image of Africa is dominated by pictures of children with distended bellies and nightmare eyes, too listless to fan the flies from their parched lips. Latter-day Pan-Africanists stand loftily on the principle that Africa must solve its own problems without European interference, but most lack the will and the moral power to move toward solutions. The rest of the world, with an attitude of sneering contempt, superficially complies with the request for nonintervention, while allowing shipments of firearms to visionless warlords. The peoples of Africa are hardly unique, of course, in their willingness to do violence to one another. European civilization since 1914 has given ample evidence of its own tribalistic propensities. Ethnocentrism, religious terrorism, the reverberations of Stalinism, continue to haunt Europe. Tribal nationalism in Africa has been no better, and no worse.

Many Afrocentrists focus inordinately on the romanticization of pharaohs, preferring to ignore the real Africa, where cruel, illiterate thugs terrorize the populations of cities lacking plumbing, electricity, or hospitals. Their war masks are no longer ancestral but – like their shoes, their shirts, and their firearms – are manufactured on other continents. Admittedly, not all Afrocentrists ignore the outrages of war, famine, and economic helplessness. On the contrary, as historian Daryl M. Scott has observed with support from the writings of Sterling Stuckey, "black nationalists have been black people's harshest critics." To that observation I will add that contemporary Afrocentrists and Pan-Africanists follow the thinking of Martin R. Delany, who opined, long ago, that the world looks upon all Africans "with feelings of commiseration, sorrow, and contempt."[6]

> Cast again your eyes widespread over the ocean – see the vessels in every direction with their white sheets spread to the winds of heaven, freighted with the commerce, merchandise and wealth of many nations. Look as you pass along through the cities, at the great and massive buildings – the beautiful and extensive structures of architecture – behold the ten thousand cupolas, with their spires all reared up towards heaven, intersecting the territory of the clouds – all standing up as mighty living monuments of the industry, enterprise, and intelligence of the white man. And yet, with all these living truths, rebuking us with scorn, we strut about, place our hands akimbo, straighten up ourselves to our greatest height, and talk loudly about being "as good as any body. . . ."
> By their literary attainments, they [whites] are the contributors to, authors and teachers of, literature, science, religion, law, medicine, and all other useful attainments that the world now makes use of. *We have no reference to ancient times – we speak of modern things.*[7]

Despite this talk of "modern things," Delany and his contemporaries, faced with the "living truths" of European dominance, felt compelled to maintain the discourse that one sociologist, Orlando Patterson, has called "contributionism," and another, St. Clair Drake, has called "vindicationism."[8] The contributionist or vindicationist tradition, nurtured by Delany and others, asserted that the African peoples had once been something more than objects of pity and contempt – that they had been contributors to civilization "from the earliest period of the history of nations."[9] The preceding chapters have illustrated how journalists, pamphleteers, and historians, both amateur and professional, crusaded throughout the nineteenth century, ferreting through the Bible and the classics in search of proof that ancient empires had been founded, or deeply influenced, by black people. Their efforts were expected to provide the necessary refutation of widespread racist beliefs that black people were semihumans, impassive brutes, or improvident clowns, who could do nothing more than crudely imitate the achievements of the white race and must remain perpetual objects of condescending charity.

Afrocentrism is closely associated with what I call "civilizationism." It is linked with the symbolic quest for "the lost cities of Africa," and implies indirectly that the worth of a people is demonstrated by its capacity for "civilization." It also implicitly defines as civilized only those cultures that have built cities with paved thoroughfares and stately mansions. Such societies are considered superior to cultures that inhabit quaint villages with adobe houses and thatched roofs. In addition, civilizationism refers to a unilinear path of progress that replicates, or at least resembles, the history of Western Europe in the development of literature, the arts, and the sciences. When linked to civilizationism, Afrocentrism is obsessed with proving that African peoples were the founders of monumental, city-building nations in the past, and demonstrating that ancient black cultures made a seminal contribution to the history of mathematics and letters.[10]

Because early vindicationists were not cultural relativists, they believed it necessary to establish the relationship of Africa's darker peoples to Egypt. From their perspective of cultural absolutism, the Nile valley was the only region of Africa that could claim a true "civilization." Since contemporary black Egyptocentrists are not cultural relativists, they continue to be obsessed with the color of the pyramid builders. They have asserted, reasonably enough, that on the basis of surviving self-representations, those people encompassed the full color range found among present-day Egyptians. Thus, many Egyptians of the third millennium B.C. would probably have been indistinguishable from a good part of the African American population today. This observation would seem innocuous, but while it has seemed perfectly reasonable to some scholars, it has raised the hackles of others.

Martin Bernal has broadly sketched the outlines of this African American historiography, as it relates to Egypt, but his obvious seriousness and touching sincerity have led him to oversimplify its various manifestations with respect to time and place.[11] Critics and sympathizers of Afrocentrism today are likely to take arguments that are part of nineteenth-century anthropological or theological debates, remove them from their contexts, and support them or attack them as if they were expressions of more recent controversies. This is, at best, bad scholarship that reveals a lack of skill in the historical contexts of mythology. At worst, it indicates either a fundamental hostility or an attitude of condescension toward African Americans.

One hesitates to criticize Bernal's attempts, because they have been well-meaning and sympathetic, but other commentators have been less benign. Mary Lefkowitz has published a double-spaced diatribe that unfortunately serves far more effectively than all the tirades of Afrocentric "true believers" to guarantee the survival of extravagant Egyptocentric mythologies, and to reinforce tendencies toward black separatism. To point the finger of derision at mystical or semireligious views developed by exasperated people, some of whom had been slaves and living under conditions of constant humiliation one hundred years ago, reveals a lack of compassion that increases confusion and exacerbates ill will.

In the absence of reliable evidence, attempts to know the races of long-dead Egyptian queens fall into the realm of abstract theory. Marcus Garvey once asked, "Who and what is a Negro?"[12] Similar questions are raised by members of other ethnicities, as, for example, the question that has recently received much attention in Israel as to who is Jewish. Many African Americans are blue-eyed blondes or else have blue-eyed blondes among their immediate kin. This is one reason why Afrocentrists and other African Americans tend to define "black" more loosely than do people of Lefkowitz's background. In any issue of *Ebony* magazine, taken at random, one is likely to find "black" models who are more Caucasian in appearance than the famous bust of Nefertiti in Berlin.[13] Whether or not the Macedonian Ptolemies were originally blondes, and to what extent generations of marrying their siblings would have preserved their contestable Aryan purity, seems irrelevant to the Afrocentrist debate. The Ptolemaic dynasty was established more than twenty centuries after the Pyramid of Cheops was built, and a thousand after Nefertiti. The color of Cleopatra would seem to be completely irrelevant to any discussion of the race of the pyramid architects.

I fail to see any intelligence in Professor Lefkowitz's speculations on such subjects as William Shakespeare's opinions on the color of Cleopatra.[14] Debates over the color of Cleopatra resemble, indeed, the debates over whether Shakespeare actually wrote the plays of Shakespeare.[15] I have made no attempt to revisit discussions of Herodotus and Diodorus Siculus, who have been discussed with numbing repetitiveness by Egyptocentrists since Volney mentioned them in the eighteenth century. Nothing new has been said of these authors since Volney, and the possibility that anything new will ever be said is remote. Martin Bernal has reiterated the old speculations in his *Black Athena*, and the contributors to *Black Athena Revisited* have provided equally speculative assertions. I do not see how Herodotus or Diodorus could have spoken with much authority to modern scholars, as neither of them was in a position to know very much about the third millennium B.C. They were born more than twenty centuries after the construction of the pyramids – closer in time to Cleopatra, and to us. Their writings, like those of Shakespeare, represent mere speculative exegeses on myth, legend, and folklore.[16]

Many Afrocentrists, who should know better, are also to blame for recirculating insupportable myths and legends that only evoke cynicism and ridicule. I have expressed my disregard for ahistorical treatments of the debate over the meaning of Afrocentric culture. I have insisted, for example, that treatments of Egyptocentrism and ethnology in Frederick Douglass must take account of the early influences of Lamarck and the later influences of Darwin on Douglass's thinking. An appreciation of nineteenth-century ethnology will go far to explain the attitudes of nineteenth-century African Americans toward the definition of culture. It will also help to explain why Frederick Douglass and Alexander Crummell never became cultural relativists, and why Edward Wilmot Blyden did.[17]

In this connection, I have already observed that Frederick Douglass's attitudes toward black Africans, as opposed to mulatto Egyptians, were disturbingly negative. Crummell rejected Egypt, but showed a respect for the physical beauty and intelligence of West African peoples. Douglass's claims regarding Egypt were accompanied by negative ideas concerning West Africa and its peoples:

> The form of the negro . . . has often been the subject of remark. His flat feet, long arms, high cheek bones and retreating forehead are especially dwelt upon, to his disparagement, and just as if there were no white people with precisely the same peculiarities. . . .
>
> Need we go behind the vicissitudes of barbarism for an explanation of the gaunt, wiry ape like appearance of some of the genuine negroes? Need we look higher than a vertical sun, or lower than the damp, black soil of the Niger, the Gambia, the Senegal, with their heavy and enervating miasma, rising ever from the rank growing and decaying vegetation, for an explanation of the negro's color?[18]

Most of the nineteenth-century black thinkers experienced the tendency of contemporary ethnologists to conflate the concepts of race and culture. Theirs was the age of Gobineau, an age of cultural absolutism, in which Africans were seen as racially inferior and believed to be culturally inferior, as a necessary result of their racial incapacities. Blyden, who was a half generation younger than Douglass and Crummell, lived well into the age of Franz Boas. He studied African languages and religions, as well as contemporary ethnology, which was beginning to attack white supremacy. He contemplated the new cultural relativism that was beginning to suggest that African cultures, although different, were not necessarily inferior.

The attempt to discover primal truths in the mysterious lore of lost civilizations has been important to the world of letters throughout recorded history. During the classical period, the Middle Ages, and again in the Renaissance, pseudohistoriographies were continually invented and repeatedly reinvigorated. Even during the eighteenth century, the so-called age of reason, pseudohistory thrived in organizations such as the Freemasons and the Rosicrucians, as Martin Bernal has briefly indicated. Much has been made in recent years of the supposed connections between Afrocentrism and Freemasonry. Indeed, the historiography of secret societies has steadily influenced all American popular culture since the eighteenth century, but a more constant influence on Afrocentrism is to be found in Christian traditions of biblical interpretation, which represented perfectly legitimate scholarship in its time.[19]

I have therefore emphasized writings of the Reverends J. W. C. Pennington and Alexander Crummell, who accepted the biblical account of creation, as their contemporary Gobineau apparently did. Nineteenth-century vindicationists frequently discussed the origins of races in terms of accounts they found in Genesis. I have noted, however, various biblical interpretations among nineteenth-century vindicationists. David Walker asserted that the Egyptians and the Carthaginians were black, while Pennington accepted the blackness of the Egyptians but not the Carthaginians. Alexander Crummell often expressed his lack of regard for the Egyptians and, as we have seen, was unwilling to associate black Africans with the history of a people he considered decadent, depraved, abominable, and perhaps even accursed. The point is that while African Americans never lost interest in the Nilotic vindicationist tradition, some have tired of thinking of themselves in terms of Egyptology, and reconstructed themselves variously as the descendants of an ancient Hamitic, Cushite, Pelasgian, or Ethiopian race that supposedly once extended its culture across the Mediterranean.[20]

Crummell's religious conservatism and antipharaonism ironically led him to a more progressive variety of Afrocentrism than that of some of his contemporaries. Since he was hostile to Egypt, his racial vindication had to focus on West Africa, where he worked for some twenty years, off and on, as a missionary. His attitudes toward the indigenous peoples, as we have seen, were ambivalent, ranging at times from the negative to the cautiously admiring. He certainly viewed the culture of uncorrupted Africans as superior to that of

American slaves, although he believed that Africa suffered under "gross darkness." He never became a cultural relativist, judging Africa and its peoples by their own internal standards. Still, he admired Africans as pristine barbarians, praised them for their sexual chastity, and lauded the indomitable spirit of warlike tribes. It remained, as we have already seen, for younger scholars like Edward Wilmot Blyden to grasp fully the implications of culture relativism theory, and to develop a fuller appreciation for African life and customs.

In the mainstream academy of today, the nineteenth-century obsession with connections between ancient Egyptians and contemporary African Americans has practically disappeared. Even such modest claims as those once made by W. E. B. Du Bois have been pushed to the margins. Du Bois argued in *The World and Africa* that "Negroids" had influenced numerous prehistoric Mediterranean cultures, including Egypt. He based his work on the scholarship of respected contemporary white scholars including B. G. Seligman, known for his white supremacist theories and anything but an Afrocentrist.[21] It requires a "dark" sense of humor to appreciate the irony that Du Bois, while relying on Seligman, was unable to consult the work of a young African American classics professor named Frank Snowden.

> I should like to have used the researches on the Negro in classic Europe of Dr. Frank Snowden of Howard University. But classical journals in America have hitherto declined to publish his paper because it favored the Negro too much, leaving the public still to rely on Beardsley's stupid combination of scholarship and race prejudice which Johns Hopkins University published. I tried to get Dr. Snowden to let me see his manuscript, but he refused.[22]

Frank Snowden eventually found prestigious outlets for his scholarship and established himself as one of the most vocal opponents of racial romanticism. In his major work, *Blacks in Antiquity*, Snowden seemed to be concerned with demonstrating the following thesis:

> Whether in Africa or in various parts of the classical world, antipathy because of color did not arise. The Greco-Roman view of blacks was no romantic idealization of distant unknown peoples but a fundamental rejection of color as a criterion for evaluating men.[23]

John Hope Franklin, the dean of African American historians, was accused of racial romanticism when he devoted several pages to Egyptian history in the earlier editions of his authoritative textbook

From Slavery to Freedom. Orlando Patterson, in his 1978 essay "Rethinking Black History," criticized Franklin's attempt "to establish continuities between Black American and North African civilizations." Franklin had made the claim that "the culture of Egypt and Ethiopia was extended to many other parts of Africa and was fused with the indigenous cultures of those areas and with the other cultures that made their way to the western land." By the edition of 1995, Franklin, assisted by the younger African American historian Alfred Moss, had removed almost all references to Egypt.

If Franklin and Moss represent a trend in the teaching of African American history, and I believe they do, then Egyptocentrism would seem to be losing, rather than gaining, influence. It is interesting to note, in passing, that the disappearance of Nilotic references from their text coincides with the introduction of new material on gender issues. Furthermore, here as in other current textbooks, time is more likely to be allotted to the folk narratives recorded by Zora Neale Hurston than to the Nilotic mythology of Drusilla Dunjee Houston.[24] Egyptocentrism's campus followers, despite the inordinate publicity they receive, are decidedly a minority. Although it would be foolish to maintain that there is no interest in Egypt in contemporary black studies departments, it is safe to say that the dominant tendencies in major departments are Marxist, feminist, or primitivist. Sometimes they are an amalgamation of all three tendencies subsumed under the slogan of "gender, race, and class."

Despite its occasionally overzealous enthusiasm, and its civilizationist presuppositions, Egyptocentric Afrocentrism is not all bad. By focusing on George James, Martin Bernal, Pauline Hopkins, and Drusilla Dunjee Houston, it advances an agenda that is preeminently "high cultural." It reveals a desire on the part of those who pursue it to associate their history with "the best that has been known or said in the world." At a time when much of American culture is obsessed with the profane traditions of "gangsta rap" and "signifying monkeys," it is fortunate that some young black Americans are thinking and debating about the works of Homer, Herodotus, and Diodorus. Molefi Asante is typical of Afrocentrists who have tended to avoid the scatological. Even when they deal with the raunchier aspects of folklore, they tend to clean it up, as Langston Hughes was wont to do. Asante's bowdlerized version of the saga of "Shine and the *Titanic*," for example, is stripped of the profanity that characterizes the various authentic versions.[25]

Gangsta rap and bawdy sagas notwithstanding, there are pockets of cultural conservatism among religiously based black communities, whose members cherish nuclear "family values" and strive toward "respectability," and who tire of having their culture defined in terms of "signifying monkeys." Regardless of how one feels about Louis Farrakhan's sincerity or his foolish ethnic hostilities, he has undeniable appeal to many black social conservatives. Many of the men who attended his 1995 March on Washington did so neither because they endorse his ethnic antagonisms, nor because they enjoy two-hour discourses on numerology, but because black nationalism symbolizes the rejection of the scatological values that predominate in media-generated images of black vernacular culture. It is to be remembered that the Nation of Islam, like most black nationalist organizations, supports a "civilizationist" view of history.[26]

African American studies have been rooted in the anthropological tradition of Melville Herskovits, ever since Du Bois glowingly reviewed his *The Myth of the Negro Past* in 1941. The only important African American scholar to reject Herskovits was E. Franklin Frazier, but in this, as in many other things, he represented a tendency that has not prevailed. It was amusing to note during the 1960s that many of those who admired other aspects of Frazier's work, for example, his attack on the "Black Bourgeoisie," were unaware of his adamant refusal to accept the thesis that African Americans were culturally an African people. Pat Ryan observed years ago – and his observation has stood the test of time – that the stronger influence on black studies has come not from the African American scholar E. Franklin Frazier, but from the Jewish American scholar Melville Herskovits.[27]

In Chapter 2 we have witnessed this influence as it manifests itself in the work of Sterling Stuckey. In his magisterial work *Slave Culture*, Stuckey pays tribute to Du Bois's interpretation of the African influence in ancient Egypt, but does not address the role of Egypt in black popular culture. The work and its index contain several prominent references to Herskovits, but Garvey and his monumentalist, empire-building Egyptocentrism are missing, as Professor Dean Robinson has observed, from Stuckey's treatment of nationalist theory. The Garveyite conception of African history and culture is likewise neglected in Henry Louis Gates's discipline-shaping *Signifying Monkey*. The Afrocentrism of both scholars is mainly in the anthropological tradition of Herskovits.[28]

Le Roi Jones, a major spokesman for militant black nationalism even before he changed his name to Amiri Baraka, cited, with approval, Herskovits's contention that "most of the attitudes, customs, and cultural characteristics of the American Negro can be traced directly, or indirectly, back to Africa." Pat Ryan was the first scholar, so far as I know, to observe the paradox of black nationalist gravitation to Herskovits. In a similar vein, however, the late Professor Willie Lee Rose saw the irony in the pronounced intellectual kinship between Herskovits and militant black cultural nationalists. She doubted "that Herskovits would have approved of the style of the arguments now becoming, quite suddenly, all the rage in the late sixties." Be that as it may, just about every African American historian, regardless of race, creed, or political affiliation, seems to pay homage to Herskovits. His supporters range from extreme Afrocentrists like Molefi Asante to Benjamin Quarles, the late teleologue of American assimilation.[29]

Since cultural relativism is so frequently introduced into discussions of Afrocentrism, I have attempted to relate the Afrocentrism of the nineteenth century to the nascent discourse of cultural relativism, and to place that discourse within its historical context. Other scholars have discussed the history of nineteenth-century anthropology with far greater authority than I can profess, and I have alluded to the work of Vernon Williams and George Stocking, among others. In Chapter 8 I offered my own superficial sketch of the cultural relativism debate as it affected the development of Afrocentrism, but, of course, the bibliography on the subject is sophisticated and voluminous. Serious students are advised to consult the bibliographies and appendixes to such works as Vernon Williams's *Rethinking Race*.[30]

Attitudes of antimodernism have been an element of American intellectual life since the romantic movement of the nineteenth century, coexisting in an uneasy and contradictory relationship with the cult of modernism, the love of the machine, and the worship of science. The attitudes of antimodernism that flourished in connection with the spirit of New England transcendentalism provided a background against which the primitivism of the Negro could be appreciated. If there had been no elements of antimodernism in the Christianity of Stowe, she would not have rhapsodized on the messianic potential of Africa's "childlike" race. If New England transcendentalists had been radical advocates of progress and modernity, they would never have contributed to the portrayal of Africans as innocent primitives.[31]

Sterling Brown was on the right track with his assertion that Negro renaissance modernists redeemed nineteenth-century racialist stereotypes in their depiction of African American culture. But whereas Stowe had seen the uncorrupted African as predisposed to Christian virtue, New Negroes saw Africans as transcending any need for Christianity. Committed to the cult of "primitivism," New Negroes admired African natives because they were presumably innocent of the influences of both Christianity and civilization. For Christianity and civilization enervated the virility of primitive tribes. The Christian tradition of the noble savage was supplanted by Robert E. Park's conception of the Negro as "the lady of the races," and by Vachel Lindsay's "Boomlay, boomlay, boomlay Boom!"[32]

Ironically, antimodernism was accompanied by the eventual triumph of Harlem Renaissance "modernism" and the rise of negritude. Traditional ideas of the "femininity," sensuality, and aestheticism of the African race achieved a dominance that is retained to the present day. Within this mythology, which stressed the primal healthy eroticism of the Negro, the word civilization itself evolved into a synonym for decadence. The myth of the sexual, aesthetic, and moral healthiness of the African was given a Freudian twist, but was still rooted in the noble savage traditions of the eighteenth century.

Primitivism is, in a sense, antimodernism; it is associated with the idea that civilization is a cancer – a sickness in the bosom of humanity, and that it leads inevitably to a sapping of creativity and an enslavement of the spirit. Both in the classics and in the Bible, civilization was associated with degeneracy. It was in cities like Sodom, Gomorrah, Nineveh, Babylon, Persepolis, and Rome that the laws of God and nature were most frequently violated. Similar ideas are familiar to anyone who has casually encountered the ideas of Jean Jacques Rousseau, Oswald Spengler, or Sigmund Freud. Civilization, according to Spengler, is "dead culture"; according to Freud it breeds, by its very nature, "discontent."[33]

Afrocentrism has, paradoxically, manifested itself in terms of both "civilizationism" and "primitivism," but the human imagination is never daunted by the need to reconcile opposites. Primitivism assumes that Africans are wiser than Europeans, because Africans have not been caught up in the mythology of progress and the mad rush to impose technological slavery on the universe. In a contradictory vein, Afrocentrists are obsessed with demonstrating that black cultures have met the criteria of being called civilized. They reconcile these opposites by asserting that Africa has produced civilizations that have miraculously retained the spiritual health and humanism of the so-called primitive, and that the African American soul remains an "oasis of simple faith and virtue in a dusty desert of dollars."[34]

The African American historiography of decline is a utopianism of the past, based on the belief that African Americans were much less than their ancestors had been, but another tradition foresaw, and rejoiced at, a day when they would achieve all the benefits of first-class American citizenship. Notwithstanding all the talk of decline, whether from virile barbarians or noble savages or stately Ethiopians, they worked out a historiography of progress that became at least as prevalent as the historiography of decline. There developed an alternative utopian teleology in African American thought, which advanced the idea of unstoppable progress toward a racially enlightened and egalitarian society in the future.

This progressive approach to history was the dominant tendency in the nineteenth century, as Leonard Sweet has deftly illustrated. Sweet makes the point that much of what appears to be black nationalism or ethnochauvinism is, ironically, a form of integrationist rhetoric.[35] We have seen how Frederick Douglass used Egyptocentric arguments in 1854 to demonstrate the fitness of African Americans for inclusion in American society. James Anderson has shown how Richard R. Wright, Sr., testified before Congress on the ancient achievements of Africans to demonstrate that African Americans could and should be educated, as other American citizens were.[36] Booker T. Washington, George Washington Williams, and Carter G. Woodson all used Afrocentric arguments, not to push for separatism but to buttress their position that the ancestral heritage of African Americans made them suitable for citizenship in the United States. The standard authorized view of African American history declares a messianic role for African Americans, usually not as a separatist doctrine but, more often, as a means of arguing for full integration into the American future.[37]

Messianic assimilationism has permeated such textbooks as W. E. B. Du Bois, *The Gift of Black Folk*, which portrays African Americans as the hope of the world. "Thus the emancipation of the Negro slave in America becomes through his own determined effort simply one step toward the emancipation of all men." Benjamin Quarles, *The Negro in the Making of America,* describes African American history "as a lesson-bearing component of the current global struggle for human rights." John Hope Franklin's *From Slavery to Freedom* endowed African Americans with the mission of "carrying forward the struggle at home, for the sake of America's role, and abroad, for the sake of the survival of the world." Even Lerone Bennett's *Before the Mayflower,* with its Egyptocentric opening chapters, ends with a vision of "American renewal" with "the highest level of black participation in history."[38]

In higher education, Afrocentrism is certainly present, along with other forms of black nationalism and Pan-Africanism, but it is more common among working-class students than among Ivy League professors. Nicholas Lehmann conducted a series of interviews at Temple University and the University of Pennsylvania, primarily with young black males, and discovered significant differences in how black studies was perceived at the two institutions. Afrocentrism, Pan-Africanism, and black nationalism were more pronounced at Temple than at the more elitist University of Pennsylvania. Perhaps Lehmann only discovered what his bias had prepared him to see, but my own, unsystematic observations on campus lead me to a similar observation. There seems to be more support for Afrocentrism, Pan-Africanism, and black nationalism among ordinary black students than among those in the elite, trend-setting institutions. One of Lehmann's informants at Temple, presumably typical, said, "I am an African man. That's who I am. That's who I'm going to be," and spoke of his allegiance to "our particular mission as African people."[39]

Lehmann felt that Afrocentrist sentiments were mainstream at Temple but that "it would be unusual to hear such sentiments or to find an avowed Afrocentrist at Penn." I would not want to give an unqualified endorsement to Lehmann's statement, nor would I reject it outright. During the eight years I taught at Brown and the semester I taught at Harvard, I discovered few Afrocentrists, and they were definitely considered exotic. There is indeed an element of class consciousness in Afrocentrism – and a gender element as well. Despite the missionary tendencies of Ivy-trained professors at working-class streetcar colleges in Philadelphia, Indianapolis, and Detroit, young working-class black males in colleges outside the Ivy League remain stubbornly Egyptocentric and black nationalistic.

They bring this Egyptocentrism with them to the classroom; they do not discover it there, because Egyptocentrism is not, essentially, a movement of the universities. These institutions tend to support and perpetuate anthropological Afrocentrism as represented in the professional networks dominating the major research universities. It is the pseudoproletarian, primitivist, and modernist approaches to African American studies that dominate black studies programs today – traditions that oppose or ignore the biblical and Nilotic traditions of Afrocentrism. But with the advent of desk top publishing, these traditions have received new life among the masses, despite the opposition of mainstream black intellectuals.

At present, African Americans who are literate but nonacademic continue to patronize bookstores that emphasize Afrocentrism, black nationalism, and Pan-Africanism. Some black students come to the university hoping to encounter in their black studies courses names with which they are familiar from their local churches and black bookstores. They are often disappointed to discover that the black studies movement in the university is far removed from the Egyptocentric vindicationist black studies movement of the grass roots. Unaware of the politics of the intellectual world, and unsophisticated with respect to scholarly methods, ordinary African Americans sometimes fail to understand why it is that serious academics dread being associated with the intellectual thuggery of Leonard Jeffries and Ron Karenga.

The romantic nostalgia and fundamentalism of young Afrocentrists do not dominate black studies programs, however – nor should they. Afrocentrism in this form is quasi-religious, and based on the assertion of belief; it is not grounded in critical inquiry. One would not expect to see university religious studies departments dominated by Christian fundamentalists or proselytizing for the religious right. Nor is it expected that Judaic studies departments in public universities should be centers for the promotion of Orthodox Jewish religious doctrine. Egyptocentric belief systems and stolen legacy doctrines may be legitimately discussed and analyzed in tax-supported universities, but the only legitimate place for indoctrination is in a black Yeshiva or black Notre Dame, financially maintained by its own believers.

Within American life, no group has ever had complete and exclusive control over its own identity. Group identity, like individual identity, depends on relationships to those persons and groups – whether hostile or friendly – to whom sociologists refer as "significant others." Eugene Genovese, in his influential study of the origins of African American culture, *Roll Jordan Roll*, provided a living illustration of the fact that persons outside a given ethnic group become participants in the shaping of its identity, simply through the process of observing it. Gertrude Stein sketched with poignant beauty, but did not invent the primitivist mythologies about African Americans that dominate her tone poem *Melanctha*. The creation of *Melanctha* symbolized Stein's "radical" departure from the imposed rules of her middle-class Jewish American ethnicity, which she found stifling.[40]

Even those who are opposed to such concepts as Afrocentrism and multiculturalism must admit that neither seems destined to disappear overnight. Afrocentrism is one form of that romantic nationalism which, in the words of Roger Abrahams, "does not demand cultural truth, but culturally derived symbols around which the people may rally."[41] It will survive for the same reasons and to the same extent that an identifiable black population in the United States is likely to survive. There are several reasons for this: First, most black Americans do not desire biological amalgamation. Second, large numbers of black and white Americans are committed to the ideal of multiculturalism, because they believe that racial and cultural diversity are beneficial to the United States. Third, some white people are still committed to the self-evident "truth," pontificated by Thomas Jefferson, that African Americans must be prevented from biological amalgamation with the rest of the population.

But American society, like Jefferson himself, has never been pragmatically committed to the eradication of the black population, whether by amalgamation or deportation or extermination. Many Americans are disgusted by the wickedness of the idea of ethnic cleansing, whether on the biological or on the cultural level. It seems likely, therefore, that there will be a separate black population in America, with its own historical myths and values, for the foreseeable future.

NOTES

═══════

Chapter 1

1. The ideology of progress has been defended by some and attacked by other African American scholars. For example, Donna Richards and Cornell West represent dramatically conflicting views. See Donna Richards, "European Mythology: The Ideology of 'Progress,' " in Molefi K. Asante and Abdul S. Vandi, eds., *Contemporary Black Thought: Alternative Analyses in Social and Behavioral Science* (Beverly Hills, CA: Sage, 1980). Cornell West, on the other hand, encourages and identifies with what he calls "a broader progressive perspective" in *Race Matters* (Boston: Beacon Press, 1993), pp. 57, 59, 64, 65, 66. For more general readings on progress, see notes to Chapter 3.

2. Molefi K. Asante insists that Du Bois was "not Afrocentric," in *Afrocentricity: The Theory of Social Change* (Buffalo: Amulefe, 1980), p. 20. Du Bois used the term in his "Provisional Draft: Not for General Distribution: Proposed Plans for an Encyclopedia Africana." The document is filed with Du Bois's letter to Daniel Walden, dated September 21, 1961, which Professor Walden generously donated to the Rare Books Room at the Pennsylvania State University library. Although there is uncertainty concerning the date of the Provisional Draft, there is no doubt concerning the date of *Information Report* No. 2, mentioned above, which was published by the Secretariat for an Encyclopedia Africana in Accra (1962).

3. Blurbs are by definition positive, and an intelligent self-promoter must never turn down a chance to blurb a book, as Gates and Baker did for Molefi Asante, *The Afrocentric Idea* (Philadelphia: Temple University Press, 1987), and *Kemet, Afrocentricity, and Knowledge* (Trenton, NJ: Africa World Press, 1990).

4. Abdul Aziz Hagg Hilmy to W. E. B. Du Bois, n.d., published in *Information Report* No. 2 (September 1962), p. 2. From 1958 to 1961, Egypt was joined with Syria to form the United Arab Republic.

5. Mary Lefkowitz, *Not Out of Africa: How Afrocentrism Became an Excuse to Teach Myth as History* (New York: Basic Books, 1996). August Meier re-

view of Lefkowitz, *Not Out of Africa*, in *Journal of American History* (December 1996): 988.

6. Drake, "Bibliographic essay," in *Black Folk Here and There: An Essay in History and Anthropology* (Los Angeles: Center for Afro American Studies, University of California, vol. 1, 1987; vol. 2, 1990), vol. 1, pp. 309–32.

7. For methods of cultural history, see Henry Nash Smith, *Virgin Land: The American West as Symbol and Myth* (Cambridge, MA: Harvard University Press, 1950); David Brion Davis, *The Slave Power Conspiracy and the Paranoid Style* (Baton Rouge: Louisiana State University Press, 1970); Carl Bode, *The Anatomy of Popular Culture, 1840–1861* (Berkeley: University of California Press, 1959).

8. Lefkowitz, *Not Out of Africa*, p. 133

9. Frank Snowden, *Blacks in Antiquity: Ethiopians in the Greco-Roman Experience* (Cambridge, MA: Harvard University Press, 1970), pp. 188–95.

10. Wilson J. Moses, *Black Messiahs and Uncle Toms: Social and Literary Interpretations of a Religious Myth* (University Park: Pennsylvania State University Press, 1982), p. 77. Lawrence W. Levine, *Black Culture and Black Consciousness: Afro-American Folk Thought from Slavery to Freedom* (New York: Oxford University Press, 1987). Sterling Stuckey, *Slave Culture: Nationalist Theory and the Foundations of Black America* (New York: Oxford, 1987). Theophus Smith, *Conjuring Culture: Biblical Formations of Black America* (New York: Oxford University Press, 1994).

11. Burkhard Bilger, "The Last Black Classicist," *The Sciences* (March/April, 1977): 16–19. John Bracey in conversation with the author.

12. Gerald Early, in *Civilization: The Magazine of the Library of Congress* (July/August 1995): 39, kindly attributes to me the observation that Afrocentrism is a "historiography of decline." Arthur Herman, *The Idea of Decline in Western History* (New York: Free Press, 1997). Lewis Henry Resek discusses Du Bois as a progressive in his "W. E. B. Du Bois Proposes a Science of Equality," in Lewis Henry Resek, ed., *The Progressives* (Indianapolis: Bobbs-Merrill, 1967), pp. 43–44.

13. Lefkowitz, *Not Out of Africa*. Mary R. Lefkowitz and Guy MacLean Rogers, *Black Athena Revisited* (Chapel Hill: University of North Carolina Press, 1996).

14. Constantin François Volney, *The Ruins, or Meditation on the Revolutions of Empires* (Paris, 1791; 2nd American ed., 1890; repr. Baltimore: Black Classic Press, 1991).

15. St. Clair Drake, *Black Folk Here and There*. A solidly researched survey of early Egyptocentric writing, though less sarcastic in tone, is Dickson D. Bruce, Jr., "Ancient Africa and the Early Black American Historians, 1883–1915," *American Quarterly* 36 (1984): 684–99.

16. Lefkowitz, *Not Out of Africa*, pp. 105–7. Bernal, *Black Athena: The Afroasiatic Roots of Classical Civilization*, vol. 1 (New Brunswick, NJ: Rutgers University Press, 1987), pp. 25–26, 173–77. One finds no Egyptocentrism in Charles Wesley's *Prince Hall: Life and Legacy* (Washington, DC: United Supreme Council, 1983). Egyptians are similarly neglected in William

H. Grimshaw, *Official History of Freemasonry Among the Colored People of North America* (New York: Broadway Publishing Company, 1903).

17. Wesley, *Prince Hall*, pp. 1–10.

18. Grimshaw, *Official History*, pp. 11–22.

19. Martin Delany, *The Origins and Objects of Ancient Freemasonry: Its Introduction into the United States and Legitimacy among Colored Men.*

20. See, for example, Monostato's aria "Alles fühlt," in Mozart's *Zauberflöte*, act 2, scene 8.

21. George G. M. James, *Stolen Legacy* (New York: Philosophical Library, 1954). In my experience, having taught at several universities, James's popularity is strongest among black male students of urban, working-class background. During the late 1980s, while teaching at Boston University I encountered a black male student organization called "Men of Stolen Legacy." As previously noted, Henry Louis Gates blurbed Asante's *Afrocentric Idea* in 1987, but Gates soon disassociated himself from "Asante, and all these guys," as reported in *The Detroit News*, January 21, 1991. Historian Arthur M. Schlesinger, Jr., overlooking Gates's past and present association with Afrocentrism, quoted this source offering Gates as a representative of "serious black scholars." See Arthur M. Schlesinger, Jr., *The Disuniting of America: Reflections on a Multicultural Society* (New York: Norton, 1992), p. 95.

22. Molefe Kete Asante, "On the Wings of Nonsense," *Black Books Bulletin: Words Work* 16, nos. 1–2 (1993–94): 39.

23. Glenn Loury, "Color Blinded," *Arion: A Journal of Humanities and the Classics* (Winter 1997): 183–84.

24. Lefkowitz implies Afrocentrism is anti-Semitic in *Not Out of Africa*, pp. 52, 172. She calls it "hate literature" in *Alternatives to Afrocentrism* (New York: Manhattan Institute, 1994), p. 31.

25. Vernon Williams, Jr., *Rethinking Race: Franz Boas and His Contemporaries* (Lexington: University of Kentucky Press, 1996).

26. Franz Boas, *Atlanta University Leaflet* No. 19, quoted in W. E. Burghardt Du Bois, *The World and Africa: An Inquiry into the Part Which Africa Has Played in World History* (1946; repr. New York: International Publishers, 1965), p. 153.

27. Pat Ryan, "White Experts, Black Experts and Black Studies," *Black Academy Review* 1, no. 1 (Spring 1970): 52–65. Melville Herskovits, *The Myth of the Negro Past* (1941; repr. Boston: Beacon Press, 1958).

28. LeRoi Jones, *Blues People* (New York: Morrow, 1963).

29. Bronislaw Malinowski, "The Pan-African Problem of Cultural Contact," *American Journal of Sociology* 43, no. 6 (1943): 649–66.

30. Roger Bastide, *Les Amériques noires*, published in English as *African Civilizations in the New World* (New York: Harper Torchbooks, 1971).

31. Robert Farris Thompson, *Flash of the Spirit: African and Afro-American Art and Philosophy* (New York: Random House, 1983). Roger D. Abrahams, *Deep Down in the Jungle: Negro Folklore from the Streets of Philadelphia*, rev. ed. (Chicago: Aldine, 1970).

32. Henry Louis Gates, *The Signifying Monkey: A Theory of African-American Literary Criticism* (New York: Oxford University Press, 1988), p. 4.

33. Stuckey, *Slave Culture*, pp. vii, viii.

34. Henry Highland Garnet, "Speech Before the New England Colored Citizen's Convention," *Weekly Anglo-African*, September 10, 1859, quoted in Earl Ofari, *Let Your Motto Be Resistance: The Life and Thought of Henry Highland Garnet* (Boston: Beacon Press, 1972).

35. Robert G. Weisbord, *Ebony Kinship: Africa, Africans, and the Afro-American* (Westport, CT: Greenwood Press, 1973), discusses the relationship of the Pan-Africanist to Zionism, pp. 142, 144. Jacob Drachler, *Black Homeland/Black Diaspora: Cross-Currents of the African Relationship* (Port Washington, NY: Kennikat Press, 1975), discusses the black nationalist–Zionist relationship, particularly with respect to the Pan-Africanist Edward Wilmot Blyden's admiration for Theodore Herzl, pp. 3, 53.

36. Alexander Crummell, "Eulogium on Clarkson" (1846), repr. in his *Africa and America: Addresses and Discourses* (Springfield, MA: Willey, 1891), p. 202. Elijah Muhammad, *Message to the Blackman* (Chicago: Muhammad Mosque of Islam Number 2, 1965), p. 51. Arthur Huff Faussett, *Black Gods of the Metropolis* (Philadelphia: University of Pennsylvania Press, 1944; repr. 1971), p. 42. Claude Andrew Clegg, *An Original Man: The Life and Times of Elijah Muhammad* (New York: St. Martin's Press, 1997), p. 20. Richard Brent Turner, *Islam in the African-American Experience* (Bloomington: Indiana University Press, 1997), pp. 90–92. Mattias Gardell, *In the Name of Elijah Muhammad: Louis Farrakhan and the Nation of Islam* (Durham: Duke University Press), pp. 37–46.

37. Douglass Bush, *Mythology and the Renaissance Tradition in English Poetry* (Minneapolis: University of Minnesota Press, 1932), p. 38.

38. Jasper Griffin in *New York Review of Books*, June 20, 1996, pp. 67–73.

39. Orlando Patterson, "Rethinking Black History," *Harvard Educational Review* 41, no. 3 (August 1971): 297–315.

40. C. S. Lewis *The Discarded Image* (Cambridge: Cambridge University Press, 1962).

41. Joseph Conrad, *Heart of Darkness* (1902).

42. For discussion of African American folkish constructions of history, see Miles Mark Fisher, *Negro Slave Songs in the United States* (1953, 1981; New York: Citadel Press, 1990). Lawrence W. Levine, *Black Culture and Black Consciousness*. Sterling Stuckey, "Through the Prism of Folklore," *Massachusetts Review* 9, no. 3 (Summer 1968).

Chapter 2

1. W. E. B. Du Bois to Edward Wilmot Blyden, April 5, 1909, in Herbert Aptheker, ed., *The Correspondence of W. E. B. Du Bois*, vol. 1 (Amherst: University of Massachusetts Press, 1973). For Blyden on the "African Personality," see his "Lecture to the Young Men's Literary Association of Sierra Leone, May 19th, 1893," *Sierra Leone Times*, May 27, 1893, reprinted in Hollis R. Lynch, ed., *Black Spokesman: Selected Published Writ-*

ings of Edward Wilmot Blyden (New York: Humanties Press, 1971), pp. 200–204. Secretariat for an *Encyclopedia Africana Information Report,* No. 2, p. 2. W. E. B. Du Bois, "On the Beginnings of the [Encyclopedia Africana] Project," reprinted from the front page of the magazine section, Baltimore *Afro-American,* October 21, 1961, and reprinted in Julius Lester, ed., *The Seventh Son: The Thought and Writings of W. E. B. Du Bois* (New York: Vintage, 1971), vol. 2, p. 724. Du Bois accepted the idea that white people could study Africa from the African point of view, and as the *Information Reports* reveal, he systematically solicited the participation of white scholars.

2. Molefi K. Asante, *Kemet, Afrocentricity, and Knowledge* (Trenton, NJ: Africa World Press, 1990), pp. 8–9. The definition of African in *Kemet,* p. 18, is confusing since representatives of every racial type can be found in "some region of the continent."

3. "African personality" borrowed by Asante from Blyden in Asante, *Kemet,* p. 113. Even under the traditional system of racial distinctions there was some ambiguity as to what was considered "Negro," since definitions were set by state rather than national legislation. In Virginia, a person having less than one-fourth Negro ancestry could be found legally white. In Louisiana, the one-drop rule prevailed. Gilbert Thomas Stephenson, *Race Distinctions in American Law* (London: D. Appleton, 1910), p. 15, points out that in 1910 an octoroon female would have been judged *legally* white in the question of the validity of her marriage to a white male. Stephenson implies recognition, however, that her fraternal twin brother, if he were recognized as a Negro in his local community, might have been deemed functionally black with respect to such a practical question as exercise of the franchise (p. 19).

4. For romantic racialism, see George Frederickson, *The Black Image in the White Mind* (New York: Harper & Row, 1971), p. 101.

5. The diversity argument against Afrocentrism is stated in Louis Wilson, "Africa and the Afrocentrists," in John J. Miller, ed., *Alternatives to Afrocentrism* (New York: Manhattan Institute, 1994), pp. 23–36. The unity of African cultures is asserted by British historian Basil Davidson in *The African Genius: An Introduction to African Cultural and Social History* (Boston: Little, Brown, 1969).

6. Asante, *Kemet,* p. 18.

7. Cheikh Anta Diop, *The African Origin of Civilization: Myth or Reality,* trans. from the French by Mercer Cook (New York: Lawrence Hill, 1994). Archeological arguments are also important to the discussion of Ethiopians in the ancient world in Frank Snowden, *Blacks in Antiquity: Ethiopians in the Greco-Roman Experience* (Cambridge, MA: Harvard University Press, 1970). Snowden belongs to a traditional school of vindicationist writers who abjure the designation "Afrocentric."

8. Marcus Garvey, "Who and What Is a Negro?" in Amy Jacques Garvey, ed., *Philosophy and Opinions of Marcus Garvey* (New York: University Publishing House, 1925), vol. 2, pp. 18–21.

9. Stephenson, *Race Distinctions in American Law.* Michael Banton, *Racial*

Consciousness (London: Longman Group, 1988). Michael Omi and Howard Winant, *Racial Formation in the United States* (New York: Routledge, 1994). Kenneth R. Manning, "Race, Science, and Identity," in Gerald Early, ed., *Lure and Loathing: Essays on Race, Identity, and the Ambivalence of Assimilation* (New York: Allen Lane/Penguin, 1993).

10. Molefi K. Asante, *The Afrocentric Idea* (Philadelphia: Temple University Press, 1987), p. 125. On the same page Asante defines Afrocentricity as "the most complete philosophical totalization of the African being at the center of his or her existence."

11. Ali Mazrui, *The African Condition: A Political Diagnosis. The Reith Lectures* (London: Heinemann, 1980), pp. 26–28.

12. This problem of self-doubt was poignantly addressed by Du Bois in his essay "Of Alexander Crummell," in *The Souls of Black Folk* (Chicago: McClurg, 1903). A still controversial exposition of the damaged black psyche thesis is Abraham Kardiner and Lionel Ovesey, *The Mark of Oppression: Explorations in the Personality of the American Negro* (New York: Meridian, 1962). E. Franklin Frazier endorsed the work of Kardiner and Ovesey and asserted that the psychic trauma of slavery was a persistent factor in the personality of African Americans during the twentieth century, in "The Failure of the Negro Intellectual," *Negro Digest* (February 1962): 26–36. For the "Pathology of the Ghetto" thesis, see Kenneth Clarke, *Dark Ghetto: Dilemmas of Social Power* (New York: Harper, 1965), pp. 81–110. Malcolm X's statement on black demoralization and loss of confidence is in *Malcolm X: On Afro-American History* (New York: Merit Publishers, 1967), p. 4.

13. An incisive appraisal of the damaged psyche controversy is Daryl Michael Scott, *Contempt and Pity: Social Policy and the Image of the Damaged Black Psyche, 1880–1996* (Chapel Hill: University of North Carolina Press, 1997), pp. 193–94. In addition to the evidence cited by Scott, see Na'im Akbar, *Chains and Images of Psychological Slavery* (Jersey City: New Mind Productions, 1991), and Kwabena Faheem Ashanti, *Psychotechnology of Brainwashing: Africentric Passage* (Durham, NC: Tone Books, 1993).

14. Molefi K. Asante, *Afrocentricity: The Theory of Social Change* (Buffalo: Amulefe, 1980), p. 39. Aimé Césaire, *Return to My Native Land*, trans. Anna Bostock and John Berger (Baltimore: Penguin, 1969), p. 72.

15. Cheikh Anta Diop, *Civilization or Barbarism: An Authentic Anthropology* (New York: Lawrence Hill Books, 1991), pp. 217, 218, 224.

16. St. Clair Drake, *Black Folk Here and There: An Essay in History and Anthropology*, vol. 1. pp. 1–11.

17. St. Clair Drake utilizes the term "vindicationism," within the context of Karl Mannheim's concept of "partial perspective," in *Black Folk Here and There*, pp. 1–11.

18. Orlando Patterson, "Rethinking Black History," *Harvard Educational Review* 41 (August 1971): 297–315. John Marrant, *A Sermon Preached on the 24th Day of June 1789, Being the Festival of Saint John the Baptist, at the Request of the Right Worshipful the Grand Master Prince Hall, and the Rest of the Brethren of the African Lodge of the Honorable Society of Free and Accepted*

Masons in Boston By the Reverend Brother Marrant, Chaplain (Boston, 1789); repr. in Adam Potkay and Sandra Burr, eds., *Black Atlantic Writers of the Eighteenth Century: Living the New Exodus in England and the Americas* (New York: St. Martin's Press, 1996), pp. 110–11. Joel Augustus Rogers, *World's Great Men of Color*, 2 vols. (New York: Helga M. Rogers, 1947; repr. New York: Collier, 1972).

19. *Freedom's Journal*, New York, April 6, 1827.

20. Samuel Ringgold Ward, *Autobiography of a Fugitive Negro: His Anti-Slavery Labours in the United States, Canada and England* (London: J. Snow, 1855). William Wells Brown, *The Black Man, His Antecedents, His Genius, and His Achievements* (New York: Thomas Hamilton, 1863). J. W. C. Pennington, *A Text Book of the Origin and History, &c. &c of the Colored People* (Hartford: L. Skinner, 1841), p. 30. Frederick Douglass, "The Claims of the Negro Ethnologically Considered [1854]," in Philip Foner, ed., *The Life and Writings of Frederick Douglass* (New York: International Publishers, 1950), vol. 2, p. 301. Drusilla Dunjee Houston, *Wonderful Ethiopians of the Ancient Cushite Empire* (Oklahoma City: Universal Publishing Company, 1926). Martin Bernal, *Black Athena: The Afroasiatic Roots of Classical Civilization*, 2 vols. (New Brunswick, NJ: Rutgers University Press, 1987–91). For an excellent alternative discussion of some of these materials, with a focus on the later nineteenth century, see Dickson D. Bruce, Jr., "Ancient Africa and the Early Black American Historians, 1883–1915," *American Quarterly* 36 (1984): 684–99.

21. Sterling Stuckey, *Slave Culture: Nationalist Theory and the Foundations of Black America* (New York: Oxford University Press, 1987), p. ix.

22. Molefi K. Asante, in an imaginative and synthetic work based on wide reading, argues the centrality of Egyptian culture to the rest of Africa and hence to African Americans; see Asante, *Kemet*. For centrality of Egypt to all African cultures, see p. 57. For indivisible unity of all Old World and New World African cultures, see p. 15.

23. Asante, *Kemet*, esp. pp. 47–110.

24. Kwabena Faheem Ashanti, *Psychotechnology of Brainwashing* (Durham, NC: Tone Books, 1993), p. 26. Theophile Obenga, *Ancient Egypt and Black Africa* (London: Karnak House, 1992). Runoko Rashidi, *Introduction to the Study of African Classical Civilization* (London: Karnak House, 1992). Na'im Akbar, *Light from Ancient Africa* (Tallahassee, FL: Mind Publications, 1994). Asar Jubal, *Black Truth* (Long Beach, CA: Black Truth Enterprises, 1992).

25. From a printed leaflet republished in Herbert Aptheker, ed., *A Documentary History of the Negro People in the United States*, vol. 1 (New York: Citadel Press, 1971), pp. 7–8.

26. Petition to the General Court of Massachusetts, January 4, 1787, the African Petition, Massachusetts Archives, Unenacted Legislation; House Document #2358, excerpted in Sidney Kaplan and Emma Nogrady Kaplan, *The Black Presence in the Era of the American Revolution* (Amherst: University of Massachusetts Press, 1989), pp. 207–8.

27. James Forten to Esteemed Friend [Paul Cuffe], January 25, 1817, re-

printed in Sheldon H. Harris, *Paul Cuffe: Black America and the African Return* (New York: Simon & Schuster, 1972), p. 244. Lamont D. Thomas, *Paul Cuffe: Black Entrepreneur and Pan-Africanist* (Urbana: University of Illinois Press, 1986), pp. 115–16. Julie Winch, *Philadelphia's Black Elite: Activism, Accommodation, and the Struggle for Autonomy, 1787–1848* (Philadelphia: Temple University Press, 1988), p. 35.

28. For Henry Highland Garnet's statement, see Earl Ofari, *Let Your Motto Be Resistance: The Life and Thought of Henry Highland Garnet* (Boston: Beacon Press, 1972), p. 86. *The Weekly Anglo-African*, September 5, 1859, repr. in Sterling Stuckey, *The Ideological Origins of Black Nationalism* (Boston: Beacon Press, 1972), p. 183. For Martin R. Delany's statement, see Delany, *Official Report of the Niger Valley Exploring Party* (New York: Thomas Hamilton, 1861), repr. in Howard H. Bell, ed., *Search for a Place: Black Separatism and Africa, 1860* (Ann Arbor: University of Michigan Press, 1971), p. 121. For an overview of the Back to Africa movement, see Wilson J. Moses, *Classical Black Nationalism: From the American Revolution to Marcus Garvey* (New York: New York University Press, 1996), pp. 1–44. For a broader definition of black nationalism, see Wilson J. Moses, *The Golden Age of Black Nationalism, 1850–1925* (Hamden, CT: Archon Books, 1978; repr. New York: Oxford University Press, 1988).

29. African redemptionism is brilliantly treated in St. Clair Drake, *The Redemption of Africa and Black Religion* (Chicago: Third World Press, 1970). Observations on Marxism are my own.

30. Drake, *Redemption of Africa*, pp. 54–70. Edward Wilmot Blyden's praise for Muslims and Jews is in Hollis Lynch, ed., *Black Spokesman: Selected Writings of Edward Wilmot Blyden* (New York: Humanities Press, 1971). See especially Blyden's essays "The Jewish Question" (1898), in *Black Spokesman*, pp. 209–14, and "Islam in the Western Soudan" (1902), in *Black Spokesman*, pp. 303–6.

31. W. E. B. Du Bois, *The Gift of Black Folk* (Boston: Stratford, 1924), p. 188. Edmund David Cronon, *Black Moses: The Story of Marcus Garvey and the Universal Negro Improvement Association* (Madison: University of Wisconsin Press, 1966), pp. 178–80.

32. Martin Luther King, *Stride Toward Freedom* (New York: Harper, 1958), p. 200.

33. Edward Wilmot Blyden, *Christianity, Islam, and the Negro Race* (London: Whittingham, 1887), p. 116, cites the passage in its translation by Alexander Pope. Crummell alluded to it in "A Defence of the Negro Race," in *Africa and America* (Springfield, MA: Willey, 1891), p. 125. Du Bois also alluded to the verse in *The World and Africa* (New York: Viking Press, 1947), p. 119.

34. Cheikh Anta Diop, *The African Origins of Civilization*, pp. 111–12.

35. George Wells Parker, *The Children of the Sun* (Hamitic League of the World, 1918). Michael Bradley, *The Ice Man Inheritance: Prehistoric Sources of Western Man's Sexism and Aggression*, with an introduction by John Henrik Clarke (New York: Kayode Publications, 1991).

36. John Henrik Clarke, in his introduction to Bradley's *Ice Man Inheritance*,

endorses, with some reservations, Bradley's views. Chancellor Williams, *The Destruction of Black Civilization: Great Issues of a Race from 4500 B.C. to 2000 A.D.* (Chicago: Third World Press, 1974).

37. Melville J. Herskovits, *The Myth of the Negro Past* (1941; repr. Boston: Beacon Press, 1958), p. 55.

38. Bronislaw Malinowski, "The Pan-African Problem of Culture Contact," *American Journal of Sociology* 43, no. 6 (1943): 649–66.

39. Sterling Stuckey, *Slave Culture*, pp. vii – x.

40. Henry Louis Gates, *The Signifying Monkey: A Theory of African-American Literary Criticism* (New York: Oxford University Press, 1988), p. 4. For systematic scholarly discussion of profane narrative tradition among black Americans, see Roger D. Abrahams, *Deep Down in the Jungle*, rev. ed. (Chicago: Aldine, 1970); Roger D. Abrahams, *Positively Black* (Englewood Cliffs, NJ: Prentice-Hall, 1970); Bruce Jackson, *Get Your Ass in the Water and Swim Like Me* (Cambridge, MA: Harvard University Press, 1974).

41. In discussing West African mythology and the trickster, Gates acknowledges his intellectual indebtedness to Robert Farris Thompson, *Flash of the Spirit: African and Afro-American Art and Philosophy* (New York: Random House, 1983).

42. Carter G. Woodson, *The African Background Outlined* (Washington, DC: Association for the Study of Negro Life and History, 1936), pp. 168–78; Jahmheinz Jahn, *Neo-African Literature: A History of Black Writing* (New York: Grove Press, 1968), pp. 15–25; and Roger Bastide, *African Civilizations in the New World* (New York: Harper Torchbooks, 1971).

43. Cheikh Anta Diop, *The African Origins of Civilization.* See notes to illustrations, pp. 29–42.

44. Leo Frobenius, *Atlantis* (Munich, 1921–28). Frobenius, *The Childhood of Man*, trans. A. H. Keane (London: Seely & Company, 1909).

45. Bastide, *African Civilizations in the New World*, p. 224.

46. Harold W. Turner, "Tribal Religious Movements," in *Encyclopedia Britannica* (1979).

47. William E. Cross, "The Negro to Black Conversion Experience," *Black World* (July 1971): 13–27.

48. George M. James, *Stolen Legacy* (New York: Philosophical Library, 1954). Mary Lefkowitz, "The Origins of Stolen Legacy," in Miller, ed., *Alternatives to Afrocentrism*, pp. 27–31.

49. Many of Thomas Jefferson's references to the Jewish religion are disturbing, but must be understood within the context of his times. I refer the reader to Thomas Jefferson, *Writings*, ed. Merrill D. Peterson (New York: Library Classics of the United States, 1984), pp. 1121, 1300, 1301, 1473, 1431, 1437, 1438.

50. See Stephenson, *Race Distinctions in American Law.* For a more recent sociological formulation of what is meant by "race," see F. James Davis, *Who Is Black? One Nation's Definition* (University Park: Pennsylvania State University Press, 1991). Also see Kathy Russell, Midge Wilson, and Ronald Hall, *The Color Complex: The Politics of Skin Color Among African*

Americans (New York: Doubleday, 1992). A typically Afrocentrist formulation of racial theory is John G. Jackson, *Ethiopia and the Origin of Civilization* (1939; repr. Baltimore: Black Classic Press, 1985).

51. Dorothy Nelkin, "Science, Religion and the Creation–Evolution Controversy," *The Drew Gateway* 57, no. 2 (Winter 1986): 46–59. Dorothy Nelkin, *The Creation Controversy: Science or Scripture in the Schools* (New York: Norton, 1982). Dorothy Nelkin, "Science, Rationality, and the Creation-Evolution Dispute," *Social Education* 46 (April 1982), repr. in *The Drew Gateway* 57, no. 2 (Winter 1986): 46–59.

52. A recent example is Theophus Smith, *Conjuring Culture: Biblical Formations of Black America* (New York: Oxford University Press, 1994). Smith himself acknowledges his indebtedness to this tradition. See also Gayraud S. Wilmore, *Black Religion and Black Radicalism: An Examination of the Black Experience in Religion* (Garden City, NY: Doubleday, Anchor Books, 1973). An alternative view recognizing the importance of religious institutions to black culture, but written in a tone of seething hostility, is E. Franklin Frazier, *The Negro Church in America* (New York: Schocken Books, 1964).

53. Herbert Butterfield, *The Whig Interpretation of History* (New York: Norton, 1965).

54. Anthony Appiah, "The Uncompleted Argument: Du Bois and the Illusion of Race," in Henry Louis Gates, ed., *"Race," Writing, and Difference* (Chicago: University of Chicago Press, 1985), pp. 21–37.

55. Arthur, comte de Gobineau, 1816–82, author of the treatise *On the Inequality of Races*, is discussed at greater length in Chapter 3. Also discussed in a later chapter is the work of Octave Mannoni, *Prospero and Caliban: The Psychology of Colonization* (New York: Praeger, 1964). Du Bois, "The Riddle of the Sphinx," is in his *Darkwater: Voices from Within the Veil* (New York: Harcourt Brace, 1920). Cheikh Antah Diop's discomfort with the negritude poets, as previously mentioned, is in *Civilization or Barbarism*, pp. 217, 218, 224.

56. John Hope Franklin, in a letter to the editors of *The New York Review of Books* (September 26, 1991), says of African American scholars that "seeking diligently to qualify as scholars of authority and having been rebuffed by white scholars in other fields, they retreated to the study of Negroes." David Nicholson, Review of Houston Baker, *Rap, Race, and the Academy*, in *The Washington Post*, June 13, 1993.

57. A point I have discussed in several previous works, e.g., in the preface and first chapter of *The Golden Age of Black Nationalism, 1850–1925*. This idea is developed more fully in Chapter 3 of the present work.

58. Snowden, *Blacks in Antiquity*, pp. 120, 289–90.

Chapter 3

1. Literature that discusses the self-image of African Americans in relation to religious themes is voluminous. For some examples, see Benjamin Mays, *The Negro's God as Reflected in His Literature* (New York: Chapman &

Grimes, 1938); Leonard Sweet, *Black Images of America, 1784–1870* (New York: Norton, 1976); Gayraud S. Wilmore, *Black Religion and Black Radicalism: An Examination of the Black Experience in Religion* (Garden City, NY: Doubleday, 1973); David E. Swift, *Black Prophets of Justice: Activist Clergy Before the Civil War* (Baton Rouge: Louisiana State University Press, 1989); Theophus H. Smith, *Conjuring Culture: Biblical Formations of Black America* (New York: Oxford University Press, 1994); George Frederickson, *Black Liberation: A Comparative History of Black Ideologies in the United States and South Africa* (New York: Oxford University Press, 1995).

2. See Claude Lévi-Strauss, "The Structural Study of Myth," in Thomas Albert Sebeok, ed., *Myth: A Symposium* (Philadelphia: American Folklore Society, 1955).

3. Olaudah Equiano, *The Interesting Narrative and Other Writings*, ed. Vincent Carretta (New York: Penguin, 1995), pp. 40, 43, 44–45. The *Narrative* was first published in London, 1789. Carretta's text is based on the London edition of 1794. Allison identifies the Baptist divine Dr. John Gill as author of *Exposition of the Holy Scriptures* (1766), and John Clarke as translator of *Truth of the Christian, in Six Books* (1711). The latter was written by John Grotius as *De veritas religionis christianae* (1627).

4. Alexander Crummell identified his father as a Temne in the unpublished manuscript "Africa and her peoples." See Alexander Crummell, *Destiny and Race: Selected Writings*, ed. Wilson J. Moses (Amherst: University of Massachusetts Press, 1992), p. 66.

5. T. J. Bowen, *Central Africa: Adventures and Missionary Labors in Several Countries in the Interior of Africa from 1849–1856* (Charleston, SC: The Southern Baptist Publication Society, 1857). An African American minister, the Reverend Samuel Williams, describes West African culture in sympathetic terms in *Four Years in Liberia: A Sketch of the Life of Rev. Samuel Williams with Remarks on the Missions, Manners and Customs of the Natives of Western Africa Together with an Answer to Nesbit's Book* (Philadelphia: King & Baird, 1857), pp. 39–48.

6. A guide to Pan-African theory of history, and to the related topic of civilization as historical process, as understood by nineteenth-century African Americans, is provided in the index, both in main entries and in subentries under "Crummell," in Wilson J. Moses, *Alexander Crummell: A Study of Civilization and Discontent* (New York: Oxford University Press, 1989).

7. Booker T. Washington said in *Up from Slavery* (1901), repr. in Louis Harlan, ed., *The Booker T. Washington Papers* (Urbana: University of Illinois Press, 1972), vol. 1, p. 224, that the "freedom" alluded to in these Spirituals meant "freedom of the body, and in this world." Miles Mark Fisher, in *Negro Slave Songs in the United States* (1953, 1981; New York: Citadel Press, 1990), argues that references to crossing over Jordan revealed the desire to return to the ancestral homeland, Africa.

8. Wilson J. Moses, *Black Messiahs and Uncle Toms: Social and Literary Interpretations of a Religious Myth* (1982; 2nd ed., University Park: Pennsylvania State University Press, 1992). David Howard-Pitney, *The Afro-American Jer-*

emiad: *Appeals for Justice in America* (Philadelphia: Temple University Press, 1990). St. Clair Drake, *The Redemption of Africa and Black Religion* (Chicago: Third World Press, 1970), pp. 41–53.

9. Richard Allen and Absalom Jones, "A Short Address to the Friends of Him Who Hath No Helper," in Dorothy Porter, ed., *Negro Protest Pamphlets: A Compendium* (New York: Arno Press, 1969).

10. Phillis Wheatley, "To the University of Cambridge in New England" (1773), reprinted in Benjamin Brawley, ed., *Early Negro American Writers* (Chapel Hill: University of North Carolina Press, 1935), p. 36.

11. Charles Wesley, *Prince Hall: Life and Legacy* (Washington, DC: United Supreme Council, 1983); William Grimshaw, *Official History of Freemasonry Among the Colored People in North America* (New York: Broadway Publishing Company, 1903).

12. See, for example, Grimshaw, *Official History of Freemasonry,* who makes only a passing reference to "the mysteries of the Egyptians passed through Moses to the Jewish people, and thence disseminated among the Greeks and Romans," p. 2, but devotes a chapter to Solomon's Temple, pp. 11–22.

13. Albert Gallatin Mackey, *Encyclopedia of Freemasonry* (1898), vol. 1, p. 189, cites Abbé Robin as the first one to attribute Freemasonry to the Egyptians. Mackey also footnotes M. Alexander Lenoir, *La Franche Maçinnerie rendue à sa veritable origene* (Paris, 1914), as one of the first. Also see George Oliver, *Signs and Symbols Illustrated and Explained in a Course of Twelve Lectures On Freemasonry,* new ed. (London: Sherwood Gilbert & Piper, 1837). Lecture I of Oliver's *Signs and Symbols* is entitled "On the Heiroglyphical System of the Ancients." Albert G. Mackey, in his *Encyclopaedia of Freemasonry,* says that Cagliostro spoke of Egyptian Masonry and cites George Costron, but Cagliostro is treated as an imposter. In Berlin in 1770 a work was published entitled *Crata Repoa: oder Einweihung der Egeptischen Priester.* Mackey compares it to the work of Abbé Terrason and believes that it was influenced by Freemasonry, not the other way around. Both works show Masonic influences. For African American Freemasonry, see Donn A. Cass, *Negro Freemasonry and Segregation* (Chicago, 1957); George W. Crawford, *Prince Hall and His Followers* (New York, 1914); William Grimshaw, *Official History of Freemasonry;* Prince Hall, *A Charge Delivered to the African Lodge, June 24th, 1797, at Menotomy by the Right Worshipful Prince Hall* (Boston, 1797); Lewis Hayden, *Masonry Among Colored Men in Massachusetts* (Boston, 1871); William H. Upton, *Negro Masonry* (Cambridge, MA, 1899); Harold Van Buren Voorhis, *Negro Masonry in the United States* (New York, 1940); Charles Wesley, *Prince Hall.*

14. Sidney Kaplan and Emma Nogrady Kaplan, *The Black Presence in the Era of the American Revolution* (Amherst: University of Massachusetts Press, 1989), pp. 202–14.

15. Mackey, *The Encyclopaedia of Freemasonry,* vol. 1, p. 189. Also see Albert Gallatin Mackey, *The History of Freemasonry: Its Legendary Origin* (New York: Gramercy Books, 1996), where the same author discusses Egyptocentric traditions but stresses biblical myths to a greater extent. Martin Bernal

seems to view Egyptocentrism as the essential element of Freemasonry, and curiously underplays biblical elements in *Black Athena: The Afroasiatic Roots of Classical Civilization* (New Brunswick, NJ: Rutgers University Press, 1987), pp. 25–26, 27, 168, 173–77, 180–88. Of additional interest is Manly P. Hall, *An Encyclopedic Outline of Masonic, Hermetic, Qabbalistic and Rosicrucian Symbolical Philosophy* (Los Angeles: The Philosophical Research Society, 1988).

16. John Marrant, *A Sermon Preached on the 24th Day of June 1789, Being the Festival of Saint John the Baptist, at the Request of the Right Worshipful the Grand Master Prince Hall, and the Rest of the Brethren of the African Lodge of the Honorable Society of Free and Accepted Masons in Boston by the Reverend Brother Marrant, Chaplain* (Boston: The Bible and Heart, 1789); repr. in Adam Potkay and Sandra Burr, eds., *Black Atlantic Writers of the Eighteenth Century: Living the New Exodus in England and the Americas* (New York: St. Martin's Press, 1996), pp. 110–11.

17. Prince Hall, *A Charge Delivered to the African Lodge.*

18. George Shepperson, "Ethiopianism and African Nationalism," *Phylon* 14, no. 1 (1953), 9–18. Drake, *The Redemption of Africa*, p. 50.

19. Percy B. Shelley's "Ozymandias," in *The Complete Poetical Works of Percy Bysshe Shelley*, ed. Thomas Hutchinson (London: Oxford University Press, 1961), p. 550. Anonymous, *The Sons of Africans: An Essay on Freedom with Observations on the Origin of Slavery, by a Member of the African Society of Boston* (Boston: Printed for the Members of the Society, 1808); repr. in Dorothy Porter, ed., *Early Negro Writing, 1760–1837* (Baltimore: Black Classic Press, 1995), p. 15. William Hamilton, *An Oration on the Abolition of the Slave Trade, Delivered in the Episcopal Asbury African Church in Elizabeth St. New York, January 2, 1815* (New York: Printed by C. W. Bunce, for the N.Y. African Society, 1815); repr. in Porter, ed., *Early Negro Writing*, pp. 392–94.

20. Anonymous, "Mutability of Human Affairs," *Freedom's Journal*, New York, April 6 and 20, 1827. John A. Wilson, *Signs and Wonders upon Pharaoh: A History of American Egyptology* (Chicago: University of Chicago Press), p. 37.

21. Ernest L. Tuveson, *Redeemer Nation: The Idea of America's Millennial Role* (Chicago: University of Chicago Press, 1968). Conrad Cherry, ed., *God's New Israel: Religious Interpretations of American Destiny* (Englewood Cliffs, NJ: Prentice-Hall, 1971). H. Richard Niebuhr, *The Kingdom of God in America* (New York: Harper & Brothers, 1937).

22. Stow Persons, "The Cyclical Theory of History in Eighteenth Century America," *American Quarterly* 6, no. 2 (Summer 1954): 147–63. Persons quotes from Henry Saint-John Bolingbroke, *Letters on the Spirit of Patriotism: on the Idea of a Patriot King: and on the State of Parties at the Accession of King George the First*, new ed. (London: Cadell, 1738), p. 128.

23. Johann Gottfried von Herder, *Ideen zur Philosophie der Geschichte der Menscheit* (1784–91); abridged trans. edited by Frank E. Manuel as *Reflections on the Philosophy of the History of Mankind* (Chicago: University of Chicago Press, 1968), pp. 268, 398.

24. Winthrop S. Hudson, ed., *Nationalism and Religion in America: Concepts of American Identity and Mission* (New York: Harper & Row, 1970).

25. The bibliography on Jefferson's attitudes on slavery and African Americans is enormous. Of seminal influence is Winthrop S. Jordan, *White Over Black: American Attitudes Toward the Negro, 1550–1812* (Baltimore: Pelican Books, 1969), pp. 429–82. Also noteworthy is John Chester Miller, *The Wolf by the Ears: Thomas Jefferson and Slavery* (New York: Free Press, 1977).

26. Thomas Jefferson, *Notes on the State of Virginia*, ed. William Peden (Chapel Hill: University of North Carolina Press, 1955), pp. 137–38.

27. Constantin François Volney, *The Ruins, or Meditation on the Revolutions of Empires* (Paris, 1791); repr. of the Peter Eckler edition, 1890 (Baltimore: Black Classic Press, 1991). The first English translation of Volney's *Ruins* was published in 1797. A second English edition, "done under the inspection of the author," was published in Paris in 1802. A partial discussion of the publishing history is contained in the Eckler edition. Jefferson threatening slaves with a whip is in Fawn Brodie, *Thomas Jefferson: An Intimate Biography* (New York: Bantam Books, 1975), p. 377.

28. Volney, *The Ruins*, p. 15.

29. Ibid., pp. 16–19.

30. Henri Gregoire, *The Literature of Negroes or an Enquiry Concerning Their Intellectual Faculties*, trans. D. B. Warden, repr. of the 1810 edition (College Park, MD: McGrath, 1967). For Jefferson's reactions to Gregoire, see Jordan, *White Over Black*, pp. 453–54. Extended discussion of Jefferson's attitudes on slavery is in Miller, *The Wolf by the Ears*.

31. David Walker's *Appeal in Four Articles: Together with a Preamble, to the Coloured Citizens of the World, but in Particular and Very Expressly to Those of the United States of America*, 3d ed. (Boston: David Walker, 1830), repr. in Sterling Stuckey, *The Ideological Origins of Black Nationalism* (Boston: Beacon Press, 1972), p. 44.

32. *Walker's Appeal*, Stuckey ed., pp. 43–45. Charles Gibson, *The Black Legend: Anti-Spanish Attitudes in the Old World and the New* (New York: Knopf, 1971).

33. Alexander Crummell, "The Destined Superiority of the Negro," in Crummell, *The Greatness of Christ and Other Sermons* (New York: Thomas Whittaker, 1882).

34. Maria Stewart, "Introduction," *Productions of Mrs. Maria W. Stewart, Presented to the First Africa Baptist Church & Society, of the City of Boston* (Boston: Friends of Freedom and Virtue, 1835), p. 20.

35. *Walker's Appeal*, p. 58.

36. Hosea Easton, *A Treatise on the Intellectual Character and Civil and Political Condition of the Colored People of the U. States and the Prejudice Exercised Towards Them: With a Sermon on the Duty of the Church to Them* (Boston: Isaac Knapp, 1837), pp. 9, 18, 19, 20.

37. For Hamites, see James W. C. Pennington, *A Text Book of the Origin and History, &c. &c of the Colored People* (Hartford: L. Skinner, 1841). For more recent discussion, see St. Clair Drake, *Black Folk Here and There: An Essay in History and Anthropology*, 2 vols. (Los Angeles: Center for Afro-

American Studies, University of California, Los Angeles, 1987–90), which discusses the Hamitic myth at various points throughout the text. The terms "Ham," "Hamite," and "Hamitic myth" are extensively indexed in vol. 1 and 2.

38. Pennington, *Text Book*, pp. 10–11, 14–15, 32–38.

39. Alexander Crummell, "The Negro Race Not Under a Curse," originally published in the *London Observer* (1852) and republished in Alexander Crummell, *The Future of Africa: Being Addresses, Sermons, etc. Delivered in the Republic of Liberia* (New York: Scribner, 1862), pp. 327–54.

40. Samuel Ringgold Ward, *The Autobiography of a Fugitive Negro: His Anti-Slavery Labours in the United States, Canada, & England* (London: John Snow, 1855), p. 273; the citation of Macaulay is in ibid., p. 275.

41. Ward, *Autobiography*. An example of the pro-slavery argument based on Noah's curse is Thornton Stringfellow's *Scriptural and Statistical Views in Favor of Slavery* (Richmond, VA: J. W. Randolph, 1856).

42. F[rances] E[llen] W[atkins] Harper, *Moses: A Story of the Nile* (Philadelphia: Merrihew & Son, 1869), p. 12.

43. F. E. W. Harper, "Ethiopia," in Benjamin Brawley, *Early Negro American Writers*, p. 293.

44. Frances Ellen Watkins, "Our Greatest Want," *The Anglo-African Magazine* 1, no. 6 (June 1859): 160.

45. Ward, *Autobiography*, p. 274.

46. Hollis Read, *The Negro Problem Solved; or Africa as She Was, as She Is, and as She Shall Be: Her Curse and Her Cure* (New York: A. A. Constantine, 1864), pp. 13–97. Quotations are taken from the table of contents.

47. William Wells Brown, *The Black Man, His Antecedents, His Genius, and His Achievements* (New York: Thomas Hamilton, 1863), pp. 32–33.

48. Brown, *The Black Man*, pp. 33–34, does not identify the specific works or editions of Cicero or Caesar with which he was familiar. Macaulay's passing remark on the ancient Britons is on p. 2 of his *History of England from the Accession of King James the Second* (1848, 1855, 1861).

49. Brown, *The Black Man*, p. 30.

50. Alexander Crummell, *The Greatness of Christ and Other Sermons*, pp. 294–95.

51. For Rousseau, see William Rose Benét, *The Reader's Encyclopedia* (New York: Harper & Row, 1987), s.v. "Noble Savage." Also see A. Owen Aldridge, "Primitivism in the Eighteenth Century," in Philip P. Wiener, ed. *Dictionary of the History of Ideas* (New York: Charles Scribner's Sons, 1968), vol. 3, pp. 598–604.

52. One theory holds that the term "noble savage" was coined by John Dryden in his *Conquest of Granada* (1672). See Benét, *The Reader's Encyclopedia*, p. 698. Aphra Behn (1640–89), in her best-known novel, *Oroonoko or The Royal Slave* (1688), develops the images of both the noble savage and the virile barbarian.

53. Edith Hamilton briefly sketches the imputed characteristics of both Hyperboreans and Ethiopians in her *Mythology: Timeless Tales of Gods and Heroes* (Boston: Little, Brown, 1940).

54. Harper's lines are reprinted in William Robinson Jr., ed., *Early American Poets* (Dubuque, IA: William C. Brown, 1969), p. 29.

55. Henry W. Longfellow's lengthy poem *Song of Hiawatha* is among the "best loved poems of the American people." Du Bois's Wagnerism is in *The Autobiography of W. E. B. Du Bois* (New York: International Publishers, 1968), pp. 156, 159, and in his *The Souls of Black Folk* (Chicago: McClurg, 1903), pp. 236, 249.

56. Crummell, *The Future of Africa.*

57. Although Crummell was not in Africa continuously during these years, he was nonetheless a citizen and continually involved in Liberian affairs. See Moses, *Alexander Crummell.*

58. Crummell, "Africa and Her People" in Moses, ed., *Destiny and Race,* p. 62.

59. Crummell, "The Need of New Ideas and New Aims for a New Era" (1885), in *Africa and America: Addresses and Discourses* (Springfield, MA: Willey, 1891), p. 32.

60. Crummell, "A Defence of the Negro Race in America from the Assaults and Charges of Rev. J. L. Tucker, D. D., of Jackson Mississippi," in *Africa and America,* p. 87.

61. Ibid., pp. 87, 89, 92, 94.

62. Crummell, "Africa and Her People," in Moses, ed., *Destiny and Race,* p. 66.

63. Crummell, "A Defence of the Negro Race," in *Africa and America,* p. 88.

64. Crummell to Domestic and Foreign Missionary Society, August 26, 1854; Crummell, "The Social Principle Among a People," in Moses, ed., *Destiny and Race,* p. 264.

65. James S. Pike, *The Prostrate State: South Carolina Under Negro Government* (1874), rep. with introduction and notes by Robert F. Durden (New York: Harper & Row, 1968), pp. 21–22.

66. Douglass's statement of faith in "moral government of the universe" is in John Blassingame and John R. McKivigan, eds., *The Frederick Douglass Papers* (New Haven: Yale University Press, 1991), vol. 4, p. 229. Douglass's theory of moral progress is the subject of Chapter 4 of the present volume. J. W. C. Pennington on moral government is in *The Anglo-African Magazine* 1, no. 11 (Nov. 1859): 345. See Wilson J. Moses, *Alexander Crummell,* pp. 101–2, for discussion of moral government. The linear development of civilization can be traced through the index of Moses, *Alexander Crummell.*

67. Howard Brotz, ed., *Negro Social and Political Thought, 1850–1920* (New York: Basic Books, 1966), p. 193. For the term "African Movement," see William E. Bittle and Gilbert Geis, *The Longest Way Home: Chief Alfred C. Sam's Back-to-Africa Movement* (Detroit: Wayne State University Press, 1964), p. 83; Robert A. Hill, ed., *The Marcus Garvey and Universal Negro Improvement Association Papers* (Berkeley: University of California Press, 1983), vol. 1, p. 541; W. E. B. Du Bois, "Reconstruction and Africa," *Crisis* (February 1919), repr. in Meyer Weinberg, ed., *W. E. B. Du Bois: A Reader* (New York: Harper & Row, 1970), p. 373; J. Ayodele Langley, *Pan-Africanism and Nationalism in West Africa, 1900–1945: A Study in Ide-*

ology and Social Classes (Oxford: Oxford University Press, 1973), pp. 24, 41–58, 113, 156.

68. See Alexander Crummell, "The Destined Superiority of the Negro" (1877), and "Civilization, the Primal Need of the Race" (1898), in Wilson J. Moses, ed., *Destiny and Race* (Amherst: University of Massachusetts Press, 1992).

69. Anna Julia Cooper, *A Voice from the South* (Xenia, OH: Aldine, 1892), p. 13.

70. Frazelia Campbell, "Tacitus' German Women," *AME Church Review* 2 (July [1886?]): 167.

71. Edward Wilmot Blyden, *Christianity, Islam and the Negro Race* (London: Whittingham, 1887; repr. Edinburgh: Edinburgh University Press, 1967), p. 116.

72. The full title is "Ethiopia's stretching out her hands unto God; or, Africa's Service to the World," in Blyden, *Christianity, Islam and the Negro Race*, p. 113.

73. Edward W. Blyden, *Black Spokesman: Selected Published Writings of Edward Wilmot Blyden*, ed. Hollis Lynch (New York: Humanities Press, 1971), pp. 152–53.

74. Blyden, "Christian Missions in West Africa," in *Christianity, Islam and the Negro Race*, pp. 58–59.

75. Hollis R. Lynch, *Edward Wilmot Blyden: Pan-Negro Patriot, 1832–1912* (London: Oxford University Press, 1964), pp. 79–80.

76. Hollis Read, *The Negro Problem Solved*, p. 387, quotes approvingly from Stowe's *Uncle Tom's Cabin*, but does not give edition or place of publication.

77. Arthur, comte de Gobineau (1816–82), was the author of *Essai sur l'Inegalité des Races Humaines*, usually translated as *The Inequality of Human Races*, although an influential American edition appeared in 1856 as *The Moral and Intellectual Diversity of Races, with Particular Reference to Their Respective Influence in the Civil and Political History of Mankind. From the French by Count A. de Gobineau: With an Analytical Introduction and Copious Historical Notes. By H. Hotz. To Which is Added an Appendix Containing a Summary of the Latest Scientific Facts Bearing upon the Question of Unity or Plurality of Species by J. C. Nott* (Philadelphia, Lippincott, 1856). For fuller discussion of Gobineau and his influences, see Michael D. Biddiss, *Father of Racist Ideology: The Social and Political Thought of Count Gobineau* (Weybright & Talley, 1970); Jacques Barzun, *Race: A Study in Superstition* (New York: Harper, 1965), pp. 50–78; Thomas F. Gossett, *Race: The History of an Idea in America* (New York: Schocken Books, 1965), pp. 342–47; Ashley Montague, *Man's Most Dangerous Myth: The Fallacy of Race* (New York: Meridian, 1965), pp. 56–58; George Frederickson, *The Black Image in the White Mind* (New York: Harper & Row, 1971), pp. 69, 79; George Wells Parker, *The Children of the Sun* (n.p.: The Hamitic League of the World, 1918; repr. Baltimore: Black Classic Press, 1981).

78. Martin R. Delany, *Official Report of the Niger Valley Exploring Party* (New York: Thomas Hamilton, 1861), pp. 133–37.

79. For example, see his theory on the origins of color, in Martin R. Delany,

Principia of Ethnology: The Origin of Races and Color with an Archeological Compendium of Ethiopian and Egyptian Civilization from Years of Careful Examination and Enquiry (Philadelphia: Harper & Brothers, 1879), pp. 20–27.

80. Martin R. Delany, *The Condition Elevation, Emigration, and Destiny of the Colored People of the United States* (Philadelphia: Published by the author, 1852), p. 37.

81. Delany, *Principia of Ethnology*, p. 10.

82. Ibid., pp. 11–12.

83. Ibid., p. 90.

84. Ibid.

85. T. J. Bowen, *Central Africa*. Samuel Williams, *Four Years in Liberia: A Sketch of the Life of the Rev. Samuel Williams*. Delany's reference to Bowen's work is in his *Official Report of the Niger Valley Exploring Party*, p. 36. Crummell's condemnation of African customs is in Alexander Crummell, *The Future of Africa*, p. 220; also see Wilson J. Moses, *Alexander Crummell*, p. 184.

86. Frederick Douglass, "Address Before the Tennessee Colored Agricultural and Mechanical Association, [1873]," in Brotz, ed., *Negro Social and Political Thought, 1850–1920*, pp. 288–89. Frederick Douglass, "The Claims of the Negro Ethnologically Considered [1854]," in Philip Foner, ed., *The Life and Writings of Frederick Douglass* (New York: International, 1950), vol. 2, p. 301.

87. Lewis Henry Morgan divides human progress into the three stages enumerated in the title of his *Ancient Society, or Researches in the Lines of Human Progress from Savagery Through Barbarism and Civilization* (1877; repr. New York: World Publishing, 1963), pp. 3–12.

88. Crummell, "The Negro Race Not Under a Curse," in Crummell, *The Future of Africa*, pp. 327–54.

89. Crummell's hostility to mulattoes was expressed in a letter to John E. Bruce, August 1897, in Moses, ed., *Destiny and Race*, pp. 87–88.

90. For "Aethiopia's blameless race," see Crummell, "A Defence of the Negro Race," in *Africa and America*, p. 125. Crummell on Egyptian abominations is in "The Destined Superiority of the Negro," in *The Greatness of Christ, and Other Sermons*, pp. 332–52, repr. in Moses, ed., *Destiny and Race*, p. 196. For citation of Blumenbach, see Alexander Crummell, "The Attitude of the American Mind Toward the Negro Intellect," *American Negro Academy Papers*, No. 3 (Washington, DC: American Negro Academy, 1898), p. 10n.

91. Alexander Crummell, "The Greatness of Christ" (December 25, 1897), in *The Greatness of Christ*, p. 11.

92. See Alexander Crummell, "Eulogium on the Life and Character of Thomas Clarkson, Esq. of England," New York, December 26, 1846, repr. in *Africa and America*, p. 202. The correct form is "Shishak." The inversion of letters "a" and "k" probably occurred in the conversion of handwriting to printed text. The Lybian Shishak usurped the throne of the pharaohs in the tenth century. See W. E. B. Du Bois, *The World and Africa* (New York: Viking Press, 1947), p. 135.

93. Alexander Crummell, "The Destined Superiority of the Negro," in

Crummell, *The Greatness of Christ,* repr. in Moses, ed., *Destiny and Race,* pp. 201–2.

94. Rufus L. Perry, *The Cushite or the Children of Ham (The Negro Race) as Seen by the Ancient Historians and Poets,* with an introduction by T. McCants Stewart (New York: Brooklyn Literary Union, 1887), p. 8.

95. Africanus Horton, *West African Countries and Peoples, British and Native. With the Requirements Necessary for Establishing That Self-Government Recommended by the Committee of the House of Commons 1865; and a Vindication of the African Race* (London, 1868). Quoted in Davidson Nicol, ed., *Black Nationalism in Africa, 1867: Extracts from the . . . Writings of Africanus Horton* (London: Longmans, Green, 1969), pp. 18–19.

96. See Hazel Carby's introduction to *The Magazine Novels of Pauline Hopkins* (New York: Oxford, 1988). Also see Pauline Hopkins, "Venus and Apollo Modelled from Ethiopians," *Colored American* 6 (May/June 1903): 465.

97. Hopkins, "Of One Blood," *Colored American* (March 1903): 342, and continuing discussion on pp. 343–45.

98. Anthony Appiah, *In My Father's House: Africa in the Philosophy of Culture* (New York: Oxford University Press, 1993), chap. 1, esp. pp. 20–21. Hopkins, "Venus and Apollo . . ." *Colored American* 6 (May/June, 1903): 465.

99. William L. Hansbury, *Africa and Africans as Seen by Classical Writers* (Washington, DC: Howard University Press, 1960). Frank Snowden, *Blacks in Antiquity: Ethiopians in the Greco-Roman Experience* (Cambridge, MA: Harvard University Press, 1970), pp. 120, 289, n. 89, 290.

100. Orlando Patterson, "African American History," *Harvard Educational Review* 41 (August 1971).

101. John E. Bruce, in "Bruce Grit's Column," *Negro World,* February 12, 1921.

102. Joel Augustus Rogers, *From Superman to Man* (New York: J. A. Rogers, 1917).

103. Ibid., pp. 18, 19, 20.

104. Joel Augustus Rogers, *Sex and Race* (New York: Helga M. Rogers, 1944), vol. 3, p. 179.

105. Oswald Spengler, *The Hour of Decision,* trans. Charles Francis Atkinson (New York: Knopf, 1934), p. 219.

106. "The Regeneration of Africa" by P. Ka Isaka Seme, a young Zulu, Curtis Medal Orations, First Prize, April 5, 1906, Columbia University, in William H. Ferris, *The African Abroad or His Evolution Under Caucasian Milieu* (New Haven: Tuttle, Morehouse & Taylor, 1913), pp. 436–40. A few lines of this oration appear verbatim in Monroe Work, "The Passing Tradition and the African Civilization," *Journal of Negro History* (January 1916): 34–41. Work does not attribute them to Seme, however, but to "a German writer," unidentified. The present author surmises that both Seme and Work may have derived the phraseology from the voluminous writings of Leo Frobenius, who may also have influenced Spengler.

107. Dorothy Porter describes the history of these associations in "The Or-

ganized Educational Activities of Negro Literary Societies," *Journal of Negro Education* 5 (October 1936): 556–66. John W. Cromwell, *History of the Bethel Literary and Historical Association, Being a Paper Read Before the Association . . . on Founders Day*, February 24, 1896 (Washington, DC: H. L. Pendleton, 1896). Adelaide Cromwell Gulliver, "Minutes of the Negro American Society," *Journal of Negro History* 44, no. 1 (Winter 1979): 59–69. Alfred A. Moss, *The American Negro Academy: Voice of the Talented Tenth* (Baton Rouge: Louisiana State University Press, 1981). Jacqueline Goggin, *Carter G. Woodson: A Life in Black History* (Baton Rouge: Louisiana State University Press, 1993).

108. George Wells Parker, "The African Origin of the Grecian Civilization," in *Journal of Negro History* 2, no. 3 (July 1917): 334–44. For a brief discussion of Parker and the Hamitic League, see *Garvey Papers*, ed. Hill, vol. 1, pp. 522–23. Also see letter of George Wells Parker to John E. Bruce in *Garvey Papers*, ed. Hill, vol. 2, pp. 279–80.

109. See St. Clair Drake, "The Responsibility of Men of Culture for Destroying the Hamitic Myth," in *Presence Africaine* [English ed.] (February–May, 1959): pp. 521–32. Edith R. Sanders, "The Hamitic Hypothesis: Its Origin and Functions in Time Perspective," *Journal of African History* 10, no. 4 (1969): 521–32. W. E. B. Du Bois, *The Negro* (1915; repr. New York: Oxford University Press, 1970), p. 9. Another version of the Hamitic hypothesis, articulated by G. Sergi, was favorably received by William H. Ferris, who adapted Sergi to his vindicationist views in *The African Abroad*, vol. 1, p. 444; vol. 2, pp. 552–64. Ferris read Sergi far more positively in 1913 than Drake did in "Responsibility of Men." Clearly African Americans did not react negatively to the Hamitic hypothesis until after C. G. Seligman published *Races of Africa* (New York: Home University Library, 1930). But Seligman, too, could be adapted to vindicationist purposes, and Du Bois relied on some of his studies in *The World and Africa* (New York International, 1948), pp. 97, 107.

110. George Wells Parker, *Children of the Sun* (Omaha[?]: Hamitic League of the World, 1918).

111. Drusilla Dunjee Houston, *Wonderful Ethiopians of the Ancient Cushite Empire* (Oklahoma City: Universal Publishing House, 1926), pp. 1–11.

112. Richard B. Turner, "The Ahmadiyya Mission to Blacks in the United States in the 1920s," *Journal of Religious Thought* 44, no. 2 (Winter–Spring, 1988).

113. Charles C. Seifert, *The Negro's or Ethiopian's Contribution to Art* (The Author, 1938; repr. Baltimore: Black Classic Press, n.d.). John G. Jackson, *Ethiopia and the Origin of Civilization* (The Author, 1939; repr. Baltimore: Black Classic Press, n.d.). Anna Melissa Graves, *Africa: The Wonder and the Glory* (Baltimore: Waverly Press, 1942; repr. Baltimore: Black Classic Press, n.d.). Sterling R. Means, *Ethiopia and the Missing Link in African History* (Harrisburg, PA: Atlantis Publishing Company, 1945); chap. 5: "Black Egypt and Her Negro Pharaohs," pp. 53–65, was reprinted as Sterling Means, *Black Egypt and Her Negro Pharaohs* (Baltimore: Black Classic Press, 1978).

114. W. E. B. Du Bois, *Black Folk Then and Now* (New York: Henry Holt, 1939), p. 22.

115. George G. M. James, *Stolen Legacy* (New York: Philosophical Library, 1954). Martin Bernal, *Black Athena: The Afroasiatic Roots of Classical Civilization*, vol. 1 (New Brunswick, NJ: Rutgers University Press, 1987), pp. 173–77. Bernal's observations are borne out by Erik Iverson, *The Myth of Egypt and Its Hieroglyphs in European Tradition* (Princeton: Princeton University Press, 1961). One should also be familiar with the Renaissance tradition of interpretive mythology as discussed in such works as Jean Seznec, *The Survival of the Pagan Gods* (New York: Bolingen Foundation, 1953), and Edgar Wind, *Pagan Mysteries of the Renaissance* (New Haven: Yale University Press, 1958). The bibliographies in both works serve as guides to the traditional intellectual construction of Egypt before the Enlightenment.

116. Charles Wesley, *Prince Hall: Life and Legacy.* Also see Charles Wesley, *The History of Alpha Phi Alpha: A Development in College Life* (Chicago: Foundation Publishers, 1959).

117. Chancellor Williams, *The Destruction of Black Civilization* (Chicago: Third World Press, 1974), p. 49. Another example of anti-Islamic Afrocentrism is Shawna Maglanbayan, *Garvey, Lumumba, Malcolm: Black National Separatists* (Chicago: Third World Press, 1972), pp. 69–76.

118. The illustration of this paradox has dominated my work over the past twenty years, and dominates the preface and first chapter of Wilson J. Moses, *The Golden Age of Black Nationalism, 1850–1925* (Hamden, CT: Archon Books, 1978; repr. New York: Oxford University Press, 1988). The themes are given further expression and may be accessed via the index entries "Christianity," "Civilization," and "Civilizationism" in Moses, *Alexander Crummell.* The notion that complex ideas often reconcile opposites is the dominant theme of my *Black Messiahs and Uncle Toms: Social and Literary Interpretations of a Religious Myth.*

119. Anthony Appiah has appropriately noted this problem, but has been somewhat ungenerous in his interpretation. See Appiah, *My Father's House: Africa in the Philosophy of Culture* (New York: Oxford University Press, 1993), chap. 1, esp. pp. 20–21. For a remarkably self-righteous condemnation of Crummell (although not particurly Afrocentric), see George Hermon's review of Alexander Crummell, *Destiny and Race,* ed. Moses, in *Nineteenth Century Prose* 21, no. 2 (Fall 1994).

Chapter 4

1. Much has been written on the idea of progress, both as actuality and as myth. It is therefore necessary to acknowledge that any use of the words "progress" and "progressivism" in this discussion of African Americans and their writings must be informed by numerous semantical complexities, contradictions, and instances of humor. There have been myriad critiques of the ideology of progress. Some of these have been cautious and thoughtful; others have been sophomoric and naive. In 1908, the

French historian Georges Sorel published *The Illusions of Progress*, a work arguing, from a Marxist perspective, that progress as commonly understood in Western intellectual circles was little more than a justification for bourgeois dominance. Sorel was certainly aware that Marxism itself might be termed a bourgeois ideology of progress. This irony was fully appreciated by subsequent participants in the discourse, notably Bertrand Russell in his *History of Western Philosophy* (1945; New York: Simon & Schuster, 1965). See Russell's discussion of "Messiah," pp. 363–64; Karl Popper in *The Poverty of Historicism* (1957; London: Routledge, 1989), and Jacques Barzun in *Darwin, Marx and Wagner* (1941; Garden City, NY: Doubleday, Anchor Books, 1958). Other twentieth-century authors have followed Sorel in contributing to the historiography of progressivism as a sometimes naive or unexamined assumption. An exhaustive list is not necessary here, but among the more notable have been Charles and Mary Beard, *The American Spirit* (New York: Macmillan, 1942); J. B. Bury, *The Idea of Progress* (New York: Macmillan, 1932); Sidney Pollard, *The Idea of Progress* (1968; New York: Pelican Books, 1971); Bernard James, *The Death of Progress* (New York: Knopf, 1973); Bronislaw Baczko, *Lumière de l'Utopie* (Editions Payot, 1978), trans. Judith Greenberg as *Utopian Lights: The Evolution of the Social Idea of Progress* (New York: Paragon House, 1989); Christopher Lasch, *The True and Only Heaven: Progress and Its Critics* (New York: Norton, 1991). Seeking to redeem the respectability of the concept are Robert Nisbet, *History of the Idea of Progress* (New York: Basic Books, 1980), and C. Owen Paepke, *The Evolution of Progress: The End of Economic Growth and the Beginning of Human Transformation* (New York: Random House, 1993). A brilliant treatment of the idea of progress in the writings of black authors is Leonard Sweet, *Black Images of America, 1784–1870* (New York: Norton, 1976), chap. 5.

2. The terms "civilization" and "civilizationism" are thoroughly indexed and defined in Wilson J. Moses, *Alexander Crummell: A Study of Civilization and Discontent* (New York: Oxford University Press, 1989).

3. With the exception of the Druidic, each theory has been touched upon in the preceding chapter. The idea that the ancient inhabitants of Britain were black was fed by white author David MacRitchie, *Ancient and Modern Britons* (London: Kegan Paul, Trench, 1884).

4. E. B. Tylor, *Primitive Culture: Researches into the Development of Mythology, Philosophy, Religion, Language, Art, and Custom* (1871; 6th ed., London: John Murray, 1920), vol 1, pp. 35–36.

5. See Barzun, *Darwin, Marx and Wagner*. For a more recent discussion, see Carl N. Degler, *In Search of Human Nature: The Decline and Revival of Darwinism in American Social Thought* (New York: Oxford University Press, 1991).

6. Lewis H. Morgan, *Ancient Society or Researches in the Lines of Human Progress from Savagery through Barbarism to Civilization* (1877; Cleveland: World Publishing Co., 1963).

7. For influences of Darwinism on Christian evolutionism, see Richard Hofstadter, *Social Darwinism in American Thought* (1944; Boston: Beacon

Press, 1955), pp. 29–31. For more on Darwinist Christianity, see R. Jackson Wilson, ed., *Darwinism and the American Intellectual* (Chicago: Dorsey, 1989), pp. 31–68.

8. Amos G. Beman, "The Education of the Colored People," *The Anglo-African Magazine* 1, no. 11 (November 1859): 340.

9. Donna Richards, "European Mythology: The Ideology of Progress," in Molefi K. Asante and Abdul S. Vandi, eds., *Contemporary Black Thought: Alternative Analyses in Social and Behavioral Sciences* (Beverly Hills, CA: Sage, 1980).

10. E. B. Tylor, in his famous definition of "Culture or Civilization," used the terms interchangeably. See E. B. Tylor, *Primitive Culture*, vol. 1, p. 1.

11. Alexander Crummell, "The Negro Race Not Under a Curse," was originally published in the *Christian Observer* of London (September 1852). A revised version of this essay appeared in Alexander Crummell, *The Future of Africa* (New York: Scribner, 1862), p. 340. For another treatment of these themes see Werner Sollors, *Neither Black Nor White Yet Both: Thematic Explorations in Interracial Literature* (New York: Oxford University Press, 1977), pp. 78–111.

12. S. S. N., "Anglo-Saxons, and Anglo-Africans," *The Anglo-African Magazine* 1, no. 8 (August 1859): 248.

13. Ibid., p. 249.

14. Alexander Crummell, "The Destined Superiority of the Negro," in Alexander Crummell, *The Greatness of Christ and Other Sermons* (New York: Thomas Whittaker, 1882), p. 333.

15. Ibid., p. 332.

16. Crummell, "God and the Nation," in Alexander Crummell, *The Future of Africa: Being Addresses, Sermons, etc., etc., Delivered in the Republic of Liberia* (New York: Scribner, 1862), p. 157.

17. Crummell cites Georg Barthold Niebuhr in "The Progress of Civilization Along the West Coast of Africa," in Crummell, *The Future of Africa*, p. 107. Gibbon is cited in Tylor, *Primitive Culture*, pp. 1, 33.

18. Alexander Crummell, "The Destined Superiority of the Negro," in *The Greatness of Christ*, p. 347.

19. Alexander Crummell, "The Greatness of Christ," in *The Greatness of Christ*, pp. 1–20.

20. Alexander Crummell, "A Defence of the Negro Race," in Crummell, *Africa and America: Addresses and Discourses* (Springfield, MA: Willey, 1891), p. 92.

21. Alexander Crummell, *Africa and America*, p. 378.

22. J. W. C. Pennington, "The Great Conflict Requires Great Faith," *The Anglo-African Magazine* 1, no. 11 (November 1859): 343.

23. Martin Delany, *The Condition, Emigration, and Destiny of the Colored People of the United States* (Philadelphia: The Author, 1852), p. 43.

24. Frederick Douglass said, "In the eyes of Nicholas, the Turk was the sick man of Europe – just so as the negro is now the sick man of America." "The Black Man's Future in the Southern States," February 2, 1862, in John Blassingame et al., eds., *The Frederick Douglass Papers*, Series 1 (New

Haven: Yale University Press, 1985), vol. 3, p. 503. Alexander Crummell used the "withered arm" analogy in his "Address at the Anniversary Meeting of the Massachusetts Colonization Society," in Alexander Crummell and Edward Wilmot Blyden, *Liberia, the Land of Promise* (Washington, DC: American Colonization Society, 1861).

25. Martin R. Delany, *Condition . . . of the Colored People*, p. 37.

26. Ibid., pp. 17, 37.

27. Ibid., p. 39.

28. Ibid., p. 172.

29. J. W. C. Pennington, "The Self-Redeeming Power of the Colored Races of the World," *The Anglo-African Magazine* 1, no. 10 (October 1859): 314.

30. Ibid. Also see Pennington, "The Great Conflict Requires Great Strength," *The Anglo-African Magazine* 1, no. 10 (October 1859): 344–45.

31. Edward Wilmot Blyden, *Christianity, Islam and the Negro Race*, ed. Christopher Fyfe (1887; repr. Edinburgh: Edinburgh University Press, 1967), p. 247.

32. See Alexander Crummell, "Destined Superiority of the Negro," in *The Greatness of Christ*, p. 343.

33. Frederick Douglass to Harriet Beecher Stowe, March 8, 1853, repr. in Philip S. Foner, ed., *The Life and Writings of Frederick Douglass* (New York: International, 1950), p. 233.

34. *Douglass Papers*, vol. 3, p. 507.

35. James M'Cune [McCune] Smith, "On the Fourteenth Query of Thomas Jefferson's Notes on Virginia," *The Anglo-African Magazine* 1, no. 8 (August 1859): 237.

36. Amos G. Beman "The Education of the Colored People," *The Anglo-African Magazine* 1, no. 11 (1859): 339.

37. Wilson J. Moses, "Writing Freely? Frederick Douglass and the Constraints of Racialized Writing," in Eric J. Sundquist, ed., *Frederick Douglass: New Literary and Critical Essays* (Cambridge University Press, 1990), and "Where Honor Is Due: Frederick Douglass as Typical Black Man," *Prospects: An Annual of American Cultural Studies* 17 (1992).

38. See Charles Beard's introduction to Bury, *The Idea of Progress*, as cited in note 1.

39. Waldo E. Martin, Jr., *The Mind of Frederick Douglass* (Chapel Hill: University of North Carolina Press, 1984), pp. 92, 178.

40. Waldo Martin refers to Douglass as "a child of the enlightenment," in *The Mind of Frederick Douglass*, pp. ix – x.

41. *Douglass Papers*, vol. 2, p. 504.

42. Waldo Martin, *The Mind of Frederick Douglass*, p. 282; cf. pp. 109, 243.

43. Brotz, *Negro Social and Political Thought, 1850–1925* (1964; New Brunswick, NJ: Transaction, 1992), Introduction, esp. p. xxvi. Brotz is hostile not so much to multiculturalism or cultural relativity as to affirmative action. Like many opponents of affirmative action, he seems intentionally to conflate the two concepts.

44. Alexander Crummell on slave culture as the white man's creation and method of oppression is in "A Defence of the Negro Race," in *Africa and America*, pp. 91–97. For Brotz on "different methods of culture," see *Negro Social and Political Thought* (1992), p. xxv.

45. In recent years, multiculturalism and cultural relativism have come under attack, but not only from such neoconservatives as Howard Brotz, Diane Ravitch, and Eugene Genovese in the *New Republic*. An attack from a liberal perspective was recently leveled by Patricia Rengel, chief legislative counsel of Amnesty International USA, who spoke of the need to "meet the challenge of some Asian governments that continue to argue cultural relativism." International feminists have rejected the relativist argument when speaking out against such tribalistic practices as "female circumcision." Both progressives and conservatives view multiculturalism as coming dangerously close to moral relativism. Patricia Rengel, Letter to the Editor, *Wall Street Journal*, July 26, 1993.

46. Waldo Martin discusses Douglass's rejection of polygenesis in *The Mind of Frederick Douglass*, pp. 226, 232–34, 243–44.

47. Frederick Douglass, "The Claims of the Negro Ethnologically Considered: An Address Delivered in Hudson, Ohio, on 12 July 1854," in *Douglass Papers*, vol. 2, pp. 497–525.

48. "Claims of the Negro," *Douglass Papers*, vol. 2, p. 515.

49. James M'Cune Smith, "Civilization: Its Dependence on Physical Circumstances," *The Anglo-African Magazine* 1, no. 1 (January 1859): 7.

50. James M'Cune Smith, "On the Fourteenth Query of Thomas Jefferson's Notes on Virginia," *The Anglo-African Magazine* 1, no. 8 (August 1859): 231, 237.

51. Douglass, "Claims of the Negro," *Douglass Papers*, vol. 2, p. 521.

52. Ibid., vol. 2, p. 502.

53. Ibid., vol. 2, p. 515.

54. Ibid., vol. 2, p. 507.

55. Introduction to Douglass, "Claims of the Negro," *Douglass Papers*, vol. 2, p. 498.

56. Thomas F. Gossett, *Race: The History of an Idea in America* (New York: Schocken Books, 1965), pp. 64–65.

57. Frederick Douglass, "Great Is the Miracle of Human Speech: An Address Delivered in Washington D.C., on 31 August 1891." Reported in *Washington Bee*, September 5, 1891. Other texts in *Washington Evening Star*, September 1, 1891; *Washington Post*, September 1, 1891. The text quoted here is from *Douglass Papers*, vol. 5, p. 476.

58. David Swift, *Black Prophets of Justice: Activist Clergy Before the Civil War* (Baton Rouge: Louisiana State University Press, 1989), p. 255. Joel Schorr, "The Rivalry Between Frederick Douglass and Henry Highland Garnet," *Journal of Negro History* 64 (1979): 30–38.

59. Frederick Douglass disparaged Truth's speaking style in "Lessons of the Hour" (1894), repr. in Philip S. Foner ed., *The Life and Writings of Frederick Douglass* (New York: International 1955), vol. 4, p. 507. Douglass

himself relates the "is God dead?" episode in *The Life and Times of Frederick Douglass* (1893; repr. New York: Literary Classics of the United States, 1994), p. 719.

60. David Blight attributes a strong faith in God and in Providence to Douglass, in *Frederick Douglass' Civil War: Keeping Faith in Jubilee* (Baton Rouge: Louisiana State University Press, 1989), pp. 6–13.

61. Douglass, "Claims of the Negro," *Douglass Papers*, vol. 2, p. 525.

62. Blight, *Douglass' Civil War*, pp. 103–21.

63. Daniel A. Payne, "An Open Letter to the Colored People," in William Wells Brown, *The Black Man, His Antecedents, His Genius, and His Achievements* (New York: Thomas Hamilton, 1863), pp. 208–11.

64. Frederick Douglass, "The Slaveholders' Rebellion," in *Douglass Papers*, vol. 3, p. 541.

65. Waldo Martin, *The Mind of Frederick Douglass*, pp. 178–80.

66. *Douglass Papers*, vol. 5, p. 137.

67. *Douglass Papers*, vol. 5, p. 129. According to the editors of the *Frederick Douglass Papers*, "Douglass first met Ingersol in the late 1860s when he took Douglass into his home as a guest after all Peoria hotels had refused him a room," vol. 5, p. 190. Cf. Douglass's journal observation that "men like Ingersol would have been speedily disposed of had they lived in Avignon in the day of its glory." *Douglass Papers*, vol. 5, p. 312. The phrase "moral government of the universe" is in an address entitled "This Decision Has Humbled the Nation," Washington, DC, October 22, 1883. *Douglass Papers*, vol. 5, p. 117.

68. Jean Baptiste de Lamarck (1744–1829) was perhaps the most influential evolutionist of the nineteenth century, prior to Charles Darwin. He theorized that individuals transmitted their distinctive acquired characteristics to their progeny as their bodies produced "subtle fluids" in response to environmental challenges. Darwin did not challenge Lamarck's belief that acquired traits could be inherited in *The Origin of Species* (London: John Murray, 1859). It was Herbert Spencer, not Darwin, who coined the phrase "survival of the fittest" as the basis of his moral science. Although commonly viewed as the consummate "social Darwinist," Spencer had published his seminal essay, "Progress: Its Law and Cause," in 1857, repr. Spencer, *Illustrations of Universal Progress* (London: D. Appleton & Co., 1864). Thomas Henry Huxley attacked the views of Spencer and the social Darwinists in his *Evolution and Ethics* (London: Macmillan, 1893).

69. Waldo Martin, *The Mind of Frederick Douglass*, p. 249.

70. Frederick Douglass, " 'It Moves' or the Philosophy of Reform," in *Douglass Papers*, vol. 5, p. 129. Waldo Martin in *Mind of Douglass*, p. 249, observes a shift toward Darwin and away from Lamarck, although he is disinclined to grant that Douglass's aversion to biological evolutionism diminished over time.

71. *Douglass Papers*, vol. 5, p. 124. There is a legend that Galileo softly spoke the words "And yet it moves" as he rose from his knees before the Inquisition.

72. For "whiggish history," see Herbert Butterfield, *The Whig Interpretation of History* (1931; repr. New York: Norton, 1965).
73. *Douglass Papers*, vol. 5, p. 137.
74. *Douglass Papers*, vol. 4, p. 229; vol. 5, pp. 80, 129. On the power of science and reason to bring about progressive change, independent of direct Providential intervention, see Douglass, "Pictures and Progress," in *Douglass Papers*, vol. 3, pp. 471–72, and " 'It Moves,' " vol. 5, pp. 131, 137. On witch burning, see *Douglass Papers*, vol. 5, p. 133.
75. Alexander Crummell, "The Social Principle Among a People," in *The Greatness of Christ*, pp. 285–311.
76. Gossett, *Race: The History of an Idea in America*, p. 345.
77. Frederic Barnard attributes multiculturalism to Vico and Herder in his article on "Culture" in *Dictionary of the History of Ideas* (New York: Scribner, 1968), vol. 1, p. 620. Douglass was in the tradition that Barnard attributes to Condorcet, i.e., he believed that social and moral progress resulted from the natural increase of scientific understanding, p. 620.
78. I develop this theme at some length in *The Golden Age of Black Nationalism, 1850–1925* (Harmiden, CT: Archon Books, 1978; repr. Oxford University Press, 1988) pp. 21, 25, 49.
79. Wilson J. Moses, "The Conservation of Races and the American Negro Academy: Nationalism, Materialism, and Hero Worship," *Massachusetts Review* (Summer 1993): 275–94, discusses Crummell's and Du Bois's disagreements with Douglass.
80. On Douglass's relationship with Martin Delany, see Robert S. Levine, *Martin Delany, Frederick Douglass and the Politics of Representative Identity* (Chapel Hill: University of North Carolina Press, 1997). Levine is correct in stressing the cordiality of the eventual break with Delany, and the fact that Douglass continued to speak well of Delany after the break.
81. "Mutability of Human Affairs," *Freedom's Journal*, April 6 and 20, 1827.
82. In later years Douglass spoke against "the alleged duty of colored men to patronize colored newspapers, and this simply because they happened to be edited and published by colored men, and not because of their intrinsic value." Frederick Douglass, "The Nation's Problem: A Speech Delivered Before the Bethel Literary Society in Washington, D.C., April 16, 1889," was originally published as a pamphlet (Washington, DC, 1889). Reprinted in *Douglass Papers*, vol. 5, p. 416.
83. See his editorial "Horace Greeley and Colonization," *Frederick Douglass' Paper* (February 26, 1852), repr. in Foner, ed., *Life and Writings of Douglass*, vol. 2, pp. 172–73. "The Present Condition and Future Prospects of the Negro People" (1853), repr. in *Douglass Papers*, vol. 2, p. 427.
84. "The Industrial College," *Frederick Douglass' Paper* (September 23, 1853), in Foner, ed., *Life and Writings of Douglass*, vol. 2, pp. 272–76.
85. Douglass admitted that he was not suited to the bank's presidency, as his life's work had been theoretical rather than practical. The black congressman John Mercer Langston advised him against taking the position and worked against his appointment. See Carl R. Osthaus, *Freedmen, Phi-*

lanthropy and Fraud: A History of the Freedman's Savings Bank (Urbana: University of Illinois Press, 1976), p. 185.

86. Douglass, "Our Composite Nationality," *Douglass Papers*, vol. 4, p. 259.

87. "At Last, At Last, the Black Man Has a Future," April 22, 1870, in *Douglass Papers*, vol. 4, pp. 265–72.

88. Frederick Douglass, "The Nation's Problem," in *Douglass Papers*, vol. 5, p. 415.

89. Jefferson's opinions on deism and unitarianism are difficult to sort through because he used the terms in ways that were idiosyncratic for his times. Jefferson referred to his beliefs as Unitarianism, although he never belonged to a church of that denomination and most of his contemporaries would have designated his beliefs as deism. See Thomas Jefferson to Benjamin Waterhouse, June 26, 1822, in Thomas Jefferson, *Writings*, ed. Merrill D. Peterson (New York: Literary Classics of the United States, 1984), p. 1459. Jefferson quirkily reserved the term "deism" for other purposes, however: "JEWS. I. Their system was Deism; that is, the belief of one only God. But their ideas of him & of his attributes were degrading & injurious." Thomas Jefferson to Benjamin Rush, April 21, 1803, in Jefferson, *Writings*, pp. 1124–25. Jefferson makes other observations on Jewish religion that apply to the first century A.D. and that, although disturbing to modern sympathies, cannot be appraised in post-Holocaust terms.

90. Frederick Douglass, "The Nation's Problem" (1889), repr. in *Douglass Papers*, vol. 5, p. 416.

91. See the article "Politics," in Stephen Thernstrom, ed., in *Harvard Encyclopedia of American Ethnic Groups* (Cambridge, MA: Harvard University Press, 1980), pp. 803–13. Bruce Stave, ed., *Urban Bosses, Machines, and Progressive Reformers* (Lexington, MA: D.C. Heath, 1972). Terrence J. McDonald's introduction to William L. Riordon, ed., *Plunkitt of Tammany Hall* (Boston: Bedford Books, 1994).

92. Kenneth Warren, creatively and unconventionally but nonetheless accurately, places Douglass within the framework of "progressivism," in "Frederick Douglass's Life and Times: Progressive Rhetoric and the Problem of Consistency," in Sundquist, ed., *Frederick Douglass*, esp. pp. 253–59. Richard Hofstadter explains why progressives opposed ethnic politics, in *The Age of Reform* (New York: Vintage, 1955), pp. 131–73. For Douglass on the assimilation of the Chinese and other ethnicities, see *Our Composite Nationality* (1869), repr. in *Douglass Papers*, vol. 4, pp. 257–59.

93. Mary Lefkowitz, *Not Out of Africa: How Afrocentrism Became an Excuse to Teach Myth as History* (New York: Basic Books, 1996), p. 127; Douglass, *Claims of the Negro Ethnologically Considered* (1854), repr. in *Douglass Papers*, vol. 2, pp. 514–20.

94. Douglass, *Claims of the Negro*, in *Douglass Papers*, vol. 2, p. 523.

95. See *Douglass Papers*, vol. 5, pp. 210, 215–16, 225, 530.

96. Frederick Douglass, "My Foreign Travels," *Douglass Papers*, vol. 5, pp. 335–37.

97. Edward Wilmot Blyden, *African Life and Customs* (London: C. M. Phillips, 1908), pp. 7–9, 11, 17.

98. Anna Julia Cooper, *A Voice from the South: By a Black Woman of the South* (Xenia, OH: Aldine, 1892), pp. 13–18.

99. Barbara Welter, "The Cult of True Womanhood, 1820–1860," in *Dimity Convictions: The American Woman in the Nineteenth Century* (Columbus: University of Ohio Press, 1976), pp. 21–41. Also see Hazel V. Carby's index references to the cult of true womanhood in *Reconstructing Womanhood* (New York: Oxford University Press, 1987); Cooper, *Voice from the South*, p. 10.

100. Cooper, *Voice from the South*, pp. 9–11.

101. Frances Ellen Watson Harper, *Iola Leroy; or Shadows Uplifted* (Philadelphia: Garrigues Brothers, 1892); repr. with an introduction by Hazel Carby (Boston: Beacon Press, 1987), pp. 225–26.

102. Harper, *Iola Leroy*, p. 233.

103. Blyden refers to "M. Finot, 'Race Prejudice,'" in *African Life and Customs* (London: C. M. Phillips, 1908), pp. 7, 8, 9.

104. W. E. B. Du Bois, *The Conservation of Races, American Negro Academy Papers*, No. 2 (Washington, DC: American Negro Academy, 1897), p. 15. Booker T. Washington, *Black Belt Diamonds: Gems from the Speeches, Addresses, and Talks to Students of Booker T. Washington, Selected and Arranged by Victoria Earle Matthews*, intoduction by T. Thomas Fortune (New York: Fortune & Scott, 1898), p. 63.

Chapter 5

1. Ralph Waldo Emerson, "Self Reliance" (1841), repr. in *The Selected Writings of Ralph Waldo Emerson*, ed. Brooks Atkinson (New York: Modern Library, 1950), p. 152.

2. W. E. B. Du Bois, "Jim Crow," *Crisis* (August 1919). Reprinted in Meyer Weinberg, ed., *W. E. B. Du Bois: A Reader* (New York: Harper & Row, 1970), p. 268.

3. W. E. B. Du Bois, *Dusk of Dawn: An Essay Toward an Autobiography of a Race Concept* (New York: Harcourt Brace & World, 1940), pp. 173–220. For Bismarck, see *The Autobiography of W. E. B. Du Bois*, ed. Herbert Aptheker (New York: International Publishers, 1968), p. 126. For Stalinism, see *The Autobiography*, pp. 27, 40, and "Dr. Du Bois on Stalin: 'He Knew the Common Man . . . Followed His Fate,'" *National Guardian*, March 16, 1953, repr. in Julius Lester, ed., *The Seventh Son: The Thought and Writings of W. E. B. Du Bois* (New York: Vintage, 1971), pp. 617–19. Alison Davis, *Leadership, Love and Aggression* (New York: Harcourt Brace Jovanovich, 1983), pp. 105–6, speaks of Du Bois's "Tamburlanian ambitions."

4. For his early and positive reflections on the potential of the church, see W. E. B. Du Bois, ed., *The Negro Church* (Atlanta: Atlanta University Press, Atlanta Study No. 8, 1903). Reprinted in Lester, ed., *The Seventh Son*.

Also see W. E. Burghardt Du Bois, *The Philadelphia Negro: A Social Study* (Philadelphia: University of Pennsylvania, 1899), pp. 389–93.

5. W. E. Burghardt Du Bois, *The Souls of Black Folk* (Chicago: McClurg, 1903), p. 206.

6. Ibid., pp. 80, 203.

7. See "Of the Faith of the Fathers," in Du Bois, *The Souls of Black Folk*, pp. 189–214. Interesting questions concerning the social importance of black religion are raised in Gary T. Marx, "Religion: Opiate or Inspiration of Civil Rights Militancy," in Marx, *Protest and Prejudice* (New York: Harper, 1969).

8. For Du Bois's mystical quasi-religious streak, see Vincent Harding, "W. E. B. Du Bois and the Black Messianic Vision," in John Henrik Clarke et al., *Black Titan: W. E. B. Du Bois* (Boston: Beacon Press, 1970), pp. 52–68.

9. "Arminianism" refers to the doctrines of Dutch theologian Jacobus Arminius, originally Jacob Harmensen (1560–1609), who modified the strict Calvinistic conception of predestination and asserted the compatability of free will with divine knowledge of the future. The influence of Arminianism on American religion comes mainly through Wesleyanism and the Great Awakening of 1739–42. See Alan Heimert and Perry Miller, eds., *The Great Awakening* (Indianapolis: Bobbs-Merrill, 1967), which includes an excellent introduction. William G. McLoughlin speaks of the influence of Arminianism on American evangelical religion in *The American Evangelicals, 1800–1900* (New York: Harper & Row, 1968), p. 10. For a more recent discussion of American puritanism, see Andrew Delbanco, *The Puritan Ordeal* (Cambridge, MA: Harvard University Press, 1989).

10. I have obviously borrowed the term "righteous empire" from Martin Marty, *Righteous Empire* (New York: Dial Press, 1970). In a similar vein, see Ernest L. Tuveson, *Redeemer Nation: The Idea of America's Millennial Role* (Chicago: University of Chicago Press, 1968). Conrad Cherry, ed., *God's New Israel: Religious Interpretations of American Destiny* (Englewood Cliffs, NJ: Prentice-Hall, 1971).

11. The roots of social gospel in American perfectionism can be seen in T. L. Smith, *Revivalism and Social Reform* (New York: Harper & Row, 1965). Also see H. Richard Niebuhr, *The Kingdom of God in America* (New York: Harper & Brothers, 1937).

12. Philip S. Foner, ed., *Black Socialist Preacher: The Teachings of Reverend George Washington Woodby and His Disciple, Reverend G. W. Slater* (San Francisco: Synthesis, 1983).

13. The self-help doctrine is seen in Booker T. Washington, *Character Building* (New York: Doubleday, Page, 1902). Also see Booker T. Washington, *Black Belt Diamonds* (New York: Fortune & Scott, 1898). For African Americans and socially conscious religion, see Gayraud S. Wilmore, *Black Religion and Black Radicalism: An Examination of the Black Experience in Religion* (Garden City, NY: Doubleday, Anchor Books, 1973).

14. For Daniel Alexander Payne's attack on "Africanisms" in the black church, see his *Recollections of Seventy Years* (Nashville: AME Sunday School Union, 1888), pp. 253–54. For a discussion of Payne's opinions, see Sterling Stuckey, *Slave Culture: Nationalist Theory and the Foundations of Black America* (New York: Oxford University Press, 1987), pp. 92–93. For another view of black mass religion that emphasizes strains of militant Christianity, see Vincent Harding, "Religion and Resistance Among Antebellum Negroes, 1800–1860," in August Meier and Elliott Rudwick, eds., *The Making of Black America*, vol. 1: *The Origins of Black Americans* (New York: Atheneum, 1971).

15. McLoughlin, *The American Evangelicals*, p. 14. McLoughlin was no doubt thinking of Emerson's indictment of American evangelicals for dwelling "with noxious exaggeration about the person of Jesus." See *The Selected Writings of Ralph Waldo Emerson*, ed. Atkinson, p. 73.

16. Sheila Walker, *Ceremonial Spirit Possession in Africa and Afro-America* (Leiden: Brill, 1972). Sterling Stuckey also discusses ceremonial spirit possession in connection with the African American ritual of the "ring shout." See Stuckey, *Slave Culture*, pp. 3–53.

17. Du Bois, ed., *The Negro Church*, vol. 1, p. 256.

18. Du Bois, "The New Negro Church" (1917?), in *Against Racism: Unpublished Essays, Papers, Addresses, 1887–1961*, ed. Herbert Aptheker (Amherst: University of Massachusetts Press, 1985), pp. 83–85.

19. Du Bois, *Autobiography*, pp. 285–86. W. E. B. Du Bois, "Credo," in *Darkwater: Voices from Within the Veil* (New York: Harcourt Brace & Rowe, 1919), pp. 3–4. Herbert Aptheker, "Introduction" to W. E. B. Du Bois, *Prayers for Dark People*, ed. Aptheker (Amherst: University of Massachusetts Press, 1980).

20. See Crummell's sermon "The Second Coming," MSC 234, Alexander Crummell Papers, The Schomburg Collection, New York Public Library, available on microfilm.

21. W. E. B. Du Bois, ed., *The Negro Church*, in Lester, *The Seventh Son*, pp. 257–69.

22. Melville Herskovits, *The Myth of the Negro Past* (1941; repr. Boston: Beacon Press, 1958), chap. 7, p. 207. E. Franklin Frazier, *The Negro in the United States* (New York: Macmillan, 1957), pp. 334–59. Albert J. Raboteau, *Slave Religion* (New York: Oxford University Press, 1978), pp. 7–16, 85–86. Jon Butler, *Awash in a Sea of Faith: Christianizing the American People* (Cambridge, MA: Harvard University Press, 1990), pp. 129–63. Continuities with West African religions are a constant theme of a well-informed and brilliantly imaginative text by Theophus Smith, *Conjuring Culture: Biblical Formations of Black America* (New York: Oxford University Press, 1994).

23. Clifton H. Johnson, ed., *God Struck Me Dead* (Philadelphia: Pilgrim Press, 1969), contains autobiographical accounts of the evangelical conversion experience taken from slave narratives collected by the Federal Writers Project during the 1930s.

24. Arthur S. Hudson, *Nationalism and Religion in America* (New York: Harper & Row, 1970), argues that Protestant ideology influences all Americans, including non-Christians.

25. Du Bois's early religious development is discussed by David Lewis in his erudite and exhaustive *W. E. B. Du Bois: Biography of a Race* (New York: Henry Holt, 1993), pp. 48–50. Du Bois, *Autobiography*, pp. 83, 90, 88, 105, 285.

26. Du Bois, *Autobiography*, pp. 280, 285.

27. Ibid, pp. 279, 280.

28. "Tonight I hit the bars! If I should lose my way, then fasten this slip in my button-hole, and send me home. Name: _____ Address _____ The money for the night-taxi is to be found in the right vest pocket." *The Papers of W. E. B. Du Bois* (Sanford, NC: Microfilming Corporation of America, 1980–81), microfilm frame 00215.

29. W. E. B. Du Bois, "Die Negerfrage in den Vereinigten Staaten," *Archiv für Sozialwissenschaft u. Politik* (1906): 22. Du Bois, *The Story of Benjamin Franklin* (Vienna: World Peace Council, 1956), repr. Herbert Aptheker, ed., *Pamphlets and Leaflets by W. E. B. Du Bois* (White Plains, NY: Kraus-Thomson Organization, 1986), pp. 309–28. Du Bois, *The Philadelphia Negro*, pp. 385–93.

30. Du Bois, *Dusk of Dawn: An Essay Toward an Autobiography of a Race Concept* (New York: Harcourt, Brace & World, 1940), p. 56. Elliot M. Rudwick, *W. E. B. Du Bois: Propagandist of the Negro Protest* (New York: Atheneum, 1969), p. 28, mentions Du Bois's hostility to noisy religiosity in the college chapel, but provides no source. Du Bois describes meeting Crummell in *The Souls of Black Folk*, p. 216.

31. J. W. C. Pennington also attempted, unsuccessfully to become matriculated at Yale. See R. J. M. Blackett, *Beating Against the Barriers* (Baton Rouge: Louisiana State University Press, 1986), p. 11. For the connection between Crummell and Alexander Du Bois, see Wilson J. Moses, *Alexander Crummell: A Study of Civilization and Discontent* (New York: Oxford University Press, 1989), pp. 30–31; for meeting with W. E. B. Du Bois, see ibid., p. 247, and Wilson J. Moses, "The Conservation of Races and the American Negro Academy: Nationalism, Materialism, and Hero Worship," *Massachusetts Review* (Summer 1993): 275–95.

32. For possible influence of Nathaniel Taylor, see Moses, *Alexander Crummell*, pp. 30, 291. Also see *The Alexander Crummell Papers*, microform edition (White Plains, NY: Kraus-Thomson Organization, 1972), Nathaniel Taylor Lecture, microfilm reel 12.

33. For discussion of natural morality and so-called design argument, see index references to William Whewell and William Paley in Moses, *Crummell*. For Crummell's reading of Saint Paul, see Moses, *Crummell*, pp. 117–18, 212–13.

34. For Crummell's hostility to antinomianism and to the excesses of enthusiasm, see Moses, *Crummell*, pp. 116–17, 193–94.

35. J. Saunders Redding viewed Washington's entire career as a facile blend of opportunism, naiveté, and hypocrisy. See the copious index refer-

ences to Washington in Redding, *They Came in Chains: Americans from Africa* (New York: Lippincott, 1950), esp. pp. 195–97.

36. Louis Harlan notes that contemporary reviewers compared Washington's autobiography to that of Benjamin Franklin in Harlan, *Booker T. Washington: The Making of a Black Leader, 1856–1901* (New York: Oxford University Press, 1972), p. 249. Max Weber's well-known references to the Calvinistic basis of Franklin's philosophy are an essential element of *The Protestant Ethic and the Spirit of Capitalism.* Despite the paucity of direct references to Franklin in the writings of Du Bois and Washington, both men can be viewed as illustrations of Weber's thesis as to the pervasiveness of Franklinian ideals in America.

37. Du Bois, *The Philadelphia Negro.* Du Bois, Washington, and Weber were all indebted to Franklin.

38. Du Bois, *Prayers for Dark People,* ed. Aptheker, p. viii.

39. W. E. B. Du Bois, *John Brown* (1909; repr. New York: International Publishers, 1962), p. 19.

40. W. E. B. Du Bois, *The Quest of the Silver Fleece* (Chicago: McClurg, 1911), p. 374.

41. W. E. B. Du Bois, *Dark Princess* (New York: Harcourt Brace, 1928), p. 279.

42. Du Bois, *Prayers for Dark People,* p. 62.

43. Alexander Crummell, "Keep Your Hand on the Plough," in Wilson J. Moses, ed., *Destiny and Race* (Amherst: University of Massachusetts Press, 1992).

44. Francis J. Grimké, "Billy Sunday's Campaign in Washington D.C., March 1918," in *Works of Francis J. Grimké,* ed. Carter G. Woodson (Washington, DC: Associated Publishers, 1942), vol. 1, pp. 554–58.

45. Du Bois, *Dusk of Dawn,* pp. 173–220.

46. W. E. B. Du Bois, *The Ordeal of Mansart* (New York: Masses and Mainstream, 1957), pp. 36–37.

47. Wilson J. Moses, *The Golden Age of Black Nationalism, 1850–1925* (Hamden, CT: Archon Books, 1978; repr. New York: Oxford University Press, 1988), pp. 257–61, 267, 268.

48. Emerson, "Divinity School Address," in *Writings,* ed. Atkinson, p. 73.

49. Du Bois, *Autobiography,* p. 285.

50. Du Bois, *The Souls of Black Folk,* p. 3.

51. Lerone Bennett, *Pioneers in Protest* (Baltimore: Penguin Books, 1969), pp. 241–56.

52. Martin Luther King, "Honoring Dr. Du Bois," in *Black Titan,* pp. 181–82. Charles T. Davis, *Black Is the Color of the Cosmos,* ed. Henry Louis Gates, Jr. (New York: Garland, 1982), pp. 219–20. In a similar vein, see Harold R. Isaacs, "Pan Africanism as Romantic Racialism," in his *The New World of Negro Americans* (New York: John Day, 1963), and Harding, "W. E. B. Du Bois and the Black Messianic Vision," in *Black Titan,* pp. 52–68.

53. W. E. B. Du Bois, "Easter Emancipation, 1863–1913," in *Creative Writings by W. E. B. Du Bois,* ed. Herbert Aptheker (White Plains, NY: Kraus-

Thomson, 1985), pp. 28–32; repr. as "Children of the Moon," in Du Bois, *Darkwater*, pp. 187–92.

54. Du Bois's tribute to the "unbending righteousness" of Crummell is in *The Souls of Black Folk*, p. 226. Du Bois's homage to Stalin is in "He Knew the Common Man . . . Followed His Fate," *National Guardian* (March 16, 1953), repr. in Lester, ed., *The Seventh Son*, pp. 617–19. Du Bois's opinions on Nkrumah are conveniently indexed in Lester, ed., *The Seventh Son*. For more on Nkrumah, see Ali Mazrui, "Kwame Nkrumah: The Leninist Czar," in S. Okechukwu Mezu, *Black Leaders of the Centuries* (Buffalo: Black Academy Press), p. 249.

55. W. E. B. Du Bois, *The Conservation of Races*, American Negro Academy Occasional Papers, No. 2 (Washington, DC: American Negro Academy, 1897).

56. Du Bois, ed., *The Negro Church*, in Lester, ed., *The Seventh Son*, vol. 1, pp. 253–54.

57. Lester, ed., *The Seventh Son*, vol. 1, pp. 256, 478.

58. On Herder, see K. R. Minogue, *Nationalism* (New York: Penguin Books, 1970), p. 58. Also see Hans Kohn's article "Nationalism," in Philip P. Wiener, ed., *A Dictionary of the History of Ideas* (New York: Scribner, 1973), vol. 3, pp. 324–39. Cf. W. E. B. Du Bois, *Conservation of Races*, pp. 7, 15.

59. Anthony Appiah alludes to my representation of Johann Gottfried von Herder, the German philosopher of history, in his *My Father's House* (New York: Oxford University Press, 1992), p. 20. My interpretation is a bit different than Professor Appiah's, and I would not, even by implication, associate Herder with the origins of German racialism in the twentieth century.

60. *Crisis* (February 1925), repr. in *W. E. B. Du Bois: A Reader*, ed. Meyer Weinberg (New York: Harper & Row, 1970), p. 378.

61. Oswald Spengler, *The Decline of the West*, trans. Charles Francis Atkinson (New York: Knopf, 1926). Originally published as *Der Untergang des Abendlandes, Gestalt und Wirklichkeit* (Munich: C. H. Beck'sche Verlasbuchhandlung, 1918), p. 31. My references are to the twenty-seventh printing of March 1988. Robert E. Park, "Culture and Civilization," was first published in Robert E. Park, *Race and Culture*, ed. Everett Cherrington Hughes et al. (New York: Free Press, 1950), pp. 15–23.

62. Hans Kohn speaks of the wedding of German nationalism to cosmopolitanism. See his article "Nationalism," in Wiener, ed., *Dictionary of the History of Ideas* (New York: Scribner, 1973), vol. 3, pp. 324–39. K. R. Minogue, *Nationalism* (New York: Pelican Books, 1968), pp. 26–27, remarks the importance of Jacob and Wilhelm Grimm to German nationalism.

63. "What Is Civilization? Africa's Answer," *Forum* (February 1925), reprinted in *W. E. B. Du Bois: A Reader*, pp. 374–81. Crummell, *The Future of Africa*, p. 107, 157

64. "What Is Civilization?" in *W. E. B. Du Bois: A Reader*, p. 374.

65. Ibid., pp. 376, 378.

66. Park himself made the analogy between his concepts and those of Tön-

nies in "Culture and Civilization." See Park, *Race and Culture*, p. 12. "What Is Civilization?" in *W. E. B. Du Bois: A Reader*, pp. 376–77.

67. Du Bois dated the experience in 1886, "at the time I was a youth of eighteen." See "What Is Civilization?" in *W. E. B. Du Bois: A Reader*, pp. 380–81. Cf. Percy Shelley's "Hymn to Intellectual Beauty" for a similar sequence of images and the theme of demoniac possession, "I shrieked and clapped my hands with ecstasy," in *The Complete Poetical Works of Percy Bysshe Shelley*, ed. Thomas Hutchinson (London: Oxford University Press, 1961), p. 531. W. E. B. Du Bois, "Africa and the American Negro Intelligentsia," *Presence Africaine* (December 1954–January 1955), repr. in *W. E. B. Du Bois: A Reader*, p. 384.

68. "What Is Civilization?" in *W. E. B. Du Bois: A Reader*, p. 380.

69. W. E. B. Du Bois, "Mencken," *Crisis* (October, 1927), in Weinberg, *W. E. B. Du Bois: A Reader*, p. 262. Du Bois's treatment of Coleridge-Taylor, an essay entitled "The Immortal Child," is in his *Darkwater* (New York: Harcourt, Brace & Rowe, 1920), pp. 193–217.

70. The conference was perhaps nothing more than a literary invention, although Hayford may have been recollecting any of several meetings treating on the problem of African interests held in Gold Coast during the first decade of the twentieth century. Du Bois organized his conference of 1919.

71. J[oseph] E[phraim] Casely Hayford, *Ethiopia Unbound: Studies in Race Emancipation* (London: Phillips, 1911), p. 181.

72. See, for example, the quotation in Du Bois, *Darkwater*, p. 167, which is taken from J. E. Casely Hayford, *Gold Coast Native Institutions* (London: Sweet & Maxwell, 1903), p. 77. The same work is quoted in W. E. B. Du Bois, *The Negro* (1915; repr. New York: Oxford University Press, 1970), p. 71.

73. Moses, "The Conservation of Races," p. 283.

74. The present author concurs with the judgment of the late Professor Rayford W. Logan, editor of the *Dictionary of American Negro Biography* (New York: Norton, 1982), who says, p. 222: "Despite its verbiage and erudite digressions, *The African Abroad* [New Haven: Tuttle, Morehouse, & Taylor, 1913] has been a valuable source for later historians."

75. Du Bois, "What Is Civilization?" in *W. E. B. Du Bois: A Reader*, p. 378.

76. Du Bois, *The Negro*, p. 17.

77. This poem by Du Bois was originally published in *The Horizon* 2 (November 1907) as "The Burden of Black Women," and reprinted in *Crisis* 9 (November 1914). It was published again, with some interesting alterations, as "The Riddle of the Sphinx" in *Darkwater*, pp. 53–55. For publication histories of this and other poems, I am indebted to the very useful notes of Herbert Aptheker, ed., in *Creative Writings by W. E. B. Du Bois*, p. 12.

78. *Crisis* (April 1924): 273–74; reprinted in Lester, ed., *The Seventh Son*, vol. 2, p. 351.

79. There is some disagreement as to the numbering of the Pan-African Congresses. Richard B. Moore credits Walters and Williams with the or-

ganization of the first Pan-African Congress in London in 1900, and views Du Bois's Paris Congress of 1919 as the Second Pan-African Congress. See Richard B. Moore, "Du Bois and Pan-African," in John Henrik Clarke et al., *Black Titan: W. E. B. Du Bois* (Boston: Beacon Press, 1970), pp. 187–212.

80. In *Dusk of Dawn*, p. 278, Du Bois says the 1923 meetings were held in London, Paris, and Lisbon. In another article he is unclear as to whether a Paris meeting actually took place. W. E. B. Du Bois, "The Pan-African Movement," in George Padmore, ed., *Colonial and Coloured Unity* (Manchester, UK, n.d.), pp. 13–26, repr. in Elie Kedourie, ed., *Nationalism in Asia and Africa* (New York: Meridian Books, 1970), pp. 372–87.

81. Du Bois, "The Pan-African Movement," in Kedourie, *Nationalism in Asia and Africa*, p. 375.

82. W. E. B. Du Bois, "Reconstruction and Africa," *Crisis* (February 1919), repr. in *W. E. B. Du Bois: A Reader*, p. 372.

83. An article in *Negro World* (April 5, 1919) reported that "An Address Denouncing W. E. B. Du Bois" was announced by Garvey at an "enthusiastic convention" meeting of March 25, 1919.

84. Du Bois, *Autobiography*, p. 280.

85. Hermann Hesse's short story "Der Europaer" (1917), in *Gesammelte Erzählungen*, vol. 3, 1903–18 (Frankfurt am Main: Suhrkamp, 1997).

86. Du Bois, *Darkwater*, pp. 39–40.

87. Robert Ezra Park, *Race and Culture: Essays in the Sociology of Contemporary Man* (New York: The Free Press of Glencoe, 1950), pp. 12, 23.

88. Sigmund Freud, *The Future of an Illusion*, ed. and trans. James Strachey (New York: Norton, 1961), p. 6. Originally published as *Die Zukunft Einer Illusion* (Leipzig, Vienna and Zurich: Internationaler Psychoanalytischer Verlag, 1927).

89. *Crisis* (May 1934), repr. in Nathan Huggins, ed., *W. E. B. Du Bois: Writings* (New York: The Library of America, 1986), p. 1252.

90. See Du Bois, "An Essay Toward a History of the Black Man in the Great War," in *Crisis* (June 1919). "The Social Principle Among a People" was published in Alexander Crummell, *The Greatness of Christ and Other Sermons* (New York: Thomas Whittaker, 1882). Delany also uses the phrase "nations within nations," in Martin R. Delany, *The Condition, Elevation, Emigration and Destiny of the Colored People of the United States* (Philadelphia: The Author, 1852), p. 13.

91. Du Bois, "Counsels of Despair," in *Crisis* (June 1934), repr. in Huggins, ed., *Du Bois*, pp. 1258–59.

92. Du Bois, *Dusk of Dawn*, p. 219.

93. The allusion to Revelation 21:1, "a new heaven and a new Earth," with which Du Bois ended this chapter of *Dusk of Dawn*, is interesting because the same words were used by Booker T. Washington at the conclusion of his "Atlanta Exposition Address."

94. W. E. B. Du Bois, ed., *An Appeal to the World* (New York: NAACP, 1947), was a 155-page document with an introduction by Du Bois and various

subsections written by others. The above quotations are from Philip S. Foner, ed., *W. E. B. Du Bois Speaks: Speeches and Addresses, 1920–1963* (New York: Pathfinder Press, 1970), pp. 204, 220. Du Bois had used the "nation within a nation" analogy previously, as we have seen.

95. Du Bois, *Autobiography*, p. 403.

96. Citation of Hayford and other quotations from Du Bois, *Autobiography*, pp. 403–4.

97. W. E. B. Du Bois, "The Saga of Nkrumah," *National Guardian* (July 30, 1956), repr. in Lester, ed., *The Seventh Son*, vol. 2, p. 638.

98. Bennett, *Pioneers in Protest*, p. 243.

99. W. E. B. Du Bois, "Ghana Calls," *Freedomways* (Winter 1962), repr. in Aptheker, ed., *Creative Writing by W. E. B. Du Bois*, pp. 52–55.

100. W. E. B. Du Bois to Edward Wilmot Blyden, April 5, 1909, in Herbert Aptheker, ed., *The Correspondence of W. E. B. Du Bois* (Amherst: University of Massachusetts Press, 1973), vol. 1. p. 146. Also see description of the project in his article on "Pushkin," *Phylon* 1 (3rd Quarter, 1940): 265–69.

101. Du Bois, "On the Beginnings of the [Encylopedia Africana] Project," reprinted from the front page of the magazine section, Baltimore *Afro-American*, October 21, 1961, in Lester, ed., *The Seventh Son*, vol. 2. p. 724.

102. Secretariat for an Encyclopedia Africana, *Information Report*, No. 2 (September 1962), p. 2. The author is, presumably, W. E. B. Du Bois, speaking for the Secretariat in his capacity as director of the project.

103. Du Bois, "Pushkin," 265–69.

104. Ibid., p. 269

105. Du Bois, "On My Character," in *Autobiography*, pp. 277–88.

106. Du Bois's essay on Bismarck, his Fisk graduation address of 1888, has never been printed in any readily available anthology. It is available both in handwriting and in typescript in the microfilm edition of the W. E. B. Du Bois Papers. His eulogy of Stalin is in Lester, ed., *The Seventh Son*, pp. 617–19.

107. Du Bois, "Ghana Calls," *Freedomways*.

Chapter 6

1. William H. Ferris, *The African Abroad or His Evolution in Western Civilization, Tracing His Development Under Caucasian Milieu* (New Haven: Tuttle, Morehouse, & Taylor, 1913). Stephen Fox, *The Guardian of Boston: William Monroe Trotter* (New York: Atheneum, 1970), is a brilliantly researched, well-written, and sympathetic interpretation of its primary subject, but Fox's observations on Ferris (p. 109) seem insensitive to the emotional pain that he endured. For another analysis of Ferris's career, see Kevin Gaines, *Uplifting the Race: Black Leadership, Politics, and Culture in the Twentieth Century* (Chapel Hill: University of North Carolina Press, 1996), pp. 100–27. Interesting questions about the treatment of African

Americans in American intellectual history have been raised by David Lewis in "Radical History: Toward Inclusiveness," *Journal of American History* 76, no. 2 (September 1989): 473.

2. A reading of the autobiographical sections of Ferris's *The African Abroad* should reveal the poignant applicability of the familiar lines from T. S. Eliot, "The Lovesong of J. Alfred Prufrock." The cultural literacy controversy was largely inspired by E. D. Hirsch, *Cultural Literacy: What Every American Needs to Know* (Boston: Houghton Mifflin, 1987). For more on the controversy, see Christopher Hitchens, "Why We Don't Know What We Don't Know," *New York Times Magazine*, May 14, 1990, pp. 32–33, 59–62. A balanced and qualified defense of some components of Afrocentrism within the cultural literacy debate is Glenn Loury, "The Hard Questions: Pride and Prejudice," in *The New Republic* (May 19, 1997): 25. Also see Loury's "Color Blinded," *Arion: A Journal of Humanities and the Classics* (Winter 1997): 183–84.

3. Booker T. Washington, *My Larger Education: Being Chapters from My Experience* (Garden City: Doubleday, Page, 1911), pp. 114–15.

4. Dudley Randall, "Booker T. and W.E.B.," in Rosey E. Pool, ed., *Beyond the Blues: New Poems by American Negroes* (Lympne, Kent, UK: Hand & Flower, 1962).

5. Anonymous, "The Negro at Harvard University," rep. from *McClure's Magazine* by *Alexander's Magazine* (June 15, 1905). G. David Houston, "The Negro Graduates of Harvard University, 1905," *Alexander's Magazine*, July 15, 1905. For a critique of Washington's educational policy, see C. Vann Woodward, *Origins of the New South, 1877–1913* (Baton Rouge: Louisiana State University Press, 1951); also see August Meier and Elliott Rudwick, *From Plantation to Ghetto* (New York: Hill & Wang, 1970), pp. 201–2.

6. E. Franklin Frazier, *Black Bourgeoisie* (New York: Collier, 1962), p. 203 n. 12.

7. William H. Ferris, *Alexander Crummell: An Apostle of Negro Culture*, American Negro Academy Occasional Papers, No. 20 (Washington, DC: American Negro Academy, 1920), p. 7.

8. Wilson J. Moses, *Alexander Crummell: A Study of Civilization and Discontent* (New York: Oxford University Press, 1990), pp. 242–44.

9. J. W. E. Bowen, ed., *Africa and the American Negro: Addresses and Proceedings of the Congress on Africa, Held Under the Auspices of the Stewart Missionary Foundation for Africa of Gannon Theological Seminary in Connection with the Cotton States and International Exposition, December 13–15, 1895* (Atlanta: Gannon Theological Seminary, 1896), p. 138.

10. Those in attendance included poet Paul Laurence Dunbar; clergyman Walter B. Hayson; sociologist Kelly Miller; and publisher John W. Cromwell. See Alfred A. Moss, *The American Negro Academy: Voice of the Talented Tenth* (Baton Rouge: Louisiana State University Press, 1981), p. 27. A printed version of the constitution provided to the present author by Dr. Adelaide Cromwell from the papers of John Wesley Cromwell specifies that membership is to be limited at fifty; cf. Moss, *American Negro Acad-*

emy, pp. 24–25, who conveys the information that Crummell's original draft of the constitution planned to limit membership to forty.

11. Du Bois's theory of the Talented Tenth prescribed that an elite of highly educated black leaders should dedicate their lives to uplifting the black masses. That Du Bois derived the idea from Crummell was suggested in John H. Bracey, August Meier, and Eliot Rudwick, eds., *Black Nationalism in America* (Indianapolis: Bobbs-Merrill, 1970), p. 123. Compare Alexander Crummell, "Civilization, the Primal Need of the Race," in American Negro Academy Occasional Papers, No. 3 (Washington: American Negro Academy, 1898), to W. E. B. Du Bois, "The Talented Tenth," in Booker T. Washington et al., *The Negro Problem* (New York: James Pott, 1903), pp. 31–75.

12. Quoted in *The People's Advocate*, February 14, 1880, microfilm available from the Library of Congress.

13. Alexander Crummell, "Common Sense in Common Schooling," in his *Africa and America: Addresses and Discourses* (Springfield, MA: Willey, 1891), pp. 328–33.

14. Dorothy Porter, "The Organized Educational Activities of Negro Literary Societies, 1828–1846," *Journal of Negro Education* (October 1936): 556–66. Moss, *American Negro Academy*.

15. Alexander Crummell, "The Attitude of the American Mind Toward the Negro Intellect," in American Negro Academy Occasional Papers, No. 3. (Washington, DC, American Negro Academy, 1898), pp. 15, 16.

16. J. Saunders Redding, *They Came in Chains* (New York: Lippincott, 1969), pp. 196–97. Lerone Bennett, *Before the Mayflower* (Baltimore: Penguin, 1966), pp. 227–29. Louis R. Harlan, *Booker T. Washington: The Making of a Black Leader* (New York: Oxford University Press, 1972), pp. 222–23, 226–27.

17. Responses to Washington's "Atlanta Exposition Address" are contained in *The Booker T. Washington Papers*, ed. Louis R. Harlan, vol. 4 (Urbana: University of Illinois Press, 1975); statements of Du Bois, Blyden, and Cansler on pp. 26–27, 30–31.

18. The problematic nature of Crummell's original reaction to the proposal of an American Negro Academy is discussed in Moses, *Alexander Crummell*, pp. 75–78.

19. Crummell, "The Social Principle Among a People," a Thanksgiving Sermon delivered in Washington, DC, 1875, was reprinted in his *The Greatness of Christ and Other Sermons* (New York: Thomas Whittaker, 1882), pp. 296, 297–98.

20. August Meier, *Negro Thought in America: Racial Ideologies in the Age of Booker T. Washington* (Ann Arbor: University of Michigan Press, 1963), p. 267, detects in the rhetoric of ANA founders the idea that "Negroes . . . were too impressed by material things." See John Oldfield, *Alexander Crummell and the Creation of an African Church in Liberia* (Queenstown, Ont.: Edwin Mellen, 1990), pp. 122–23; Moss, *American Negro Academy*, pp. 22–23; and Moses, *Alexander Crummell*, pp. 261–69.

21. For organization of the American Negro Academy, see Moss, *American*

Negro Academy, pp. 1–57. Also see Moses, *Alexander Crummell,* pp. 258–75. Both Moss and Moses base their studies of the academy on documents in the possession of Dr. Adelaide Cromwell, especially the typescript verbatim account of Edward J. Beckham, stenographer, entitled "Organization of the Academy for the Promotion of Intellectual Enterprise Among American Negroes," and an untitled manuscript document in the handwriting of John Wesley Cromwell that describes the early organizational meetings of December 18, 1896, through February 15, 1897, as well as the official organizational meeting of March 5, 1897.

22. Crummell to John W. Cromwell, October 5, 1897, Bruce Papers, Schomburg Collection. Gregory U. Rigsby, *Alexander Crummell: Pioneer in Nineteenth Century Pan-African Thought* (New York: Greenwood Press, 1987), p. 166–67. Moses, *Alexander Crummell,* p. 261.

23. Oldfield, in *Alexander Crummell,* p. 123, asserts that Crummell's increasing dissatisfaction with the leadership of Booker T. Washington "eventually led to the organization of the American Negro Academy," indicating fundamental agreement with the present author in *Alexander Crummell,* p. 261–70.

24. Crummell's reference to Dickens's Gradgrind is in his "The Attitude of the American Mind," p. 16.

25. W. E. B. Du Bois, *The Conservation of Races,* published as American Negro Academy Occasional Paper No. 2. (Washington, DC, 1897), p. 7. For solicitation of paper, see Moss, *American Negro Academy,* p. 31. For differences of opinion between Douglass and Crummell see Moses, *Alexander Crummell,* pp. 226–27, 289–92. A public confrontation between Douglass and Crummell at Storer College on May 30, 1885, is mentioned in Alexander Crummell, *Africa and America: Addresses and Discourses* (Springfield, MA: Willey, 1891), pp. iv – v.

26. Joseph de Maistre (1753–1821) was a reactionary, a major figure of the counter-Enlightenment and a royalist who believed that Western civilization should submit to the temporal authority of the pope. Du Bois's ironic resemblance to de Maistre consists in his suspicion of the mob, his occasional revolt against rationalism, his tendency to revere ancient traditions, and his belief in the enlightened despotism of big government.

27. Ferris, quoted in Beckham, "Organization of the Academy," p. 20.

28. Crummell's theories on African and slave cultures are discussed at length in Moses, *Alexander Crummell,* pp. 93–94, and 278–79. Also see Crummell, *Africa and America,* pp. 91–97.

29. Crummell on revivals in Moses, *Alexander Crummell,* pp. 193–94

30. Crummell, "Civilization, the Primal Need of the Race," p. 4. See William Whewell, *Lectures on the History of Moral Philosophy* (Cambridge: Deighton Bell, 1862). Also see discussion of Whewell in Moses, *Alexander Crummell,* pp. 75–78.

31. Crummell, "Civilization, the Primal Need of the Race," p. 5.

32. Joel Williamson, "W. E. B. Du Bois as a Hegelian," in David G. Sansing, ed., *What Was Freedom's Price?* (Jackson: University Press of Mississippi,

1978), pp. 21–49, 116–18. Hegelian themes are apparent in Du Bois's poem "Hymn to the Peoples," in W. E. Burghardt Du Bois, *Darkwater: Voices from Within the Veil* (New York: Harcourt Brace, 1920), pp. 275–76.

33. Crummell, "Civilization, the Primal Need of the Race," p. 6

34. The speaker is not clearly identified in Beckham, "Organization of the Academy," p. 20.

35. Booker T. Washington, *My Larger Education*, pp. 134–36.

36. John Dewey, *My Pedagogic Creed* (New York: E. L. Kellogg, 1897). Washington's experiences of 1875 antedated the rise of Deweyan influences, and since it is normal to view Dewey's approaches as "pragmatic" and "progressive," we should in all fairness apply the same terms to Washington's. Lewis Harlan is sensitive to the analogue, but demurs at overstressing the point, in Harlan, *Booker T. Washington: The Wizard of Tuskegee, 1901–1915* (New York: Oxford University Press, 1983), pp. 144, 151.

37. Thomas A. Dixon, Jr., "Booker T. Washington and the Negro," *Saturday Evening Post* (August 19, 1905): 1–3; repr. Stanley Feldstein, ed., *The Poisoned Tongue: A Documentary History of American Racism and Prejudice* (New York: Morrow, 1972), p. 203.

38. Du Bois refers to Marcus Tullius Cicero (106–43 B.C.), whose oration on behalf of Archeas the poet included a defense of poetry and an argument that idle moments were better spent in the pursuit of books and ideas than in wasteful and harmful pastimes.

39. Crummell says in "Civilization, the Primal Need of the Race" that "civilization never seeks permanent abidence on the heights of Olympus . . . she descends . . . meeting the minutest of human needs" (pp. 5–6).

40. Scarborough, *The Educated Negro and His Mission,* American Negro Academy Occasional Papers, No. 8 (Washington, DC: American Negro Academy, 1903), p. 5. "Ich dien" is the motto of the Prince of Wales.

41. Ferris, *The African Abroad,* vol. 2, pp. 822–52.

42. Ferris quotes Volney at length in *The African Abroad,* vol. 1, pp. 444, 449–50. Ferris also quotes at length from Franz Boas, *The Anthropological Position of the Negro,* and G. A. Hoskins, *Travels in Ethiopia above the Second Cataract of the Nile* (London: Brown, Green, Longman, 1835). See Ferris, *The African Abroad,* vol. 1, pp. 455–60 and p. 471.

43. Ferris pays tribute to Giuseppe Sergi, *The Mediteranean Race,* but provides no publication details or page references. He also cites William Z. Ripley, *The Races of Europe* (New York: Appleton & Company, 1899).

44. Ripley, *The Races of Europe,* cited in Ferris's *The African Abroad,* vol. 2, p. 525.

45. Ferris, *The African Abroad,* vol. 2, p. 525.

46. Marcus Garvey, *Philosphy and Opinions of Marcus Garvey,* ed. Amy Jacques Garvey (New York: International Publishing House, 1925), vol. 2, p. 18.

47. Eugène Henri Paul Gauguin (1848–1903), a French painter whose life has influenced popular myths concerning the socialization of modern artists. Midway through his thirties, he quit his job as a brokerage clerk and left his wife and five children to become a painter. He spent his

later years in Tahiti, and is known for his vibrant portraits of native women.

48. Some of these points were made in my article "More Stately Mansions: New Negro Movements and Langston Hughes' Literary Theory," *The Langston Hughes Review* (Spring, 1985): 40–46; repr. Moses, *The Wings of Ethiopia: Studies in African American Life and Letters* (Ames: Iowa State University Press, 1990), pp. 265–66.

49. Tony Martin demonstrates the role of bourgeois intellectuals in the Garvey movement; see his *Literary Garveyism: Garvey, Black Arts and the Harlem Renaissance* (Dover, MA: Majority Press, 1983). Judith Stein stresses even more the importance of class in *The Garvey Movement in the World of Marcus Garvey: Race and Class in Modern Society* (Baton Rouge: Louisiana State University Press, 1986).

50. Ferris, *The African Abroad*, vol. 1, p. 309.

51. For Thomas Jefferson's attitudes and comparisons, see Wilson J. Moses, ed., *Classical Black Nationalism from the American Revolution to Marcus Garvey* (New York: New York University Press, 1996), pp. 12, 46–47, 81–82. For Crummell on boasting of bastardy, see Wilson J. Moses, ed., *Destiny and Race: Selected Writings, 1840–1898 / Alexander Crummell* (Amherst: University of Massachusetts Press, 1992), pp. 87–88.

52. Ferris, *The African Abroad*, vol. 1, p. 131.

Chapter 7

1. W. A. Domingo, Account of Marcus Garvey's St. Mark's Church Hall Lecture, in Robert A. Hill, Jr., ed., *The Marcus Garvey and Universal Negro Improvement Association Papers* (Berkeley: University of California Press, 1983), vol. 1, p. 191. For "energetic" and "wide-awake" see William H. Ferris on Garvey, in *Marcus Garvey Papers*, vol. 1, p. 75n.

2. See Marcus Garvey, *The Tragedy of White Injustice* (London: Marcus Garvey, 1935), p. 6, in which Jesus Christ is endowed with a "blood of Negro tie," and where Asian races and heroes conveniently slip into and out of black identities.

3. Marcus Garvey, *Philosophy and Opinions of Marcus Garvey*, ed. Amy Jacques Garvey (New York: International Publishing House, 1925), vol. 2, p. 19.

4. Marcus Garvey speaking at Madison Square Garden, October 30, 1919, printed in *Garvey Papers*, vol. 2, p. 129.

5. The phraseology is from Henry Highland Garnet, in the *Weekly Anglo-African*, September 10, 1859, quoted in Earl Ofari, *Let Your Motto Be Resistance* (Boston: Beacon Press, 1972), p. 86.

6. Garvey praises Booker T. Washington's avoidance of public agitation in *Philosophy and Opinions*, vol. 2, p. 38, and calls political agitation "a losing game," in ibid., p. 106.

7. *Negro World*, September 29, 1928.

8. Oswald Spengler, *The Decline of the West*, trans. Charles Francis Atkinson (New York: Knopf, 1926). Cf. Du Bois, "What Is Civilization? Africa's Answer," *Forum*, February 1925; repr. in Meyer Weinberg, ed., *W. E. B.*

Du Bois: A Reader (New York: Harper & Row, 1970), p. 374. Civilization was linked to discontent by Garvey (*Philosophy and Opinions*, vol. 1, p. 31) six years before Sigmund Freud published *Das Unbehagen in der Kultur*, translated in 1930 as *Civilization and Its Discontents*, although Freud's suggestion for the English translation was *Man's Discomfort in Civilization*. See James Strachey's introduction to *Civilization and Its Discontents* (New York: Norton, 1961), pp. 3–4. Marcus Garvey spoke of the poison of civilization in "Present Day Civilization," *Philosophy and Opinions*, vol. 1, p. 31.

9. Ibid., vol. 2, pp. 119–20.

10. David Shi, *Facing Facts: Realism in American Thought and Culture, 1850–1920* (New York: Oxford University Press, 1995), p. 276.

11. Alexander Crummell, "The Solution of Problems: The Duty and Destiny of Man, Annual Commencement Sermon, Wilberforce University, June 1895," *AME Church Review*, April 1896.

12. Hans Kohn emphasizes "humanitarian democrat and cosmopolitan pacifist" in his article "Nationalism," in Philip P. Wiener, ed., *Dictionary of the History of Ideas: Studies of Selected Pivotal Ideas* (New York: Scribner, 1973), p. 326. In the same vein, see Raymond Williams's essay "Culture," in *Keywords: A Vocabulary of Culture and Society* (New York: Oxford University Press, 1976), p. 79.

13. Arthur Joseph dè Gobineau, *The Inequality of Human Races*, is discussed in Jacques Barzun, *Race: A Study in Modern Superstition*, rev. ed. (New York: Harper & Row, 1965); Thomas F. Gossett, *Race: The History of an Idea in America* (New York: Schocken Books, 1965); Ashley Montague, *Man's Most Dangerous Myth: The Fallacy of Race* (New York: World Publishing, 1964). Gobineau's influences on nineteenth-century Americans are discussed in George Frederickson, *The Black Image in the White Mind* (New York: Harper & Row, 1971). Gobineau's influences on negritude are discussed in James Arnold, *Modernism and Negritude: The Poetry and Poetics of Aimé Césaire* (Cambridge, MA: Harvard University Press, 1981), pp. 40–41.

14. Tylor, *Primitive Culture: Researches into the Development of Mythology, Philosophy, Religion, Language, Art and Custom* (London: John Murray, 1920), and George W. Stocking, *Race, Culture, and Evolution: Essays in the History of Anthropology* (New York: Free Press, 1968; repr. Chicago: University of Chicago Press, 1982), p. 90. Cf. A. L. Kroeber and Clyde Kluckhohn, *Culture: A Review of Concepts and Definitions* (New York: Vintage, 1952).

15. See Alain Locke's appraisal of Morgan, Spencer, and Tylor in "The Concept of Race as Applied to Social Culture," *Howard Review* 1 (1924): 290–99, repr. in Leonard Harris, *The Philosophy of Alain Locke: The Harlem Renaissance and Beyond* (Philadelphia: Temple University Press, 1989), p. 197.

16. Lewis H. Morgan, *Ancient Society* (1877; Calcutta, 1958), pp. 562–63

17. Sumner, *Folkways* (1906; repr. New York: Dover, 1959), pp. 12–13.

18. Herder, quoted in Raymond Williams, *Keywords*, p. 79.

19. Although Park was critical of Sumner, he accepted the underlying thesis

of his Folkways. See Robert E. Park, *Race and Culture: Essays in the Sociology of Contemporary Man* (New York: Free Press, 1950), pp. xi–xiv, and numerous indexed references. Frazier was suspicious of multiculturalism and completely rejected romantic racialism, but was influenced profoundly by other aspects of Park's analysis. For discussion, see James E. Blackwell and Morris Janowitz, *Black Sociologists: Historical and Contemporary Perspectives* (Chicago: University of Chicago Press, 1974), pp. 85–115. Also see Anthony M. Platt, *E. Franklin Frazier Reconsidered* (New Brunswick, NJ: Rutgers University Press, 1991), pp. 85–90.

20. Robert E. Park, "Education and Its Relation to the Conflict and Fusion of Cultures: With Special Reference to the Problems of the Immigrant, the Negro, and Missions," *Publications of the American Sociological Society* 13 (December 1918): 59, repr. in Park, *Race and Culture*, p. 280. George Frederickson, *The Black Image in the White Mind*, cites this famous quotation from Park on p. 327, and discusses Gobineau and his influence on American thought on pp. 69, 79, 101, 132–33. Dean Grodzins reminded the present author of Parker's romantic racialism in a letter of August 22, 1996, where he generously directed me to the Parker quotation; see Theodore Parker, *Works* (Boston: American Unitarian Association, 1907–13), vol. 14, pp. 273–75.

21. *Liberator*, March 12, 1858. Citation provided by Grodzins.

22. Edward Wilmot Blyden, *African Life and Customs* (London: C. M. Phillips, 1908), p. 9. Blyden on "African Personality" in Hollis Lynch, ed., *Black Spokesman: Selected Published Writings of Edward Wilmot Blyden* (New York: Humanities Press, 1971), 187–214. Douglass on multiculturalism is in John Blassingame et al., eds., *The Frederick Douglass Papers*, Series 1 (New Haven: Yale University Press, 1982), vol. 2, p. 507.

23. William S. Willis, Jr., "Skeletons in the Anthropological Closet," in Dell Hynes, ed., *Reinventing Anthropology* (New York: Random House, 1972), p. 140, touches on this problem only by implication.

24. Vernon Williams, Jr., *Rethinking Race: Franz Boas and His Contemporaries* (Lexington: University Press of Kentucky, 1996), pp. 102, 104–16.

25. Melville Herskovits, "The Negro's Americanism," in Alain Locke, ed., *The New Negro* (New York: Charles Boni), p. 359.

26. Melville Herskovits, "Ethnohistory," in *The New World Negro: Selected Papers in Afroamerican Studies* (Bloomington: Indiana University Press, 1966), p. 122.

27. Willis, "Skeletons," p. 140.

28. Ibid.

29. Bronislaw Malinowski, "The Pan-African Problem of Culture Contact," *American Journal of Sociology* 48, no. 6 (1943): 649–65.

30. Ibid., p. 665.

31. For the seminal discussion of this Caliban theme, see Octave Mannoni, *Prospero and Caliban: The Psychology of Colonization* (New York: Praeger, 1964); originally published as *Psychologie de la Colonisation* (Paris: Editions du Seuil, 1950). Also see the reaction of Frantz Fanon, *Black Skin, White Masks* (New York: Grove Press, 1967), pp. 83–108.

Chapter 8

1. Gwendolyn Bennett's "Heritage" is less frequently mentioned than Countee Cullen's poem by the same name. Both are anthologized in Alain Locke, ed., *The New Negro* (New York: Albert & Charles Boni, 1925). Langston Hughes's poem "Nude Young Dancer" is also in *The New Negro.*
2. Vachel Lindsay's "The Congo" is widely anthologized; e.g., see Norman Foerster, ed., *American Poetry and Prose* (Boston: Houghton Mifflin, 1957).
3. George Hutchinson observes negative reactions to the poem in *The Harlem Renaissance in Black and White* (Cambridge, MA: Harvard University Press, 1995), p. 148.
4. Langston Hughes, "The Negro Speaks of Rivers," in James Weldon Johnson, ed., *The Book of American Negro Poetry* (New York: Harcourt Brace & World, 1931). Du Bois's poem "The Riddle of the Sphinx" has a somewhat complicated publishing history. See Herbert Aptheker, ed., *Creative Writings by W. E. B. Du Bois* (Amherst: University of Massachusetts Press, 1980), p. 12. The best known version is in Du Bois, *Darkwater: Voices from Within the Veil* (New York: Harcourt Brace, 1920), pp. 53–55.
5. Fred McElroy brought to my attention an early use of the "New Negro," in Edward M. Brawley, *The Negro Baptist Pulpit* (1890; repr. Freeport, NY: Books for Libraries, 1971), pp. 238–44. The construct "Harlem Renaissance" is challenged by Sterling A. Brown in "The New Negro in Literature, 1925–1955," in *The New Negro Thirty Years Afterward: Papers Contributed to the Sixteenth Annual Spring Conference at the Division of Social Sciences* (Washington, DC: Howard University Press, 1955), pp. 57–71. Also see the introduction to Michael W. Peplo and Arthur P. Davis, *The New Negro Renaissance: An Anthology* (New York: Rinehart, 1975).
6. For notes on the publishing history and significance of Locke's *The New Negro*, see Robert Hayden's "Introduction" in Alain Locke, ed., *The New Negro* (New York: Atheneum, 1968), and Arnold Rampersad's edition of Alain Locke, ed., *The New Negro* (New York: Atheneum, 1992). Also see the good discussion by George Hutchinson in *The Harlem Renaissance in Black and White* (Cambridge, MA: Harvard University Press, 1995), pp. 396–433.
7. William B. Harvey, "The Philosophical Anthropology of Alain Locke," in Russell J. Linnemann, ed., *Alain Locke: Reflections on a Modern Renaissance Man* (Baton Rouge: Louisiana State University Press, 1982), pp. 17–28. Alain Locke, "The Concept of Race as Applied to Social Culture," *Howard Review* (1924), repr. in Leonard Harris, ed., *The Philosophy of Alain Locke* (Philadelphia: Temple University Press, 1989), pp. 187–200.
8. Linnemann, *Alain Locke*, p. 23. Harris, ed., *Philosophy of Locke*, pp. 56–57.
9. Leonard Harris, ed., *Philosophy of Locke*, p. 77.
10. Henry Louis Gates, Jr., "Beyond the Culture Wars: Identities in Dia-

logue," in *Profession 93* (New York: Modern Language Association, 1993), p. 11.

11. Patricia Rengel, Letter to the editor, *Wall Street Journal,* July 26, 1993. Also Dinesh D'Souza in *Wall Street Journal,* July 27, 1993.

12. Robert Hayden viewed the Harlem Renaissance as "clearly integrationist, not separatist," in his "Introduction" to *The New Negro,* p. xiii. However, Charles T. Davis emphasized the movement's and Locke's nationalistic tendencies in "Prose Literature of Racial Defense, 1917–1924: A Preface to the Harlem Renaissance" (1942), published in Davis, *Black Is the Color of the Cosmos: Essays on Afro-American Literature and Culture, 1942–1981* (Washington, DC: Howard University Press, 1982), p. 178.

13. Locke, ed., *The New Negro,* p. 256.

14. Michael Winston has brilliantly and succinctly described Locke's indebtedness to Mason, and her influence on the Harlem Renaissance in general. See his article on Locke in Rayford W. Logan and Michael R. Winston, *Dictionary of American Negro Biography,* p. 401. For additional discussion of Mason and of the Harlem Renaissance, see David Levering Lewis, *When Harlem Was in Vogue* (New York: Random House, Vintage Books, 1982).

15. Locke, ed., *The New Negro,* p. 254.

16. Quoted by Michael R. Winston in "Alain Leroy Locke," *Dictionary of American Negro Biography,* p. 401.

17. W. E. Burghardt Du Bois, *The World and Africa: An Inquiry into the Part Which Africa Has Played in World History* (1946; repr. New York: International Publishers, 1956), pp. 150, 156–57.

18. Sterling A. Brown, "The New Negro in Literature, 1925–1955," in *The New Negro Thirty Years Afterward,* p. 58. Alain Locke, "Art or Propaganda?" *Harlem: A Forum of Negro Life* 1 (November 1928): 12, quoted in Brown, p. 59.

19. Nathan Huggins, *Harlem Renaissance* (New York: Oxford, 1971), p. 308.

20. Lewis, *When Harlem Was in Vogue,* p. 304.

21. See Harold Cruse, *The Crisis of the Negro Intellectual* (New York: Morrow, 1967). The problem persisted into the thirties, as Cruse points out, when the Works Progress Administration and the Communist Party became important agencies for the support of black artists and intellectuals.

22. W. E. B. Du Bois, "Mencken" *Crisis* (October 1927).

23. W. E. B. Du Bois, *"Home to Harlem,* and *Quicksand,"* reviewed in *Crisis* (June 1928). Weinberg's observation is in Meyer Weinberg, ed., *W. E. B. Du Bois: A Reader* (New York: Harper & Row, 1970), p. 262.

24. W. E. B. Du Bois, "The Negro College," *Crisis* (August 1933).

25 Marcus Garvey, *"Home to Harlem:* An Insult to the Race," *Negro World,* September 29, 1928, also denounced Du Bois as one of those "prostitutes" who obeyed the injunctions of white publishers.

26. Frazier, "La Bourgeoisie Noire," in V. F. Calverton, ed., *Anthology of American Negro Literature* (New York: Modern Library, 1929), p. 385.

27. The present author once encountered a reader for a major journal who

had no knowledge of Ferris, confusing him with a living folklorist of the same name.

28. Martin Kilson, "Paradoxes of Blackness: Notes on the Crisis of Black Intellectuals," *Dissent* (January 1, 1988): 73.

29. For the career and ideology of the Rev. Youngblood, see Samuel G. Freedman, *Upon This Rock: The Miracles of a Black Church* (New York: HarperCollins, 1993).

30. Wilson J. Moses, *The Golden Age of Black Nationalism, 1850–1925* (Hamden, CT: Archon Books, 1978; repr. New York: Oxford University Press, 1988), pp. 20–21, 59–61; cf. Alfred A. Moss, *The American Negro Academy: Voice of the Talented Tenth* (Baton Rouge: Louisiana State University Press, 1981), p. 299. George Frederickson, *Black Liberation: A Comparative History of Black Ideologies in the United States and South Africa* (New York: Oxford University Press, 1995), p. 69.

31. Aimé Césaire "Cahier d'un retour au pays natal." The poem was originally published in French, *Volontés* (Paris), no. 20 (August 1939): 42.

32. Cheikh Anta Diop, *Civilization or Barbarism: An Authentic Anthropology* (New York: Lawrence Hill Books, 1991), pp. 217–18.

33. Jacques Barzun, *Race: A Study in Superstition* (New York: Harcourt, Brace & Co., 1937), pp. 50–77.

34. Hollis Read, *The Negro Problem Solved; or Africa as She Was, as She Is, and as She Shall Be: Her Curse and Her Cure* (New York: A. A. Constantine, 1864), p. 90. Read does not identify the quotation with which he begins this passage, nor is he obsessed with specificity in identifying his corroborative authorities. With characteristic mid-nineteenth-century abandon, he simply lists them as Pritchard, Hamilton Smith (elsewhere in the same chapter spelled Smythe?), Morton, Ritter, Trail, T. B. Hamilton, Sir William Jones.

Chapter 9

1. Secretariat of the Encyclopedia Africana, *Information Report* No. 2 (September, 1962), p. 2.

2. Secretariat of the Encyclopedia Africana, *Information Report* No. 1 (June 1962), p. 2

3. See, for example, the letters of support from Basil Davidson and Melville Herskovits in Encyclopedia Africana, *Information Report* No. 1 (June 1962), p. 4, and Jan Vansina in Encyclopedia Africana, *Information Report* No. 2 (September 1962), p. 7.

4. Under the heading "Africa and Classical Culture," the Encyclopedia Africana, *Information Report* No. 3 (December 1962), carried an excerpt from Livo Steechini, "The Historian and African Civilization," which had appeared in the *American Behavioral Scientist* (April 1962). Steechini's arguments resembled points presented earlier in Pauline Hopkins, "Venus and Apollo Modeled from Ethiopians," *Colored American* (May/June 1903): 465, and later by Martin Bernal in *Black Athena: The*

Afroasiatic Roots of Classical Civilization, 2 vols. (New Brunswick, NJ: Rutgers University Press, 1987–91).

5. *Tarzan of the Apes* was first filmed as a silent in 1917. *Trader Horn*, the first movie to be filmed in Africa, was made in 1931.

6. Daryl Michael Scott, *Contempt and Pity: Social Policy and the Image of the Damaged Black Psyche, 1880–1996* (Chapel Hill: University of North Carolina Press, 1997), pp. 193–94, 197–98. Scott cites Stuckey's introduction to *The Ideological Origins of Black Nationalism* (Boston: Beacon Press, 1972), pp. 10–11. Martin R. Delany, *The Condition, Elevation, Emigration and Destiny of the Colored People of the United States Politically Considered* (Philadelphia: The Author, 1852), p. 43.

7. Martin R. Delany, *The Condition of the Colored People*, pp. 43–45. Emphasis added.

8. Orlando Patterson, "Rethinking Black History," *Harvard Educational Review* 41 (August 1971): 297–315. Vindicationism is copiously indexed in St. Clair Drake, *Black Folk Here and There* (Los Angeles: Center for Afro-American Studies, University of California at Los Angeles, 1987), vol. 1.

9. Delany, *Condition of the Colored People*, p. 53.

10. I have defined "civilizationism" at length in *Alexander Crummell: A Study of Civilization and Discontent* (New York: Oxford University Press, 1989), where the index entry is extended. Also see the index entry "Civilization" in Moses, *The Golden Age of Black Nationalism, 1850–1925* (Hamden, CT: Archon Books, 1978; repr. New York: Oxford University Press, 1988). Extreme hostility toward the concept of civilization as progress has been expressed by Orlando Patterson in "Rethinking Black History," p. 308. For an entirely different perspective, see Basil Davidson, *The Lost Cities of Africa* (Boston: Little, Brown, 1970).

11. Martin Bernal, *Black Athena*, vol. 2, pp. 435–38.

12. Marcus Garvey, *Philosophy and Opinions of Marcus Garvey*, ed. Amy Jacques Garvey (New York: Universal Publishing House, 1925), vol. 2, p. 18.

13. See, for example, the photo of entertainer Halle Berry on the cover of *Ebony* (March 1997). First-century depictions of Cleopatra tend to resemble Barbra Streisand.

14. Mary Lefkowitz, *Not Out of Africa: How Afrocentrism Became an Excuse to Teach Myth as History* (New York: Basic Books, 1996), pp. 38, 39, 40, 47.

15. A recent contribution to this discussion is Joseph Sobran, *Alias Shakespeare: Solving the Greatest Literary Mystery of All Time* (New York: Free Press, 1997). Reviewed in the *Wall Street Journal*, May 1 and May 15, 1997.

16. Mary Lefkowitz and Guy MacLean Rogers, *Black Athena Revisited* (Chapel Hill: University of North Carolina Press, 1996). While this very interesting book is predominantly scholarly, a great deal is also polemical. Black chauvinists and Afrocentrists will harvest much grist for their mills, and much will be readily convertible to their own rhetorical agenda.

17. Problems of nineteenth-century ethnology are complicated by the fact that so many misconceptions prevail. E. B. Tylor, while presumed to be a founder of cultural relativism, expressed extremely racist ideas respecting black people. Herbert Spencer is commonly described as a social

Darwinist when, in fact, his theories predate publication of *The Origin of Species*. Darwin is presumed to have repudiated Lamarck, although he clung to Lamarckian views. William Graham Sumner, although a social Darwinist, denounced "ethnocentrism."

18. Frederick Douglass, "The Claims of the Negro Ethnologically Considered," in John Blassingame et al., eds., *The Frederick Douglass Papers*, Series 1 (New Haven: Yale University Press, 1982), vol. 2, pp. 520–21.

19. Martin Bernal, *Black Athena*, pp. 25–26, 27, 168, 173–77, 180, 485.

20. Arthur, comte de Gobineau (1816–82), *The Moral and Intellectual Diversity of Races, With Particular Reference to Their Respective Influence in the Civil and Political History of Mankind*, trans. H. Hotz (Philadelphia: Lippincott, 1856), chap. 11. Also see Michael D. Biddis, *Father of Racist Ideology* (New York: Weybright & Talley, 1970), p. 118. Also see Chapter 3 of the present work.

21. Du Bois, *The World and Africa* (New York: International Publishers, 1947; repr. 1965); for "Mediterranean Negroids," see p. 87; Seligman is cited on pp. 97, 107.

22. W. E. B. Du Bois, *The World and Africa*, p. x.

23. Frank M. Snowden, Jr., *Blacks in Antiquity* (Cambridge, MA: Harvard University Press, 1970), p. 217.

24. Zora Neale Hurston, *Mules and Men* (Philadelphia: Lippincott, 1935). Drusilla Houston, *Wonderful Ethiopians of the Ancient Cushite Empire* (Oklahoma City: Universal Publishing Company, 1926; repr. Baltimore: Black Classic Press, 1985), is an influential Afrocentric work that includes considerable feminist ideology.

25. There are at least two versions of Matthew Arnold's famous "best that has been. . . ." See *Oxford Dictionary of Quotations* (London: Oxford University Press, 1966), pp. 19, 20. The saga of Shine belongs to the genre of urban folklore referred to by cultural anthropologists as the "toast." Shine is a black shiphand on the *Titanic*, who swims to shore after the liner hits an iceberg, mocking the wealthy white passengers as he strokes. Molefi K. Asante, *The Afrocentric Idea* (Philadelphia: Temple University Press, 1987), pp. 80, 101–3, 106, 116. Asante's version should be compared to those presented in Roger D. Abrahams, *Deep Down in the Jungle* (Chicago: Aldine, 1970), pp. 97–108. Also see Bruce Jackson, ed., *Get Your Ass in the Water and Swim Like Me: Narrative Poetry from Black Oral Tradition* (Rounder Records, n.p., n.d.).

26. E. U. Essien-Udom is one of the few scholars who have seen any relationship between the Nation of Islam and its Christian precursors. See Essien-Udom, *Black Nationalism: A Search for an Identity in America* (Chicago: University of Chicago Press, 1962), pp. 17–26.

27. Melville J. Herskovits, *The Myth of the Negro Past* (New York: Harper & Brothers, 1941). See W. E. B. Du Bois review in *Annals of the American Academy of Political and Social Sciences* 222 (July 1942): 226–27. This and another review of the same work are reprinted in Herbert Aptheker, ed., *Book Reviews by W. E. B. Du Bois* (Millwood, NY: KTO Press, 1977). For personal and intellectual conflict between Frazier and Herskovits, see

Pat Ryan, "White Experts, Black Experts, and Black Studies," *Black Academy Review* 1, no. 1 (Spring 1970): 57–60.

28. Until I read Robinson's unpublished book manuscript "To Forge a Nation," it had not occurred to me that Marcus Garvey was so conspicuously absent from Sterling Stuckey's *Slave Culture: Nationalist Theory and the Foundations of Black America* (New York: Oxford University Press, 1987).

29. Le Roi Jones, *Blues People: Negro Music in White America* (New York: William Morrow, 1963), p. 7; Pat Ryan, "White Experts, Black Experts, and Black Studies," p. 58; Willie Lee Rose, *Slavery and Freedom* (New York: Oxford University Press, 1982), p. 194; Molefi K. Asante, *The Afrocentric Idea* (Philadelphia: Temple University Press, 1987), pp. 19, 52, 56; Benjamin Quarles, *The Negro in the Making of America* (New York: Collier-Macmillan, 1964; rev. ed., Macmillan, 1969); repr. with a new preface and a new introduction by V. P. Franklin (New York: Touchstone Books, 1996), p. 37.

30. William Stanton, *The Leopard's Spots* (Chicago: University of Chicago Press, 1960). John S. Haller, *Outcasts of Evolution* (Urbana: University of Illinois Press, 1971). Hamilton Cravens, *Triumphs of Evolution* (Philadelphia: University of Pennsylvania Press, 1978). Marvin Harris, *The Rise of Anthropological Theory: A History of Theories of Culture* (New York: Crowell, 1968). Audrey Smedley, *Race in North America: Origin and Evolution of a World View* (Boulder, CO: Westview Press, 1993). Dorothy Ross, *Origins of American Social Science* (Cambridge: Cambridge University Press, 1991). Vernon Williams, Jr., *Rethinking Race* (Lexington: University of Kentucky Press, 1996).

31. See George Frederickson's copious index entries under "romantic racism" in *The Black Image in the White Mind: The Debate on Afro-American Character and Destiny, 1817–1914* (New York: Harper Torchbook, 1917). Also see Frederickson, *The Black Image*, p. 327.

32. Sterling Brown, "Negro Character as Seen by White Authors," *Journal of Negro Education* (April 1933). Park, "Education and Its Relation . . . ," as cited in *Publlications of the American Sociological Society* 13 (December 1918): 59.

33. The fact that Freud attributed *unbehagen*, in fact, to *Kultur*, not *Zivilization*, is presumed by his translators to be of limited consequence, perhaps because Freud expressed his disdain for any attempt to distinguish between the concepts of culture and those of civilization. Sigmund Freud, *The Future of an Illusion* (1927; New York: Norton, 1961), p. 6.

34. W. E. B. Du Bois, *The Souls of Black Folk* (Chicago: McClurg, 1903), p. 12.

35. Leonard I. Sweet, *Black Images of America, 1874–1870* (New York: Norton, 1976), pp. 69–124. This was the most imaginative discussion of African American historiography published in the 1970s, although the publishers were guilty of slipshod editing, poor binding, halfhearted advertising, and lackadaisical distribution.

36. James D. Anderson, *The Education of Blacks in the South, 1860–1935*

(Chapel Hill: University of North Carolina Press, 1988), pp. 29–30. I am indebted to Lloyd Monroe for bringing this aspect of Anderson's book to my attention.

37. Booker T. Washington, *The Story of the Negro: The Rise of the Race from Slavery* (New York: Doubleday, Page, 1909). George Washington Williams, *History of the Negro Race in America, from 1619 to 1880* (New York: G. P. Putnam's Sons, 1883), and Carter G. Woodson, *The African Background Outlined, or Handbook for the Study of the Negro* (Washington, DC: Associated Publishers, 1936).

38. W. E. B. Du Bois, *The Gift of Black Folk* (Boston: The Stratford Company, 1924), p. 258. Benjamin Quarles, *The Negro in the Making of America* (New York: Touchstone Books, 1987), p. 20. John Hope Franklin, *From Slavery to Freedom* (New York: McGraw-Hill, 1994), p. 527. Lerone Bennett, *Before the Mayflower* (New York: Penguin Books, 1988), p. 442.

39. Nicholas Lehmann, "Black Nationalism on Campus," *Atlantic Monthly* (January 1993): 31–47, passim.

40. Eugene Genovese, *Roll Jordan Roll: The World the Slaves Made* (New York: Vintage Books, 1976). Genovese's work followed in the pattern of the pioneering work of John Blassingame, *The Slave Community: Plantation Life in the Antebellum South* (New York: Oxford University Press, 1972), and Sterling Stuckey, "Through the Prism of Folklore," *Massachussetts Review* 9, no. 3 (Summer 1968). Works of similar thrust are Lawrence Levine's *Black Culture and Black Consciousness: Afro-American Folk Thought from Slavery to Freedom* (New York: Oxford University Press, 1978), and Mechal Sobel, *The World They Made Together: Black and White Values in Eighteenth Century Virginia* (Princeton, NJ: Princeton University Press, 1987). Works in this vein were harshly criticized by Kenneth S. Lynn in "Regressive Historians," *The American Scholar* (Autumn 1978): 471–500.

41. Roger D. Abrahams, *Positively Black* (Englewood Cliffs, NJ: Prentice-Hall, 1970), p. 150.

INDEX